THE AXE AND THE OATH

THE AXE AND THE OATH

ORDINARY LIFE IN THE MIDDLE AGES

ROBERT FOSSIER

Translated by Lydia G. Cochrane

PRINCETON UNIVERSITY PRESS
PRINCETON AND OXFORD

Original edition published under the title *Ces gens du Moyen Âge* by Robert Fossier.
World copyright © LIBRAIRIE ARTHEME FAYARD, 2007.

English translation copyright © 2010 by Princeton University Press
Published by Princeton University Press, 41 William Street,
Princeton, New Jersey 08540
In the United Kingdom: Princeton University Press, 6 Oxford Street,
Woodstock, Oxfordshire OX20 1TW

Library of Congress Cataloging-in-Publication Data

Fossier, Robert.
[Ces gens du Moyen Âge. English]
The axe and the oath : ordinary life in the Middle Ages / Robert Fossier ;
translated by Lydia G. Cochrane.
p.   cm.
ISBN 978-0-691-14312-5 (cloth : alk. paper)
1. Civilization, Medieval. 2. Middle Ages. 3. Europe—Social life and customs.
4. Europe—Social conditions—To 1492. I. Title.
CB351.F68513 2010
940.1—dc22   2010004039

British Library Cataloging-in-Publication Data is available

Ouvrage publié avec le concours du Ministère français chargé de la culture—
Centre national du livre. This work is published with support from the
French Ministry of Culture/Centre national du livre.

This book has been composed in Minion with Old Claude display

Printed on acid-free paper. ∞

press.princeton.edu

Printed in the United States of America

1   3   5   7   9   10   8   6   4   2

CONTENTS

Preface   IX

PART ONE: MAN AND THE WORLD

CHAPTER 1: *Naked Man*   3

A Fragile Creature   3

 An Ungainly Being   3

 Fairly Content with Himself   5

 But Are There Nonetheless Nuances?   8

But a Threatened Creature   11

 Does Man Really Know Himself?   11

 "Abnormal" Assaults on Man   16

 The Illness That Lies in Wait   19

 The Black Death   23

 Can Those Men Be Counted?   27

CHAPTER 2: *The Ages of Life*   37

From the Child to the Man   38

 Expecting a Baby   38

 When the Child Arrives   41

 "Childhoods"   44

 The Child in the Midst of the Family   48

Man in His Private Life   51

 As Time Goes By   52

 Nourishing the Body   59

 The Shaping of Taste   67

 Adorning the Body   69

Man, Woman, and the Others   77

 The Two Sexes Face-to-Face   78

Sexual Concerns   82

Living by the Fire and by the Pot   87

The Chains of Marriage   91

. . . And Their Locks   96

Kin   102

. . . And "Relations"   107

The Workplace   108

The House   109

. . . And What Was Found in the House   115

Man Is Born to Toil   117

But What Work?   121

And Tools?   127

The End of Life   131

The Elderly   132

The "Passage"   136

After Death   139

CHAPTER 3: *Nature*   145

The Weather   145

The Paleo-Environment   146

What Did They See or Feel?   149

Fire and Water   154

Fire, the Symbol of Life and Death   154

Saving and Beneficent Water   157

The Sea, Horrible and a Temptress   160

The Products of the Earth   164

Mastering the Soil   165

Making the Earth Render   168

Grasses and Vines   171

The Trees and the Forest   175

The Forest, Overwhelming and Sacred   175

The Forest, Necessary and Nourishing   180

And the People of the Forest?   183

CHAPTER 4: *And the Animals?*   186

Man and Beast   187

    Fear and Disgust   187

    Respect and Affection   189

Knowing and Understanding   194

    What Are the Beasts?   195

    Penetrating This World   198

Utilize and Destroy   202

    The Services of the Beast   203

    Killing: Man's Job   208

    A Contrasting Balance Sheet   215

PART TWO: MAN IN HIMSELF

CHAPTER 5: *Man in Himself*   223

Living in a Group   224

    Why Come Together?   225

    How to Assemble?   229

    Where to Gather?   235

    Laughter and Games   246

Precautions and Deviations   252

    Order and the "Orders"   254

    Peace and Honor   260

    Law and Power   265

    Gaps   276

    And People from Elsewhere   285

CHAPTER 6: *Knowledge*   292

The Innate   293

    Memory   293

    The Imaginary   298

    Measurement   303

Acquisitions   310

Act, Image, Word   312

Writing   317

What to Learn?   323

And Where?   329

Expression   335

Who Wrote and What Did They Write?   336

For Whom and Why Did Authors Write?   341

The Artist's Part   343

CHAPTER 7: *And the Soul*   348

Good and Evil   350

The End of Dualism   351

Virtue and Temptation   356

Sin and Pardon   362

Faith and Salvation   365

Dogma and the Rites of Medieval Christian Faith   366

The Church   371

The Other World   376

CONCLUSION   382

PREFACE

"We of the Middle Ages, we know all that," states one of the characters in a play by an author who wrote a century ago. That ludicrous statement was intended to raise a smile from a literate audience, but how about the others? How about those for whom the "Middle Ages" is a vast plain with uncertain contours in which collective memory sets into action kings, monks, knights, and merchants placed somewhere between a cathedral and a castle with a keep, with all of them, men and women, bathed in a "medieval" atmosphere of violence, piety, and occasional feast days? The politicians, journalists, and media people who perform before our eyes dip into that mix, usually in total ignorance, for their peremptory and hasty judgments. This is all very *moyenâgeux*, a term and an attitude that we can leave to the music hall repertory of the Châtelet and say "medieval" or "Middle Ages," which cover the same area with no hint of condescension.

Several decades ago, Lucien Febvre (and Fernand Braudel after him, although less aggressively) laughed at those who claimed to approach and describe those men and women as they changed and multiplied over a thousand years. The two scholars agreed, as Marc Bloch had established once and for all, that the territory of history was the human condition, man or men in society, but they considered it pure fiction to seek an unchanging prototype over such a long time span. "Medieval man" did not exist. Yet, this was the title that Jacques Le Goff gave, some twenty years ago, to the essay that served as an introduction to a collective work by ten well-known scholars. Le Goff avoided the creation of a general model, however, by offering a series of portraits of "social types" (in fact, in English translation the book is titled "Medieval Callings"): the monk, the warrior, the city dweller, the peasant, the intellectual, the artist, the merchant, the saint, the marginal man—and women and the family. Those portraits drew their art and their color from the entire complex of actions, shared the imaginary and the systems of representation and categorization that shaped the flow of economic and social life. What emerged was a medieval typology—cast within specific categories accessible to modern readers—of elements that also contributed to an understanding of the problems that assail us today.

This is not my approach. Besides, why should anyone continue or even return to that fresco by adding further "types of men" or offering nuances and new details? Such a task, carried out sector by sector, would be interminable, tedious, and unproductive; moreover, it would be far beyond my competence. Instead, it is striking, in this work and in others of more modest ambitions, that although the authors show little surprise at the fact, all of those men, no matter what their origin, clearly ate, slept, walked, defecated, copulated, and even thought in the same ways that we do. We too eat with our fingers, cover our sexual parts (which, incidentally, we make use of in an identical manner); we too protect ourselves from the rain as best we can; we laugh or cry out just as people did in the times of Charlemagne, Saint Louis, or Napoleon. Naturally, I am well aware of the contingencies of daily life or of a given time period, the weight of thought or of fashion, but to look at him in his ordinary life, yesterday as today, man is merely a bipedal mammal who needs oxygen, water, calcium, and proteins to subsist on the portions that emerge at the surface of a ball of iron and nickel with three-fourths of its surface covered with salt water, living on landmasses occupied by an ocean of vegetation peopled by thousands of other species. Man is, in short, only a "human beast." It is that *bête humaine* that interests me, and Lucien Febvre was quite wrong to think that ten or twelve centuries could change him.

The reader may judge these thoughts provocative and react with a bit of anger, but the discomfort that he feels will simply illustrate my point. The reader's reaction shows, in fact, that he cannot shake off the basic idea that underlies his thought. Man is an exceptional being because he was willed by the divine Spirit or, if he rejects that convenient postulate, because he is an animal endowed with superior qualities. However, anyone can see that man's life is ceaselessly threatened by the liquid, the vegetable, and the animal, all of which besiege him; that life is an unceasing combat to avoid death; and that perhaps, in the long—very long—history of our planet, his passage will leave no deeper trace than that of the coelacanths or the dinosaurs that lived hundreds of thousands of years before him. Let us then be more modest, and begin examining ourselves less complacently.

In attempting to shake up "certitudes," my hope is to lead the eventual reader to raise questions about them, naturally leaving open the possibility of returning to them if they prove the better choice. I am aware that my proposed course has some weaknesses. What is important is that the being that I will attempt to describe in his body, his soul, his brain, and his environment has to be inserted into a context, which is that of my sources, or at least those that I can master. I cannot claim to describe the fellah of the age of the pharaohs or the Tibetan monk any more than I can evoke the courtier at Versailles or the miner in *Germinal*. It is only within the Middle Ages that I feel myself somewhat at home, although my profession has of course led me to frequent the Athenian hoplite or the Reichshoffen cuirassier for a short time. As it happens, the period of the "Middle Ages" has specific traits, as does any other stage in the human adventure: I cannot hide them, thus calming the posthumous anger of Lucien Febvre. What is more, we need to agree about what was or were the "Middle Ages," an expression invented for the use of the university by Guizot or perhaps even by Bossuet. Was this a segment of time in which the economy and society had certain distinct traits—"feudalism," as Marx would have it? But, really, did people eat "feudally"? Was it a time of triumphant militant and generalized Christianity? But can we say that the epidemic known as the *mal des ardents* was an effect of the Gospel according to Saint John? Enough of that. Such niggling objections serve no purpose. My documentation and most of the scholarly works that I intend to pillage or draw from concern the period between Charlemagne and Francis I; like all other scholars and with the same debatable arguments, I will even concentrate on the period between the twelfth century and the fourteenth century, the very period targeted by the "medieval" banquets and parades that municipalities put on to raise money. Still worse: I will choose most of my examples from France, northern France in particular, because it is the area I know best.

I haven't quite finished with my attempt to turn aside facile criticism: the man about whom I will speak is neither a knight nor a monk; he is not a bishop or a "great man," neither is he a bourgeois, a merchant, a lord, or a man of letters. He is a man worried about the rain and the wolf, concerned about wine, his strongbox, the fetus, fire, the axe, the neighbors, sworn oaths, salvation—all those things that people speak to us about only occasionally or by preterition and through the distorting prism of political institutions, social hierarchies, juridical rules, or the precepts of faith. Thus no economic exposé will be found here, no chart of technical achievements, no class struggle: just a poor everyday man.

One last word: I have borrowed almost everything from others, and I do not cite them. But, as is usually said in hastily prepared acknowledgments, they will recognize themselves. Here and there I have added a thought or two of my own, especially on the import of what is "natural" and on the "misery" of man. I take responsibility for these, as well as for everything summarized and all simplifications and neglect of chronological or geographical nuances that are sure to set the "specialists'" teeth on edge. But that is the price of all pillage.

Have I clearly stated my goals? Now all I have to do is achieve them.

THE AXE AND THE OATH

PART ONE

MAN AND THE WORLD

Here, then, is an animated being who normally lives in an airy environment composed for the most part of oxygen, nitrogen, and hydrogen. He belongs to the order of the vertebrates, and is a mammal with a regular cycle of reproduction normally accomplished by the union of the two sexes. It is indispensable to know something about his origin and the stages of his evolution if we want to follow the ways through which his "thought" gradually enslaved a part—a very small part—of Creation. Today even those men who have the modesty or humility necessary to attempt an approach to this question hesitate and quarrel. Brandishing a mandible or a coccyx, they combat one another in the profound night that covers all new discoveries and stretches back hundreds of millions of years, as they try to discern how we have moved from a marginal chimpanzee to Sigmund Freud.

Men of the Middle Ages asked themselves no questions of this sort, nor did those of the centuries that followed, almost up to our own day. Man was a creation willed by the Supreme Being when he had finished creating the world, a crowning achievement to his labors and created in his image. Woman followed soon after, as a sort of corrective to what should have been perfect from the start. In that conception of things, does the origin of man pose no problem, and is what some find disturbing about it simply God's punishment for some original sin? Would it were so!

NAKED MAN

I want to ask the reader—and I admit that this is a difficult exercise—to leave aside for the moment all traditional schemas and try to describe and evaluate the human being.

A FRAGILE CREATURE

An Ungainly Being

This heading may seem shocking, but it is the result of archaeological, textual, physical—I was about to say zoological—observations based on bodies found intact, gripped in ice or encased in mud: mummies of holy men or great personages; skeletons, entire or partial, recovered from a necropolis; the remains of clothing or tools in which places, dates, and conditions of conservation are but anecdotal details. Iconography, painted or sculpted, differs from these indisputable remains only in the care it takes to highlight a detail: a gesture, stature, a gaze. Reasonably, the variations between these men and our contemporaries are negligible. They may be a bit shorter, if we can judge by the equipment of daily life, but with more muscular vigor, as illustrated by the surprising exploits of the warrior or the woodsman. Is this a question of alimentation? Or perhaps of lifestyle? Besides, in the cemetery, who is capable of distinguishing the tibia of a vigorous serf from that of a sickly lord?

Let us stop contemplating ourselves with delight, as we have done for thousands of years, the female sex even more than the male, and say with brutal clarity that man is an ugly and weak creature. To be sure, we might grant some grace to curves or rounded body parts, at least according to our own criteria of beauty, but how many ungraceful, if not downright ridiculous bodily elements we have: our feet with their useless toes, our rumpled and immobile ears, our heads much too small for the rest of the body (something that Greek sculptors, as friends of harmony, attempted to correct), man's genitals or woman's breasts! Is this purely a question of aesthetics? There is worse, however. Bipedal and plantigrade, man walks, runs, and jumps much less well than the quadrupeds; his lower members are quite atrophied and so weak they would make any carnivorous animal laugh; his fingernails are useless, and what remains of his teeth are not much better; the hair on his body is little protection from rain and snow; copulation forces him into grotesque postures (a defect that he shares, it is true, with many other mammals); with old age his stature shrinks, his flesh sags, his organs betray him. Still worse, his senses are extraordinarily weak: he cannot see very far and not at all at night; he perceives only a small part of the noises and sound waves that surround him; his sense of smell is completely null, and his tactile sense mediocre. His flesh is said to be tasteless and too salty, his smell is stomach-turning, or at least that is the point of view of other animals, those, precisely, whose grace, suppleness, sight, and perception astonish and charm us: the bird gliding on high, the fish swimming with the stream, the feline about to pounce. If we stopped admiring ourselves one thing would be clear. Man is a creature to which Creation was unfair. And yet . . .

And yet, how can anyone deny that man has planted his mark deeply on the emergent portions of the planet. He must have been given some particularity to compensate for the mediocre baggage with which he began. If we posit that man is an exceptional creature willed by the Supreme Being, no explanation is necessary. In the Middle Ages no one worried about the question. That there are in the world "white people," "black people," and "yellow people," small and tall people, the good and the bad, geniuses and idiots, and even Christians, Jews, and Muslims was all a part of a superior design the aims of which escaped man's understanding Here Below and might perhaps be revealed to him On High. As a result, there is no trace, during those centuries, that anyone sought (and, for even greater reason, found) the two criteria, one positive and one negative, that make man an exceptional zoological case, whereas today there are very few—even among those of deep spiritual conviction—who will not accept the notion. Man is the only mammal who can oppose his thumbs to the other fingers of his hands, a condition that is unique to him and is indispensable for seizing, transforming, and using tools or for the manipulation of fire. This skill, necessary for everything from chipping flint to building and operating a computer, is the indisputable base of man's superiority over the other animals. The master of fire and the master of the object, man is also, on the other hand, the only mammal, if not the only animated being, who destroys and kills out of hatred or for pleasure, without being pushed to it by fear, hunger, or some sexual impulse. He is the most dreaded and the most pitiless of predators.

Fairly Content with Himself

Persuaded that they were what God willed, men of the medieval centuries necessarily attributed the ugliness and weaknesses that they saw in those around them to that same divine will, but as an alteration of God's original work. Physical or moral imperfections bore the stigmata of divine discontent. If someone had a despicable soul, bodily sufferings, or a heavy conscience, it was because he or she had sinned, and such a one was inevitably described or painted as "ugly" or infirm. Iconography and profane literature leave no doubt about this: Jews, "Saracens," and the crippled were, in principle, "ugly," with grimacing expressions, misshapen bodies, members out of proportion, repugnant skin lesions, a hairy body and a red face, and with abnormal or disturbing nose, eyes, and ears. The effect of such traits was to discourage charity or understanding. The medieval world had little pity for the unlucky and the *disgraciés*, in the root sense of the word. The blind man's mistakes were laughed at, the sick were excluded and the weak scorned. No one sought to understand either the Jew or the infidel. At best, they were feared and people fled from them; at the worst, they were exterminated, "thrusting the sword into the stomach as far as it could go," as the saintly King Louis put it. Not that there were no movements in the direction of mutual aid, especially from the Church, but charity only rarely included recognition of others. At best, it was the alms of a slight pity or indulgence. Such modest signs of opening up to the other were always stained by a bit of hesitation, even remorse. This was because such victims of the divine anger were surely guilty either of not seeing where true faith lay or of having slighted it. Salvation did not pass that way, but by an utterly personal life of faith and hope. It was better to give a vineyard to the Church than a kiss to a leper. This rejection was not uniquely moral; it was social as well. As written works or paintings were done for "the right people," which meant exclusively the aristocracy until the end of the twelfth century and the "bourgeois" as well after that time, the cowardly knight, the depraved cleric, or the vulgar peasant were "ugly" or at best ridiculous.

The ideas of Good and Evil, the Beautiful and the Ugly are by no means universal. Anyone who does not understand that evident truth risks many disappointments, today more than ever, when we are confronted with other cultures and other systems of thought. These different scales of value expose us, and probably the others as well, to serious errors of evaluation, hasty condemnations, and fearful disorders. For Christians of the Middle Ages in the West, long enclosed within a limited and fairly homogeneous geographical framework of populations of Indo-European, Celtic, Germanic, or Mediterranean origin, the notion of the Beautiful might easily have been uniform. There were only differences of detail between the Celtic horseman and the Roman legionnaire, the Greek Aphrodite and the Germanic Virgin. The canons of Praxiteles or Apelles are quite close to those of the painters of the pre-Renaissance or the Gothic of Amiens: stature in general shorter than 1.75 meters for a man; a head measuring one-seventh of the body's height; an oval face with deep-set eyes, a strong nose, but fine lips; a light skin more rose than brown; thin fingers, moderate body hair, but abundant hair on the head. Naturally, I am well aware that people tended to be bigger to the north of the continent than the south, browner in the south than in the north, and that there were more round skulls in the west and the south than toward the east or the north. In my opinion, all of these "ethnic" nuances are negligible variations in comparison with Semites, Asiatics, or blacks of all sorts. It is striking to note that the prototypes praised by the poets of the *langue d'oc* and the authors of romances of the *langue d'oïl* or depicted in frescoes and miniatures actually do have these traits, to the point that, at times despite reality, they are applied indifferently to specific models, which the painter or writer refuses to see.

Beauty is what God has willed, and given that he made man in his image, man will have what are presumed to be his features; the angels, John the Baptist, and Jesus all resemble one another, as do the Virgins from century to century. This means that we end up with a curious contradiction: No one is unaware that, according to Scripture, it was amid the Jews that God the Father chose to become incarnate; that the prophets, the apostles, and Paul himself were Jews, which means that they were "ugly," according to Western criteria. However, none of the representations of them that were made bear Semitic features—not the Christ, or the twelve apostles, or the archangels or the precursors. Local models wiped out reality, or else it was generally admitted that all those figures were no longer Jews and no longer ugly, given that they recognized the Messiah.

But Are There Nonetheless Nuances?

If a man of those times ventured out of his universe of white-skinned Christians, he immediately lost his critical spirit. This does not mean that he failed to find virtue in someone like Saladin or Avicenna, or even in a learned rabbi, but that he saw only moral traits in such men. Viewed from the outside, all of them were "black men" because black pertains to the night, the unknown, and danger. Turks, Saracens, and Mongols were thought to have black skin, but not the Jews, because they had struck an alliance with God, even if they later killed God. Also, they all had a human appearance. But beyond them, all of the beings sculpted by the artist of Vézelay, imagined by Mandeville in his room in London, or whom Pian del Carpini or Marco Polo encountered on the routes of central Asia are monstrous, a veritable human bestiary. They are deformed, and certain parts of their bodies are hypertrophied or stupefying: their skin, horns, ears, feet, "marvelous" faces are the result of a mixture of Western phantasms and Persian, Indian, or Chinese legends.

When the Christian described these men on his return to his familiar world, he was not indifferent to the nuances I have referred to, nor was he blinded by the prototypes, but his observations were only rarely descriptive and physical. The *langue d'oc* poet and the *langue d'oïl* romancer, the warrior author of the sagas or of the *chansons de gestes* took note of people's stature, hair, and complexion, but they seldom escaped reproducing the topoi; a beard is "flowing," hair is "of gold, " lips are "scarlet," the complexion is "like a rose," muscles are "supple," a man is "tall and slim," and when a young man jumps on his horse or the sweet young thing offers a flower to her lover, the admiring circle of "friends" is not surprised and offers noisy approbation. Obviously, as the rustic at the plow or the weaver at his loom is never described, the historian usually says nothing about them. Exceptional circumstances are needed in order to arouse curiosity, such as the fabulous exploits of the companions of Roland or the searchers for the Holy Grail, which go far beyond all verisimilitude, even granted an exceptional sportive vigor. But these tours de force that undoubtedly set youthful warriors atingle may have been created as instruction, not as description.

Finally, attention seems to focus on the general comportment of the individual. One might even stretch things a bit and say that vision was sociological rather than physiological. For example, if the obesity of a king was noted and deplored, it was not in order to allude to his off-kilter diet or out of concern for his health; it was because the function, here a public one, and the activity, here equestrian and warlike, of the king were being flouted, in which case obesity is a sin, a fault, a "disgrace." Much attention was paid to people's gaze, the mirror of the soul; it bore witness to the sentiments that animate the man who is being described or depicted, much more than was true of acts, gestures, or costume. An artist's times impose certain requirements on him. It has been observed that hardly anyone laughs in Roman frescoes and statues, just as if an anguish of the present weighed on the times. In medieval art, eyes are often shown bulging or fearful, as a sort of reflection of those old "terrors of the year 1000" that some people today try so violently to deny or disguise. Peace, to the contrary, can be read in the reposed features of depictions of the *Beau Dieu* or on the unwrinkled faces of people in thirteenth-century miniatures. The "Reims smile" is not the product of the genial chisel of an inspired artist. It comes from his models.

Still, a chronicler who wanted to "place" his heroes had to find something that set them apart. As he usually cared little for form, he sought a comportment in which the physical supports or enlightens the moral. And without always knowing that he is doing so, he falls back on Galen or Hippocrates. Man has a "temperament," a "humor" that is the result of unequal combinations, within his body, of the four principles of life admitted by ancient, and later Arabic, medicine. He is phlegmatic, melancholic, choleric, or sanguine. The poet leaves it to the physicians (*physici*) to seek the causes of this; he himself is only interested in its effects in daily life or in social relations, as seen in alimentation, activities, moral or physical reactions, and an entire range of virtues or faults.

A final domain, blood, is more under control today. That blood flowed as freely in those centuries as it does today (and perhaps more freely) is unimportant. What matters is that the spectator of those years seemed unmoved at the sight. Artists multiplied severed heads from which blood spurted, the gaping wounds of Christ, body parts strewn about the battlefield, leaving a red tide of blood, cuirasses out of which blood gushes like a fountain. The poet was not far behind, with broken skulls, severed arms, pierced stomachs, and more. Was this due to ignorance, or partial ignorance, of the role of blood in life? Does it show less sensitivity to the pain of the wound? Or resignation before a death that was close, probable, and inevitable? There was nothing resembling the emotion that flowing blood prompts today, at least in certain parts of the world (happily, those in which we live, for elsewhere it is a different story). It is not that blood did not matter to men of those times, but rather that they saw in it an element of the transmission of life, even of virtues. The Germanic custom of drinking the blood of a warhorse in order to fill oneself with his courage and strength may be pure invention on the part of a startled chronicler. On the other hand, the importance attached to the woman's menstrual cycles is clear in the first blood carefully conserved in the home, the solemn publicity given to the renewed cycle in the churching of women, and the prohibition of sexual relations during menstruation.

Serology has made enough progress today for biologists to seek connections between the various blood groups and the ability of the individuals within them to withstand aggression from microbes or viruses. In the Middle Ages people noticed it when a certain man (unfortunately, only those of high rank were observed) presented signs of being affected when his neighbor was not, and in times of epidemics these facts were even more evident. In the midst of a contaminated household certain groups seemed untouched, and for no apparent reason. In this connection, the pandemics of plague in the fourteenth and fifteenth centuries (to which I shall return) present a striking case in point. There were small groups of healthy people in the middle of an ocean of contagion. Unhappily for the historian, such observations were rarely specific or numerical; still, they may explain the undisputable diversity of estimates that researchers have offered concerning human losses on such occasions. I myself was long unaware, for example, that individuals of the B blood group are not receptive to the plague bacillus, and where that group was in the majority—in Hungary, for example—the disease had many fewer victims. Blood groups have been so mixed in the intervening centuries that any satisfactory estimate of their distribution in the Middle Ages is out of the question. Hypotheses have not been lacking, however, some of them perhaps hazardous, such as those offered in Great Britain to explain the movements, conditions, and stages of Saxons as they populated the British Isles.

BUT A THREATENED CREATURE

Does Man Really Know Himself?

Our societies, which think of themselves as "evolved," have fallen into a sort of cult of the body. Seized by panic before aging and imbued with reverence for the remedies that crowd our medicine chests, we crowd establishments for "getting into shape" and even sue physicians whose art has not kept its promises or fulfilled expectations. The Mediterranean world—that of antiquity and our own—is more strongly inclined in this direction than any other. But today we have available a store of knowledge about pathology and we have highly skilled caregivers who dissipate our fears and our ignorance—at least in theory. Historians, swept along for about a century by that nosologic wave, have provided a number of studies on the medieval body, searching for traces of illnesses, sounding their psychological effects, and even promoting some of them (the bubonic plague, most obviously) to figure as factors— demographic ones primarily, more than economic and even social—in the evolution of the medieval centuries. In this way, they have thrown a good deal of light on the illness of the great of that world, on mass epidemics, and on Judeo-Greek and Arabic science, and they have catalogued the signs, written and unwritten, of diseases, offered serious diagnoses, and sketched out their evolution. And all of this labor is admirable.

Admirable, but superficial, for in those days as today, although people were and are under "stress" (a term that dates to 1953 in this usage!) from bouts of the plague or the brutal progress of AIDS, little is known about corns on toes, a runny nose, or a lazy colon, those "minor miseries" that nonetheless destroy the body's harmony. I cannot answer the question that heads this section for our own times, but for the Middle Ages, the response is categorically negative. Besides, how could those men have had access, before the twelfth century, to the medical treatises that arrived from or were soon to be written or translated in Cordova, Palermo, Salerno, and Montpellier? We are not even sure that the monks who followed Peter the Venerable in the mid-twelfth century or the princes who were advised by *physici* were truly aware of the demands and the weaknesses of their bodies. As for the others, how could they have raised questions about what was evidently a reflection of the will of God? The stillborn baby, the child born with defects, and the chronically ill, but also the deaf, the blind, and the dumb were the price to pay for God's wrath. These were all quite naturally punishments for a sin committed by such people or by their parents, for transgressions that were inherited, as was the condition of servitude. There was no remedy and no appeal to that judgment. As for violent death in combat, at the turn of a forest path, or by accident, it bore a defamatory condemnation: no confession, no salvation.

Still, the Christian found it difficult to accept this dogmatic "double or quits," and he sought recourse, without making too much display of rancor toward arbitrary decisions that might come from On High. First of all, there were intermediaries to which one had access to soften the rigor of the Judge. The veneration of relics and pilgrimages to holy places expanded along with the influence of the Church. As was often the case, at least in Western Europe, the Church was skilled at seizing interested devotional practices, many of which predated it: a minor healing god, a stone, or a thaumaturgic spring were embraced and placed under the guidance of a saint, real or invented, who was reputed to have healing powers. Each of these saints had his "specialty" connected with the details of his life or martyrdom. One healed pimples, another specialized in fever or pain, his efficacy proven by miracles that were sought avidly. Some scholars have even investigated the recrudescence of these cults in the eleventh century and later. Could they be used to evaluate the spread of a particular disease? In any event, the miracles that took place, as simply described in a large number of texts, offer a panoply of the more current afflictions that reflects more illnesses due to dietary insufficiencies than to wounds or organic diseases. As for the Virgin, whose cult grew exponentially after 1150, spurred on by the Cistercians, she was more useful for healing the soul than the body, and prayers were addressed to her more as a mother than a miracle worker. It is true that the Church never dared to allow the cult of the Virgin to develop to the point where she became a mother goddess, a Christian Cybele. She was a virgin, and thus could not serve as the emblem of fertility.

Pilgrimages and offerings were works of piety, and the monks rejoiced in them. But were their prayers efficacious? Would it not be better to address oneself—but in secret, of course—to powers that were expert in the art of interrogating the stars, which could only have an effect outside of time, or instead to concoct remedies outside the limits of an infernal etiology? Magicians or sorcerers are particularly appreciated today by all historians proud of their acquisitions in anthropology or sociology, and the "inverted" world delights all of the disciples (be they close or not) of Freud, Mauss, or Lévi-Strauss. Moreover, the innumerable trials that were held, between the fifteenth century and the nineteenth, to judge those who were the masters of "maleficent" forces provide fodder for thick commentaries. It is true that, in general, we have only the dossiers of the prosecution in such trials. In the thirteenth century the *exempla* of the Dominicans, who obviously condemned such practices (kinesthetic gestures and chiropractics, repetitive formulas and invocations, rites founded on vegetal substances or on the virtues of water) show that their place, at the heart of the rural world at least, was generally admitted and of capital importance. Efforts to heal the body were much more frequent than those touching the soul, and because the Church did not admit that such efforts could alter the divine will, those who claimed to take the place of God in combating the ills that he set loose had to be condemned and even burned. If need be, an accusation of heresy justified the pyre for the sorcerers, although in reality more bonesetters were burned than evil spirits.

The Dominicans' *exempla* and the *fabliaux* also gave women, old women in particular, a role as intermediaries between this dark world and bodily failings. They were the ones who seemed quickest to respond to practices that have elicited laughter from the finely tuned "scientific" minds of the age known as "modern." Today, however, disguised as "medicine lite," phytotherapy, cures to restore youth, and a recourse to "natural" remedies are all the rage, and creams, ointments, infusions, purgatives, massages, or kinestherapeutic manipulation rival "psychological aids" and "restorative cells" in appealing to a grotesque degree to our bewildered ego. We are told to follow a certain diet or consume a particular plant; what is more, most of the recipes that we know from the Middle Ages were found in medical treatises.

If women are in the front rank here it is because Eve was halfway to being a sorceress, and any mother knew recipes to cure her children. Men, more observers than traditionalists, contributed experience gained from their herds and flocks and, more rarely, their travels. There is one exception, however: the Jews. They went from one village to another, street by street, carrying sachets, phials, and amulets; they were skilled in examining urine, purging and bleeding, placing splints correctly, setting cupping glasses, and taking a pulse. They had accumulated that knowledge and practical experience thanks to their thousand-year history in Mediterranean and Eastern cultures. They had assimilated the synthetic hypotheses of Greco-Roman medicine and the analytical experience of Hindu and Iranian physicians, and throughout the Islamic world had carried their store of knowledge from one community to another. The most learned among them translated Avicenna and Galen and wrote commentaries on Constantine the African; they followed Maimonides and taught Averroes. It was the Jews, modest representatives of science, who cared for the sick. It is true that they soon paid a price for their efforts. Because they had knowledge, because people consulted them at every turn, their destiny was bound with their success. Should they fail to cure patients during an epidemic, it was thought that because they were familiar with the disease, they must have unleashed it.

In order to cure the sick with other weapons than "old wives'" recipes, one had to know how the body was made. This was beyond the expertise of the commonality. The soldier had seen stomachs slashed open and bleeding wounds; the peasant had some idea of the skeleton of the animals that he butchered; all women were gynecologists. But no one had an overall view or guessed the role of the heart or the brain. Even when an epidemic struck, no one grasped the idea of contagion, thus no one seized (or combated) the idea of a transmitting agent. Besides, that ignorance, which was defeated by popular medicine only in the nineteenth century, was not total, given that—either by experience or intuition— a number of therapeutic practices were known: trephination, cauterizing wounds with fire, the reduction of fractures, plasters, opiates, tourniquets, cupping glasses, and emetics achieved their aims and give proof that some accurate observations were made about blood, bones, and skin. It is true that a *physicus* or a *mire* was often called on to intervene. In 800 some more learned practitioners even managed to draw up a list of medicinal plants in a capitulary, but theory long remained at the level of that of the humors of Hippocrates, Galen, and Oribasius. Persian contributions, via Salerno or Montpellier, to what was known about the harmony of organic function, the circulation of the blood, the role of spinal marrow, and even the idea of hereditary qualities, came from Spain and the Balearic Islands in the late twelfth century, but they ran afoul of the Church's prohibitions, in Troyes in 1163, for example, and in the Lateran Council of 1215. The very idea of putting a scalpel to a human body was condemned; it was equated with "black magic." At the same time, however, animal cadavers were not only carved up by butchers but also used for scientific purposes. Beginning at what date were human autopsies performed? Clandestinely, on disinterred bodies, perhaps around 1190 or 1230 in Venice; on the dead bodies of condemned criminals a little later, also in Italy. Emperor Frederick II, a great innovator in this as in other fields, advised and encouraged dissection in Sicily after 1240, and after 1290 it was authorized in Bologna and Padua. Moreover, scholars in northern Europe in particular (a fact that deserves comment)—Albertus Magnus, Neckam, Cantimpré, and Roger Bacon among them—rushed to sample the delights of experimental science. This break with the older empiricism is a new chapter in the history of thought. The fourteenth and fifteenth centuries witnessed the birth of a new scientific medicine. But where did ordinary people stand in all this?

"Abnormal" Assaults on Man

Bombarded by medical jargon that gives us the illusion of knowledge, we are quick to lose sight of the primitive form of illness. In our own disordered societies, popular diagnostics point to allergies to everything and to nothing; to stress, which is a convenient excuse for any illness; or to a mutant virus when those who should know have nothing useful to say. In daily life, a cold, a stomachache, an itch, "kidney trouble," or headaches are our common lot.

We hardly speak of them: how could people of the Middle Ages have done so, in a society that was more accustomed than our own to the blows of fortune? Terms like *flux de ventre, catarrhres, langueur, pestilence*, or *fièvres* did not have a clear medical definition. Infirmities, inborn or acquired, went untreated and were not talked about. The weak used a stick to walk, the deaf used a hand as a trumpet, and mockery greeted the gesticulations of the mute. As for the blind, doubtless the low and flickering light of the hearth or the candle increased their numbers, but their confusion was met with laughter, and nothing was done to aid the myopic between Nero's first-century amethyst and Bacon's thirteenth-century magnifying glass.

Behavioral anomalies are more striking. When they affect the great of this world they are noted, but they are not corrected. The chronicles stigmatize obesity at every turn and laugh at the knight whose girth makes it difficult for him to ride a horse, but they say nothing about his gluttony. They note complacently that men were well aware of their corpulence, as when Louis VI and his enemy William the Conqueror teased each other for it. Drunkenness was, please pardon the expression, drawn from the same barrel. Humble or great, many drank too much, to the point of passing out. What is known about the amount of wine or other alcoholic beverages absorbed by adults of both sexes, at all social levels, and of all ages—from a liter to a liter and a half on a daily basis (although the alcoholic content is unclear)—explains the phenomenon. Moreover, in lands in which grapes were cultivated, opinion was always indulgent toward drunkenness when it did not result in dishonorable conduct. It is well known that John Lackland drank too much, as did his enemy Philip Augustus, and that their behavior was related to cirrhosis of the liver; it is also known that, somewhat later, Charles the Bold, who was drunk one day out of two, died an absurd death because of his addiction. Saint Louis, who was known for his austere piety, forced the closure and emptying of the taverns of Paris in the evening, but was he obeyed elsewhere?

Excessive eating and drinking led to other excesses that were attributed to weakness of character and were deplored with a smile. Sexual attitudes and sexual practices, to which I shall return, also caused physical ills that were encouraged by an abusive use of aphrodisiacs. But such effects were not categorized as illnesses any more than was excessive eating. In contrast, there were behaviors that today are explained psychosomatically and that at the time seemed to compromise the Hippocratic harmony. One of these—drugs, with all of their psychic, nervous, and organic effects—has now become a widespread social scourge. Unhappily, the loss of self-possession that the use of drugs brings with it was considered, in those distant times, a submission to the forces of evil, which means that drug use was more likely equated with sin and vice—which were not talked about openly—than with a physical addiction that could be combated. Drug use, not denounced, was thus not described or much investigated. It is clear that it was present, however. In the Frankish states of the East or in the nearer lands of Islam, the mastication or smoking of Indian hemp was certainly practiced more widely than just among the Muslim sects of Lebanon or the Atlas Mountains. In Europe itself, powders made from poppies picked in Asia were known in Italy before 1200 or 1250, and were transported in bundles of "spices" or in medicinal phials. The strange visions, psychedelic impressions, and cerebral troubles brought on by the consumption of such substances were beyond the powers of description of a user, but when he could hold a brush, the result was the fantastic visions of Hieronymous Bosch. Opium can be absorbed without any desire to draw troubled inner illumination from it, and some scholars today feel that ergotism can be connected with involuntary drug use. The sources speak at length of it, and although no one had any idea of the origin of the illness or its remedies, the epidemic nature of the *mal des ardents* and the *feu saint Antoine* (Saint Anthony's fire) struck people's imaginations and aroused the chroniclers' emotions. Attested to as early as 872 in northern Europe, in the tenth century in central France, and by the end of the eleventh century throughout

Southern France, the disease came, without any possible doubt, from the hallucinogenic effects of ergot, a microscopic fungus somewhat like a morel mushroom, invisible to the naked eye, that lived in the ears of grains, rye in particular, entire fields of which it contaminated. Everyone who ate the rye fell sick, and opinion saw maleficent contagion at work. The symptoms were dizziness, confusion, delirium, followed by a burning sensation and a intense fever, which, taken together, give the impression of a drug or an epidemic disease. In all times and all places ergotism, which was not always deadly, accompanied rye, the use of which declined at the end of the Middle Ages; the disease disappeared when nitrate fertilizers were introduced.

Just as ergotism was taken to be an epidemic plague and using hashish considered a punishable offense, the origins of cerebral asthenia—the complex mix of anguish, paralysis, frustration and fatigue that plagues almost all of our own contemporaries under the name of stress or nervous tension—were similarly misunderstood. The terms used in medieval times show that sick people were more likely to be depressed than abnormally excited. The words used to describe their suffering were *langor*, *stupor*, and *indolentia*. Naturally, noise, agitated movement, and overwork seem to us reason enough for a breakdown of nervous resistance. In the centuries of the Middle Ages, when these were obviously less, people looked to character to explain depression. Someone inactive was simply useless. Moreover, there was no such thing as vacations, leisure time, or retirement homes. The idle person was rejected, even scorned; he was not an invalid to be cured or a weak person to be supported. Leisure was a luxury for the powerful or a vocation for the monk.

The Illness That Lies in Wait

Nonetheless, not all medieval men and women were cripples, drunkards, drug addicts, or depressives; still, they suffered from illnesses just as we do—more precisely, though, not the same illnesses. Oddly, cancer, which nibbles at our subconscious when it is not attacking our organs, is never mentioned. Its basic cause, which is the disturbance of cellular life, hence a direct attack on the principles of harmony inherited from the ancient world, should have struck both the scholars and the common people, but no: total silence! Obviously, some signs are reported that might be or certainly are indications of cancer. The word "tumor" and even the word "cancer" appear in the sources, but in the sense of a swelling or of pustules. The notion that it spreads from one organ to another (which we call metastasis) was denied, as was the corruption of one body by another, perhaps, where the learned were concerned, because of what Aristotle had to say on the topic. There is no mention of cancer and, no less curiously, no allusion to the respiratory system, for catarrh can be many things. The handkerchief was a medieval "invention," but there is no mention in the sources of blowing one's nose, spitting, or coughing.

In the final analysis, the common man seems to have paid attention only to what he could plainly see, which was his skin; to his stomach, which worried him; and to a fever, which he took as a preliminary sign of illness. What was known as *flux de ventre* was one of the most frequently mentioned causes of the death of an important personage, and probably of more humble ones as well. What did it include? Was it a simple intestinal or gastric disturbance? In the fifteenth century, the sources speak of purgatives, plasters, imbibing oils, and, with a touch of reality, polluted waters, or the bad air of the streets. But people were also aware that there were more serious forms of the complaint that might be judged contagious. Did anyone isolate the symptoms of dysentery, typhoid fever, or scurvy? A high fever, diarrhea, thirst, and "malignant" pains were noted and—correctly enough—attributed to insects or the ingestion of or simple contact with tainted foods or impure liquids. By its effects the disease was thought to be contagious, because it struck entire groups of people who lived in unhygienic environments, such as poor people in the cities, soldiers on the battlefield, and starving peasants. Some went so far as to speak of an epidemic. The presence of *flux de ventre* was widely noted in the sixth century and in the twelfth century in the armies of Italy, Aquitaine, and wherever famine ruled. Thirty thousand people may have died of it in England in 1406. But the size of these and other statistics are proof of the chronicler's fears more than of the real extent of the disease. People were treated with bleeding and purging, which aggravated the illness, or with unguents and pulverized herbs, which were better but did not save either Saint Louis or John XXII.

Fever was just a symptom, and it was quickly noted. But when it was intense, chronic, or the source of pain or vomiting, it could be the sign of a specific disease. At the time, *fièvre jaune, quarte, miliaire,* or *suette* (yellow fever, quartan ague, miliary fever, sweating fever)—all manifestations that today's medical science differentiates—were seen as simple variants of the *peste des marais,* or malaria, the *paludisme* of hot, humid, and unhealthy climates. It is probable that a connection was established between these various forms of the disease and the sting of insects, but the repetitive nature of the bouts of fever or hepatic deficiencies meant that the disease was treated only superficially by compresses or opium-based potions, and many people, from crusaders in the Levant to peasants who lived by the sea, died of it. On the other hand, grippe, which is viral in origin and the symptoms of which are a cough, a headache, and a high contagiousness, was seldom identified. There is notice of waves of the grippe in 972, of two or three other occurrences in the twelfth century and of more in the fourteenth century, but nothing distinguishes it from a "classic" fever except for fits of "catarrhal" coughing. The *hoquette* that the Bourgeois de Paris complains of in 1420 because it interrupted sermons was probably whooping cough.

A man can conceal his pains and bring down his fever, but he cannot hide skin lesions. I have already spoken of the importance (even if only symbolic) of that fleshly envelope, which is and has always been the reflection of a person's good health, wealth, physical beauty, and even moral stature. Powders and creams were invented to cover the injuries of age and the imperfections of one's traits. On this level, the Middle Ages would have few lessons to learn from the frenzied publicity we are subjected to today. Unfortunately it does little good to hide wrinkles and revive one's complexion when disease is plainly visible. Pimples, pustules, and red discoloration did not escape the painter, and not only when a taste for realism guided the paintbrush in the fifteenth century. But it is leprosy that remains the emblem of the Middle Ages in the common subconscious. How many images there are, and how many narrations that evoke the leper, covered with repugnant crusts and ugly scales (*lepra* in Greek), in rags, shaking a rattle, and constrained to take refuge alone in a dreadful lair, far from all normal life. Lepers accounted for from 2 to 3 percent of the population, the historians learnedly tell us; in France alone around 1300 there were more than four thousand asylums to receive them—*lazarets, maladreries, léproseries*, and hospices—and from the ninth century on, innumerable laws dictated that someone suspected of leprosy be isolated and that his house, his clothing, and all the movable goods that he may have touched be burned. Today there is ample doubt about these measures, as the illness is still current in Asia and its various aspects are better known. In the Middle Ages lepers went into the city, gave witness in legal documents, received and managed wealth; some of them had a function at the court or in commerce, to the point that one of their number, Baldwin IV, was king of Jerusalem. At a certain moment, leprosy declined. It may have given way to the tuberculosis bacillus, with which it is incompatible and which was not mentioned until the late fourteenth century. It is true that a few *cagots* remained isolated from society up to the seventeenth century, but these were more likely to be outcasts than sick persons. What are we to think? The exterior signs of leprosy are well known: patches of darkened skin, buboes and ganglions, nodules that eat away at the joints and the cartilage of the hands or the nose, bouts of fever, even gradual paralysis. But all of these signs, which can lead to death, are far from being attested everywhere. Was leprosy perhaps confused with other highly visible dermic infections such as erysipelas, eczema, psoriasis, naevus (birthmarks, moles), none of which is contagious? One might well wonder whether the terrible reputation of leprosy is not based in large part on its psychological significance. Repulsive, subject to uncontrollable sexual impulses (the possibility was raised of delivering Iseut over to them), bearing their probable faults on their faces, accused of poisoning wells and infecting grains and even farm animals, lepers were the "untouchables" of the Christian West, symbols of Evil, of Sin, and of the Impure. Thus they must be excluded and kept away from the faithful.

Of all of these afflictions, men of antiquity and of the Middle Ages mention one only in a whisper and we are still struck by its extranatural aspect. A man—or a woman, for that matter—speaks and acts normally amid others when, suddenly, he stiffens, turns white, drops to the ground, is seized by convulsions, then falls into something much resembling a coma. After an hour or two he gets up and has no memory of the crisis. He has clearly been "possessed" by the Holy Spirit. This was the *haut mal*, the *mal sacré*, that picked its victim as an instant receptacle of a superhuman power. Before the nineteenth century made progress in medical science regarding the nervous system, epilepsy was taken for a sign of divine favor and the epileptic for a messenger from the Other World. He was not pitied; he was not subjected to treatment; he was respected and feared, whether he was Caesar himself or a poor laborer.

The Black Death

These days, when human life weighs less when it is that of the poor or the inhabitants of "undeveloped" lands, we react differently to demographic disasters. Besides, our means of information—our "media"—take great pains to make this so. The "developed" world is moved when two soldiers are killed in a surprise attack, two hundred die in an attack, or two thousand are crushed when a tower collapses, but when seven hundred "indigenous persons" kill each other with our weapons or thousands perish in an earthquake, we are hardly touched—if it all occurs far from where we are. We ought to judge disasters equally and use words such as "genocide" with prudence. The two abominable and stupid world wars of the first half of the twentieth century produced some 50–60 million dead in five years, which may be modest, all things considered, in the face of the 120 million natives killed with alcohol, smallpox, and measles by the "glorious" conquerors of Mexico and South America. It is true that in the world wars those who died were supposedly defending a land or an idea, and that in Central and South America those who remained received the true Faith. But what can we say about those who died of the "Black Death"— the 20 to 25 million Christians who lay in the streets swollen with black buboes and who had demanded and received nothing?

We need to look more closely at the plague. So much has been thought, studied, and written about this scourge that I can hardly hope to say anything new. Just about everything provided by the sources is known. This means that I will concentrate on a few aspects that could be judged secondary. First of all concerning the nature of the plague. The persistence of points of concentration of the disease in central and eastern Asia has permitted us to study it in depth, beginning with the works of Yersin at the end of the nineteenth century. The two contagious forms of the disease—the pulmonary, which is 100 percent fatal, and the bubonic, from which one out of four persons can hope to escape after four days—have neither the same gravity nor the same exterior signs. The first form was dominant in the fourteenth-century epidemic (but not in later occurrences), which explains the terror inspired by its approach, as it was incurable and its incubation period was only a few hours or days. However, to the extent to which contemporaries noted such nuances, it was the "black" plague (the word was first used only in the sixteenth century)—the less deadly form with inflamed buboes, the survivors of which were immunized against recurrences—that was the most often described and feared. It was also the variety that recurred up to the late fifteenth century, leaving behind an increasing number of survivors.

Next, the conditions of contagion. People were persuaded that, like other maladies thought to be contagious, only the touch of the sick person or his clothing transmitted the disease. This means that fire was seldom used to destroy the clothing and the objects of the dead person, and no one dared to go so far as to incinerate cadavers in a Christian society that prohibited cremation. Identifying the agents of propagation was a complete fiasco. The common people blamed astral conjunctions, poison thrown into the wells by the Jews, or, more simply, divine fury; the learned themselves—at least those who held a pen—saw nothing, never noticing the rats who carried contaminated fleas, or even flea bites. Hence all the therapeutic measures that were imagined were just the opposite of what should have been done. Bleeding the victim and lancing the buboes only aggravated the symptoms of the disease and contaminated the caregivers; opium compresses or plasters made of bird organs had no effect on the humid breath of the patient, the source of pulmonary contagion. As for crowding into the city to flee a plague-ridden village, it was obviously the opposite of what should have been done.

Thanks to defective observation of the disease and useless prophylaxis, the epidemic of 1348–51 swept away something like 30 percent of the population of western Europe. What happened next is often neglected. First, the historian is struck by the extreme inequality of the damage from one region to another, which in fact poses a number of problems. Although our sources are fairly well distributed geographically, their authors are unaware of what was occurring in adjoining territories. Here and there the disease did not strike at all. No one thought of taking any precautions (even though the bacillus crossed the Channel in less than ten days!). Some have sought local causes to explain why certain areas escaped the plague—fewer roads, waterways, or cities—even though contrary examples abounded. Today scholars tend instead to look to specific and individual resistance. In fact, the recurrences of the epidemic in 1372–75, 1399–1400, 1412, and up to the end of the fifteenth century, were less spectacular, hence were less often noted, in spite of an equal virulence of the disease. We have the impression that this was because recurrences chose their victims: children, old people, and pregnant women. Beyond a degree of simply getting used to attacks of the plague, as seen in the maintenance of economic activity and a rise in population rates, certain individuals may have escaped contagion through a serological immunization, and, as I have already mentioned, people in the B blood group seem to have had a natural resistance to the plague bacillus, which means that its predominance in populations of pure Celtic or Asiatic origin (Hungarians, for example) may perhaps explain the "white spots" on the map of the plague.

Let me add two further observations. First of all, if the arrival of the plague and its lightning-fast propagation were striking for their swiftness and prompted unreasoning panic, it is far from true that the high number of deaths was due only to the virulence of the bacillus. Contemporaries hardly remarked on contagion at the time. They sought an explanation in unfavorable astral conjunctions, which may have been connected with climatic variations. Historians today find other causes in archival documents. Disquieting demographic statistics or financial accounts, a changing economic situation, and an accumulation of social difficulties make the period from 1310 to 1340 a phase of depression with a background of natural calamities and political troubles. The only detailed demographic document that has come down to us—an extraordinary relic—is a register of births and deaths in the small village of Givry in Burgundy, south of Dijon. This famous document attests to a death rate that was growing beginning as early as 1320, even if it increases by leaps and bounds with the arrival of the plague. Morbid manifestations in art or in deviant religious customs also preceded the plague, and a number of Jews were massacred before those dates. In any event, the plague struck men who were already weakened, if not already sick. Inversely, the gradual decline of the Black Death was not only due to a lessened virulence of the bacillus, but also to an economic recovery and a population increase that led to the reoccupation of abandoned lands and hamlets. Throughout the West, that recovery occurred between 1430 and 1480, according to region, but the disease continued for some time to come.

A second remark pertains to a fact that is too often neglected, which is the relative abundance of sources that throw light on the plague of the fourteenth century. This abundance minimizes earlier assaults of the disease, in classical antiquity and above all in the sixth and seventh centuries, when it ravaged the coasts of the Mediterranean. Although we know next to nothing about these epidemics, scholars today agree that they were the point of departure for the profound and durable political and economic decline of the southern flank of Christianity in its younger years, which may partially explain the brutal expansion of Islam over ruined terrains and weakened men, a highly important phenomenon in the history of the world. This means that we need to pose a similar question regarding the epidemic of the fourteenth and fifteenth centuries. What is usually stressed is the leveling off of the relative overpopulation of Europe, the reshaping of the rural habitat, strong variations in prices and wages (not necessarily in a negative direction), or the woes of the feudal system. If we look closer at the situation, the social upsets, a thirst for gold, and the redistribution of wealth that came after the epidemics lasted much longer than the period of the biological decline of the disease. Just as the plague that is foolishly called Justinian must be one of the pillars of the Muslim phenomenon, so the plague of the late Middle Ages lies at the origin of the colonial expansion of Europe of the sixteenth century. The presumed "rebirth" of classical antiquity had nothing to do with it.

Can Those Men Be Counted?

I have not yet attempted to estimate the number of men and women I am trying to survey. As Marc Bloch pointed out, we cannot judge the daily life and the work activities of past populations when we lack basic figures. Unfortunately, we do not know the numbers, or, rather, our data are few, sparse, disputable, and late; before the fifteenth century at the least, they defy all certitude. The reason for this lies not only in the archives, although it is true that here, as in other domains, the losses have been immense. Worse, in all of the centuries of the Middle Ages, figures were not given their real arithmetical values except in ecclesiastical computation. That "turn of mind" probably had psychological causes, for example, a clear indifference to exactitude in accounting that is not found in other cultures, notably Oriental or Semitic. Figures had only symbolic value. One, three, seven, and twelve were God, the Trinity, or figures found in the Bible; and as for six and its multiple six times six, they were the sign of what cannot be counted with the fingers of one hand, thus, what surpasses immediate understanding, whether what was in question was the dead or the living, years of age, or degrees of kinship. This disdain for figures affected measurement as well. Someone would sell "a wood," bequeath "his land," and give "what he has." Even when a number appears, the historian's despair remains because he does not know how to interpret "a wood of one hundred pigs." Are there actual pigs in the woods? Is this an evaluation of how much land will feed a hundred pigs? Even games of dice, which persisted throughout the Middle Ages, are given over to the intervention of chance, hence of God, and their outcomes are more psychological than actuarial. In the domain that I am reviewing a certain indifference with regard to the number of individuals can be justified, since any need for precision—for fiscal reasons, for example—is lacking. What is more, men are ceaselessly in movement. They do not know how old they are and cannot name their cousins. As late as 1427, we can find Florentines who do not know how many children they have. It was perhaps only the powerful who kept track, but only out of a familial, fiscal, or political interest, not out of a spirit of geometry. The researcher has few tools with which to pierce that wall of ignorance. There are no serious lists, and in particular no complete ones, of tenants, taxpayers, or conscripts, especially in the countryside or before the fifteenth century. The best we can do is to survey a series of witnesses, the genealogies of lords or princes, and fragmentary chronicles, and try to glean from them pieces of a broader picture. And even then, how many unknown persons will be left out: the newborn, those absent for the moment, the extremely old, or the miserably poor? As for the female sex, the "male Middle Ages"—to make use of a totally exaggerated formula—thrusts women out of economic or political texts, which are men's work, and out of articles of law, which are sexless. The same male viewpoint is capable of leaving women out completely, as in certain phases of "machismo" that require explanation, for example, in northern France between 1100 and 1175.

This means that a demographer has little to go on. The situation is better than it was a few decades ago, when scholars had to be content with vague adjectives or adverbs and took refuge behind a few famous documents whose reputation came from their very rarity. Among these are the *Domesday Book* from eleventh-century England, a text filled with uncertain data; the *État des feux* of 1328, which never clearly defines just what is meant by a "fire"; and the Tuscan *Catasto* of 1427, which cannot without exaggeration be called a typical example of a census. Still, we can attempt to enumerate questions and analyze responses. The overall evolution of the population first. Except for some regions that I shall not examine, the curve was ascendant, with a population that tripled between the years 1000 and 1300. This datum is uncontested, but historians debate about the chronological framework. A large majority of them hold for a strong rise in population in the seventh and eighth centuries, if not from the late sixth century, and another rise at the end of the Carolingian age. Others, among whom I count myself, see in this rise only a recuperation, probably even only a partial one, from the decline of the third to fifth centuries. These historians search in vain for capitularies noting births and worry about ambiguous or disappointing archaeological information. All scholars agree, however, regarding the years following the year 1000, when there was a sure but uneven rise in human population, weakening after 1250 or 1270, with an average (completely theoretical, of course) annual growth of 0.7 percent. This figure is low, and quite inferior to the growth rates of a number of "developing" regions today and even to the growth rates attained in France in recent years. This was no "baby boom," but a movement of remarkable duration: three hundred years.

This may well explain contemporaries' indifference to the question of population figures. There are indeed a few chroniclers who speak of the human tide, but for the most part these are city people, where a population increase may have been more visible, thanks to in-migration more than to a rising birth rate. Even within the aristocracy, about whom we have more information, we can detect no sense of a disquieting numerical increase. Although the marriage of younger sons had for some time been blocked, this was done in order to avoid the division of wealth, not because the lordly dwelling risked becoming too crowded. Moreover, in the thirteenth century, the door was unbolted. This neutral attitude toward the number of the living carried over to the dead. Any attempt to count the elements of a given family structure almost always encounters large groups: six, seven, or ten children at the least, and girl children are often left out. That large number of offspring ought to have increased the growth rates noticeably, and if it failed to do so, it was because at least a third of those children died, even among the great, who had a right to expect better care: Blanche of Castile lost five of her thirteen children. That fearful infant mortality lasted throughout the thousand years of the medieval period, an issue I shall return to. As late as the fifteenth century, 42 percent of the ground space in Hungarian cemeteries was taken up by the graves of children under ten years of age, not including the stillborn, who offer a totally different theme for meditation.

The reasons for the decline in births at the end of the medieval age are quite evident. War and contraceptive practices had little to do with it; the famines that struck before the plague weakened men more than killing them off; the breakdown in family structures and its effects on relations of mutual aid counted for something. But we arrive inexorably at a basic reality. Even without the intervention of three of the "four horsemen of the Apocalypse"—war, famine, and the plague—the birth rate declined. This leads the historian to look back in time to see what had made it rise in the first place. The answer is easy to see. A richer diet reinforced man's natural defenses and brought down the death rate, particularly in infant mortality; family structure evolved at a faster rate in the direction of the isolated, child-producing conjugal couple; the practice grew of putting out babies to a wet nurse, thanks to the large number of women capable of feeding another woman's child; liberated from the amenorrhea that accompanies breast-feeding, a woman could become pregnant again sooner, thus reducing "generational intervals." How can we be sure that this does not reflect, if not a "fashion," at least a convenience, a comfort, rather than a "natalist" determination? A deliberate desire to generate children appears only with the development of privileges of primogeniture, which encouraged the search for a male heir or the desire to replace one. But this puts us in around 1050–80 and can be applied only in the lordly world. Hence our a posteriori explanations lead us to the threshold of the initial cause. If we eliminate the notion of a sudden divine tenderness for a truly weak portion of God's creation— an explanation that was considered sufficient at the time, and still is today for those of a certain turn of mind—we will have to turn to what escapes man and come back to the "natural" causes that I have already mentioned. Even if they display some hesitation, today's historians do not evade an appeal to the forces of the climate and to the history of the Earth. The "optimal" phase that has been observed after 900 or 950 lasted until around 1280 or 1300, but signs of a tipping point can be seen after 1150, when some lucid chroniclers noted unexpectedly strong tides, increased rainfall, or the retreat of a glacier. But no one could have seen in these the effect of a powerful movement of nearby ocean waters—and I am no more capable than they were of explaining it—but that slow reversal of the biotic high point of the tenth to the thirteenth centuries may easily provide an explanation for the phenomena of demographic stagnation mentioned above.

I have at times alluded to the female sex, so poorly treated in the texts. The moment will soon come to approach the woman in her dwelling. For the moment, what is important is rather to discern the ratio, or numerical relation, between the two sexes. In the animal world (or at least for terrestrial species), the reproducing male is in the minority, perhaps because he is sometimes physically eliminated when his job is done. This occurs among the insects, for example, and among certain mammals. Among humans, demographers are in agreement in estimating that the two sexes are numerically equal at birth, leaving aside surges of temporary inequality, the origin of which still escapes us. Among adults and even at puberty, however, the female sex seems to have been in the minority, particularly in the eleventh to thirteenth centuries, at a ratio of eighty to ninety females for every one hundred males. The written sources (which, admittedly, concern the more favored levels of society) show clearly a certain hunt—I was about to say "fair"—for women, who were relatively rare, hence expensive. A daughter could be married off at fifteen, and often she was "promised" even earlier; she was, in fact, the nub of the family's wealth, the jewel that commanded a certain price. Young men participated in tourneys to win her, while others walked the roads and scoured the farms. After the Church authorized remarriages, in the age of Saint Louis, widowers, who could not compete with younger men, were satisfied with the girls who were left and cost less. Women who reached the age of twenty or twenty-five and had found no takers or had successfully rejected the convent remained under the authority of their father or their brothers and provided domestic help as *fileuses* in France and "spinsters" in England. The numerical inferiority of women was abnormal. It posed problems. Some have noted that the texts say little or nothing or are capricious when it comes to women, but that is an easy way out. Others have spoken of the systematic infanticide of the weakest females, but that is technically absurd and would concern only the early Middle Ages, about which we know very little in reality. A high mortality rate due to repeated and closely spaced births—every eighteen months on the average—quite obviously would not apply to barely nubile girls, besides which, the physical resistance of the so-called weaker sex is superior to that of males. This was already noted in those days, when in fact young widows were numerous. Until something better comes along, we remain today with the idea of less care given to girl children: premature weaning, overly restricted diet, lack of medical care. But these explanations are unsatisfactory.

A final problem: I shall return in good time to the question of family structures involving both sexes and several generations, but I cannot leave the demographic domain without speaking of the *feu*, or "hearth." It is its arithmetical signification that is important here. Most of the documents that bear numerical data regarding the population express those data in terms of the *feu*, and at times even *feu fiscal*, or unit for the perception of taxes, rather than the *feu réel*, taken as a group of individuals. Vehement quarrels still divide historians in this context. Is the *feu* the basic cell of the couple and the four or five children who live under their roof, thus five or six persons who live together? Or is it rather a larger group with lateral or ascendant prolongations or even including domestic servants, according to local structures governing family groupings (and it has been estimated that up to ten or twelve individuals lived in a Jewish "hearth")? And what about the aged and isolated widow? How were newborns counted? Did the scribe who did the counting use the same calculation methods everywhere? Given that the idea of a disinterested census was foreign to those times, were exact figures furnished to the scribe according to the interests of the household? For example, if the survey was fiscal or military, did families attempt to avoid a tax or a requisition or, to the contrary, obtain a food supplement? The example of the survey of 1328 is well known for Paris: did the city have 80,000 or 200,000 inhabitants?

Thus all that we have on which to estimate population density, in various places and at various times, is the number of *feux*, which means that any attempt to translate such figures into "inhabitants per square kilometer" or square mile is problematic. It is out of the question and well beyond my aim to sketch out here a geography of human implantation and its variations. There are a few elements that seem sure, however. If we look at the years around 1300, the high point of population growth, we can see that the population of rural areas was, in France for example, roughly equal to that of 1900 and much higher than that of 2000. The reason for this is the growth of cities, which rivaled, equaled, and then swallowed up the rural population beginning in the seventeenth century and especially in the twentieth century, reversing the relationship of country dwellers and city dwellers and pushing the latter from 10 percent to 60 percent of the total population. The problems posed today by crowding in the cities and the rural exodus are well known, but they are beyond my interests here. When historiography considers tradition, it has long given western Europe, France in particular, the reputation of stability, if not immobilism, and "the old peasant traditions" and the "immutable serenity of the fields" are often attributed to the centuries of the Middle Ages. This is a serious error. In those centuries, to the contrary, if the countryside was in fact just about all there was, it was animated by what Marc Bloch called a sort of "brownian movement." Men did not stay in one place. Alone or in small groups, they came and went ceaselessly. And these were not only younger sons in search of girls, pilgrims, merchants, or soldiers, but also peasants who, from one generation to another, went to settle in another clearing, left the shore for the heights or the heights for the shore, as if impelled by some sort of material or mental discomfort. The historian is struck when he plunges into the heart of this confused mass, whether he studies a village or a seigneury, and finds perpetually changing census surveys. One result of this is that in the few regions that remained isolated—narrow valleys or unfertile lands where people did not mix or move about much—homonymy became the rule, in those days as in our own.

These observations on population shifts open up two fields of study that are clearly distinct but well defined. Anthroponymy, the study of personal names, is today the object of growing interest as a tool for prosopography in the study of families and as proof of social or economic status. It is true that we have to wait until the twelfth century at the earliest to see the ancient Roman custom of naming an individual with a given name followed by the name of his *gens*, or clan, and perhaps with a personal surname as in "Caius Julius Caesar." Next came the Germanic and Christian use of the baptismal name followed only by an indication of filiation: Jean fils de Pierre. It was in order to distinguish among all the many repetitions of "John, son of Peter" that the surname reappeared, first among men of war: "Jean Bel oeil, fils de Pierre et chevalier." Next, the byname won greater acceptance and filiation began to disappear: "Jean le grand, fils de Pierre" became just "Jean le Grand"; then, thanks to a recognition of geographical provenance made necessary precisely because of the habit of incessant moving about: "Jean le Grand, de Paris." At that point the "de" became the *particule* used by the aristocracy to distinguish the family's place of origin or principal fief. After the thirteenth century this anthroponymic switch was fully accomplished: "Jean Bel oeil" was recognizably a commoner and "Jean de Paris" an aristocrat. The commoner often took as his last name a term corresponding to his trade or his appearance, such as "Le fèvre" (like the English "Smith") or "Le gras" (the Fat Man). We would have to wait until well into the fifteenth century, however, before he would transmit that name to his heirs, who might in fact be thin and never strike an anvil. As for what the French call a *prénom* and the English call a first name or a given name, studies have pointed to regional influences, changing notions of piety, family relations, and even fashions, as well as local cults, devotional practices, and recall of ancestors.

I might note one last domain of studies in the incessant comings and goings within the population: what place should be reserved for the stranger, the person who comes from elsewhere, be it only the next village? The assimilation of the "other" is certainly more psychological than it is juridical. It touches on the domains of the heart and the mind. Hence I shall return to it. But I can suggest, even at this point, that in a society not yet enclosed within strict rules for life in common, the welcome shown to the newcomer was probably carried out without major difficulties. In France, where later arrivals made the population strongly composite, the eventual homogeneity is striking. The future may have another opinion.

Thus I come to the end of this first and external look at the human being: what is his body and what he knows about it, the care that he takes of it, and population numbers. The next step is to insert that human being into his natural environment and follow him in the ages of his life.

2

THE AGES OF LIFE

One of the strongest arguments against the notion of a "man of
the Middle Ages" rests on the simple length of that period, hence
on the inevitable changes that such a mythical being would have
undergone during the course of the centuries. That view is not
false, and I shall certainly take it into account, especially concerning cultural or even social phenomena, for I hold such changes to
be genuinely superficial, in that they do not effect the physical and
material framework within which I have placed my subject. I am
seeking the physical man, his body, his environment, and his relations with other animate beings. Given those preoccupations, can
the personal evolution of the human being be found? He is born,
he lives, and he dies, as the joking enigma of the ancient Sphinx
teaches us. Here again, there is no rupture, no indisputable opposition between the Greco-Roman infant and today's newborn, so
why should there be any difference between the Carolingian baby
and one born during the Hundred Years' War? This involves details
and a question of sources. Let us see what we know.

FROM THE CHILD TO THE MAN

Expecting a Baby

The idolatry of which today's child, and even the newborn baby, are the victim—and victim is the right word, if you think about it—in fact conceals our obsession with old age and death. The child is brand new, hence he will be used to sell face creams or automobiles. Daring pediatricians have loaded childhood with "certitudes" that have led the courts, or simple public opinion, to take as truths and proofs the infantile phantasms that an unfinished being, or at least a being "in formation" is capable of drawing from his dreams or his subconscious. That attitude of devotion that surrounds childhood is quite recent, all things considered. The centuries that preceded our own were harsh toward the young, who were mired within a severe economic or social climate in which the useful and the utilizable took first place. Going farther back in time, it has been stated that the Middle Ages, even more than "modern times," undervalued childhood and were unaware of the very notion. In the last fifteen years or so, that opinion has been seriously shaken, if not abandoned. The centuries of the Middle Ages—at least those of which something remains—illustrate this well. If the child was not king, as he is in our own day, because he lived in a world in which everyone had to defend himself while young in order to survive, he was nonetheless the object of a deep-felt tenderness, attentive care, and an upbringing that equals our own today.

But we need to look more closely at why this is so. In all centuries, it is a personal triumph if the birth of a child is for the mother the total fulfillment of her femininity and, for the father, the very expression of his virility. Such sentiments are sufficient in themselves to encourage the desire to have a child, and no human society has escaped them, despite the contortions of fashion. But, whereas our own times treat the child as a consumer, now or in the future, it was his role as a producer, and a producer of power and wealth, that dominated then. The child was not uniquely a "gift of

God," as the Church repeated, but also an element in the world of work, an instrument of authority, and a family possession. That material appearance may underlie a claimed discredit of childhood and a failure to recognize its plenitude; to the contrary, however, it was those future roles that justified the attention and the tenderness. As usually happens, and until the sixteenth century, when its ministry began to weaken, the Church saw clearly that increasing and multiplying the children of God makes them living symbols of the glory of the Most High. Obviously, some preachers grumbled that all of those children cost a lot and drained off the alms on which the Church lived. What is more, children do not grow on trees. All of them, including those who failed to blossom, were the fruit of profane embraces that God, perhaps to test his creatures, had rendered highly enjoyable, at least for the man. One could pray before and after, to be sure, but during the sex act? This was a cruel dilemma, for sexual abstinence would counter the divine plan and was hardly to be counted among human virtues.

In any event, for the laity, male and female, children were expected and hoped for. Because the Church threw a veil over this topic, it is hard to tell whether lovers or couples in a delicate situation in relation to canon law shared those sentiments. In principle, the unborn child was the issue of a legal union; still, the totally honorable position that bastards attained, especially in the fourteenth and fifteenth centuries, clearly shows that even if they were not desired, they were acknowledged, by their mothers of course, but also often by the man who begot them, who might have ignored them or pretended to do so, but who sometimes made a comfortable place for them in his family, which took them in. Unfortunately, none of the heroines of the romances of the thirteenth or fourteenth centuries is placed in a situation that would communicate to us their thoughts on the subject. But court decisions, many recipes, and penitential prescriptions offer abundant proof of the place of anticonceptional or abortive practices, and these were addressed not only to servant girls made pregnant by their masters or widows raped by a band of "youths," but to legally married couples as well. It was usually the man who took the initiative to incite his companion to get rid of an unwanted baby, and the judicial system always took his complicity for granted. Justice considered this all the more normal because, for contraception at least, the role of the man was quite evidently essential: the man controlled the positions used for sexual intercourse and its voluntary interruption, given the absence of all the many methods that have been imagined by modern technology. Our age is much concerned about such problems and has even established an entire juridical arsenal to keep watch over them. The only real difference between today and past centuries is that now such methods are openly used, as is true of other sexual behaviors to which I shall have occasion to return. Voluntary abortion, in town and even more in the country, was certainly a common practice, but it remained clandestine, hence dangerous. The Church insisted that semen be respected. In practice, the old wives' recipes are quite well known. They were usually concoctions of chamomile, ginger, and fern, along with some truly dangerous manipulations. However, the reasons for this abandonment of gestation remain totally obscure. In the fourteenth century, several "Doctors of the Faith," San Bernardino of Siena among them, reached the point of admitting that before forty days of fetal life the embryo could be destroyed, not without a whole series of penances, of course, and only provided there was a serious reason such as bad health or even extreme poverty. This is a good indication of how frequent such acts were.

So here is the child, conceived and expected. We are strangely ignorant about pregnancy. Perhaps because the hands that wielded a pen were men's and they had little interest in what was only childbirth, and perhaps also because every woman was pregnant every eighteenth months, on average, during her marriage, hence a dozen times according to the demographic norms of the age. This means that pregnancy could hardly be called an *état intéressant*, as was true until recent times. Apparently, the procedures normal to the human species pertained: nine months of pregnancy, a sagging spine, complete amenorrhea. Also probably, the old wives, experts in prediction, commented on the postures, attitudes, and "crav- ings" of their patients. Besides, if the pregnancy was going badly and was interrupted, the fault was attributed to the woman alone, and sterility was always blamed on her, even if the man's semen was known to be weak. The vase was defective, not what was poured into it. As is true today, the woman, quite naturally, but the husband as well, we are told, were deeply moved by the first movements of the fetus in utero, a positive sign that all was go- ing well. It is interesting, however, that the physicians of antiquity saw those first movements as a sign of a difficult pregnancy and a dubious childbirth.

Birth itself is also hard to grasp, for here too the man was absent, as a father or as a scribe or painter, and we have only very few and late exceptions to that rule. The woman in labor lay flat, squatted, or was simply supported by cushions. Older women pre- pared linens and water, while a *ventrière* encouraged and held the mother. The *ventrière* attempted to place the baby correctly if it should present itself badly, either by massaging the stomach or the vagina with oil or by manipulations with her bare hands. These women were experts in childbirth and seem to have acted out of good will. If the delivery did not go smoothly, and if the umbilical cord was not cut and sutured rapidly, the risks of infection were extremely high. Under such conditions of rudimentary hygiene, childbirth, in itself probably painful, involved a high risk of death. The cesarean section to save the child was not done, at least as long as the mother was alive, and we can estimate that one woman out of ten, and perhaps more, almost always first-time mothers, did not survive a difficult childbirth.

When the Child Arrives

If the mother was threatened, the newborn child's lot was scarcely more enviable. Even if he did not die upon leaving his mother's womb, his life might last only a few hours or a few days. Why should humble folk have had any more luck than the powerful, whose genealogies attest to the hecatomb of births? From 25 to 30 percent of babies were stillborn, a figure difficult to find today even in the most poverty-stricken lands. Causes of death included tetanus, meningitis, strangulation by unskilled manipulations, dysentery, and vascular insufficiencies caused by a difficult pregnancy or a premature birth. Not only was death frequently connected to childbirth, but it was considered unacceptable, unjust, and painful, as an entire familiar literature testifies. Moreover, even if the child died after only a few moments of life, it had known human breath, and, not baptized, it would go to hell, as Saint Augustine promised. How was that soul to be maintained until Judgment Day, in Limbo, that haven of expectation that permits "the process of mourning," as it is known today? *Sanctuaires de répit*, at times simple chapels placed in the countryside, preserved the connection with such souls, under the protection of the Church, and showered them with gifts and prayers. As for the tiny body, archaeology attests to the extreme rarity of burial among the baptized. Was there a special place for burial, for example, under the parvis of a church? Or, as excavations have shown, under the threshold of the paternal house, crushed under a building stone to keep some demon from seizing it to turn the dead child into a changeling of the Devil? Or, more simply, would it be thrown into the nearest stream?

So now we have a child who is born and is alive—for the moment at least. But was he really the child engendered by the father and borne by the mother? The obsession of a substitution, accidental or voluntary, by a human hand or a diabolical one, still inhabits the mothers of today. And what was to be said or done with twins? Were they not perhaps a proof of bad conduct on the part of the mother, made pregnant by two different men? Or was one of the two babies—but which one?—perhaps the diabolical double of the other? Little was known about twin births, and the rarity of twins attested in aristocratic genealogies raises the specter of infanticide, a grave crime, worse than voluntary abortion, but the only way to wash the family honor clean. In any event, the child was not a full member of the human group until he had passed through two rites of passage that signified his entry into common life.

The first of these, the bath immediately following birth, was probably the more important in the eyes of people of the time. It was a rite that reflected the pious iconography of the baby Jesus, but it was also systematic and ancestral. As is still true today, it was of course first an act of bodily hygiene that washed the child free of the traces of his stay in the maternal womb, but it was also his entry into the world of the living: first his cry, obtained if necessary by a good wallop on the buttocks, then the contact of hands and water. The ritual significance, probably of prehistoric origin, of the first bath did not escape the people of the time, and if the linens and the basin were still in female hands, the father, this time, was present.

The second rite was baptism. Here again water was involved: this was the child's entry into the world of Christians, which has provided historians with abundant testimony and explanations. I shall limit my remarks to a few nondogmatic observations. The administration of this first sacrament was not exclusively the work of the servants of God. A layman, even a woman, could perform it if the child was in peril of death. On the other hand and somewhat oddly, for a long time the Church, in its phase of the conquest of the West, tolerated, if not encouraged, the baptism of adults or at least adolescents, especially on the occasion of a feast day of reception and renewal such as Christmas, Easter, and Pentecost. Such practices, of which there is abundant archaeological proof up to the eleventh century, thus created a troublesome canonical situation. What happened to the soul of a young man who was killed before he had been "received"? Was a simple *ondoiement*—private, emergency baptism—sufficient? In any event, the relationship with God was the most important point, and the development of the custom of having god-parents corresponded to the world's taking the youthful new Christian into hand, at God's delegation, in place of his parents. That spiritual kinship, which in our own day has become totally symbolic, could substitute for natural kinship, and its effects, both psychological and material, were quite visible.

"Childhoods"

At this point we have the child, desired, delivered, and received into the Church and society. Sometimes its gender had been predicted by experienced older women, but usually it was a surprise. The child's gender prompted fewer reactions than is usually thought. One of the many arguments advanced in support of the idea of a marked preference for boys is based on the numerical superiority of adult males. As stated above, the normal ratio between males and females was equality, and eventual disproportions, aside from swings that we cannot explain, might come from the lesser care given to small girls. It has also been suggested that our documentation always emphasizes males, and that all of our calculations are thus false. If at the time, preference was indeed given to boys—and is this not still the case?—it was purely economic in nature and a simple reflection of the contemporary context, which might explain its very slow reversal today. In a society of producers and predators, it is more useful to have warriors and laborers than it is to have female spinners and cooks. As men were the only ones who wrote, they do not fail to stress their role in society, from birth on. But in reality, the true wealth of the family lay in the females, whose marriage was of prime importance and whose fertility would carry on the species. This is visible and well known in regard to the aristocracy, and was probably true elsewhere as well. The discredit from which the female sex suffered was thus much more psychological than economic in nature and was based on a supposed physical weakness and lesser productive utility. Without entering into a quarrel that began as soon as people learned to write and that would lead me beyond the scope of the present volume, I shall simply note that all serious physiological studies and economic data prove the contrary.

The mother, reinvigorated after childbirth by eating abundantly and downing a few good gulps of wine, still remained "impure." The Doctors of the Church had to go through a number of contortions to make an exception of Mary, who was conceived "immaculate." In the explosion of the cult of the Virgin in the twelfth century, it was indeed her role as a mother that the faithful emphasized. For the people, it was more important that she had borne the Child than that she had received a mysterious gift. The return of the mother into the community of Christians, the rite that washed her clean of all stain, was the *relevailles* (in English, the churching of women). This form of renewed baptism has biblical references. The Church compared it to the Presentation of the Virgin at the Temple, but was powerless to strip it of its sexual dimension. In fact, it signaled that the woman was henceforth "available" again. The rite was celebrated by manifestations of happiness that involved the entire kinship clan, if not the entire village. In general, this rite of reinsertion took place one month after the birth of a boy, two if the child was a girl, as if the impurity had been greater.

The newborn baby was fed with mother's milk, first because it was a law of nature, but also because any other sort of alimentation would keep the mother at home longer and impede her return to her economic activities. There is plenty of iconographic evidence of a woman shown spinning, cooking, and even mowing hay with her child at her breast, being fed, it seems, without any sort of "schedule." The mother's milk might prove insufficient, however, or else, as early as the twelfth century, the mother might want to stop nursing—we have lists of remedies for ending the flow of breast milk—to rid herself of an obligation she judges oppressive. This was true both of the aristocrat eager to regain her liberty and the peasant woman needed for field work. The child would then be given to a wet nurse, and candidates were not lacking, for the simple reason that a large number of mothers had children who died in childbirth. Our pediatricians today see the mother's giving up nursing as a first and almost immediate rupture, at least with her body. It is difficult to judge the matter, but it is possible that people of the time saw it as a problem, as the choice of the wet nurse was made with great care and families displayed a legitimate wariness. She must be of an age close to that of the mother, not herself pregnant, and exceptionally healthy. Moreover, nothing stopped the nurse from breast-feeding her own child along with her charge. Romances, *fabliaux*, and chronicles never fail to stress the more than fraternal, almost sexual, affection between "milk brothers" or to make good use of the image of the "friendship" between the little noble and the little peasant who feed from the same breast.

Weaning seems to have been late, eighteen months at the earliest and sometime later for boys, as if they needed maternal protection for a longer time. Did the mother's milk supply dry up? Did the child's teeth begin to appear? Whatever the reason, the child underwent a second break with his mother. Apparently, because mothers knew or felt that such a separation was coming, it occurred slowly, step by step. But if the child felt the shock, the mother went on to a new stage because the amenorrhea that accompanied breast feeding came to an end and she could conceive again. This inevitably determined the rhythm of a woman's fertility at about a year and a half between births if she breast-fed. If not, the births were more closely spread, and the "revolution of the nurses," as it has been called, figured among the possible causes of demographic increase in the twelfth and thirteenth centuries.

With a child born every eighteen months, motherhood that began at sixteen or eighteen years of age, and a life expectancy estimated to be from forty to sixty years, a married woman might have from ten to fifteen pregnancies in her lifetime. Taking infant mortality into account, the average number of surviving children per couple was from 4.5 to 6.5. These figures, which seem high from the viewpoint of France today, explain the population increase discussed above. All of the aristocratic genealogies show comparable figures. Why should things have been different for the humble? That is, unless miserable poverty pushed them to infanticide or to child abandonment. The first of these was dramatic, criminal, and obviously it was hidden, but it surfaces in the reasons adduced in *lettres de rémission* giving royal pardon in cases of a child who is *encis*, or killed by suffocation in the bed of its parents, dying "fortuitously." Child abandonment, which was less consistently hidden and considered less grave, was even the object of regulation and publicity. Monks and friars and charitable Christian laymen picked up newborns left on the steps of a church and placed them piously in hospices built for that purpose. Are we so sure that such practices are exclusively "medieval"?

Moreover, even if the very young child escaped that gloomy fate, he, and more particularly she, remained exposed, up to four or five years of age, to contagious and sometimes fatal childhood diseases—chicken pox, measles, scarlet fever, whooping cough—but also to such disturbances as intestinal fevers. It is quite probable that little attention was paid to such illnesses and that, to the end of early childhood, an ungrateful Nature was permitted to do her will, sweeping away a certain number of otherwise healthy children. In the cemeteries the skeletons of young children under seven years of age account for some 20 percent of the dead. From another point of view, stories of miracles, which usually provide one traditional source of information on the health of the faithful, only rarely involve small children, as if the Virgin or the saints saw little point in manifesting themselves for such young and fragile creatures, victims of "deferred death." So were children ignored, as used to be thought? Certainly not, given that the heroes of the romances complain bitterly when a child dies and signs of parental affection are clear in iconography. The Church even expressed its irritation over the kisses, caresses, and baby talk that minimized the presence of God in favor of his creatures. There was at least a certain fatalism accompanying the pain and sorrow in face of the all too inevitable death that surrounded childhood.

Iconography, medical treatises, and the biographies of famous men abound in details about early childhood. The baby was tightly swaddled, his arms pinned to his side, although at times his feet were left bare. He was bathed frequently, up to three times a day, and changed even more often. This was women's work. Men seemed to have been shocked by a baby's nudity and visibly turned away from the sight; on the other hand, we have depictions of men feeding mush to a baby or giving it a pacifier. When the child reached the age of one, he was helped to walk with the aid of a walker, but anything like a playpen or crawling on all fours were systematically discouraged. The first may have been seen as a reflection of fetal enclosure, and the second as a return to animal life, condemned by God. Archaeology has given ample justification to the many depictions of such toys as rattles, marbles, wax dolls, play dishes, little wooden weapons, or toy horses and soldiers. As in all centuries, toys are the reflection of what the child saw around him, and I shall leave it to the psychiatrists to determine which of them substituted for the mother, which expressed opposition to the adult, or which reflected intelligence or displayed character. Similarly, my chosen field of observation does not permit me to discern the adult disciplining of childhood games that classical antiquity found so interesting, the share of psychic transgressions they display and that philosophers love, or the part played by the Demon against whom the preachers thundered. The child had his foods, his clothing, his furniture, and his own toys. He was not the ageless midget depicted for so long by so many historians.

The Child in the Midst of the Family

Until the end of *infantia* and the beginning of *pueritia*, the child enjoyed a quite special place in society. He was not, as was thought in the nineteenth century, a simple smaller copy of the adult, but nor was he the fully realized being enjoying his originality that a number of "thinkers" of today would have us believe. He was a work in progress, but one with a noticeable role in human evolution. He was the link between the here and now, from which he came and the mark of which he bore, and his future as a man, as both ancient philosophy and Christian conviction imagined it. The child was thus holy. He was perhaps even within the host of the Eucharistic sacrament. His words were the echo of the Divine; his acts were to be interpreted as religious signs; he alone was the depositary of the will of the dead, which he expressed in his unclear speech. Not that anyone should stand in drop-jawed admiration before that half of God, as is often the case today. To the contrary, the Church recommended that the child not be interrogated or even gazed at with too much insistence, as that would spoil him. Besides, might not the Demon inhabit him at certain moments? This is why the cult of the Holy Innocents was such a tremendous success, and why people prayed to guardian angels to watch over the child's conduct. Should he fall short of expectations, he must be punished, at times severely; when he cried, it was because Evil was inhabiting him and he should be beaten. That severity was not a relic of the paternal omnipotence of antiquity; it was a form of service to God.

It is within this domain of the relations between the child and his family environment that our moral evaluations have gradually changed. Parental rigidity is neither indifference nor disdain; it is governed by the religious. This is why the father and the mother, in equal measure, overflow with affection for the child and manifest it by their caresses and an almost fearful attention. Some have sought to discern an evolution in these sentiments. After the mid-thirteenth century, they believe they can trace a progress in the place occupied by the father, perhaps because the development of schools gradually removed the mother from the role that had been hers in the elementary education of children. Above and beyond their common affection, the parents played a different role. The father took care of enlightening the soul of the child, teaching him what *auctoritas* meant, that of the Almighty in particular; the mother watched over the health of his body and taught him the rudiments that furnished his young brain. Some educational manuals (which concern the adolescent more than the child) have come down to us, and some of them are even the work of women, a rare occurrence in the history of medieval literature. But they resemble many other written sources in that they are works of theory, generally reserved for the rich: princes, as in the ninth century; future clerics in the twelfth century; the daughters of knights in the fourteenth century; and the children of burghers in the fifteenth century. However, we possess more treatises on horse medicine than on pediatrics. Moreover, in the age bracket in question here, the reactions of the medieval child to his parents are totally beyond our ken. Hagiography does indeed include some "young people" who attempt the "death of the father," but it is often purely a romantic fiction imagined by an aged monk.

There is one domain that merits a pause. The child almost always had brothers and sisters, uncles and aunts, at times grandparents. If the common adage of "brother, a friend given by Nature" is a pious thought that is quite obviously contradicted by many examples in all epochs, perhaps in the centuries of the Middle Ages people regarded it more charitably. Elder brothers and sisters indisputably exerted an influence on their younger siblings, the girls in particular, who were subjected to the authority and the interests of the eldest brother when the parents died. Traces of this dominance remain in French culture. In contrast, two other aspects of the medieval picture have disappeared or at least faded. Although we catch glimpses of the role of the older sister as a substitute for the mother, the role of the mother's brother, the maternal uncle, who substituted for a dead or failing father, was visible everywhere. Examples of this "nepotism" in the etymological sense of the term abound from Charlemagne to Louis XIV. The reason for this is well known. The "matrimonial model" (to which I shall return) united two beings of quite dissimilar ages. As natural evidence shows (but the notion is widely flouted today), the child has a vital need to feel both the male and the female gaze concentrated on him. If the father cannot satisfy this need because he is too aged or too often absent, another man of the same blood and roughly the same age as the mother will substitute for him. When that happened, the social effects were considerable, since two lineages combined to surround the child, then the adolescent, and finally the adult, and help him in his "establishment." How many laborers inherited from their uncle, how many younger sons owed their Church appointment to one, how many knights got ahead thanks to the "friendship" of a great man! As for the grandparents, who today are an indispensable counterweight to parental excesses, they were almost nonexistent in the Middle Ages. If they were still present after surmounting the barrier of sixty years of age, they were hardly ever mentioned, since they were canceled from active life, the only life worthy of interest. I shall return to the place occupied by such "formidable oldsters," who, in the lands of Roman law in particular, long retained control of the management of their wealth, but such examples are all the more apt to be cited because they were few and far between.

Our young child has now passed beyond the perils of childhood disease. He has become acquainted with domestic work and perhaps with rustic tasks and even military ones. He knows his letters, at times his numbers. When the bishop passes through the parish, he will confirm his baptismal vows. He is no longer an *infans*, but a *puer* (and his sister a *puella*). He is eight years old, twelve at the most. His life truly begins.

MAN IN HIS PRIVATE LIFE

The opposition of public life, which emerges from the mass of people, and private life, which is the realm of the individual, has been a solid notion among historians since ancient times. Power, wealth, regulations, and of course the economy, social hierarchy and even religious beliefs have been marked by this idea, and its evolution through time or its variety over space has formed the web of history. What is public jumps up before our eyes, because it is what is highlighted by our written, painted, or sculpted sources. What is private—that is, the modest personal framework within which the human moves—is closed, inaccessible to the outsider's gaze, hence amply hidden from the gaze of the student of the Middle Ages. In order to reach the private sphere, we have to draw information from the bits that "the house" has left behind: anecdotes gleaned from the *dits* or the *fabliaux*; fragments of individual account books, postdeath inventories, and even testaments; the details of a miniature; the artifacts found in archaeological digs. All this is tenuous and highly debatable. To be sure, changes have taken place over the course of centuries. For example, after the plague, at a moment in which distaste for a world in ruins, the *contemptus mundi* gripped people's minds and more importance was attached to the sphere of the particular than had been the case before. But is this so sure? Are we not perhaps victims of a simple evolution in our sources, which grew closer to the individual in a dawn of "humanism"? There is greater emphasis on towns and cities, and we know more about some levels of society than others. It has been noted that in romantic tales the aristocracy appears in over 18 percent of plots, clerics in 9 percent, merchants in a 33 percent of them, while the rest of society—peasants and marginal people—do not reach 50 percent, which is far less than their presence was in the real world. At least such sources no longer talk ceaselessly of monks and knights, bishops and lawyers at Parliament, master cloth merchants, and *échevins* and similar magistrates. These men may well have eaten and slept like the rest of humanity, but their private lives bear little interest for me.

As Time Goes By

Our triumphant species was endowed by the Creator with capacities of perception that, although inferior to those of other animals, are not null. Today, blinded by the flash of electricity, deafened by mechanical hullabaloo, trading speech for a keyboard, breathing in chemical effluvia, dispensed from using our sense of touch to finger anything whatever, and tasting only frozen foods, we have lost the complete use of our senses. Unfortunately, it is really difficult to measure the state of those same senses in the Middle Ages, for, once again, our sources provide only fugitive bits of information.

"Sight is life" an advertisement proclaims. And a person whom illness or fate has made blind inspires our compassion and receives our aid. In the Middle Ages, he inspired laughter. The calamity of blindness was taken as a just divine punishment, and the "miracles" that restored sight only happened to innocent children or virtuous hermits. The confusion of the blind was an excellent source of humor. This is all the more surprising when we think that night, which plunges all men in darkness, had a sinister reputation. Still, disdain for the blind could very well be a sign that blindness was, precisely, a negligible exception to the general rule. On the other hand, we might well wonder about the quality of anyone's sight, for it was subjected to the incessant trembling of a capricious hearth fire, a vacillating candle flame, a smoky torch, or a dying oil lamp. It might happen that a chronicler laughs at a captain unable to see the approaching enemy, at a merchant who mixes up his bails of wool, or at an accountant incapable of drawing up an exact inventory. As for the correction of deficient sight, we have to wait until the fourteenth century to find any mention or depiction of corrective glasses, set on the nose of a scribe or an officer of justice. These are usually faceted precious stones, beryl among others, the same sort of colorless emerald used in the *béricles* and *besicles* (spectacles) of later days but that were more like monocular magnifying glasses such as the one Nero had used many centuries earlier.

Could men hear any better? Here again, how are we to distinguish deafness from distraction? The searcher for the Holy Grail who fails to hear the warnings of the green dwarf in the forest, or the king who nods off and is plunged into madness by the sound of a lance on a helmet—are they deaf? To my knowledge, there is no image of a person with a hand held up to a deficient ear like an ear trumpet. Still, in a civilization in which orality ruled, it would be good to know if people heard the cry of a watchman on top of a bell tower warning of a band of mercenary soldiers passing by or the tempting cries of merchants in Paris and elsewhere. Or, at the other end of the scale, the murmurs of a Cathar *parfait* in the ear of one of their faithful as he died or the breathy predictions of a sorcerer in a trance. There is another problem, one more pressing than all the others. We have of course been told of the excellent acoustics of many church naves and of the high level of skill of their architects in obtaining a good resonance for chants and melodies, but when the crowd was large, tightly packed, and absorbed sounds, how could anyone grasp the preacher's words, whether he was speaking in Latin or the vernacular? Did it help to do away with side aisles, as was the case in some of the Dominicans' buildings? It is hard to accept the idea that Saint Bernard, haranguing a thousand crusaders at the foot of the hill leading up to the Basilica of Sainte-Madeleine in Vézelay, could have made himself heard everywhere, any more than Jesus "on the Mount" in years past. And if his words were passed from mouth to mouth all the way to the most distant of the faithful, what was left of their meaning when they arrived?

We are struck by the extreme sensitivity of the sense of touch in a number of domestic or wild animals. Among humans, it is by the mouth, to which he brought all objects, that the nursing child made contact with the world in which he lived. As an adult he did not abandon that first form of knowledge. In the Middle Ages the kiss, the *adoratio*, reigned supreme. It appeared in the kiss of union and peace given on the mouth of others; in the kiss of submission and devotion placed on the hand or on the foot of the master, or on the relic; in the kiss of tenderness or pleasure on the body of the child or the lover. These gestures, which are still familiar to us, manifested the union between the carnal and the symbolic. The Middle Ages was a culture of the gesture: gestures of the entire body, as in the dance of peasants on a feast day or even that of clerics performing sacred rites; but also gestures that served to externalize the soul, from the simple salutation with a nod of the head to kneeling in humiliation or devotion. Contagion from one domain to another is easily explained. In antiquity the joined hands of the slave who gives himself to a master were later those of the vassal placing his hands in those of his lord, or of the Christian praying to God—that is, after the prayerful attitude changed, in the early Middle Ages, from the arms raised to the sky of the believer of ancient times. Such gestures had to remain contained, however. Disorderly exaggeration would remove all of their symbolic value.

Kings and pontiffs were immobile, their instruments of command in hand, and the dance itself stayed close to its sacred sense. It was a pleasurable but pious action, not a lubricious or demoniacal trance. That was left to sorcerers or those possessed by the Devil.

The hand played the most prominent role in such gestures, probably because it is the part of the body that most distinguishes the human species from other living creatures. The *manus* was the emblem of authority. It was the hand of God thrust out from the clouds by which the will of the Creator was made known; it was the hand of the father putting his daughter's hand into that of her future husband; it was that of the prince or the dignitary placing his hand on the crown that was the sign of his power or on the parchment written in his name; it was the hand of the aged knight striking the nape of the neck of a young warrior with a *collée*, thus promoting him to the ranks of the *militia*; it was the hand of the merchant who seals his intention to keep his promise with a buyer with a handshake or a *paumée*. Many of these gestures have come down to us: the oath sworn before a judge, right hand raised but bare; the soldier's salute, his hand touching his hat, before a superior officer; even the worldly *baisemain*, a hypocritical homage to female power.

The "reasons" behind these gestures are not the only aspects of the question that have been studied, along with their gradual weakening under the effect of reading and writing. Archaeology, always searching for material signs of daily life, has observed tools, tool hafts, jug handles, and door handles with the same care as it has the height or the strength of men of those times. It has reached the conclusion that this was a world of right-handed people. This remark is hardly new. The discredit of the left side, the *sinistra* of ancient Rome, can be read as far back as the first traces that man has left of his passage on the earth. I have no competence for debating the hypotheses (or even the certitudes) that attribute a great motor force and a more lively impulsive force to the left hemisphere of the brain, which commands the right side of our bodies, and even less regarding the consequences—neurological first, then psychological—to which this innate situation leads. Everything permits us to suppose that in medieval times as in our own day, the right dominated the left, and that scribes must have been taught to hold the pen, whether a feather or a reed, with their right hand. This is what is generally attested to in the iconography of the period, but only "generally," as we possess a certain number of painted scenes or narrations in which a warrior in combat, a pilgrim on the road, or a prince "in majesty" is clearly ambidextrous. As for the scribes themselves, scholars have done their best to find left-handed writers, and they have found signs of them here and there. If the second testament of Philip Augustus and the first manuscript of Guibert of Nogent in the twelfth century are indeed autographs, as has been suggested, were these two men perhaps left-handed, or thwarted lefthanders?

There is another sense that is purely animal in its raw manifestations, which is the perception of the passage of time. Our cardiac rhythms and our psychic equilibrium are as sensitive to it as are plants and other living beings. We who are slaves to our watches and our calenders do not pay the attention to passing time that our ancestors—even our near ancestors—did. Naturally, the return of hot or cold weather did not require any long reflection, any more than the succession of days and nights. The sun, the work of God, took care of all that. The working day began when the sun lit up the barn or the workshop and stopped when it set, and even in the city, working at night—*le travail au noir*—was not permitted, a topic to which I shall return. The divisions into "hours," which were estimated at twelve for the day and four for the night (the *quart* of the sentinels), were founded on the ancient duodecimal calculation, but in northern Europe they were inevitably unequal in length according to the season. In principle, this was good enough for the peasant and the working man. Anyone who wanted to know more had two ways to do so. As the sun progressed through the sky, the sun dial projected the shadow of its indicator onto a flat dial marked with twelve lines—provided the sun was shining! If the sun was hidden, one had to rely on the bells that rang at regular intervals from the nearest church or monastery to signal the moment for the offices that the clerics, the monks in particular, were expected to attend: prime at sunrise, tierce four divisions later, sext at midday, none four "hours" after that, and vespers at sunset. At night the bells were rung in three-hour intervals: compline at the first, matins at the second, and laud three "hours" before prime. In the middle of the year, in France at the spring equinox, for example, bells would ring at six o'clock, at ten, at two in the afternoon, at six, at nine, at midnight, and at three in the morning.

This unequal division of "hours" was extremely inconvenient. When the moment came to set the time for a meeting, to execute a contract, or to put a judgment into writing, it just did not work. The men of classical antiquity had been aware of the problem, and the ancient Greeks used devices that measured specific amounts of water or sand passing from one receptacle, called a clepsydra (a word that means "which steals water" in Greek), to another. But although a mechanism marking equal divisions of time—twenty-four in one day, still following the duodecimal system—seems to have been conceived in antiquity, it was not applied. Or, rather, its use spread only very late, its application was slow, and it was used especially in the cities, where there was a more urgent need to keep track of working hours or set times for meetings. We have images of such devices from the early thirteenth century and examples of others from the fourteenth. A public clock, placed in a communal bell tower, as was the case in Caen in 1317, led to the triumph of "merchants' time" over "Church time."

Counting hours was important for ordinary life, but keeping track of days and months was less so. This is perhaps why the biblical or the Greco-Roman legacy held firm. This is still the case in France now that the genial invention of the "revolutionary" calendar has unfortunately been forgotten. The Lord's day was the only break in the numbered succession of the *feriae* that ran from Sunday (*prima feria*) to Saturday, even though it was only at the end of the week that the Creator finished his work. The division of the Roman month into calendes, nones, and ides was respected as well, along with the old pagan names, Germanized here and there, of the days of the week and the months of the year. Apparently no one was surprised that the Christian Church should adopt such a system. It is true that it was a matter of interest only to clerics and scribes. The commonality cared not a whit, recognizing only the days celebrating some saint (often a local one) or some episode in the life of Christ. Moreover, variations were incessant, following the customs of the place, even when it came to fixing the date on which taxes were due. As for ritual holidays, they shed their ancient connections and were whitewashed as Christian celebrations. Solstices and equinoxes became Christmas, Ascension Day, Saint John's or Saint Michael's Day. Judaic souvenirs connected with agrarian life or "sacred" history remained, but disguised, in such feasts as Easter, Pentecost, and even Lent. That left Sundays, where it was often the village priest who gave them a name by borrowing a few words from the Epistle of the day. Little memory is left of these except for Quasimodo, or Low Sunday.

The succession of the years presented a problem for the thinkers. For the commonality, the use of continuous numbers—which seem natural to Westerners of the Christian and Muslim worlds, but not to Asiatics—was of little interest in the ordinary life of the peasant or the artisan, who did not write and whose personal memory was hazy. Was he even conscious of the transition from one year to another? The tangle of "styles," followed only by those who knew, was just as variable as it was unreasoned: Christmas? Easter? The Annunciation? Epiphany? On what basis? The foundation of Rome? An old notion empty of all meaning. The birth of Jesus? But Christmas is a fiction, and the guess made of its date in the sixth century was wrong, in all probability at least four years too early. The Hegira of the Prophet? But those "voyages" to Medina were repeated and often based on oral tradition alone. It made more sense to do as the simple people did, either give each year an original name, as was done in China (but this required an excellent memory) or count years from when the nearest bishop had received his miter or the local prince his crown. But this moment had to be known, and the clerical mind was tortuous. Should one count years from his anointing? his coronation? his designation? his consecration?

Whether they were counted or not, the daytime hours went by, and there had to be ways to keep track of them. But not before previously having passed through the night, that half of the day in which men and beasts, for all practical purposes without light and unable to work, were delivered over to darkness, the unknown, and danger. Rarely depicted but often described, night was the unavoidable moment in which man was dispossessed of himself. Night was "horrific"; devils and sorcerers made use of it to set their traps: it caused panic, nightmares, or lubricious temptations. More cruelly, it was the setting for brutalities, in times of peace as in war, and for thefts and rapes. More than 55 percent of the crimes that we can account for, thanks to *lettres de rémission,* were nocturnal. People had to defend themselves, close themselves in, and consult one another to grasp or interpret the noises, stirrings, and faint lights that animated the darkness. The night might even be tamed and made the setting for embraces and pleasure, or else for noble thoughts. How many Christians found or returned to the faith thanks to the night! But when Prime rang out from the bell tower, it was time to begin living again.

Nourishing the Body

One must "eat to live," to be sure, but could not one also "live to eat"? In a world in which half the population did not eat its fill and a large part of the other half ate only enough to sustain life, how could anyone not dream of a Land of Cocagne all made of sugar cakes (which is the meaning of the word *cocagne*) or a palace of Dame Tartine? Were these infantile phantasms? Not a bit. From the twelfth century, when the land of plenty is described from a distance, to Bosch or Breughel, who reveled in it, satiation was the hope of hollow stomachs, gigantic bellyfuls in an unbridled feast—profane, not religious—at which one could go to ruin with drunken sprees for six months. This was because all too often the inevitable privations engendered by a capricious Nature were joined by sudden food shortages: a series of disastrous harvests due to bad weather and, on the human side, too many mouths to be fed, with no reserves, no commerce to help out, and no advanced tools. Throughout the West this happened in the eleventh century and again in the fourteenth century, and I have already recalled the wasted terrain that awaited the plague bacillus. Cannibalism occurred: Raoul le Glabre, a cleric with a full stomach, describes it with an almost morbid delectation in Burgundy around 1090.

Happily, killing one's neighbor in order to eat him was not a common occurrence. Normally, Nature nourished men as she had since Neolithic times, when they began to solicit her. For once, it is relatively easy to describe the situation and to draw up counts. The study of medieval alimentation, ranging from the botanical quality of grain to the number of places at table, has made considerable progress recently. We have medical treatises that include recipes and dietetic prescriptions; account books regarding foodstuffs (but all too often for the highest levels of society alone); depictions of banquets, most of them exceptional occasions; narrations or fables; princely chronicles; archaeological observations regarding the dentition or the bone structure of skeletons; and studies of the use of culinary equipment. We can thus hope for some meaningful statistics. According to gender, age, work expectations, and even climatic conditions, an adult needed from 2,500 to 4,000 calories per day. As it happens, data drawn from the sources just mentioned completely upsets this medical parameter. In the ninth century, men put to hard labor under the *corvée* and men stationed in watch towers in the fourteenth century consumed approximately 6,000 calories per day; sailors in the thirteenth century and laborers in the twelfth century consumed over 3,500 calories daily. And the sources say nothing of "open air" produce that agricultural workers, for example, may have consumed. Combining data leads to at least one conclusion. Contrary to tenacious popular opinion, and except for intervals of sudden famine, people ate enough and even too much in the western Europe of the Middle Ages. But a weak physical resistance to outside attacks contradicts that statement, which means that in the Middle Ages people ate much, but badly.

It was the imbalance among protein-bearing foods that explains a situation that was reliant not on choice but necessity. Carbohydrates accounted for up to 80 percent of the calorie load, which is excessive. It was bread, or rather the various cereal flours, that formed the base of what people ate. In a variety of shapes and forms—*miches, navettes, bâtons longs, galettes,* and *boulettes*—or stirred into gruels, soups, or stews, bread was king. It was white bread more often that is reported. Rye had a poor reputation (as we have seen), and oats and barley were rarely used in the human diet (although animals ate them). In the lands of northwestern Europe and in the Mediterranean regions, grains served to make a thick soup, the Saxon porridge, *gaumel* in Artois, *polenta* in Italy, semolina in the Maghreb. Where the soil was not good enough for wheat, which produced white bread, a mixture of wheat and rye called *méteil* was used. As for the various varieties of what we call "pasta"—noodles, macaroni, lasagna—they are attested to in the early part of the early Middle Ages, but were simply a particular way of working flour. And we can add to these carbohydrates the starchy beans, vetches, peas, and lentils that grew amid the grain (hence were called *petits blés*). Bread is the first of the Eucharistic "species," hence it appears everywhere. It was the only product whose price, which fluctuated according to the wheat harvest, was supervised and even set by the local authorities. We in France forget that this was true in our own country until only a few decades ago. In lands that depended largely on cereals, the economic place, symbolic value, and proportional presence in people's diet of bread can be measured. But by the same token, bread occupied too great a place in the diet. People consumed from 1.6 to 2 kilos of bread per day, and other foods were known as *companaticum*, "what you eat with bread."

Added to these starches, there was what haunts our "diets" today: sugar. Curiously enough, little is known about sugar in the Middle Ages, although desserts and *oublies* (rolled wafers) served at the end of a meal were rich in it. Sugar beets existed but were fodder for cattle; Arab traders brought sugarcane to Sicily and Andalusia as early as the ninth century, but it remained scarce, costly, and almost exotic. This left honey collected from the hive, but, as we shall see, medieval tastes were less attracted to it than our own.

Where food is concerned, we think first of animal proteins, the basic aliment for physical effort, but disappointment awaits us. Despite the traditional and false image of medieval tables sagging under the weight of roasted boars and enormous hams, meat was quite rare. It could be found, to be sure, boiled in the pot or salted, cut into small pieces in the soup, and even—infrequently—roasted. No, it was not true that the lords ate nothing but venison, the bourgeoisie nothing but beef, the peasants nothing but pork, and students nothing but mutton. Everyone ate everything. Excavations of food storehouses and accounts of table expenses attest to this. Every sort of animal was eaten, including horses and even dogs (yes, dogs!). Their bones bear indisputable traces of being cut up. To be sure, according to the region and the moment in time, on the one hand, and local tastes and the consumers' level in society, on the other, one animal was butchered in preference to another. Pork tended to be eaten salted, cured, or as sausages in the winter; mutton (and sheep were raised above all for their wool) provided its offal in the summer; beef was found everywhere and accounted for 20 percent of total meat consumption. As for venison (deer for the most part), after the tenth century and, except in zones of intense forest hunting, it accounts for no more than 5 percent of the bones found. All of that furnished, in view of the portions we can account for, a bit less than from 80 to 100 grams per day, which is not much. So did people eat rabbit? partridge? even eggs? Archaeology is silent on the question. Their carcasses may have been tossed to the dogs, who dragged them about. Still, the texts abound in allusions to pullets, chickens, and eggs paid as quit rent, with amounts specified. Where did these all end up? High-flown narrations speak to us of peacocks, pheasant, and swans carefully arranged on the banquet table, but this was an affair of the wealthy.

What is left is fish. Another disappointment! Even though every year millions of herring swam through the Pas de Calais (or, from the English point of view, the Strait of Dover) and abbeys disputed the profits that could be drawn from them, law suits regarding ponds and rivers, fishing devices and fishmongers' stalls encumber our archives, and the emblem of Christianity is the fish (or *ichthys* in Greek: *Iesus Christos Theou uios sôter*: Jesus Christ, son of God, savior), fish hardly ever appears on a banquet menu and disappears almost entirely from the peasant's table. Better (or worse), there are few traces of fish spines. Is this because deep-sea fishing lacked technical know-how and remained too close to the coasts? Or is it because procedures for salting (for white herring) or smoking (for sour herring) remained poor, to the point that what was not immediately consumed would rot? Or is it because the fresh-water fish in the rivers went above all to the monks' refectories? All that we have are lists: perch, carp, eel, pike, herring, whiting, salmon, and cod. I should also mention in passing (given that I cannot say more about them) that mussels and oysters were less prized than in antiquity, but are found in middens. Snails and frogs seem to have been a novelty.

We consume too many lipids and too much fat, as our silhouettes show. Obesity does not seem to have been a threat for medieval men, for they made little use of fats, preferring boiled food to fried. Even milk, presumed to be a complete nourishment, was considered good for the newborn at the maternal breast, but cow's milk and that of the she-ass and the goat were considered heavy and not eaten except curdled, drained, and mixed into soup. To be sure, milk was made into cheeses that were appreciated; the *formaticum* (fresh cheese in wicker containers) triumphed in Gaul and in Italy, but the more authentic *caseum*, in a linguistic irony, took over in Saxon lands (and in Spain). These cheeses were the object of an advantageous trade, and certain of them—brie, Holland, Chester, Parmesan—began to be distinguished from the others, but they hardly even appear, unless as a morning snack like the one that Robin brings to Marion. Butter, simply stored in pots, went rancid rapidly, and people preferred to cook with lard or vegetable oil, as well as with olive oil near the Mediterranean, walnut oil or poppy-seed oil more to the north. Unless a whale, perhaps weary of living, washed ashore, thus providing the villagers with enough *grapois*—whale blubber, fat and flesh—to last a year. This was a rare gift, however.

Bread and its like, a piece of cheese, a bit of meat would do, but a *potage* required other things: *herbes* gathered in the garden and in the forest. The range of vegetable products available was large. All the ones we know were there except for tomatoes and potatoes, both of which came from across the Atlantic, as is known. There was cabbage, to begin with, then carrots and parsnips, garlic and onions (reputed to be the richest of vegetables), watercress, lettuce, artichokes, cucumbers, spinach, asparagus, and more. The more affluent thought little of these products snatched from the soil, which they judged to be bland, earthy tasting, and vulgar; they preferred foods that came from trees or bushes: apples, pears, walnuts, figs, chestnuts, olives, quince, cherries, medlars, and even oranges and lemons if they could be had. And grapes, the glory of the West? On a few princely tables, perhaps; the rest—all the rest—went to the wine press.

And finally we come to the wine, the second "species" of the Eucharist, the symbol of renewal, the drink of the Bible, of Cana, and of the Last Supper. So many studies and books have been written on the vineyard, its working, and its harvest, and on the various stages of wine-making and commercialization, that I cannot claim to add anything. I shall limit myself to a few simple remarks. First of all, wine appeared on all tables, in all rooms, and in all cellars; and it was much the same everywhere. The distinctions that we love to make between varieties and regions had hardly appeared in France. There was Gaillac-Bordeaux, Hermitage-Bourgogne, and "France" (that is, what was consumed from Chartres to Reims).

At the court of Philip Augustus, himself something of a connoisseur, the "battle of the wines" sought to establish a hierarchy, but the list actually followed the king's preferences. It was only in the fourteenth century that distinctions became clearer. Second, the wines drunk were for the most part white wines. Only the *claret* of Bordeaux (of which the English imported up to 700,000 hectoliters per year in the fourteenth century) was a rosé. But the pope's wine and the wine of the dukes of Burgundy of that same period were reds, and their prestige grew over the centuries. As for more exotic wines, malvasia from eastern lands, muscat from Italy, Grenache from Portugal, they would not likely be found in thatched cottages. Third, the wine of the Middle Ages was not the wine we know. Its alcohol content, thanks to still rudimentary wine-making processes, was at best from 7 to 10 percent. Kept (but not more than one year, after which it would turn) in barrels made of resinous wood, it must have recalled the ancient wine of the amphoras, with a spicy and somewhat bitter flavor. On the other hand, and this is an essential point, the volume of wine that was consumed was enormous. From one to three liters per day per person, women and monks included. This was a prodigious amount of wine to absorb, but its effect was lessened by its modest alcohol content.

But what could people drink instead? Water? Yes, obviously, but water from fountains and wells was subject to the caprices of the weather, for river water might invite colic or the *flux de ventre* that we encounter so often in texts. Beer, then? Yes, beer is attested to from classical antiquity, and its production increased enormously after the thirteenth century. Once again, however, it was not the beer that we know. The Celtic *cervoise* and the Saxon ale were bitter and brownish and made from fermented oats. The yellower color of Germanic beer came from the use of barley and, at the end of the Middle Ages, the addition of hops. People drank beer, however, in the northern portions of the continent, in Scotland, Frisia, and on the shores of the Baltic, where grape vines were consistently planted but gave only a thin stream of acidic liquid. It would be nice if there were no more wordy attempts to justify planting entire hectares of wine grapes purely to satisfy the village cure's need to fill the priestly chalice day by day. And as for laymen taking communion in wine, it is an archaic memory that, in any event, would certainly not empty out the wine barrels!

All this heavy food—several kilos per day—and all these liquids, how were they consumed? With some exceptions related to the constraints of living in the north, where an odd imbalance between day and night or the extreme cold demanded some adjustment, the schedule for meals followed the ancient habits, which were also those of common sense. On rising, between six o'clock and eight, according to the season, came the "break" of the nightly fast, the *disjejunium*, which occurred at Prime and might consist of a bit of cheese and a glass of wine (reputed to enhance the ladies' complexion). The *prandium*, or principal meal, was eaten fairly early, at sext, or between the eleventh and thirteenth hour (one P.M. in modern terms), after the first half of the working day. The *cena* was eaten early, from sixteen to nineteen hours (four P.M. to seven P.M.), because for six to eight months of the year the sun set before nineteen hours, after which people would have to eat by candlelight. The English, perhaps a hungrier people, found that dining at the hour of none was late, and they shifted this meal early in the day, so that "noon" and "after noon" marked their day. People ate seated, as was true in antiquity despite depictions of reclining Roman diners, a custom restricted to the wealthy and that made it difficult to cut food with a knife. Tables were boards or planks on trestles; people sat on benches or sacks stuffed with straw; much later, but not in every house, there would be a table and chairs. The food was cooked in a cauldron hung over the fireplace or, if called for, on a spit; breads and cakes came from the domestic oven, located somewhat apart. Humble folk used table linens only on holidays; a hand or sleeve sufficed for wiping one's mouth, and it was not until the age of Francis I that people wiped their mouths with a napkin, as did the king. The pot was placed amidst the diners. They had wooden or metal bowls, sometimes shared with another person, and a goblet. Each one helped himself from the pot with his knife, a polyvalent piece of "flatware," or with his hand for cold food, perhaps using a *tranchoir*, a slice of stale bread or a small wooden slab. Spoons were only used as ladles; sauces and soups were poured into the individual bowls from which they were drunk directly. As for the fork, its first example dates from the fifteenth century, when it was made of precious metal and was reserved to princely company. People washed their hands before the meal, without the complicated and symbolic ritual imposed on the knights of the Round Table. Hands were washed again afterward—for good reason—in the tub in which the dishware would be washed. As for the gravy-soaked *tranchoirs*, the crumbs, and other bits remaining on or under the table, the dogs that waited underfoot made sure that they disappeared.

The Shaping of Taste

What I am describing here is the ordinary custom of common people. This is not what the texts and the miniatures tell us about, but uniquely what archaeology exposes through an observation of utensils and culinary leftovers. Other sources evoke the exceptional. Obviously, at times archaeological investigation can come upon a peasant feast or a good supper given by a wealthy merchant, which imitated "princely" tables. Such special occasions required not only the zeal of the mistress of the house—perhaps like the young and inexperienced woman whom the "Ménagier de Paris" bombarded with advice in the fifteenth century, or like one of the *maîtres queux* of King Charles V for whom Taillevent provided recipes in his *Viandier*—but also an entire set of rites and habits or customs that take us very far from the common people.

The "princely" table required personnel and space. In the royal palace around 1330 there were seventy-five cooks, thirty-three wine stewards, twenty-one bakers, men (and some women) arranged in a strict hierarchy, and who were often persons of long experience. Also needed were specialized kitchens, sideboards and buffets, musicians on the stage, and turning spits. The guests' places were arranged in order of importance at the table of the master or across from it, thus *en haut* or *en bout*—at the head of the table or the foot—where the least of them would dine on what was left, if they had anything at all. Ducal banquets in Burgundy in the fifteenth century might be served to more than three hundred guests, but twenty was an average number for a banquet offered by the church. The meal usually was divided into three "services," each of which included a complete range of dishes, which usually arrived cold, thanks to the distance between the kitchens and the banqueting hall. There would be red meats and fowl, interspersed with jellied dishes and cakes, fruits with the main dish, spicy foods at the end as a *boute-hors* (literally, a "kick-out"). Between each service there were pauses at which drink and *entremets*—biscuits to nibble and custards—would be served. The notion of a "menu" of dishes served in a logical order appeared only quite late and is thought to be Slavic in origin.

A meal of this sort lasted several hours and could be renewed over two or three days. This is what explains the extraordinary volume of foods consumed and enumerated in the account books. To take one example from a hundred others from the late Middle Ages, when figures are available, in three days thirty guests absorbed 4 calves, 40 pigs, 80 chickens, 10 young goats, 25 cheeses, 210 baked goods, tarts or biscuits, and 1,800 *oublies*; and they drank 450 liters of wine, without counting the bread and water. How can we not suspect that a sizable proportion of a feast of this sort made its way to the kitchens or the pantry?

Enormous displays such as this have anchored in the popular mind the idea of a "medieval" cuisine that is absurd and vaguely repugnant. On the one hand, cabbage without bacon; on the other, gigantic dishes dripping with grease, all more or less spoiled and prepared by ignorant cooks. We see the situation more clearly today. It was during the course of the thousand years of the Middle Ages that Western culinary tastes were slowly formed, at least the tastes that persist in face of the invasion of the more ostentatious, largely exotic, and always artificial customs purveyed by fashion. It is possible that taste, here and there, took on a "regional" tone, and in France we cling to the idea of "local" cuisine. In reality, these are recent traditions, strongly subjected to the immediate geographical contingencies. The basic tastes in foods—for bread, red meat, and wine—were, to the contrary, solidly established, and they showed a preference for light cooking and an attention to contrasting flavors. Medieval diners may have appreciated the mixture of sweet and sour more than we do, or a juxtaposition of contrasts: goat *à l'orange*, cod *à la bière*. The principal difference, however, may lie in a taste for spices, which were mixed in with everything. It is not that they were necessary, as is ceaselessly repeated, to dissimulate foods of doubtful freshness, but rather because spices had the symbolic value of the unexpected and the strange. This is why mustard and peppers were considered too vulgar, given that they were less costly than clove, cinnamon, nutmeg, or cardamom, which hinted of a mythical Orient. Some 80 percent of medieval recipes call for the addition of spices. It is by their variety that we evaluate the "social level" of a dinner. Salt and pepper for the simple people; cinnamon and *graines de paradis* (amomum seeds) for the rich.

Adorning the Body

The knight redolent of perfume (aromatic oils, for the most part) and who encounters a *vilain* finds him, the authors of romances tell us, to be black, hairy, dirty, and smelly. There is some class disdain here, but there is also a historic error, for people did not wash themselves any better in a castle than they did in a cottage or a workshop. Moreover, they washed as much, if not more, than people did in the "Grand Siècle" or the "Belle Époque." Above all, collective memory has retained, with images to prove it, the public baths, which had become places of clandestine pleasure. That evolution seems to have taken place in the fourteenth and fifteenth centuries, or at least that is when there is abundant mention of it. This forgets that medieval baths were a reflection, somewhat faded to be sure, of their ancient counterparts, which were places for bathing, sport, distraction, and lewd behavior. That "institution" of the Roman world was urban par excellence, to the point that wherever Rome wanted to leave its mark, even in a country area, it opened baths. In medieval times as well, baths were an urban phenomenon and were claimed to be of remote origin. The buildings that contained the baths were much more modest than the Roman ones, however. As far as we can tell, they included one or several connected rooms with an access walk and large wooden tubs filled by a hydraulic system with an intake system connected to a local fountain or a nearby watercourse. The tubs could contain a dozen or so bathers, both men and women, who immersed themselves waist high, which of course led to the baths' shady reputation. Some miniatures show, behind the bathing room, a number of beds that did not serve exclusively for repose. The "clients" of the baths kept their heads covered, which might seem surprising, but permits us to eliminate the hypothesis (concerning the women at least) that these were simple brothels or *maisons de passe*, given that "professionals" usually wore their hair loose. At the entrance one could rent a canvas towel and a cake of soap made of a mixture of oils, grease, and ashes. The tubs were heated from beneath, as in antiquity, by fire-resistant bricks; a *fontanier* supervised the heating process, and there was personnel that circulated to prevent theft of the bathers' personal effects. The municipal authorities in Italy and in southern France and representatives of the royal powers in the north did their best to provide as honest as possible an organization for this "public service," which seems to have paid rather well.

But not everyone had enough money to go to the baths, and there were none in the countryside. Still, there is no lack of narrations or images of bathing: a young Grail seeker bathed by maidens; a lady being scrubbed down in a tub by a servant woman; a country man splashing about in a fountain. In one's own home, and according to the household's level of wealth, there would be a special room in the castle, a corner of the kitchen in a bourgeois house, a simple tub or even just a pail in the cottage. In the fourteenth century there is even mention of a basin filled with a pitcher and emptying through a plug hole. The water was brought in from outside the house, from the well or the fountain, unless there was a water carrier who went through the streets, as in Italy. The custom was to wash one's feet before going to bed, wash one's face on rising, wash one's hands before passing to the dinner table, and to clean one's teeth, on occasion, with powdered cuttlebone. In country areas a complete bath would only have occurred for a family festive occasion.

Our sources are utterly silent—even the most ribald of the *fabliaux*—when it comes to the evacuation of human excrement and urine. Such acts, which are obviously vital and constant, are covered with a thick veil: Out of modesty? Disdain? Humiliation in the face of these imperious needs? The chronicles remain mute. All of those kings, lords, bishops, and knights never have natural needs to be satisfied, whether it is in the middle of a battle or in the middle of a sermon. Still, we are told that William the Bastard, fleeing before his barons in revolt, was nearly taken by them because he had to get off his horse for a moment. Much later, what would have happened if Henry III had not been on his *chaise percée* when his assassin surprised him, or Napoleon not been beset by severe intestinal pains at Waterloo? We know a lot more about the job of spreading out the soiled straw of the stables than we do about what happened to human wastes, essential though they were for fertilizing the nearby garden. This means we know just about nothing on the topic. In the countryside people probably used the spaces that nature offered, and the woods and the streams, with an occasional bucket, could do the job. For the cities we have iconography and archaeology to inform us. There were public latrines offering pierced planks set on top of log segments placed over the rivers or in the ditches by the city walls. In private houses, there was sometimes an outhouse in the courtyard. We even have a representation of one of these with a picture of a chamber pot on it. Or there might be a conduit that opened out to the exterior in a corbeled overhang, and too bad for passersby! The high point was reached in the fifteenth century with a *chambre de retrait* with a seat and drainage taken care of by a terra-cotta pipe reaching to a ditch or a sewer and an open *éventoir* that assured the airing out of this *aisance*. As for what happened after using such conveniences, there was no paper before the fifteenth century, cotton was too expensive, and using personal linen was unthinkable. So what did they use: Leaves? Nothing at all?

There remains the question of clothing. "Remains" is not the right term, for just as much as today, clothing came immediately after nourishment in men's daily preoccupations. Naturally, the role of clothing as a "social marker" was clearer in the cities or in the castle than it was in the country, but even in rural areas, on festive occasions embroideries, decorative belts, or costly fichus came out of the coffers to be exhibited with pride. Everywhere and for everyone, it was "the habit that makes the monk," and not the reverse. A romantic image often contrasts a white and nude antiquity and a Middle Ages wrapped in leather and iron. That image is largely a question of climate, however, and the essential difference lies elsewhere. Much clearer and even radical changes in how people thought of clothing took place. As usual, I am battling clichés here. No, the typical Roman was not a magistrate draped in an immaculate toga with fine open sandals on his feet, but rather a peasant with a short skirt and a bloused top, as shown in mosaics depicting country scenes. In later centuries (but when and how?) changes began to take place and items of clothing were introduced that had been unknown in classical antiquity—Mediterranean antiquity, that is, since some innovations had Celtic, Germanic, at times even Asiatic origins. Buttons and buttonholes gradually replaced the buckle and the hook and eye; thin laces replaced thongs and straps; men began to wear hats, not to mention the gloves and handkerchiefs that came from colder lands. Male costume is better known because it is more widely depicted. It also offers the clearest novelties: trousers with legs instead of a short skirt or the bouffant breeches of Oriental knights. Trousers became the rule for the field worker, the artisan, and of course the warrior. Only the clergy, the monks, and the powerful continued to wear a robe.

We know too little about what underclothes were worn in antiquity to judge whether or not the medieval age brought any innovations. What the *fabliaux* and the *lettres de rémission* call *petits draps* were quite short pants that laced at the waist and somewhat longer shirts made of linen or hemp. Women covered their upper torso with a chemisette reaching up to the neck and pinned in with needles, but we know nothing before the fifteenth century about whether they wore a brassiere or a corset reaching up to the breasts. Obviously, we know more about outer garments: men wore a long short-sleeved shirt called a *bliaud*, breeches in a thicker cloth that covered the stomach, the thighs, and that were sometimes fixed below the knees, and stockings down to the feet, attached above the knee by garters. Over all of this men wore a vest, short or long, called a *jacque* and women wore a vestlike *surcot* or a *gonnelle* and a woolen dress, which was always long. The vocabulary of clothing is very rich, and it probably conceals a great many regional particularities, but once we admit that there were local customs, professional necessities, and climatic constraints, there is a clear homogeneity in these clothing items. People did not wear different clothes inside and outside of the house; they wore the same things from morning to night; there were no special night clothes (people probably wore a chemise and certainly a nightcap). When the weather was cold, they layered up.

Naturally, I am not speaking here only of the common people. It is generally agreed that a number of things distinguished "quality": the choice of cloth, silk for some, linen for the less fortunate; the use of dye for all or part of the jerkin (*justaucorps*) or the breeches; scarlet or green rather than the "horizon blue" derived from woad or pastel worn by the common people; the use of furs such as rabbit, squirrel, or, more rarely, ermine; for the fourteenth-century courtier, a tendency toward a thinner silhouette with the breeches cut closer to the legs and a tighter doublet; a display of jewels or precious stones mounted in earrings, necklaces, sleeve buttons, or clasps. These additions to the costume of wealthy burghers or noble lords and ladies were not to be found among the humble, with three somewhat surprising exceptions all through the Middle Ages.

First, medieval clothing had no pockets, an inconvenience sometimes shared with women's clothing today. Where was one to keep a handkerchief, gloves, coins, keys, a knife? In his or her belt. This item of clothing was the only one that the peasant would put away in a chest and wear only on the occasion of a festivity or a visit. It might be a wide leather strap with nailheads, decorated by a showy buckle, from which to hang a purse, a key ring, a cutlass, and, if one's employment demanded it, a counting stick or a calamus. Although "a golden belt is worth less than a good reputation" it still contributed to one.

The second domain is even more surprising. It is shoes. This time, the phenomenon was reversed; toward the end of the Middle Ages we do indeed find costly extravagances such as women's *poulaines*, doeskin slippers with sharply pointed toes, raised up and held by a chain of precious metal attached to the ankle; or, earlier in the period, the sumptuously decorated slippers of princes and high clergy. But aside from these exceptions (which would be the delight of elegant consumers today), shoes seem to have been quite ordinary. Archaeologists have recovered a surprising quantity of them. More often than not, they began with a simple sole of untreated leather or wood (in the case of the *sabot*) that wore out fairly quickly. Onto this was fixed or sewn a stocking-shaped, ankle-high upper portion resembling that of a light boot made of cloth or supple leather and tightened by means of laces or thin cords. The wealthy might have embroidery on their shoes, but the extremely precarious nature of footwear in general explains why they were replaced roughly every three months and why the profession of shoemaker was one of the most active and the most prosperous. In 1296 there were 130 shoemakers' shops in Paris, and the "trade" was almost the first to receive statutes of its own, which it did in 1100. In contrast, those who made wooden *sabots* or *tatons*, which were like scuffs and were worn indoors, came in for little consideration and had only rustics as customers.

Customs in a third domain—hair and coiffure—were so close to our own that they deserve somewhat fuller treatment. Male hair styles, beards, and mustaches followed fashions that we can easily trace thanks to iconography, as is true for antiquity as well. But although fashion has no reasonable explanation, we can assume that professional contingencies or people's interest in distinguishing themselves from others can lead to a particular practice. If the layman wears a beard, the cleric will be clean-shaven; when the laity is clean-shaven, however, the monk will show off his full beard. If a warrior wears an open helmet, as he did until the mid-twelfth century, he will cut his hair short but keep his beard; when he wears a closed helmet he will shave both head and beard. A dyer will shave off his beard to avoid getting dye on it, but a merchant will add to the dignity of his commerce by wearing a beard. For women the situation was much more complex, as it is today. In most cases female hair was more abundant than men's. It was bound up, if only for convenience in daily activities, in braids and tresses, or at times in a various sorts of chignons (called *truffeaux*). The large amount of wood, bone, and ivory combs found among archaeological artifacts is a good indication of the medieval interest in hair, and variation in the distance between the teeth of a comb, the care taken in its decoration, and the quality of the work that went into making it show the importance of combs, even in a modest social milieu. Only mirrors rival them in number and quality in the artifacts found in excavated dwellings. Men could of course have used them for their hair or their beards, but they are usually viewed as related to women's interest in their outer appearance. Can we be satisfied with taking such objects as proof of a coquetry or a desire for an attractive appearance inherent to all women? That would be too simple. Female hair is the very emblem of sexuality. Undone, it is erotic, the appeal shared by Eve, Mary Magdalen, and the *filles communes* in the street. Female hair could be displayed at home, but outside the private area should be hidden, as it is charged with what is secret and sacred in the house, which is not the business of outsiders. Some sort of enveloping headdress, even just a tight kerchief, would keep it sheltered from the concupiscent gaze of men and the obscene curiosity of strangers. There is no "religious sign" in this and no mark of "male tyranny," but only a barrier between the interior and the exterior. Even in the early twentieth century, to say of a French women that she was *une femme en cheveux* because she wore no kerchief, no hat, no "veil," indicated that she was of little account, even someone not to know. Thus an abyss separates our old customs, which still pertain in certain cultures, and today's extravagant display of flying female hair, frantically agitated before our eyes by an advertising industry that does not even know that it is depraved.

If fashion dictated how men wore their hair, it had less effect on head coverings. These obeyed natural constraints, like those of climate, and safety precautions such as being able to ward off blows; they were also a way to mark respect toward a master or toward God. From earliest antiquity to our own day, the historian of "the hat" can find little that is not extremely banal: a tight woolen cap for cold weather or to wear to bed at night; something lined, shaped like a balaclava, or with ear flaps for hunting or working in the woods; a straw hat, conical or brimmed little "boater" for summer's heat; a skullcap for the priest or the Jew in prayer; a felt hat with a visor or flaps for the merchant, the magistrate, or the officer. All of these cases, in all centuries, derive from customs and commodities whose meaning matters little. I should note, however, that the extravagant fourteenth- and fifteenth-century headgear, female in particular, that never fails to adorn the heads of paid actors in "medieval" parades, holds no more interest for the history of common folk of the age—which is what interests me—than the prodigious constructions of felt, veils, and flowers worn by the ladies of the court or the *haute bourgeoisie* from Louis XIV to La Belle Époque do for the world described by Zola.

I have spent much time over this perishable body that will be covered, at the end of life, by no more than a thin winding-sheet or nothing at all. But, as I said at the beginning, clothing, even of the most modest sort, occupies a sizable place in household economy. One example to end with: for a man of the people at the end of the fourteenth century, underclothes would cost eighteen sous, breeches (*chausses* or *braies*) twelve sous, his cape and hat sixteen sous, his shoes and gloves four, and if he wore a fur-lined cloak, twelve more. This amounts to a total expenditure of about three livres, the price of a workhorse or a hectare of land, whereas the daily pay for a worker at the same period would be at best six deniers, or two hundred times less. This means that it cost a small fortune to dress properly, and not much less to eat enough. Life as a couple was costly. But what about the sentimental life of the couple?

MAN, WOMAN, AND THE OTHERS

Nature dictates that, except for surprising exceptions, all of which are external to the realm of the vertebrates, species are perpetuated by the union of the male and the female. And this union does not imply the preeminence of one sex over the other, be it sexual, mental, or physical, and I will leave it up to the few proponents of outmoded attitudes to dispute that evident truth. That union can be a one-time occurrence, the result of a purely animal urge, or it can be repeated and durable, thus setting off the founding of a social life in common, first at the simplest level of the couple, then at that of the family and the tribe and even beyond when groups begin to multiply. It is the human species that occupies me here, but I will not forget that such ties exist outside of our own species, as people of the Middle Ages were well aware. They had observed conjugal ties, even familial ones, among many of the animals who lived in proximity to them, such as rats, wolves, and a number of felines and cervidae. This behavioral trait even struck them so strongly that they "sexualized" the heroes in many of their descriptions of animal stories. This occurs in the *Roman de Renart* and the *Roman de Fauvel* and in a number of the offshoots of Aesop's *Fables* known as *ysopets*. Still, it is the human being who occupies me here.

The Two Sexes Face-to-Face

A reasoned study of the behaviors of the female and the male is one of the major fields of human reflection. Since societies began to leave traces of themselves in writing, in deeds, and by means of works —one might say, for the last twenty thousand or ten thousand years—the problem of relations between man and woman has inspired minds and conditioned attitudes. In our own time, when people attempt—and a good thing, too—to untangle many of the ties that bind us, it has been an active preoccupation. But the road to a balanced point of view is still encumbered with a priori ideas, things left unsaid, and instinctive reactions, in which furious differences inspired by superiority and inferiority complexes use scornful precepts to cover their excessive lamentation. Still, general opinion today, while pretending to deplore the fact, agrees that there is a dominant sex, the male, who sows the grain and bears the sword, and a subjected one, the female, who bears and ripens the fruit. Even outside of the strictly sexual dimension, the male is considered "strong," since he holds the reigns of society in his hand, while the female is thought "weak," even "imbecilic," in the root sense of lacking support, even though her physical resistance and her longevity are far superior to those of the "stronger" sex.

What was the situation in the Middle Ages? If I put to one side all that archaeology has revealed to us about the superiority of the woman and the occult matriarchy that women imposed inside and at times outside of the house, and if I keep to the surface, I am confronted by an incontrovertible fact. The Middle Ages were "male," just as Georges Duby said. Or at least this is true if one's conclusions are founded, as Duby's were, on written sources alone, all or nearly all which were the work of men of the Church, clerics who had no reason to know anything about the body, the head, or the soul of women, which they haughtily ignored. Moreover, women did not write. It is true that here and there we find a learned blue-stocking like Hildegard of Bingen in the eleventh century; female lovers such as Héloïse or Marie de France in the twelfth and thirteenth centuries, whose works may or may not have been written by them; vindictive and tearful ladies of the court like Christine de Pizan in the fourteenth century—without counting a queen or a countess here and there who ruled with an iron hand and acted instead of writing. But this is an infinitely small contingent, and it is not much reinforced by what some cleric credits to a lady in a *roman courtois* or a *chanson d'oc*, or even to a married woman in a *fabliau*. That leaves Joan of Arc's responses to her judges. But what did La Pucelle have to say about men?

The judgments we have are thus those of men without women, and this was all the Christian world heard, from the Roman encyclical stuffed with ancient law to the sermon of the local curé to his flock of artisans and villagers. Their sentence was cruel: Woman was "the Devil's door" and "the enemy," responsible for Adam's Fall, and the symbol of impurity, as evidenced by the blood that ran from her. She was the she-wolf cruelly devouring men, the insatiable and lustful sow. The more she attempted to be loved, the more she should be hated. Moreover, Aristotle had declared that the woman has no intelligence and does not understand what she does. Hence, Saint Jerome advises, she must be punished by beating—though "reasonably," as Beaumanoir corrects. Furthermore—but this is approaching the profane—she is chatty, a scandalmonger, capricious, and spends money too freely. Hence, silence! Keep your place and obey the master, whose qualities are all that should be seen.

Still, when they had shot all of the misogynist arrows in their quiver, some writers began to think twice. God had willed that creature and drawn her out of man. Was this a rectification to a Creation that was supposed to be perfect and complete from the beginning? Or was woman a test to which the male, the favored being in all things, was subjected? The question becomes murkier when the personage of Mary, the spouse and mother of God, is introduced into it. Mary is virgin, to be sure, and this virtue remains, in the eyes of the clerics, the ideal of female life, despite the "grow and multiply" of Scripture, which is contradictory, to say the least. Therefore there was more than the sexual aspect in the veneration that the faithful brought to Mary from the early Middle Ages and that increased notably after the twelfth century. Mary was the Mother, the protectress of a humanity in disarray; she speaks for all humanity before the Divinity, just as she did at Cana and elsewhere. But, did not Jesus willingly speak to women, to the Marys, for example, Mary of Magdala, Mary of Bethany (who were often confused in the Middle Ages), and Mary Cleopas? It was to these women that he first showed himself at the Resurrection; they bandaged his wounds and helped him by standing before the cross. He tended to pardon women more easily than men, and if there were no female apostles, it is because the Jewish world of the time, although less misogynist than many other societies, would not have understood it. This was a fatal error in the young Church, and Saint Paul made it the rule. Moreover, medieval hagiography, which was repeated from one village to another, teemed with female Christian martyrs and saints and exemplary mothers. So how were Eve and Mary to be reconciled?

Much of what the common people thought escapes us, but the anthropologists have discerned certain attitudes among men. In those days, and perhaps in all ages, the sentiments of the male were dual, but not contradictory. The first is fear of the woman, often disguised as scorn and suspicion. Because he understands nothing of the mechanisms of female sexual desire, the male denounces the ruses and the simulacra to which women have recourse in an attempt to satisfy it, and because he feels that he cannot respond to it fully, he develops, without admitting to it, what psychiatrists would call a "castration complex." On the other hand, in the display of masculine authority outside of the house there persists a feeling that inside the home female sexual power rules and that it must then be contained within those four walls. Cooping up one's wife, as "Le Ménagier de Paris" recommends, and forbidding her to show herself to full advantage is not only a way to safeguard familial honor but also a sexual precaution. Just as male adultery tends to be pardoned because it takes place outside of the home, female adultery will be punished because it generally takes place in the husband's bedroom. As for the woman's sexual avidity, it is quite simply a temptation conceived of by the Evil One and is all the more to be feared because the woman covers herself with the appearances of beauty and pleasure and the man feels himself totally disarmed by her. Adam should be stricken from human memory as a deplorable though dramatic start for the reign of males. Before the fifteenth century, what is more, no one talked of him!

A second domain lies beyond sexuality. Man indulged in acts of physical violence, to which woman responded by acts of moral violence that were more subtle and more hurtful and from which the writers of *fabliaux* drew a good deal of inspiration. As is still true today, it is men's violence that we see and deplore. In the Middle Ages such acts were excused and even encouraged as "legitimate" in the writings of the men of law. Violent outbursts were not the primary forms of an obtuse "machismo," but rather an expression of anger and disappointment, for man did not just fear woman—he did not understand her, and he lost patience. Aristotle had already shown concern over the multiple facets of the female mind, and some of the more open-minded preachers of the Middle Ages— Thomas Aquinas, for example—sought to "categorize" women. Thinkers appealed to the old theory of humors of Hippocrates and Galen to state that women were melancholic, sanguine, choleric, or phlegmatic. This was also true of men, of course, but women's psychic behavior and mental reactions depended still more closely on "signs" to be read in the stars. How to approach a woman depended on whether she was an autumn, a spring, a summer, or a winter person. This time simple folk and the learned agreed that a close connection with "Nature"—a word that pertained to the entire female being, her conduct and her sexual aspect—explained (but did not excuse) strange behaviors. Men noted, with an astonishment tinged with fear, women's ties with the dead, their knack for remembering or piercing the incomprehensible, their taste for all that was "illogical" or "unreasonable"—that is, all that was not "human" in all the senses of that word. Without going so far as to draw learned conclusions from all this, the common man noticed what was external: a taste for appearances, a cult of the body, an appetite for material wealth, and, to end the list with a quality that was not among the least of their accomplishments, the subtle authority that they exercised over children and possessions.

Unfortunately, we do not know what the second sex thought of the dominant one, because women were mute. It is not difficult to discern what they thought if we look to the charges against them that I have just listed. Whatever the context, they thought the contrary and acted accordingly. We can trace female "counterpowers," and I have already touched on them: they appeared around the hearth fire or on the bed pillow; at the "parliament of women" that took place at the fountain, the washing hut, and the mill; at the cemetery, which men feared and avoided; and in the devotions or pilgrimages specific to women. Women were zealous in the cult (or at least the somewhat sulfurous veneration) of the Magdalen, the repentant sinner and "countermark" of the Virgin. Men put their hopes in the Mother, the Spouse, and the Virgin, saintly or human, while women found a consoling patroness in Mary Magdalen.

Sexual Concerns

The Bible is formal when it states that man and woman (in the singular) will "become one body." Whether the sex act caused the Fall, as common sense would suggest, or Adam and Eve fell for some other and higher reason, sex was certainly involved in that unfortunate affair. The sex act was founded on monogamy, on the first couple, and on the procreation that would come of it. This is not at all the way the Greco-Roman world saw things, but it was the view of most of the Jewish world. Saint Paul, going far beyond what one might read in the Gospels, made monogamy the rule for Christians. The ideal would even be virginity, but since that would be going against the will of the Creator, the sex act was inevitable, although it was admissible only in view of the procreation that God expected from it. A symbol of the union of God and his Church, the sex act gives the leading role to man. It is man who will choose the moment and will limit that moment to opportune times, exclusively in view of procreation. The Fathers of the Church—all of them womanless men—competed with each other to back the "apostle," laying the foundation for dogma and trampling the traditions and customs of the ancient "pagan" world. The difficulty, soon understood, was that God's creatures—the man at least—drew an obvious pleasure from that act, which had become punishable. Moreover, polygamous practices had been inherited from other cultures. As early as the Carolingian age, Doctors of the Faith went through all manner of verbal contortions to avoid this trap. In the eleventh century, Burchard of Worms opened the way to the notion that copulation was not illicit when it took place when the woman could not conceive—on the condition that the man be unaware of that fact, of course. Albertus Magnus advised men to perform purifications before (!) and after copulation, in an anticipatory absolution. In the mid-thirteenth century Thomas Aquinas somewhat more lucidly recommended that the man draw only a *delectatio moderata* from such exercises, and it was not until the age of Jean de Meung, a hundred years later, that the *Roman de la Rose* swept away all such sham.

Obviously, from the age of Saint Paul to the pre-Renaissance, no one showed any concern about the woman. She was a simple vase into which semen was poured. Still, that passive role was not as neglected as one might fear. The protection afforded woman—in all stages of her life, virgin, pregnant, widowed—was quite real, and even the "barbarian" codes from the fifth to the ninth centuries, like Roman law, offered severe penalties and condemnations for mistreating her. The learned were well aware of this. As early as Aristotle, followed by Galen's disciples and, before the end of the twelfth century, all of the physicians who read Al-Rhazi or

Avicenna, Constantine the African, or the medical manuals from Salerno, had some idea of the genital life of women. Their descriptions of the clitoris, the vagina, the ovaries, and the menstrual cycle were not incorrect, even if they did not always seize the connections between them. They were wrong about the significance of the menstrual cycle, in that they judged menses to be an expulsion of the impure humors of the female body, and they thought that women secreted a sperm that, mixed with male sperm, was indispensable for procreation. They took good note of the strength of sexual desire among women, however, and of its inexhaustible renewal and its moments of greatest intensity, all of which was considered the very expression of lust and a danger to the soul. To be sure, these were the musings of clerics, and in the village no one read either the Irish penitentials of the tenth century or the fourteenth-century medical treatise of Guy de Chauliac, but people listened to the curé and they knew how things were at home.

What I see, first of all, are erotic manifestations that are quite different from our own. The nudity that seems nearly total in our current mores does not seem to have had the role of excitation that we give to it. The portrayal of Eve in the cathedral of Saint-Lazare in Autun is nude, but that is precisely because she is Eve. There are few if any other examples of nudity in a fresco or a piece of sculpture depicting Salome or personifications of the deadly sin of lust, and the little nude bodies that represent the souls of the dead are asexual. If domestic arrangements allowed it, spouses undressed separately, and we have seen them above bathing in mixed company in the baths, but with a hat on their head. In contrast, hair and hands were sexually charged emblems that enchanted the poets of the *langue d'oc*, as was the color of a woman's cheeks or lips. The *mille jeux d'amour* of the lovers in *Jehan et Blonde* and other *romans* are thus, above all, caresses on the face or repeated kisses that would bring a smile to the lips of more than one adolescent today.

And what about the act itself? When men decide it, the learned clerics tell us; when women want it, say the popular poets. Apart from coitus interruptus—a trustworthy contraceptive practice but one condemned by the Church as a sacrifice to pleasure before duty—the act must be completed, which implies both the consent of the woman and her orgasm, considered indispensable for a total procreation. If not, God was watching. Given that the *fabliaux* speak quite freely and even with glee of such *ébats*, it would be easy to enumerate men's failures and women's disappointments, his errors and her ruses, but there is nothing there that is not common to all ages. As for the partners' position, the Church accepted only the most "natural" one: the woman on her back, the man lying on top of her, which it considered the only position that permitted conception without excessive pleasure. That was not the opinion of the writers of classical antiquity: Ovid speaks of a dozen attitudes, body twists, and positions, including lateral ones; certain Arabic authors go so far as to describe twenty-four positions. Provocative medieval literature such as that of the Goliardic poets, but also didactic works like the *Évangile des quenouilles*, and even music, or at least what remains of it under the name of *Carmina burana*—all such sources add to what we know and must have informed men of the time, even earlier than the twelfth century, but increasingly toward the fifteenth century, when a liberalization of mores and language began to take place. Even the chroniclers, who were generally serious men and lettered clerics, abound in anecdotes about the sexual life of their heroes. We thus learn that Philip Augustus was unable to perform with his Danish wife, but his grandson Charles of Anjou was capable of doing honor to his wife five times a night, at the risk of his health. Moreover the *nouvelles* and the *devinettes* of the fourteenth and fifteenth centuries provide us with an extraordinary list of erotic and scatological terms that would even make a journalist from a scandal sheet blush.

Curiously, we know as much about a number of anomalous sexual behaviors. Greco-Roman society judged "particular" physical contacts or pleasures to be natural, because they were connected with bodily pleasure, and excusable because they had no connection to the soul. It was by establishing a necessary connection between the sex act and procreation that Christian thought rejected all physical manifestations that lay outside of the canonical norm to be immoral, abnormal, and unnatural, hence the province of sin and damnation. Even sexual relations between married couples at times when the woman was infertile were considered adulterous. This dogmatic straitjacket had no chance of containing natural impulses, those within the believing and "normal" Christian home included. Beyond sexual experiences that were illicit but admitted—that is, occasional paid fornication, a topic to which I shall return—we can observe an extreme liberality of mores. What informs us about these is the enormous mass of documents expressing indignation, condemnation, and threatening punishment (the efficacy of which it is impossible to judge) in the many penitentials of the tenth through the twelfth century, which set the tariff to each deviance from proper behavior, or in indignant pamphlets such as the *Liber Gomorranus* of the devout Peter Damian around 1050, which brandishes excommunication and acts of penitence. The efficacy of these condemnations leaves us skeptical, for during the same age, jurisprudence and collections of laws such as Gratian's *Decretals* have nothing to say about such behaviors.

Masturbation was first on this list. The sin of Onan was ranked at the same level as simony, as it was a question (for the man, at least) of wasting the seed that God had given him for the perpetuation of his people, thus it was a sort of dilapidation of wealth, almost of the community's wealth, as serious as that of Simon Magus when he attempted to purchase Christ's art of miracle making. Women were more apt to attract the condemnation of the penitentials, however—a condemnation that varied according to age, rank, condition, or the occasion. This may have been because of the large numbers of women without a man—nuns or young women— among the population. The borderline between masturbation and homosexuality is not very clear in medieval texts. Both were globally classed as sodomist acts "counter to nature," hence deserving of execration. This condemnation included a number of practices: anal intercourse, also between partners of different sexes; acts of same-sex pedophilia, contacts between men and animals, which were qualified as "bestiality"; and, of course, homosexual practices, male and female. Antiquity had left innumerable examples of these practices, which were rigorously disapproved only in cases of pedophilia, considered a cowardly violence, and bestiality, thought to be an insult to the gods. Naturally, the Church simply followed suit. Bestiality on the part of the isolated mountain herdsman was not denounced very often because it was not very visible, but when it was attested, it was punished with burning at the stake, the punishment for heresy. Pedophilia was seldom visible. In general it was a family concern and no one else's business, but when it was discovered, it was punished by taking away material possessions or by corporal punishment and no more. As for homosexuality, a topic of intense interest today, medieval social structures facilitated it with their groups of unmarried young people (male or female) who lived together in the castle or in the convent or monastery, or who gathered together in the "youth societies" of the village or the devotional associations of the towns. Such behaviors, which reflected the execrable image of the vices of Sodom and Gomorrah, were judged to compromise the health of the guilty parties but not that of the mass of the population, which is why the punishments for them remained personal and were rarely carried out in public. The most one saw were individual manifestations, the sublimated outcome of a friendship extended into the carnal. It is only in our own day that anyone has thought to seek out all the possible or actual cases of homosexuality that abound in the sources and that range from Roland and Olivier to the "mignons" of the fifteenth and sixteenth centuries. In the Middle Ages homosexuality seems to have been viewed with complacency.

Living by the Fire and by the Pot

To paraphrase Antoine Loisel, a sixteenth-century jurist: "Sleeping and eating together: This is what marriage is, it seems to me." Leaving marriage aside for the moment, along with all that it represented in medieval times, let us turn to a description of life *à feu et à pot*, as fourteenth-century men of law put it, in an attempt to put the hearth and the life of the couple into context.

For many people, historians or not, the couple is the only observable framework. It was the territory of the man, as both the law and custom proclaimed. The man held all rights over the woman who lived at his side, thanks to his *manus*, the authority conferred on him, with or without marriage, by Saint Paul or by Justinian, along with all later law systems. As we have seen, he could beat her; she owed him obedience, even above her love for her own children; she was there to give him progeny, to aid him in his salvation, and to respond to his sexual demands. The virtues expected of a woman were chastity, if not virginity; constancy in caring for the house; silence; and fidelity. It was useless for her to learn to read. Cooking and sewing were enough. This picture has been ceaselessly reproduced up to our own day, but it is false, even grotesque. I have already stressed the inequality of sexual games, the reciprocity involved in men's violence and vexations, and women's equal rights and duties in the upbringing of the child or in expectations of reverence from the child. As for the role of the woman as "housekeeper," I have insisted that the humiliating and subordinate role assigned to her is an invention of the nineteenth century. I might add here that the near absence of women in the lists of witnesses in law cases is largely due to the nature of the texts in which we search for them, since such texts usually concern real estate, in which women took no active part.

If men insisted so strongly on the control that they claimed to exert over their women, it is in large part because they feared losing it, and not without reason. The age difference between man and wife in the most usual style of marriage meant that the home sheltered a young woman of sixteen or eighteen years and an adult male ten or fifteen years older. The psychological characteristics of matrimonial ties were thus not those of our own day, where couples, married or not, tend to be roughly of the same age. The natural consequences were a tendency on the part of the husband to play the role of a father as much as a lover, relatively brief unions, the man's conviction that he knew more than his wife and the woman's belief that her personal freedom was being limited. It was this imbalance that led to bombastic pronouncements in the manuals for living together, the books of advice to the married, and the *Ménagier de Paris*. Another effect may have been more serious. The wife, younger than her husband and perhaps left too much to her own devices when he was occupied outside the house, might seek elsewhere for pleasure, leading the preachers to decry her inconstancy and bad behavior. The ménage à trois, an unfailing plot device of the *fabliaux* and even of "chevalric" romances, has no age. The poets tell us that it leads to burlesque humor; the *lettres de rémission* counter that it leads to drama. The Church might thunder away, cry dishonor and fornication, but public opinion was quite indulgent concerning adultery, and the punishments that it applied— having the guilty couple, naked and bound together on ass-back, ride through a jeering crowd—seem conceived more for laughing at the guilty for their stupidly getting caught than for punishing them for their bad deeds. Moreover, the deceived husband is always portrayed as ridiculous, or even odious.

One of the most troublesome effects of the medieval "matrimonial model" is that it left a large segment of the male population under the age of marriage (which required an "estate" of twenty-five to thirty years of age) without any licit sexual activity. The Church, guardian of public morality, saw the danger clearly. Without putting overly much conviction into it, it preached chastity or continence, but that was a lot to demand of young men. It protested about "onanism," knowing well that masturbation and fellatio were common practices among serving men and others. Adultery, which was already reprehensible, given the sacred nature of the marriage union, disturbed family order and must be combated and condemned. There was worse, however: rape, a male habit from earliest antiquity, which combined personal violence with disturbance of the social order. In the Middle Ages as in our own age, many sexual attacks were not denounced to the authorities by victims or their families because they feared dishonor.

This means that we cannot measure how widespread the problem was. The large number of laws attempting to limit rape give us a fairly good idea of its nature, however. In general rape was a collective nocturnal assault, and its victims tended to be defenseless women without a man: young girls, widows, and poor women. A certain number of the abortions in criminal records were performed to eliminate the fruit of such brutal unions. The Church floundered about among contradictions. Rape was to be condemned, but abortion even more so, and when it sought a way out its decrees clashed with people's rights. Today we consider rape a "blood crime" almost on the same level as murder, as a violent attack on the physical integrity of a weaker being, which explains the rapist's traditional excuse, the claimed "consent" of the victim. This was not the medieval attitude. The harm was not, or not only physical; it involved an attack on property, since the woman was an essential part of the family patrimony managed by the father, the husband, or the brother. Wounded pride and dishonor? Yes, but also burglary, according to civil law. Thus the punishment should be corporal punishment, though without going as far as castration, adopted in other cultures to avoid a repetition of the offense (here Abelard remains an exception), but also the payment of a stiff financial compensation to the family that had been insulted, at times coupled with a forced exile in the form of a pilgrimage or a ruinous penalty if the guilty party found pilgrimage impossible.

Adultery and sexual misconduct were reprehensible, and rape often remained hidden, hence unpunished. What to do? There was one way out, but only for men. Prostitution, physical love, regulated and at a fixed price, served to maintain social order by absorbing the irrepressible impulses of unsatisfied youths and even men of mature years. And trial documents, inquiries, narrations, and images furnish solid documentation. Far from pursuing the unreasonable utopia of preventing prostitution, as naive or ignorant moralists of all centuries have thought possible, the medieval Church saw it as the only concession that could be admitted to the tyranny of sex. It condemned prostitution, obviously, but it also closely supervised its functioning. It was in accord with the municipal officials that the Church agreed to take responsibility for *filles communes*, placing them in specialized houses that it often owned, and when the "girls" began to age and could no longer ply their trade, the Church sought lodging for them in a religious community or service in the household of a priest. In principle, the revenue from the *maisons de passe* went to the municipality, but in order to avoid seeing groups of male "professionals" employ prostitutes for their own profit, the Church did not refuse to accept gifts from the men who frequented the houses, thus in part redeeming their sins. In the city these houses, known as *abbayes, châteaux gaillards, retraites d'aisances*, or *petits bordels*, were often grouped around the churches, on the bridges, or across from the palace. Many of the "common" women were peasants who had found no other employment in the city, but it has been shown—for fifteenth-century Burgundy, for example—that a high percentage of well-established women exercised their talents in such places, and we have already seen that bathing establishments were open to a variety of paying customers. In contrast, we know nothing of what went on in the village. Probably there were some older women, promoted to the rank of *maquerelles* or bawds, who acted as procuresses. Streetwalkers (*prostitution sauvage*) seem to have been just as widespread. We know from mentions of places where fairs were held or mercenary soldiers or streams of pseudopenitents passed through, that they were followed by *meretrices*, women wearing no veil and not decently dressed who offered themselves to the first comer. When in the early twelfth century a holy man, Robert d'Arbrissel, surrounded himself with such women in order to save their souls and their bodies, the established Church found it somewhat difficult to see this simply as a pious act.

The Chains of Marriage

The situation of the woman in medieval times got bad press, and the reader will have noticed that I am trying to fight against a priori judgments. Naturally, many things changed over such a long span of time. Thanks to the use of written sources—for archaeology cannot offer clear dates in this domain, and iconography is repetitive—we can observe real fluctuations. From the end of the Carolingian period—say, 900—to around 1030 or 1050, women seem strongly present in economic or political affairs. In contrast, there is a decline in that area (a moral decline, in any event) from 1050 to 1180 or 1200. This was followed by a striking rise during the latter half of the thirteenth century and a continued high level of involvement for 150 years, followed by another decline when society began the shift to the "modern age" in the fifteenth and sixteenth centuries. Obviously, there is more than one explanation for these variations in female power: the numerical predominance of men or women; tightened or relaxed Church control; an evolution or shifts in types of activity in the economy of production; the progress or the retreat of individualism. But the underlying causes of these various contributing factors are not easily accessible, and recourse to extrahuman origins is beyond my powers. On the other hand, the evolution of Christian marriage, be it an effect or a cause, is a good field of observation.

Although it seems to me evident that the material destiny of the medieval woman does not by any means merit the hypocritical affliction that it often elicits, I have to admit that her fate as a wife—her juridical fate, at least—was, without discussion, mediocre and constitutes the principal argument for the proponents of a "male Middle Ages." In our own day we are witnessing a gradual weakening of the indissoluble bond of monogamous marriage, whether or not of religious inspiration. There are other and more supple ties, perhaps of shorter duration, that unite men and women, and this is hardly the place to discuss them. In all of the centuries of the Middle Ages, concubinage was considered illicit, open to condemnation, contrary to both morality and the divine will, and likened to pure fornication or to polygamy.

Today marriage is recognized as the founding cell of medieval society, and it is the inspiration for a superabundant historical literature, homogeneous in its conclusions, that I shall attempt to summarize. Virginity is an ideal reserved to a small handful of individuals who may or may not have volunteered for it and who were venerated but had nothing to do with daily life. Anyone who was not a virgin is necessarily part of an "order" that God places immediately after virgins: married people or *conjugati*. By entering into that state, those who had previous been called *puer* or *puella*—boy or girl—whatever their age (like Guillaume le Maréchal at forty years of age) became known as *vir* and *uxor*; they blossomed within the Christian world; they fulfilled a sort of coming into a new estate that it was normal to sacralize. The Church did not fail to do so, portraying marriage as an inviolable and perpetual contract in conformity with what Adam and Eve had known before and after the Fall. It made a seventh sacrament of it, but the last of the sacraments and one that the husband- and wife-to-be administered themselves, one to the other, with no need for the intervention of a minister of the Divinity. To break that contract would be an unacceptable rupture of faith, a "heresy." Still, that union must necessarily subscribe to God's will for the proliferation of humanity, hence it implied union of the flesh, without which the marriage, remaining *en blanc*, had no human reason for being. And since that union risked being the source of impure pleasures, it had to be surrounded by a number of guarantees of stability indispensable for its long life. The first of these was, quite evidently, the sincere consent of both spouses. Today, except for some survival of older beliefs in the "higher" reaches of society, it seems obvious that physical attraction or mental affinity justify living together. This was far from true in the Middle Ages. The girl, canon law decreed and Gratian's *Decretals* reiterated, can be married as soon as she is supposed to be nubile, which is at the age of twelve or fourteen, and the boy only a little bit later. Even if the future couple waited until they were sixteen or eighteen, how could anyone believe in the depth or the sincerity of their consent? They could refuse consent, and when that happened it was a source of scandal. Acquiescence was imposed on them—on the woman in particular—as a matter of principle. This does not mean, however, that a genuine sentiment of conjugal affection did not develop in these forced unions.

If boys and girls expressed their sentiments only later, it was the members of their family, fathers in particular, who decided. They did so by drawing from an arsenal of obvious and quite visible reasons: for a boy, in order to settle him outside of the parental group and, if possible, find an advantageous marriage for him in a hypergamy designed to consolidate or create profitable economic or political ties; for a girl, marriage, even beneath her social condition, meant ridding the family of the cost of her upkeep, given that she was not a productive force in the eyes of the father, but only a piece of goods that bore a price. This is why it should be noted that if some ethnologists stress, for example, the "market" for or even the "trafficking" of girls, it is only fair to consider that the same thing applied to boys. Naturally, these attitudes were those of the great of this world, the only people we know well (even too well). Among the common people, that is, the majority of the population, although the intervention of kin or even a quite understandable interest in the skillful management of lands or shops existed, the principle of a near equality of social levels—homogamy—seems to have been the rule in order to assure continuity in family management.

So now we have two young people destined for each other, after negotiations between fathers (or perhaps between mothers, which would have made for sharper dealings). If needed, "friends" might be consulted, even the *abbé de la jeunesse*, whom the young recognized as a sort of gang leader. Or the father might choose from among the girls at whose door the young men had left flowers or green branches on May Day. The *sponsalia* made the agreement concrete: on that occasion the engaged couple were formally presented to each other, after which they publicly pronounced the *verba de futuro* and clinked their wine glasses. Was there love at first sight? Disappointment? How are we to know? Some time went by, on occasion several months, which were probably taken up with examining and weighing the advantages of the material

promises or exploring eventual obstacles such as awkward kinships, stains on the family reputation, and false claims. The *nuptiae*
themselves were the most important part of the entire process, and
they were a mixture of Roman traditions, Christian demands, and
Germanic practices. Giving all possible publicity to the contract
established between the two families involved having crowds of
relatives and friends present, the exhibition of gifts and the bride's
trousseau, calling in musicians and buffoons, and offering meals
and parties—enough to bankrupt one fourteenth-century Genoese merchant for six months. In Italy, where abusive expenditure
was rampant, the communes even had to draw up sumptuary
laws to limit the marriage ceremony. The marriage would be celebrated in the bride's house, and the bride and groom wore their
finest clothes, as we can see in one famous example, Van Eyck's
1435 painting of Giovanni di Nicolao Arnolfini and his bride-to-be.
The man and his wife-to-be would both wear some sort of headdress, and the bride would be dressed in colored clothes, red in particular, never white. A Jewish custom required that a canopy (*pal-
lium*) be held over the couple; a Roman custom dictated that the
father of the bride take his daughter's hand in his own and place it in
the hand of the husband, thus transmitting the *manus*, or authority
over her, to him. Following a custom both Roman and Germanic,
the couple pronounced the *verba de presenti*, a formula of definitive
engagement that expressed consent, and there was little way out for
a rebellious woman to refuse to do so. In respect of an ancient symbol, the couple exchanged rings testifying to their mutual engagement, but did not necessarily place them on the third finger of the
left hand, which ancient theorists believed to be directly connected
to the heart by a blood vessel and a nerve. Two or more witnesses
were present, one of them perhaps a churchman and the other a
notary who later read out what material promises the two fathers
had made. After the ceremony in the home, the wedding party
and the guests would go in procession to the church to receive
the vows and the blessing of the Church, but this "religious" rite
was far from current before the fourteenth and fifteenth centuries,

when the clergy finally managed to impose it. Until that time, the blessing took place outside of the church, within the parvis, *ante valvas ecclesie*, or *in facie*. This might be followed by a mass of thanksgiving, but it was expensive, and many families were content with a blessing, given that it was the couple who performed the sacrament.

Also as is still true today, and if the family's purse permitted it, the family and the guests moved on in procession, displaying their finery, through a volley of tossed grain, a symbol of fertility, to a banquet. Here there is no lack of documentation regarding princely menus, but the meal was pure show for the bride, who, although present, did not eat anything. She waited for the final stage that really sealed the union. Here the women were in charge, the men remaining far from the nuptial chamber to sing or shout ribald (if not obscene) songs. The marriage bed, which had been blessed by a priest, immediately welcomed the couple. Man and wife were stripped bare by women presumed to be experienced, and the man had to submit to the *dénouement des aiguillettes*, the undoing of ribbons that had been wrapped around his penis, then unwrapped, in a rite that expressed the liberation of his virility. The couple were brought a *chaudeau*, an infusion or an aromatic wine reputed to have aphrodisiac properties, after which they were left alone. For a long time, however, custom dictated that a woman of mature years remain nearby all night to announce to all, at least if she were aware of it, that the union of the flesh had indeed taken place. As for a chastity belt to be undone or a *droit de cuissage* authorizing the local lord to deflower the bride-to-be, these are clearly "romantic" inventions, a hollow echo of a payment to the feudal master in deniers of a *formariage*, or fee due when a serf married out of the fief.

... And Their Locks

What I have described here is the ideal marriage, the Christian marriage par excellence, as it was set into place from the ninth to the twelfth centuries. Whether it involved lord or commoner, marriage obeyed the rules, but less and less as time went by. As for the juridical framework of marriage, about which I have said nothing, it colored (at times with a black brush) the physical and moral engagements of the couple.

First, we have to remember that polygamy resisted the repeated attacks of the Church. The practice was common in classical antiquity, and it persisted among the Germans and Scandinavians and in the Islamic world. It was not based, as has been ceaselessly stated, on a male egoistic and unbridled sexuality that demoted the woman to the level of a mere object of male pleasure. In a demographic situation with a high death rate (from a number of causes), it was hope of descendants that encouraged recourse to polygamy, in particular when the man controlled the wealth and had the power. Polygamy, in the form of simple concubinage, held strong even among rulers like Charlemagne who held themselves to be good Christians. It resisted in a quasi-official form almost up to the end of the twelfth century, at least among the aristocracy. In the Scandinavian world it was an established custom for every war chieftain to have several wives, or *frilla*, which meant that marriage *more danico* (Danish style), without the Church's endorsement, permitted raising several families at once. In this arrangement, there were no bastards or illegitimate heirs, and all destinies were possible: William the Conqueror offers the most famous example here. The custom was not uniquely Norman or Saxon, however: Philip I in the eleventh century, and Philip Augustus in the twelfth, never managed to obtain the pope's recognition of their mistresses as legitimate wives, and the children of these "favorites" (as they were termed at a later date) did not suffer from their illegitimate birth.

The Church set up another obstacle that had to be overcome: consanguinity. It demanded exogamic marriage—that is, marriage with no blood connection between husband and wife. That very rigorous position does not seem to have come from any fear of physical alteration of the progeny, as modern biology might suggest. The Church has been accused of harboring the dark aim of attempting to prevent or stigmatize unions that threatened to bolster the political or economic power of the lay aristocracy, its rival, henceforth constrained to the choice of an unrelated spouse. It seems more reasonable to suggest that the Church quite sincerely appropriated the taboo of parent-child or brother-sister incest that is almost inborn in the human species. As soon as the early Middle Ages, the Church extended the prohibition to the seventh degree of kinship, or the descendants of the same great-great-grandfather. Both civil law and canon law of the eleventh century repeated these demands, which means that the strong concentration of aristocratic lineages forced warriors to seek wives at a distance, almost outside of the kingdoms in which they lived, or else to face personal excommunication, interdiction on their lands, and even exile. Moreover, the threat of incest extended to godfathers and godmothers and to widowers and widows who wanted to remarry. From a practical standpoint, these strict limitations were unsustainable. People ceaselessly transgressed them, at times paying the price for it. In 1215, at the Fourth Lateran Council, the prohibition was shifted from the seventh to the fourth degree of kinship, the children of first cousins or closer. This was still too strict, and it was possible to break the law either by purchasing a dispensation (not too difficult an affair), by feigning ignorance, or, if those involved were not members of the high levels of society, by counting on an uneducated curé. Conversely, incest was an excellent excuse for repudiating a spouse, for example when the couple had not managed to produce children or, among warriors, had produced only daughters. Famous for its scandalous nature and its dramatic consequences, the rupture of the marriage between Louis VII and his queen, Aliénor (better known as Eleanor of Aquitaine), required fifteen years of royal reflection before the king realized that he and his queen were related and demanded an annulment. This prompted the Church to proclaim the need for an inquiry preceding marriage and, in 1215, to require the proclamation of bans—that is, to grant the right to marry only when it had been proven that consanguinity did not exist.

The inevitable weakening of doctrine concerning incest led to similar shifts in the area of remarriage. It was conceivable that a wife charged with sterility be repudiated (but not without greasing the palm of the Church) and be prohibited from remarrying; repudiation, in principle forbidden and in fact rare, was a sign of an ascertainable infirmity and a blemish. But widows were a totally different question. Although the widower could remarry without difficulty, the husband's death did free the widow of the *manus* that he had extended over her or of that of the head of her own family. As with vassals and lords in the warrior's world, one could not swear loyalty to two different men. However, in demographic terms there was a risk of seeing a large contingent of widows who were young and sometimes still childless. Her birth family might have trouble resigning itself to the Church's suggestion that a young widow seek the convent, nor could her kin close their eyes to the risks of her falling into dissolute ways. Furthermore, having recuperated its *manus* over the woman, her family could again hope for some profit from her. Under pressure from the aristocracy, the Church was thus persuaded to tolerate remarriage, if not at the 1215 Council, at least one or two generations later. It is true that within the more affluent levels of society, the negotiations necessary for arranging the material conditions for a second union were more difficult, as was the choice of a suitor. More often than not, the widow was led into a hypogamic marriage less brilliant than her first one. Not everyone could trade one king for another, like Eleanor of Aquitaine. In the more modest levels of society the idea arose that such a union, which was often out of balance because of the widow's age, was a reversal of the traditional order of matrimony, if not a frustration of social order. The couple often had to pay a fairly stiff *formariage* tax to the local youth and their leader, the *abbé de la jeunesse*, by offering drinks for everyone and paying for more or less erotically charged dances. Even that was not enough to prevent *charivaris*, noisy parades of young men in costume and masks, shouting obscene songs under the newlyweds' window. When the remarriage coincided with a feast day permitting the reversal of ordinary taboos—Saint Valentine's Day, Saint John's Day, or May 1—women could join in on these noisy demonstrations.

Historians, in particular those on the right, have long dissected the nature of what families promised one another on concluding a union. Because such practices drew on civil law or canon law and on Germanic or ancient customs, and because they evolved during the ten or twelve centuries of the Middle Ages and varied from one region to another, not to mention the extraordinary confusion of vocabulary that exists among the scribes and notaries, there has been a flood of minutely detailed studies on these topics. Claiming to filter them would be a vain effort, even if I were equipped to do so. This means that I shall keep to what is simplest, even simplistic. There is no mystery about the underlying principle. The solidity of a union demanded guarantees on both sides. The Church, which might have been content with words and gestures, ended up—and rather early, around the eighth century—taking charge of the secular aspects of marital arrangements, but it does not seem that it saw in them, as do the majority of historians and all of the ethnologists, the signs of a commercial transaction involving the purchase of the woman and guarantees of the execution of the sale contract. Only vestiges of these practices survive, but it is not difficult to understand how they worked. The father who gave his daughter and transmitted his own *manus* to her husband had every intention that the bride's material situation remain good. Thus he gave goods, a complete trousseau, jewels, even lands and land-rents, the value of which was displayed, complacently enumerated so as to demonstrate the rank and the expectations of the bride, who, with very few exceptions, would go to reside with her husband, now the manager of that *dos* or *dotalicium*. The dowry became a part of the bride's property—her *propres*—and its dissipation by a prodigal husband could cause lively quarrels, if not armed conflicts, between lineages. If those holdings, or even a small part of them, remained after the death of the husband, and for even greater reason if he repudiated his wife, they belonged to the woman, who could return with them to her family house. This fact was the origin of the custom that a daughter with a dowry could not claim any part of the inheritance of her family of origin. On the other hand, the husband and his father could block a portion (from 30 to 50 percent) of their own *propres*, known as *dos propter nuptias, donum,* or *douaire* (widower's dowers), which the ethnologists assimilate to the purchase price of the woman. These holdings were meant to assure the wife, should she become a widow, a portion of her husband's inheritance, thus enabling her to avoid having her children strip her of her wealth. The *douaire* was not to be touched during the marriage, and if that should indeed happen, a similar sum had to be provided in other ways. The Church kept a careful watch over such matters.

This rudimentary picture probably hides much duplicity and many quarrels. But I might note that although a woman, once married, did not have control over the management of these material guarantees—a fact that has led her to be judged, in law, as an "eternal minor"—she had a father, brothers, and other kin, sword or club in hand, who certainly had no intention of being duped. Moreover, when the question arose of the deceased husband's inheritance—equal division among the sons and unmarried daughters, with a larger share going to one of them, usually the eldest, unless there was a will directing almost all of the inheritance to one person—the wife nonetheless remained mistress of her third, or *tiers,* her *douaire*. Admittedly, there are some examples of widows stripped of everything and to whom their families of origin refused assistance that contradict my optimism, but I think them rare.

If the equality of the husband and the wife was compromised, it was reestablished in the face of death. Graves, both those of the "great" with their epitaphs and, later, their *gisants* lying flat on the tomb, but also those of the common people exhumed by archaeologists, brought together the bodies of the husband and the wife, and the *obits*—masses for the repose of the soul—make no gender distinctions. The two families competed to show pious zeal, and the Church, which received the costs, strongly backed that equality.

In a society rendered fragile by many uncontrollable perils, a man alone was lost. If he had chosen to live as a hermit or a recluse, that choice was a refusal of humanity, and the Church, if it did not dare to condemn a courage of soul of the sort, was not fond of strong minds. In the West at least, life in a group seemed to it more natural, both for its servants and for the laity. The "family" was the framework that God had willed and in which the couple or couples who functioned as its cells should be inserted. But the term "family" covered a vast set of concentric relations in the Middle Ages; it was a group whose members recognized a certain shared kinship, of blood of course, particularly for the closest circle, but also of interests in common, shared sensitivities or affect as one moves away from the couple that provided the nucleus of the relationship. Such ties wove a tangle of obligations and services within the social tissue in which affection, friendship, and interest all played a role. It moved out from lateral kinship to the structure of the lineage, then to the structure of close friends (*amis charnels*), domestic associates, clients, the greater clan, and neighbors. Thus the nature of the "family" affected all aspects of daily life, matrimonial preoccupations, the management of wealth, services of peace or war, devotions, and a common past. As we have seen with marriage, the broad range of the questions involved explains the wealth of historiographical material produced on the subject, which justifies my decision, once again, to limit myself to a simple, simplified, or even simplistic description.

Blood relations first. We have seen the role of the father in the choice of a husband or wife and in keeping an eye on the management of the dowry, the promotion of the son, and the transmission of power over the possessions of the lineage. Did he also play a role in the choice of the names given to children? Anthroponymic research or a taste for seigneurial prosopography are all the rage today. One way to establish a filiation is to search for the repetition of a "family" name from one generation to another. Is name-giving maternal in origin when the marriage is hypogamic for the wife, who thus has an interest in recalling the dignity of her former rank? Or the opposite when the husband wants to assert his superiority? Among more humble folk, the question does not seem to have been of much importance. To be sure, the range of names is often formalized by custom or fashion, but it was restricted to holy personages of the Christian belief. People were named Jean, Jacques, or Pierre, or Marie, Jeanne, or Catherine, with *le jeune* or *la petite* added if two brothers or two sisters received the same name from their father or perhaps some other authority. As for the mother, in principle mute and standing to one side, we are left to imagine the weight of her gaze as she stands behind the gesticulating father. How many medieval examples there are, inherited from ancient times, of an Oedipus complex or an abusive mother! How many difficult situations as well, that the writer of the romance or the chronicler let pass without comment: Percival kills his mother and abandons her; Guibert of Nogent can extricate himself from his mother's clutches only by becoming a monk; to pay a nocturnal visit to his wife without alerting his mother, Blanche of Castile, Saint Louis had to use a hidden stairway. And these are only three cases among a hundred others.

Collateral kin no longer have the importance in Western culture that they once had. In times past, brothers and sisters, the elder ones in particular, supervised their younger siblings and intervened in their affairs, the first with a weapon in his hand, the second with a vengeful word on her lips if the parents were absent or the honor of the group was threatened. This time the *lettres de rémission* speak of individual or group vengeance. I have already mentioned the role of the maternal uncle in substituting for an absent father. I could furnish hundreds of examples of similar "nepotic" intervention in the dubbing of a knight, an ecclesiastical promotion, a commercial association, an insurance contract, a loan of money, or a testamentary legacy. Although these customs may be weaker now, they still exist among us. Hence why linger over them?

In contrast, two aspects of kinship are more specifically medieval. The first (and I have already mentioned it) concerns illegitimate children. It is still true in today's France, in spite of the growing malleability in social customs, that civil law, which we inherit from Napoleon, if not from Louis XIV (to stop with him) shows a degree of reserve concerning the equality of rights of inheritance according to "legitimate" birth. The problem is clearly a minor one in the current dissolution of the juridical nature of the marriage union, but not in the Middle Ages, when it was connected with the ideas of an illegitimate child as the fruit of sin and stained by that sin and of a stranger who might claim a portion of the inheritance. The situation of such "natural" children, who were probably even more numerous in the country areas than they were in the cities, evolved in an increasingly favorable sense. Some illegitimate children were killed at birth or in infancy (neither pretexts nor occasions were lacking), others were abandoned, or until the eleventh century, thrust aside in humiliating domestic arrangements and after then admitted into the family entourage with a certain show of disdain. The coats of arms of "bastards" showed a "brisure" (the "bar sinister"), and they had to wear special, two-colored clothing, were subject to vexing protocols, and could aspire only to less ambitious marriages. Still, achieving the full exercise of a social function (one of Philip Augustus's bastards became a count) gradually gave them access to a life identical to that of legitimate children. Given that toward the end of the fourteenth century and in the fifteenth century (excluding royal thrones), we find bastards who led armies, were dukes, and served as councillors to princes, we might well wonder whether the demographic shock of the plague played a liberating role.

The second specifically medieval aspect of kinship is perhaps more surprising. The fate of younger sons no longer seems to have generated only more or less friendly rivalries; the adage of the brother as a "friend given by nature" was never taken seriously, the brother being more of a rival than a friend. For many centuries of the Middle Ages, younger sons were undervalued, given that it was normally the older or the oldest brother who succeeded the father. In a society basically founded on land ownership and on arms, there could be no question of sharing *auctoritas*. Primogeniture or the *droit d'aînesse* even became part of the law codes around 1050 or 1100. It was still possible, however, for a younger son, for one reason or another, to enjoy a concentration of advantages of the sort, and examples of this exist in the eleventh century. We can easily imagine the rancor and the conflicts that ensued. Customarily thrust aside in favor of the older brother, younger sons could not make a marriage that might later threaten to dissolve the family patrimony, even if they sought a wife and their fortune far from the paternal castle. A number of crusaders, especially those who settled in the Holy Land, were younger sons with no hope of a profitable return home. It was only toward the end of the thirteenth century that they were authorized to take a wife while living on the patrimonial lands, both because of demographic decline and because the system of seigneurial land tenure was weakening. This made it worth the risk of having to live with jealousy between sisters-in-law. These were of course aristocratic problems, and we have no way to measure to what extent they pertained among more humble folk. In contrast, we can presume that the situation of unmarried daughters must have been much the same in the castle and in the cottage. Young "old maids," left out as a result of bad luck, misfortune, or some unfortunate accident, had little choice. The convent? A number of female monastic institutions had such a bad reputation that it permits us to surmise that they were filled with women with little inclination for the cloistered life. An *aventure courtoise*? That depended on whether some adventure-seeker decided to encumber himself with a female companion before he abandoned her, disillusioned and "sullied," as was generally the case in the *amour courtois* glorified by the poets and dutifully reiterated by the historians. All that was left was the paternal house or a brother's house, with housekeeping, minor tasks, humiliation, and weaving as her lot. As we have seen above, in English "spinster" has two meanings.

At least closely related family members, united by blood, were aware of these ties. Historians of the law are fond of contrasting two different juridical structures within these family ties, and the sociologists distinguish two types of kinship groups. For the historians of law (and once more this is quite schematic), one of those two structures was agnatic—pyramid-shaped, with family interdependence headed by the pater familias. This was the structure that Roman law considered typical of "the family." The other was cognatic—constructed in horizontal layers with a lateral interdependence—and was more a Celtic or Germanic concept. Sociologists, on the other hand, divide family structure by types: a large family that lived by hunting or was pastoral or perhaps even itinerant, and another more narrow structure, conjugal in nature, and attached to agrarian exploitation. It is obvious that these two images do not overlap, but over a good thousand years, there must have been shifts between them. Rather than engage in a detailed examination, I shall mention two characteristics: first, the conjugal nucleus won over against all larger structures; second, the Church, by invoking the first couple, quite naturally pushed in that direction. As early as the Carolingian age, this structure was presented as the rule in the Church's dogmatic works, but it was a rule by no means universally respected at the time. Until the end of the Middle Ages, families resisted Church pressure and relied on the broader kinship group. This was more the case within the aristocracy, to be sure, but it probably was true elsewhere as well. Until the thirteenth century, there is no real estate transaction involving the patrimony that does not require the approval of members of the larger kinship group, the *laudatio parentum*, and when that larger group did not exist, the reverse move, the "lineage retrieval" taking back goods in the name of the family, obstructed any transaction that threatened the basic foundation of family stability.

... And "Relations"

Beyond this vast first circle there lay the *familia* and the *amicitia*, which had a less strong influence than close kin and whose role as a protective outer layer included an entire series of "services" rendered—protection, money, war, recommendation—more or less without repayment. These were services of people who shared a common destiny, which was the *sors* of the broader lineage; they were thus the *consortes* (members on a more or less equal basis) or the *pares* of the familial group, those who were of the same "house," known variously as *maison, casa, consorteria, consortia,* or as *casate, alberghi,* or *paraiges* in countries of Latin languages. In Italy groupings of these sorts even formed part of the urban fabric, with families inhabiting blocks of houses in closed neighborhoods guarded by towers, chains, and paid watchmen, with their own church, their tombs, and their banners. All of the participants in the group (or at least 20 percent of them) who were in the service of an illustrious lineage chose to be known by the master's name. Thus many who served the Doria family in Genoa were named "degli Doria," or "of the Doria." These were valets, publicity agents, and *sicarii* (hired thugs), but also "friends" on a somewhat higher level: favorites, counselors and accountants who formed a sort of clientele like the entourage of the Roman patrician. And why not that of a French *châtelain* or an English lord?

Still a bit more distant were neighbors, whom one met under the village elm or the arcades of a city square, at times in a procession or during the meetings of a pious confraternity, and even more probably in trade-related gatherings in the city or assizes in country areas. These were occasions for exchanging advice and support or else news and slanderous gossip. Neighbors were a protection against the isolation that was a sign of rejection of social order and passed for a demonic temptation of pride or the sin of envy. In this connection, it was adults who were more suspected of closing their door to others, since the young were apt to gather in bands—known as *brigati* in Italian towns—under the leadership of a local "abbot" (*abbé*). These youths were apprentices, lawyers' clerks, pages, stable boys, or male domestic servants; their female counterparts were chambermaids or serving girls. There were not many females among such groups, as after the age of eighteen or twenty, all the girls were married or "lost." These bands enlivened village or neighborhood celebrations and the *caroles* in which neighbors gathered to dance; they included the musicians who provided an *aubade* or a serenade at the balcony of a lovely lady, but they also included rapists and cut-purses, a poisonous and criminal excrescence of kinship structures.

THE WORKPLACE

Thus far we have brought together the several faces of a couple, its progeny, and, when needed, its collaterals and even its servants. This was the "house" or the "hearth," the kingdom of the woman, where people took shelter, ate, slept, and worked. How many were there gathered around the hearth? That certainly depended on the family structure, on social status, and on the available means of living, and the "average" figures that I have mentioned above (from 3.8 to 5.2 persons, and more in urban areas than in the countryside) are meaningless unless we speak of demographic evolution over several centuries. It is more interesting to know the internal composition of the group (when fiscal or alimentary data permit it), the "real hearth" that determined the actual structure of the family nucleus. Two urban examples, Reims in 1422 and Florence in 1427, explain and justify that diversity with only minimal differences between them. We find 37 percent of couples with unmarried children, the essential and "normal" structure, to which we can add another 11 percent without children, reaching a total of nearly half of all households; if we add the 8 percent of widows still caring for children we have more than half. At their side, however, there are 28 percent of households that were multiple, including grandparents, collaterals, *frérèches* composed of siblings and their families living together, and domestic personnel, thus falsifying any reasonable average. The remaining households, representing a sizable proportion of the population, were unmarried or at least isolated persons: abandoned widows or dowagers, old maids or aging bachelors. Four out of seven persons thus lived "normally," two lived in a group, and the seventh was one of society's leftovers.

The House

Whether it was a simple grotto or even an underground pit, or else the castle or the *ostal* of the powerful and the rich, the house was the basic cell of life, a haven of safety, a space for sociability, and a place of memory and of piety. Closed in and private, hence inaccessible to the Other, it was also an expression of charity—or of charity as it was conceived in those centuries, which was the alms of a loaf of bread or a bowl of soup offered at the door, for the beggar knocking at the door might be Jesus—or the Devil, to be sure—and there was no way to know which. That hospitality, which is so often and so willingly forgotten in our own day, was one of the natural paths to salvation.

Iconography of the house is abundant but repetitive and simplistic; the texts describe it poorly, and no floor plans exist before 1400 or even later. Here archaeology triumphs, and even more so in country areas than urban ones. Excavations of deserted villages, villages that changed, or communities built hurriedly that involved a concerted effort, private or public, have provided much data about houses, *hôtels*, streets, domestic installations, and even how the land was partitioned into plots (a topic about which I shall not speak). Hundreds of sites have been excavated since 1950 or 1960 (or are being excavated today) from Scotland to Sicily and from Andalusia to Denmark, habitats occupied from Germanic times to the Renaissance or for much shorter times. On French soil, sites such as Charavines in the Alps, Rougiers in Provence, Villiers-le-Sec in the Île de France, Rigny-Ussé in the Loire Valley, and Mondeville in Normandy, to mention only five prominent examples, have furnished more information than an entire truckload of deeds and titles. In Caen, Tours, Arles, Douai, and Paris it-self, deeply buried layers of the medieval urban habitat have been brought to light, making the city's basic structure accessible to us.

The general evolution of house construction, ignoring geo-graphical differences of detail, is fairly clear. In the Germano-Celtic world, the rural house was essentially a "hall," a long rect-angle, for example sixty meters by twenty meters, reinforced by posts and capable of sheltering up to fifty individuals and animals. Huts served for artisan activities, and closed storage pits protected reserve supplies but were located next to the principal house. The fireplace was outside, separated from the house, either for fear of fire or to serve several groups. The building materials used were local: wood, dried clay, daub made of wood chips and mud, gran-ular pisé (muddled clay). Farther to the south, where the builder's art went back to antiquity, local stone was used and construction displayed more rigor, although it would be a mistake to confuse (as is generally the case) the *villae* with several buildings, inhabited by the family of a major landholder flanked by slaves or dependent farmers, with the dwellings of tenant farmers or free peasants. As for the urban habitat, it was rudimentary in the north, and in the south it perpetuated the ancient model. This arrangement changed when its two chief supports, clan life and a predominantly pastoral society, began to break up. Specialists in this field strongly disagree about the moment when one system changed to another, flinging indisputable examples at one another. By choosing a broad range of time—the seventh to the eleventh centuries—we have some chance of getting it right. The new type of habitat was, in effect, quite different, whether the underlying cause of the change was the dissolution of the large familial group or objective economic changes such as the expansion of the culture of cereals or urban ar-tisan work. The new direction was a shift to the smaller-sized indi-vidual house of some twenty meters by six or ten meters containing one nuclear family. The animals were moved out and the fireplace was moved in. This change, which was evident in country areas, was reflected in the towns by a clear break between the lordly or bourgeois *ostal* that dominated an entire section of the town, and the artisan's dwelling, which might contain several "hearths." The apogee of this evolution can be placed at the end of the thirteenth century, and we shall have a closer look at its consequences in a moment. After the thirteenth century contrasts grew. In country areas the "block houses" were accompanied by commons but the more modest houses fell to the level of the hovel. Something similar happened in the cities. Sumptuous *hôtels* stood facing crowded lodgings. I am deliberately not discussing the later developments, the causes, or the effects of this "social fracture."

At the risk of a simplification of which I am fully aware, let me summarize what is known. In country areas in the middle of the medieval period, the house was composed of one room (two after the thirteenth century) with a floor surface of fifteen square meters or so, horizontally divided into "zones" but with no upper story, or else with a loft reached by an inside ladder. The walls, banded by a flashing at ground level and without deep foundations (which makes excavation and identification difficult), were made of boards, blocks of peat, mud, pisé, bricks, or dry stones, according to what was available locally; floors were of tamped-down soil, the roofing was thatch, shingles, flat roofing stones known as *lauzes*, or round tiles, again, according to what was available locally. The hearth was placed along one of the inside walls, with a broad flooring of crushed stone and either a hood (for the rich) or a simple hole in the roof (for the others). There was one entry door, made of rough planks, hung by hinges and provided with latches (at a later date, locks) to discourage the marauder or the intruder, but which would not stop a mercenary soldier with pillage on his mind. There were few or no windows due to the fragility of the houses, and when there were windows they had shutters that could be closed should the need arise. Everything in this rudimentary scheme was arranged to contain the nuclear family as closely as possible. The fire chased away fears and fostered a spirit of community, and the same could be said of the wife, who reigned over the household as a wealth or a danger to be guarded, while the stores of food, wine, and tools assured survival. The nearby presence of a cellar, a bread oven, and a sheepcote indicated that the owner was a wealthier man.

Curiously enough, it appears that these dwellings were not inert structures, built to last for "time immemorial." Instead, they were moved, though not very far, every time they were restored or re-constructed, and archaeology shows many in-situ modifications. Was this because building materials were generally light? Was it due to a demographic, even an economic evolution? At Wharram Percy, a Yorkshire village that has been particularly thoroughly excavated, one house went through nine successive stages over three centuries.

The dwelling changed when the wealthy owner was a warrior, showing a more hierarchical arrangement and a division into ver-tical zones. We have a good deal of information on the "castles," not only from excavations, which often have difficulty distinguishing between various construction periods, but also from complete de-scriptions, some of them famous though perhaps imaginary, such as that of the Château d'Ardres in the Boulonnais in the twelfth century. On top of a *motte*, a mound of stones and mud built up by *corvée* labor that served more to give witness to the superiority of the master than to be used in warfare, a solid tower was built. At first square and built of wood, later round and made of stone, the tower stood in isolation or, as the centuries went by, flanked by buildings. Looking beyond the evolution of military architec-ture, which is not a part of my subject, the internal arrangements were almost always the same. On the ground level or in a cellar there was storage space for foodstuffs, a water reserve or, when possible, a well, and room for horses, domestics, and the kitch-ens. Above that, on the first upper level, the only access for which was through a raised and sometimes fortified postern, there was the *aula*, a large room for gathering together one's "friends," needy relatives, and "men." The great hall served for games and for eat-ing, for the master was expected to spend freely so as to make a display of his power and his wealth; it was a place for gatherings, for example, to seek suitable candidates for an office, for a fief, or for a marriage. The private areas were on the floor above the hall. They included a fireplace; sleeping quarters for men, who could come and go as they wished; and, in particular the bedchamber of the master, the nucleus of the lineage, where the treasure chests were hidden. A still higher floor contained the quarters of the family women, a wealth to be guarded carefully, and their chatty serving women, who were not supposed to be seen on the floor below in the room where the "men" slept. The master's "retreat," also on this upper floor, was a room in which he and his kin listened to readings of poems and epic songs—or perhaps cooking recipes. At the very top, as close as possible to God, came the chapel. As castles grew in size their arrangements changed. Interior corridors replaced passageways along the curtain walls skirting the bastions; circular stairs replaced ladders; a "garden" with arbors and flower beds eventually replaced the grassy lists that lay between the inner and outer walls.

In the city, although the *hôtels* of the rich and powerful recalled the "noble" dwellings of the countryside, more ordinary dwellings had little in common with rural *chaumières*. This time, iconography tells us a good deal more than excavation. In an urban setting in which activity was constant, archaeology can only highlight particulars, whereas we possess an abundance of late medieval views of Siena, Paris, Genoa, Rouen, and many other cities. Cities were plotted as narrow parallel bands, with ten meters or so on the short side facing the street. This means that houses were longitudinal, with one room behind another, followed by an open area or a courtyard accessible from the rear. Although the outside walls were often made of mud and straw bricks supported by half-timbering, stone was preferred when it could be afforded; roofs were made of tile or slate. Because houses were built so close to one another, fire was the scourge of medieval cities. In the thirteenth century, all of Rouen burned down four different times. To prevent the frame of the house from catching fire, the axis of the roof was built perpendicular to the street and topped with a gable. Since the ground surface was limited, houses had to be built up, at times with upper levels corbeled out to gain more room, which led to the romantic and excessive look of "medieval" houses that seem to belly out, nearly touching one another over the street. At street level, next to the entry door, there was one room with a bay window that could be closed with wooden shutters. If the house was that of an artisan, this room would be his workshop and he would work in plain view of the passerby or the client. When the moment came to sell a product, he could open up the shutters, which were made of horizontal boards, to create a protected display shelf. In the rear, at times in a room giving off the courtyard, a staircase led to the upper floor or floors. If the house was relatively small, the wooden floorboards would be held up by beams resting on piles driven into the ground. When the courts pronounced a sentence that included the penalty of *abattis*, those supporting beams were sawn through, thus causing the entire house to implode. Given that this disaster caused a major hardship for the entire neighborhood, it is probable that an exorbitant fine was usually substituted for it. Unlike the thatched country cottage, the city house had a cellar with access from inside. Such basements were vaulted and could serve as a shelter should the need arise. As we have seen, the latrines were generally open to the outside; the principal hearth was on the first upper floor and might be accompanied by other more modest fireplaces on upper floors with parallel chimneys and separate conduits, thus increasing the risk of fire. This meant that several households—several *feux*—could inhabit the same house, the proprietor on the ground floor and the first floor, with poor relations, domestics, or tenants with limited revenues above them. Whereas in country areas the immediate surroundings of the house included little more than a *usoir* where a small cart could be left and a garden that was part of a larger common cultivated space, in the city, to the contrary, the courtyard behind the houses played a more individualized role. It was used for setting up tents, leaving old casks, growing carrots, fennel, and herbs for making soap or perfume, and even planting a fruit tree or two, but it was also a place to leave old tools or ashes, kitchen refuse, and even the content of chamber pots (until the cities organized a public pick-up service in the late fourteenth century at the earliest), unless the city moat was close enough at hand to resolve that problem.

... And What Was Found in the House

It should be obvious that I attach great importance to what is found in excavations. The archaeology of the deserted village or the eviscerated urban site has served me well. Suddenly, however, it is of no help. Just about everything inside such houses was made of wood; the only remaining iron items are a few tools; only a few coins represent other metals. Ceramic fragments are abundant, but in a thousand-year span, only specialists can date pots, basins, and bowls, all of which look alike to an untrained eye. Colored tiles on the floors and even on the walls in the wealthier homes interest the historian of art or of techniques, but the common people did not have them. The textiles, the leathers, and the wooden objects have disappeared, except in the very rare cases of underwater excavations. So what do we see?

"See" is the right word, for in both the cottage and the city house, people saw little unless they lived in a sunny land, where, what is more, people tended to avoid the sun. The door only had a grille or a cat door; the windows, when there were any, were cracks to let in air and were closed by shutters or, at most, with oiled cloth. With the exception of churches and a few castles, window glass, which was thick and colored like stained glass, appeared only in the fourteenth century. This means that grease or wax candles were used at night and, much more rarely, oil lamps. Domestic light was festive, almost religious, and it was the only justification for the interior decor of painted beams and wall frescoes that the rich provided for themselves. The tapestries that made the workshops of Italy, Arras, Flanders, and Angers famous in the late Middle Ages played an isothermic role, creating a cushion of air between the room and the ice-cold wall.

The house was the procreative cell, hence the bed was king among the furnishings. Beds are the personal item most represented in paintings—beds for all social environments and in almost all ages, and the inventories drawn up after a death note them before anything else. The bed was a social "marker," in particular when it had hangings, curtains that could be closed, and at times a dais. Its components were always the same, however: a wooden frame, a bedstead with feet and a high head; a webbing of interlaced ropes or hemp straps; a straw mattress or a *chutrin* stuffed with dried pea vines, straw, and grain husks; sheets of linen or hemp, rough to the touch and regularly smoothed out by being beaten with a stick; a wool "counterpane" or a featherbed; and pillows and a stiff *traversier*, or horizontal pillow. In Germanic lands, where people were more concerned about rot or vermin, a fur or animal skin was preferred. Under the bed or beside it was a *couchette* for a nursing baby, with the chamber pot, which was sometimes made of fine ceramics, nearby. The bed was up to 2.5 meters wide, which means that it could easily contain parents and children or even several adults. People usually slept half-sitting, propped up by pillows, but sick people and mothers awaiting childbirth rested stretched out. The head of the bed was always placed against a wall, a custom of all human beings from the prehistoric caverns to our own day as a way to avoid being surprised from behind by the nocturnal attack of a carnivore or an enemy.

Nothing equaled the bed among the furniture, unless it was the coffer. We still have a few fourteenth- and fifteenth-century examples, from wealthy homes, of course. They are made of oak, walnut, or pine, close with imposing locks, and are often worked, even with marquetry. All sorts of things were put in them: money, embroidered clothing, belts, arms, everything needed for writing and counting, at times even onions or a ham. In the competition for wealth, coffers and chests came right after the bed, and in all cases well ahead of all the rest of the furnishings: tables (on trestles until the fourteenth century), wooden chairs (or, more rarely, with caned seats), benches, stools, folding stools, pegged bars on the walls before armoires came into fashion in the Renaissance. As if in an inventory worthy of Jacques Prévert, the *dits* and the *fabliaux* enumerate, but without the order that I have introduced, the *outillement au vilain* that humble folk needed for daily life: a grill, hooks, spits, skewers, or *crémaillères*; terra-cotta pots that gave a certain taste to foods or tinned metal containers that smelled somewhat; various sorts of bowls, tankards, frying pans, and terrines for the *potage* and for mush; strainers, ladles, spoons big and small; a broom and shovels. On top of that and on a slightly higher level, a balance, spindles, and a spinning wheel. On the uppermost level, mirrors, combs, and jewelry.

It is obvious that all of these items, conscientiously enumerated in wills, listed in excavation reports, or mentioned in "bourgeois" poetry, aided the woman, especially in the privacy of the home, because the "tools" of the man remained outside of the house, ready for use in the fields or the workshop. The level of the home's equipment is not only strongly gendered but also reflects social differences. At Charavines two early-eleventh-century houses have been found side by side. They may have been quite different in their internal decor, which has disappeared. One of them contained gaming tables, musical instruments, and pieces of weaponry, but not the other, where all that remained were traces of looms or bits of metal. Did knights live in one house and peasants in the other? Or "knightly peasants of the year one thousand"? Debating the question would take me far afield, into a study of society, which is not my affair. We can see, however, that the houses bear traces of individuals, this time separated by their economic and social condition. Everyone labored, according to his estate. It is time we looked at work.

Man Is Born to Toil

Not only is this aphorism inaccurate; it is completely contradictory to the lessons of history. All pre-Christian civilizations—those of "classical" antiquity and probably those of the peoples whom antiquity called "barbarians"—were founded on leisure, or *otium*. The effort that was necessary—obviously necessary—to the survival of the species was furnished by slaves, while even activities that might be judged productive, for example, the hunt, the struggle for material goods, even prayer or discourse for reasons of spiritual satisfaction, had an essentially pleasure-seeking aspect. They reflected an attitude worthy of being known and praised, an attitude that was "noble" in the original sense of the word. Its contrary would be *ignobilis*, which included the activity of exchanges between men; *otium* stood counter to *negotium* or commerce. Enough word play, however. There are philosophical attitudes in which a search for pleasure in leisure is what sets social life in motion, and many have sung the praises of hedonism, but the gradual decline of slavery and the idea that labor might contain a reward of its own because it demands a difficult but salutary effort slowly opened the way to the idea of work as a means for spiritual redemption. To be sure, the biblical malediction pursuant to the Fall clearly states that toil is a punishment, and later Jesus tells Martha, when she complains of having to prepare dinner without her sister's assistance, that Mary, who was contemplative and idle, had chosen the better part. Jesus himself declares himself to be the son of a carpenter, and he recruits his apostles from among working men.

Idleness thus remained "holy" because it was only without other preoccupations that one could devote oneself to God. It was a virtue that brought men closer to what in the East would be called Nirvana and was not to be confused with laziness or sloth, a sin of resignation and inertia and an insult to humans. A further step came in the early centuries of Christianity. Work was exhausting; to give oneself over to it with determination, as monks did, was to break the body and stifle all unhealthy impulses. As monastic rules reiterated: *ora et labora*, "pray and work." At that point work shifted from being a punishment, albeit a voluntary one, to sanctification. It was work that procured liberty. It is true that slaves might have found it difficult to persuade themselves of this, but no one asked them to listen to the thinkers. In the Carolingian age it was thought that work was inherent to the sanctified human condition and that God himself had labored to create the world. In the thirteenth century Jacques de Vitry stated this clearly: "Whoever does not work does not eat."

We have no lack of sources of all sorts to tell us about the working world: statutes of trade associations, organizational texts, narratives and poems; iconography as well, such as depictions of work in calendars, and archaeology for everything regarding tools. Important chronological and technological changes undoubtedly occurred during the thousand years of the Middle Ages. Let me attempt to focus on a few constants. To begin with, vocabulary. Medieval French did not contain the word *travail*. The term *tripalium*, which is its origin, indicated a three-legged prop used to steady a horse's hindquarters while it was being shod. That the term was later used to designate an instrument of torture baldly highlights the painful and negative aspect of work. Both the texts and people of the time spoke of *labor*, *actio*, or *opus*, which designated "effort," "advance," or "piece of work," all terms that implied physical exertion. The aim, of course, was to produce an object or transmit a message. A man who worked the soil, a weaver, a merchant, but also a cleric or a warrior "worked," each according to his estate and his tools. But the attempt to describe the nature of work relations by means of a theory or a system, as many scholars have been led to do, seems particularly futile. Whether they loyally invoke Adam Smith, Ricardo, Malthus, Marx, or Weber, historians build up or tear down mechanisms that are cruelly lacking the psychological dimension, which is what matters to me in this context. Work was dominated by tacit rules that falsify any sociological description and that, in my opinion, justify the "naturalistic" option that I have chosen to adopt, as the reader will already have remarked. I see three such rules, and when they gave way to others it can be said that the Middle Ages had "ended" and "modern" times had begun.

The first rule is the very contrary of our own economic conceptions. The notion of competition did not exist. The Church stood guard against it, for it could only be the source of rivalries, jealousy, and sin. Whether they were consumed or used for artisan work, the products of the soil and livestock were the same for all, and the effort involved in making them available to the buyer should thus be equal. There was no "publicity," which was considered to be deceitful and an indication of an interest in profit; there was no "dumping" in order to lower prices, which would hurt others. And if, in the city, butchers' stalls or cloth workshops tended to be lined up on the same street (which was less often the case than is thought), it was not to juxtapose the same products and the same prices, which would be absurd, but rather because apprenticeship was served "on the job" by relatives or companions from the same locality. We should not imagine some sort of golden age, however. One man got rich through his business while another was ruined; welcome, presentation, and skill made the difference, rather than a sharper sense of profit on one side and an almost philanthropic abnegation on the other. Still, although a desire for earnings inhabits all men in all times, strict municipal laws were there to punish all infractions. If a public agent found a sheet or a length of cloth too short, too long, or too light according to established standards, it would be destroyed publicly, and the dishonest or clumsy artisan subjected to paying a fine. Even in those times of penury, a loaf of bread judged too small or too blackened was tossed into the water. In the eyes of economists, who began to teem in the sixteenth century, such stringent regulations were strangling free enterprise and, ultimately, profit, the wellspring of the economy. The consequences concern us all.

The second rule is close to the first. The objective of work was the "common profit" and "good commerce." There is doubtless some spirit of Christian charity in this, but there was also (or perhaps even more) an interest in public order, without which that objective could not be obtained or maintained. In northwestern Europe and in Italy, after some rather vague attempts to supervise the world of work in Carolingian times, the cities took over the task of supervising measures and verifying prices under the watchful eye of armed guards to avoid violence. Certain rulers became involved, but not to any great extent before 1250. At that time there was an influx into the city of unskilled rural men who mingled with the unemployed urban workers; Franciscan "little brothers" had little difficulty raising revolts among them, but it is not within my scope to speak of the *effrois*, riots, and strikes put down by the forces of order. By that time—the fourteenth and fifteenth centuries—the working world under such regulation began to suffer.

The third rule brings us closer to our own times and permits us to return to the countryside. Work was the fruit of an effort and involved a result, but these were not always the same. The warrior wins glory, but at the price of his blood; the cleric may come to be reputed for his influence, but he had to put in long years of study; the artisan and the merchant might get rich, but he ran the risks of chance and an unfavorable economic situation. But what of the peasant? His salvation was assured if he followed the rules of piety: labor that was hard and constant but peaceful and subject to few dangers aside from the caprices of nature. Besides, if what he produced seldom drew him out of mediocrity, it was never (or almost never) threatened. If one had the necessities, why adopt a spirit of enterprise? Was there, here and there, a pioneer trying to settle in a new land? Or a greedy peasant who dreamed of getting control of portions of a monastic forest that he thought might yield well? They were a minority, and such attempts can be understood only over a long time period. Here the productive spirit of initiation was eliminated, and routine and custom held back progress. This is why the historian, after paying his respects to agrarian questions between the tenth and the thirteenth centuries, plunges into the history of cities. There, at least, work takes on a certain relief.

But What Work?

The moralists and the philosophers of the twelfth and thirteenth centuries, more or less persuaded that they could create a "mirror of the world," did a good job of distinguishing between "order," social relief, and efficiency in the object of labor, but they did not attempt to characterize work by ergonomic standards. It is precisely biotechnology, however, that illuminates the form and the result of effort, definitively and more broadly than any other systematic consideration. People work for no remuneration, for wages, or in expectation of a payment, or else they do nothing and wait for the fruit of work to fall in their laps.

Each of those possibilities deserves consideration. For the first, the idea of slavery immediately comes to mind. Human cattle carried off from the battlefield or during a savage raid, slaves did all manner of labor. Traditional history closes its eyes out of modesty (or cowardice, if one prefers) at the ignominy of Greco-Roman "civilization," Byzantine hypocrisy, Muslim cynicism, and the cowardice of the Christian Church of the West, which condemned commerce in human flesh but refused slaves access to its ministry, even though Christianity made its first converts among slaves. The illustrious Carolingians made many ignoble raids beyond the Elbe among the Slavs, who lent their name, become "slaves," to the large numbers of men taken as far away as Islam or the Christian East. In order to appease a troubled conscience here and there, these subjected hordes were given a hasty baptism, and leading them to their destination was put in the hands of Jews. We need not linger long over this first group. Its numbers decreased as early as the eighth and ninth centuries, thanks to the cessation of major raids; besides, many in this subjected population obtained a bit of land to cultivate or a fixed domestic employment. Above all, slavery did not "pay." The elderly, pregnant women, and small children were responsibilities that turned no profit, and the time when one could put to death an indocile or sick slave was long past. We will have to look elsewhere.

Although it is done constantly, I shall not invoke serfdom as the "heir" to slavery. This is an intellectual facility founded on constraints of a juridical nature (and perhaps moral ones as well) that weighed on a portion of the peasantry. It is an arena littered with dead ideas, and it seems to me truly far from my purposes here to consider the provenance of those alienated, "attached" (the root meaning of *servi*) men. Besides, I am persuaded, in spite of affirmations that date to Marx or Ernst Bloch, that such a state was never generalized and was soon dissolved, and I might add that the nature of the serf's work was identical to that of the free peasant if we ignore some personal obligations that are not within my field of vision. Let us leave it to the jurists, then, to collect formal evaluations of serfdom. Standing with a pitchfork in hand or as mixed bones in the cemetery, workers, free or not, were identical.

It is instead within the family that we find unpaid workers. In the peasant group (and often in the artisan's family) a wife, children, and siblings were paid only in terms of the global earnings of the group; everyone operated for the collective interest, according to his or her age and strength. This introduced a sort of division of labor, it is true, but that differentiation was not inherent and came only from the will of a father or the prestige of an elder. Similarly, a refusal to assist the group of relatives or friends in a task considered unworthy or unpleasant, such as guarding pigs or spreading fertilizer, would lead, at the worst, to a fit of temper or being "deprived of dessert." Unpleasant tasks were absolutely typical of peasant labor, however. There was no schedule aside from the daylight hours; at harvest time or the grape-pressing season there was no repose short of exhaustion. The only profit was the result of work well done. And if a neighbor came to offer a hand, his benevolence was simply a charitable act, as the community counted on God to thank him for it. This large range of free labor, all things considered, justifies a formula that was universally valid: in the Middle Ages, everyone did everything.

At the limit between free labor and working for pay, there was a third sort that gradually disappeared from Western practices, which was working without a fixed remuneration or for a very small one, but living on the advantages attached to the activity, which might include gifts, opportunities for perquisites or fees, and small earnings resulting from the effort furnished, which at times might be personal or relatively disinterested. The range of workers of this type was very broad. It included the *ministérial*, who served as the agent or the accountant of the demesne, but also the chaplain and the bodyguards. It also included all of those, from the apprentice old-clothes dealer to the village knight, who lived with no schedule and no wages on what they could glean from their "office," which might come in the form of a portion of the taxes collected, the alms or oblations of the faithful, or the profits from occasional pillage or minor theft. It is quite probably from within this "service" personnel that "friends" were recruited; the obligated and all of those who formed the *familia* or the *casa*, as we have already seen, and who were tied—in the city in particular—to a master who granted them his friendship and his confidence.

Then we come to the group that is most familiar to us: those who are paid wages for their labor. There are so many facets to this topic that if I reviewed them all I would end up with a portrait of medieval economy. I shall therefore limit myself to its most prominent features. Such workers were paid for what they did to the profit of those who employed them. In country areas, they would be *journaliers*, day workers confined to tasks that required only physical strength, as brewers, common laborers, or share-cropping tenant farmers. This fringe of the free but impoverished peasantry was encouraged (though not created) by certain religious orders such as the Cistericians, who had no interest in opening their lands to tenants, whom they thought too demanding or too indocile. The situation of tenant farmers is difficult to grasp. Either they exploited their own lands, which would place them among the unpaid workers we have just seen, or they rented them, which would mean that once they had put aside what was necessary for survival, they owed "rent" in the form of produce or money to a master who benefited from their labor. I will spare my reader the pages and pages that would be required for a review of the various forms of tenancy—*cens, surcens, agrière, complant, métayage, mezzadria, fermage*, and many others—and will omit discussion of the "services" that were added to the rental fee. Although these lightened as the centuries passed, they amounted to obligatory labor (*corvées*) at the grape harvest, at plowing time, or in the form of guard duties. Historical literature today teems with such a broad range of studies of regional and chronological variations that I cannot possibly cope with them all, so I shall abandon the topic to those who delight in local monographic studies. Should all of those workers be considered "salaried"? Yes, because although they paid, they were paid as well, but in a way that may surprise us. They were protected, they had recourse to a judge, "common" spaces were opened for them to keep their grain, their livestock, or their wood—services that the state, since the fourteenth century, has appropriated.

Passing on to the city, things became simpler: if the apprentice was paid in kind while he learned the trade, and if the master tradesman paid himself only through his earnings, the others— *valets* or *compagnons* in a workshop, *saute-ruisseaux* or *houliers* (lawyers' errand boys and go-betweens) looking for employment expected to be paid. Once again, there is an entire range of payment schemes. Workers might be paid by the piece or by the day, with a contract or by verbal agreement, and the worker might or might not be inscribed in a guild, belong to a *métier* (though not in all cases), live in a particular part of the city, or belong to a confraternity. Workers were expected to respect the working hours that tolled from the city's belfry, but they might easily be punished if they ruined a piece of work or were discovered to be working by night (*au noir*) in their rooms doing overtime at the expense of their colleagues. The latter were called *chambrelans* or *jaunes* for the yellow flame of the candle that lit their illegal work. Should workers stop working despite the "common profit," if they fought with one another, or if they destroyed their rivals' working materials, it resulted in disturbances that were the fabric of daily life in the city: *effrois* or *émotions* or a *takehan* or *harelle* complaining of high prices, low salaries, unemployment, being cheated by the powers that be, overly acquisitive wealthy people, or competition from peasants immigrating to the city—an entire "working world" that hints strongly at poverty.

Then there were some on the fringes of the working world who did nothing. These were not the same individuals as those in the two first "orders" according to the divine scheme. The latter could seem idle, it is true, but their task was to consecrate themselves to others, not to produce goods. The cleric preached and taught in order to save or guide souls; the warrior fought for glory and spoils, to be sure, but the brilliance of his table or his deeds honored the humble more than it exasperated them. As for monks, hermits, and recluses, their idleness was holy since it put them in contact with the Holy Spirit; it was up to the faithful to persuade themselves that this was for their good. Besides those holy men and women whose time could neither be counted nor paid, there were the elderly, for whom time no longer counted and who were no longer paid. They kept track of kinships, gave advice, arbitrated disagreements, and pronounced judgment under the village elm or the arcades of the city. At the other extremity of this many-hued world were the "miserable," who were not always all that miserable: the beggars, cut-purses, armed bands of roving marauders like the *écorcheurs*, *caïmans*, or simple bandits who lurked in the woods, one or two of whom were hanged now and then to reassure the population. All of these labored too, after all, and completely at the expense of others.

Still, a panel is missing in my picture, an essential one, in my opinion, and not the least. Where are the women? "One man out of two," as the humorist says? First, they were in their private lives, where they displayed an activity and furnished efforts—even physical ones—that were equal to or surpassed those of the men laboring outside the house. Women were responsible for the fire and the food, the oven and the mill, the water from the well and aiding at harvest time. They did all of the activities reputed to be women's work: spinning and sewing, making baskets and weaving cloth that they then cropped and combed. But those repetitive tasks, about which men understood nothing, put the idea into those men's heads and into our own that, shut up in the home, the woman "did not work." That fiction was shattered in the thirteenth century, perhaps earlier, when people began to see more clearly. If it is difficult to separate the roles of men and women in country areas in the management of property, for example (who keeps the accounts? who accepts the *cens* or pays them?), it is evident that when a woman was widowed she took on the role of the deceased husband, whereas the widower remarried immediately, and not only for reasons of sexual appetite. In the city, however, as is attested by the feminization of many patronymics related to occupations, the place of women was strengthened during the final centuries of the Middle Ages. They reigned over leather-working, felt-making, and the cloth trades. It is true that a loom required more strength than they were capable of giving, as did setting a sail or brewing beer, but they were the ones who sorted the merchandise, counted it, and sold it. Iconography shows us women keeping a haberdashery or a cobbler's shop, but also a butcher shop or a grocery store. The statutes of the various trades include women among the masters of shops, the workers, and the servants. So was there parity, as contemporary women demand and as their own grandmothers would have known it? Probably not, and for all the reasons that are still put forward. Female labor outside of the domestic setting was broken up by pregnancies, limited by the rough tasks of manipulating tools, and marginalized by a fearful male prejudice that we have already encountered. We know almost nothing about inequalities in salary, which are probable but concealed by the theoretical texts. There was no female "corporation," and women scarcely had the right to any respect within the male *métiers*, or trade associations. In her own house, the woman was indeed mistress; outside of it, without being either a serving woman or an auxiliary, she remained subservient to the male gaze.

And Tools?

Historians who study the higher echelons of the working world do not find it too difficult to describe the tools that were required. A writer went to school, then to the university; he had been taught to hold a pen and to construct a sermon or participate in a *disputatio*. Memory, talent, and psychology were inborn qualities or ones encouraged by exercising the mind. The warrior had to become expert in riding a horse, using heavy and dangerous weapons, and knowing how to dodge a blow and watch out for trouble. He had little need for schooling or knowledge. Courage, an ability to size up a situation at a glance, and endurance were enough. All other men had things to learn.

First of all, they had to learn how to sustain an effort that was more physical than nervous. In reality, we are quite ignorant regarding the sports, exercises, or muscular preparation needed to maintain the resistance required by tasks that machines do for us today. I have already noted that men and women of the time were never "tired," or at least never complained of being tired. Yet, how many examples of exceptional efforts there are, at least in literature: pilgrims on foot or soldiers on campaign who march ten hours without stopping; knights in the saddle for twenty leagues; quarrymen dragging blocks of stone that weigh a ton; people in a besieged city holding out for two months with nothing but foul water to drink! When Emperor Frederick Barbarossa bathed in an icy stream at the age of eighty (to be sure, he died of it), or when Philip, the duke of Burgundy, out of his mind, wandered for three days in the forest without eating; when Roland strikes such a heavy sword blow on the helmet of a miscreant that he slices him in two, or when it takes several people to withdraw Durandal, his sword, from the ground, where Roland planted it; when someone is reported to have killed a bull with his fist, jumped over a cliff, uprooted an oak, or even (and this was a woman!) broken down a stone wall, no one marveled at it. Beside these astonishing experiences, in which imagination certainly played a part, the sports that we know, ball games or games involving skill, equitation exercises or rhythmic dances, seem mere amusements with little to do with training.

Thus one had to learn by imitation or by observation, beginning in childhood, as we have seen. The custom of calling "mother" (*mère*) the older artisan who welcomed novices to the trade was not simply a coincidence. That older artisan offered an example to the worker, to be sure, and also to the young peasant, and he also taught the tricks of the trade and passed on the techniques and the sayings that guided the newcomer's first steps. As the historians of technology believe, the shades of Varro, Vegetius, Columella, and Vitruvius hovered over this process, along with all of the "geniuses" to whom learned men (who had not always read their works) dedicated commentaries, but whose names the man on the job had never heard. Of course, the ten centuries of the Middle Ages saw progress in technology in all sectors, but in my opinion this was the result of practical observation rather than a teaching process, hence it matters little if a technique originated in Greece, Iran, China, or among the Slavs or the Celts.

For some time tools remained quite stable, to the discontent of the archaeologists, who count on artifacts to provide dates. The sickle, the flail, the hoe, the distaff, the balance, or the pitchfork are adapted to the human hand and body just as the horseshoe is to the horse's hoof. As long as human beings continued to use a tool there was little reason to change it. How are we to date them, then? A number of medieval "inventions" are simply the result of a keen observation of constant realities. Stamping on grapes to crush them in the tun, regularly beating iron made red hot in the forge involved an alternative movement of thighs or arms, which is the soul of the brace and bit and the camshaft; harnessing a horse at shoulder level or providing the saddle with a pommel and a cantle was an obvious remedy for an animal who suffocated when attached by a rope around his neck or for a warrior thrown off his horse when he attempted to charge. As for the famous plow with a share and a moldboard, the triumph of medieval agriculture, it is a natural response to a rich, thick soil that needed to be broken up before the plowshare could penetrate it, then needed to be pushed to the side to avoid having the soil fall back into the furrow. Was something similar known in ancient times? Perhaps, but the question that remains is why? Let us leave the quarrel to the experts.

Let me make myself clear. How can I deny progress in the quality, the efficacy, or the volume of work when all of these expanded greatly between the eleventh and the fourteenth centuries? This would be pure absurdity, and I too am persuaded of the economic and social "leap forward" that was an effect of the plow, and also of the fulling mill, the weaving loom with pedals, ventilation devices in the mines, lap-jointing, and horseshoes. All I am trying to do is bring these "novelties" down to the hand and the personal experience of the peasant and the craftsman or the cleric and the warrior, even though I speak less often of the latter two. I have a good guide in doing so: the Church itself. Progress did not seem a worthy goal to the Church, which feared a search for profit that would endanger salvation. Hence it condemned initiatives that lacked support in Scripture, and it mistrusted the individualism of any audacious soul who broke with the spirit of collectivity. This position was difficult to hold to at a time when the Christian world was being swept along by an increasing use of money, multiplying exchanges, and rising needs. In the twelfth century the Church charged the Cistercians with offering a rural model of a rational and, in principle, disinterested economy. In the thirteenth century it permitted the brothers of the Order of Preachers to spread the word in the cities about codes of economic good conduct. In the fourteenth century, it too was carried along by the flow.

A final observation to focus our vision. All of what I have said tends to minimize excessive differences between our own times and the centuries of the Middle Ages. I need to furnish a correction, however, or perhaps a sharper look. All of the occupations or types of work that I have summarized do not lie on exactly the same plane as our own. What I mean by this is that they were divided up differently. In the city in particular (but is not today's society a largely urban one?), a survey of types of work holds some surprises. Thanks to many of our sources—for example, the poems or *dits* of the thirteenth century (such as the *Dits de Paris*)— we find that food-related activities represented as much as half of the known trades, and those directly connected with raw materials, metals or textiles, represent almost another third. This left only 10 or 15 percent of occupations for those dedicated to intellectual activities, and only an infinitely small fringe for the "services" that we call "the tertiary sector." I should not have to point out that these proportions are totally different today, almost inverted. Is this a banal statement? Yes, of course, but it should not be neglected.

The time has come to abandon the adult man and woman, kin and neighbors, the active and the less active, but also the house and the workshop, passing time, and the common table. Bit by bit, life weakened in them, and they faced approaching death.

THE END OF LIFE

Man did not have to wait for Saint Augustine to know that he must die and did not know when. Death is the leading actor in the human adventure. Well before the West called itself Christian, death haunted people's minds; it ruled over family relations; it weighed on the economy; it commanded all meditation. Belief in the next world, both in the West and beyond, made death the foundation of fear and the threshold of hope, the end of the body and its miseries, and the beginning of the time when souls would be weighed. Since no one could avoid death's sentence, death had to be "tamed," rendered accessible, admitted as a beginning and as something desirable, thus limiting the force of our vulgar ties to things of this world. This was a hard job. Greco-Roman society, the only ancient society for which we have some notion of attitudes toward death, did not succeed in making death acceptable. It exiled the dead to an isolated necropolis outside the city or buried them along the roads. The return of the living to among the dead (or vice versa) undeniably marks a mental break of the first order. Invoking increasing massacres or terrifying epidemics is a highly insufficient response. The idea of the immortality of the soul eventually carried the day. Death was a beginning, a rite of passage that must be prepared with faith, almost with joy, so as to liberate the soul, rejoin the ancestors, our models, and accede to true light. This did not exclude either the fear of pain or the drama of separation. After the twelfth century, such concerns even grew when life "here be-low" became sweeter and more amiable, for many people at least. After the mid-fourteenth century, when human excess or the furies of nature reached a high point, death once more appeared as hid-eous and repugnant, one of the four horsemen of the Apocalypse, a view that remained true for some time.

Death was unpredictable, to be sure, but most men were con-scious of its approach.

The Elderly

It has been said that every society has the old people it deserves or it gives itself. Over a thousand years, the Middle Ages saw a num-ber of "societies of the aged" come and go. We are incapable of measuring the proportion of men and women "of great age" at that time. For one thing, and most obviously, we lack written sources, but also the very notion of age varied in its meaning and in its ef-fects. Is this not still the case? To "act your age" or "die before your time" is a question of how we view the calendar or, at most, of cor-onary vigor, but to "reason like an old man" or to "act old" is less flattering when it comes from the mouth of someone younger, and it no longer concerns "age" as such but rather behavior. These are banalities but they contain a judgment. Old age can be respectable or ridiculous; it resides more in attitudes than in arteries. During the Middle Ages, that second way of looking at old age was rarer, or at least it has left fewer traces in literary expression. The first was dominant and deserves a closer look.

Life expectancy, as the demographers who limit themselves to counting tell us (and one person who lives to the age of ninety and another who dies at ten give a life expectancy of fifty!), varied from century to century according to the standard of living, but it can be estimated that in the Middle Ages it never rose above sixty to sixty-five. I have mentioned this above. Beyond that age, one was a survivor, but not useless. There are now few older men in the mili-tary, but in the early fourteenth century, over 10 percent of men of war were over sixty. It is an error to believe that early death was widespread in the medieval world, as is shown by innumerable examples. Naturally, common sense dictates that we distinguish between types of activity, lifestyles, and genders, but the finish line is well beyond what traditional historiography teaches. All of those "oldsters" thus formed a *classe d'âge* that was held in awe and, generally speaking, respected. Not always, to be sure, as many of the *fabliaux* prove. There are many examples of an old father or grandfather shut up in the attic with a half-cloak thrown over his shoulders. In the oral tradition, such oldsters were witnesses to what had come before, and their arbitrage was sought. They told the inquirer how old they thought they were: seventy years old, eighty, only rarely more, which pleads in favor of verisimilitude. As depositories of memory (familial memory, at any rate, but on some occasions political memory), they were an indispensable link between the Here Below and the world On High, and they were often asked to recite their memories by the fireside. In a society in which little if anything was written down, they were the servants of time.

Protected, beginning in the early Middle Ages—for example, from the fees charged for drawing up agreements—the elderly were viewed more as privileged witnesses than as grandparents. As I have said above, one seldom sees them interfering in the activities of the younger generation as they do today. In the more or less romantic biographies of famous men, the figure of the grandfather is somewhat immobile; he does little except to serve as an example to be followed or to express mute disapproval. Still, how "great age" was viewed changed at the very end of the Middle Ages, when it no longer enjoyed universal reverence. What might now be called a youth culture stressed all that was young and new. After 1350 or 1400, all the heroes of literature are young and handsome, as were the "stars" of the political game and the military leaders. Like Joan of Arc, the kings, dauphins, dukes, and warriors who were lauded by the young and followed by crowds were all under thirty. This has led some to imagine a generalized rejuvenation of all administrative personnel of the time, which is an error. Prelates, magistrates, dignitaries of the court were still men of a certain age, but fashion, even that pertaining to clothing, headdress, and speech, aimed at glorifying a youthful appearance and behavior. As is true today of our yearning to seem "young," this may reflect a stronger fear of death in face of a rising death rate caused by the catastrophes of the time. People did not yet put their hopes in facial creams and surgery, but they believed in the Fountain of Youth.

Still, an old man knew that the end was near. If his organism had not given him an implacable warning, he consulted seers, had a fling with necromancy, or dabbled in astrology if he was wealthy, as did Louis XI. Some had their dreams interpreted; others, who knew how to read, drew consoling thoughts from such approved reading matter as the lives of the saints or the heroes. In the literary world, this was the age of the *artes moriendi*, "manuals of death"; preachers, the preaching friars at their head, assured the throngs that man is nothing and grace is all. On the walls of fifteenth-century churches the *danse funèbre* showed the dead of all levels of society dancing together. Was it not a comfort to know that they were all being dragged toward Judgment? Besides, was not death the beginning of a "fourth age" that opens to eternity? First the Platonic philosophers, then Augustine had said that death was only a "passage."

A passage? But it still inspired fear, and the Christian, resigned to it or not, lived a "religion of fear," thinking that he might have sinned too much, thus ruining his chances for salvation. The idea of beginning life anew, which gives Buddhists their serenity, was rejected by Christian dogma in the councils of the fifth century. The game had been played and it was useless to struggle against death. Its victory was certain. Even the thinkers who hoped that man would fight back against the inevitable, such as Avicenna in Iran and even, for a while, Bacon in the West, held only derisory weapons in a miserable pharmacopoeia of plants and unguents. The dying man, surrounded by his entire *familia*, at least in the early centuries of the Middle Ages, was alone when the "hideous" moment came.

Since nothing was considered worse than a "bad death"—one that was not foreseen or organized in a timely fashion—all necessary precautions had to be taken so as to figure among the small group of the elect. First, one's soul had to be cleansed, and the higher one's place in human society, the more soiled it was likely to be. Voluble and at times public confessions to atone for crimes or smaller bad acts were the rule. At that moment, the dying man faced the Judge. Hiding nothing and sparing no one, he was capable of trampling on the interests and even the honor of his relatives. This was a sad perspective for the entourage thus unmasked and humiliated. This was all the more true as only the ministers of God could open the gates to Heaven, and that service had to be paid. Thanks to a promise of being received as a monk *in extremis vitae* or being permitted to repose *ad sanctos* among the religious or in the sanctuary itself, one could hope to benefit in the Beyond from the support of the prayers of the religious—those of monks in particular, which were reputed to be more efficacious than those of the canons of the cathedral, who were presumed to be too busy. But in order to gain these advantages, one had to give a wood, a vineyard, the use of a *garenne* (a fishing or hunting preserve). Moreover, the men of God were sufficiently in touch with the interests of the Church to hurry to the bedside of the dying man when agony approached. His soul would be all the more assured of eternal rest if *obits*, masses on the anniversary of his death, were organized. Since vanity was very much a part of the remembrance that the dying man hoped for, these *rentes de mort* were of a price that the survivors often found crushing, enough to ruin a family, but that dazzled the world. Around 1450, the Captal of Buch, a captain with a distinguished military career but with a black soul, ordered twice as many masses as were prescribed, a hundred years later, by the very pious king of Spain, Philip II. At least we can say that this funerary debauchery gave rise to a highly interesting category of documents: obituaries or necrologies carefully kept up to date in the monasteries and friaries as a calendar of anniversary masses, or *rouleaux des morts* that circulated from one monastic institution to another listing names of the dead. The historian finds them a gushing font of family data.

Often consternated by inconsiderate donations of a fear-stricken dying relative, the family could attempt to exercise a right of *retrait* in the name of the lineage that had been stripped of its wealth. This was difficult in the face of a Church virtuously draped in the idea of the salvation of the soul, but it was easier if the dying man had drawn up a will. I cannot pause for the history of the last will and testament, which would weigh down my narration with heavy juridical considerations. I shall only say that the practice of making a will, solidly established in southern Europe from Roman times and the very early Middle Ages, gradually spread toward the north, particularly in the twelfth century, and then beyond, when customs regarding the division of an inheritance, formerly guided by lineage concerns concentrating on younger children or already dowered daughters, ceded under demographic pressure and thanks to the evolution of the family. At that time, the testament appeared to be the only way to permit satisfaction of the desires (at times the caprices) of the dying person. The corps of notaries drew a notable part of its income from wills, as might be imagined.

But now the testament has been drawn up, the pious donations have been promised, extreme unction has been administered, and the penitential wake has started. Everything is nearby, even fear. Here comes Death.

The "Passage"

This time, only a few apparent differences distinguish the rich and powerful from the men we have followed thus far. All crossed the threshold of death naked. Death, in all centuries and all localities, is an individual adventure. The moment at which the soul left the body, which medieval art renders so strongly by a small nude form escaping from the mouth of the deceased, might of course evoke tears from the family, or perhaps only from the women. Although the medieval world encountered death at every turn, it was still an occasion of surprise and pain, tragically accompanied by the moans of the dying man. This presents a somewhat more somber picture than the one the Church attempted to give of death. For the Church, the ideal was to die in one's bed, peacefully surrounded by a family in tears, uttering a few well-chosen words. This was also the image offered in iconography almost up to our own day. Clearly, reality lay elsewhere. Instead of an edifying and serene death narrated by his biographers, who claimed to have been eyewitnesses, the saintly King Louis IX, stricken with dysentery in Tunis, was very probably writhing with intestinal pains accompanied by vomiting and diarrhea when he died.

Whether death was rough or gentle when it came, it was surrounded by a web of customs. It was a passage, a mutation, and an institutional rite of life in society, even when the dying man was no longer in any condition to take part in it with any degree of lucidity. The family, even the entire village, were present, inside the house or nearby, in a sort of theatrical ostentation; a minister of God chanted invocations to pray for a good death, for pardon for sin, for eternal salvation, and for the suffering Christ to act as an aid to the moribund, should he still be able to hear and understand. All such rites were in reality much more aimed at solidifying and consolidating the community of the living than accompanying the one who was leaving this life.

That was the "good death" that followed the rules. Unfortunately, there were other kinds. I have already spoken about the newborn babies who died before they could be baptized. In Limbo, where they reposed while prayers were recited for them in special chapels and sanctuaries "of respite," they awaited a Judgment that could not condemn them. Children aborted just before they were born or were presumed dead on coming into the light of day may have been baptized or just *ondoyé* by being given a private, emergency baptism, and since that pseudosacrament could be administered by a layperson, even a criminal, eternal damnation could be avoided. Condemned criminals usually made honorable amends, and the Church permitted them to leave for the gibbet with their consciences at ease, at least in principle. Two other "bad deaths" might lead to the gates of Hell. First, there were those who had died a brutal and unexpected death—the warrior killed in combat or a murdered man—deprived of the precautions we have seen above. The warrior was probably safe, because before the battle, which might have received a priestly blessing, he may have confessed and received the host; or he may have done away with some miscreants, which would earn him pardon. If this was not the case, he could hope that a good show of remorse before witnesses or simply that proper burial might influence Judgment. Obviously, the man cut down at a turning in the wood with no chance to say a final prayer was under a greater threat. He would thus be judged on his "dossier," that is, by his family, his neighbors, and his confessor. At worst he would linger awhile in Purgatory until the wrath of the Creator subsided. In short, he was presumed to be an innocent victim and could be buried in hallowed ground.

But suicide was one threshold that the Church refused to cross. That social phenomenon (and there are "desperate" centuries) has always struck at the foundations of Christian dogma: one cannot take into one's own hands the gift of life that God has made to his creatures. Other cultures and other belief systems absorbed suicide much more easily. Thanks to a defiance of the world or out of disgust, widespread use was made of it in antiquity, and not only Greco-Roman antiquity. The Jewish religion found ways to explain suicide as a pious sacrifice; Islam in our own time furnishes incessant and bloody examples of this. But the Christian faith founded its success too firmly on the hope of a radiant Beyond to be gained thanks to efforts in this world, not to judge doing away with oneself an inconceivable and criminal act. This means that suicides are often hidden from our view, and there is no known suicide among the entire range of illustrious men and women whose cause of death can be ascertained during the thousand years of the Middle Ages. So did only poor people commit suicide, given that they might in fact have good reason to despair? Suicide is always an admission of defeat; moreover, it is an expression of self-disgust more than an attack on the Creator. That *pirouette*, as French puts it rather cruelly, is more like thumbing one's nose at the survivors than it is a salute to death. As far as we can tell from an approach unrelated to chronology, four-fifths of all suicides were men, and in medieval times three out of five of these hanged themselves and one out of four chose drowning. As is still true today, the family often refused to recognize that expression of a last will, speaking instead of illness or an accident. The Church may have been fooled, but when the act was patent the suicide was judged a criminal and his body dragged across the ground and hanged in public.

Even reduced to this brief schema, it is clear that suicide existed. How many warriors deliberately rushed into the thick of the action specifically in order to perish there, but with glory and honor? How many recluses, hermits, and perhaps also prisoners, let themselves die of hunger in their cells? How many Cathars accepted the *endura*, a voluntary death by inanition? And was all of this obscure domain that Plato admitted but Aristotle found repulsive—all of this *desesperatio*—likened to simple madness by all those good folk who had been promised happiness, but at some distant future time?

After Death

The funeral procession did not form until the body had been washed. There was little or no embalming, according to the archaeologists. The bodies of martyrs, real or claimed, and a few great rulers may have been treated, after the entrails had been removed, with balms, oils, and narcotic products, and at times, the body might even be tied up with narrow bands, but the West never used or did not discover the practices used in Egypt. At best, all that remained was a desiccated corpse in a piteous state. The official report drawn up in 1793, on the opening of the royal tombs at Saint-Denis, is horrifying. The body was buried in a winding sheet; a rich man might at times be buried in a fine suit of clothing, but the poor man had nothing but a length of sheeting. Bodies were practically never buried bare. Because wood rots, to the dismay of the archaeologists, wooden coffins were not used. The body was laid out on the ground, or it may have been placed in a stone tub, perhaps sheltered by a few tiles, more to protect the human remains from carnivores than from profanation. Burials are a favorite domain for excavation, as they reflect the practices, the various moments, and the surroundings of death. I shall limit my remarks on the topic to a few indicative points. Cremation, which was already in dispute before the triumph of Christianity, almost completely disappeared, except in the case of those condemned to die at the stake, whose ashes were scattered. This means that the dead were buried in the body. Until the eighth or ninth century, the remains were accompanied by objects, funerary offerings, perhaps arms, and small objects of private life such as jewelry or coins. These customs, which were indisputably pagan, disappeared with the Gregorian reforms toward the end of the eleventh century. Face-to-face with the Judge, the dead should be nude in his winding sheet, his sarcophagus, or his reliquary, if the body was represented by fragments of some holy personage. But, as the moralist tells us, "the world is made more of the dead than of the living." What could be done when space began to run out? Reuse a burial space, thus displacing and creating confusion among the bodies (the archaeologists' nightmare)? Create common burial trenches, thus deliberately mixing the bones, to the scandal of what remained of the family of the deceased? And what should be done when an epidemic struck, as did the plague in the fourteenth century? Burn the dead under the pretext that it was a measure of hygiene while the Church looked the other way? Naturally, the well-born who hoped to be buried next to or in the midst of monks did not want to be forgotten, and we can still see their memorial stones or the raised tombs on which they figure as *gisants*. The beauty of the funerary architecture in Saint-Denis, Fontevraud, or Champmol is indisputable. More modest burials bore only an epitaph, at times just a simple square stone with the name of the dead, perhaps placed behind an anonymous pillar, as is the case of

Pascal's tomb in Saint-Étienne-du-Mont in Paris or Bernini's tomb in Santa Maria Maggiore in Rome.

For even a deceased person of more modest rank, the funeral procession was expected to be solemn, as a man was being carried to God. When that man was a king, the ceremony had a political dimension. By the tenth century, the Church attempted to cover all possible cases by instituting an *ordo* or a *usus* for funerals. As in antiquity, mourners repeating chants and benedictions were certainly a part of the proceedings, but we know little about the organization of the Church rite itself. When the procession arrived at the burial place, the body was deposited on the ground. That was the moment for the reading out of the last gifts of the deceased in the presence of his relations and the men of the Church, at the risk of an explosion on the part of furious heirs who felt themselves cheated, as the sources attest. Except in the case of burial *ad sanctos*, the place of inhumation was the *atrium*, a public space but a holy one, and the untouchable nucleus of the community of the survivors. In medieval times the atrium played a role that we find it difficult to imagine. It might be large, even more than a hectare, and was a space of asylum and peace. No one, not even the local lord, could come into it on horseback or bearing arms; no fugitive or banished person could be seized within it; and it was where the villagers or city neighbors gathered to make decisions of a common interest, set the date for the grape harvest, or declare the taking up of arms. It was there that young wives could gather, or women after childbirth, but it was also—and nobody saw any blasphemy in this—the site of a fair dedicated to pigs or the celebration of the harvest. The Church may have frowned at some of these gatherings, but the cemetery was a part of its *dos*—its personal goods—and the place where its message had the best chance of being heard. Caring for the dead, also a responsibility of the Church, brought together all those who made a living on the death of others: professional mourners, gravediggers, masons, guards, or people who accompanied the funeral rites, not to speak of the entire corps of church personnel attached to the cult of the dead.

For the dead required a cult. First, because they were now in contact with the world of the ancestors and could thus intercede for worried survivors. A mourning period began with what is now called a *travail de deuil*, the aim of which was more to get the dead accustomed to their new state than to reassure the living. The memory of the deceased was honored in the *libri memoriales* of noble lineages that historians of the family find so precious; the family made sure that the memorial masses, or *obits*, were said properly, as already mentioned; and if the family's social rank was sufficiently high, seigneurial and even royal genealogies that are the delight of researchers today had to be drawn up in which every ancestor would find his place (be it accurate or imagined). It was apt to be the women who took charge of these marks of deference and memory, as they were reputed to have a better connection with the Other World. The point was to bring relief to the soul of the deceased, to be sure, but also and especially to strengthen family unity. Even the more humble dead had a right to dances, celebrations, prayers on the Day of the Dead, when the dead were felt to be present among their loved ones, which was followed by the prayers and veneration of the saints on All Saints' Day. Naturally—but this was done by the wealthy and more frequently after the fourteenth century—one might pay a chaplain to serve a family chapel devoted to the memory of a lineage, or a trade corporation, for that matter. Such chapels came to be lodged between the buttresses of Gothic churches, separated from the side aisles of the nave by a grille that protected the cenotaph of the ancestors and a few tombs, and rendered the works of art commissioned by members of the family inaccessible to tourists.

Whether supported by memory or rapidly forgotten, the dead plunged into the Beyond, where we shall rejoin them later. The question for those who were left behind was whether the dead person was truly dead. The Church was formal. The separation of soul and body is absolute, and only Judgment can reunite them. This involved a problem of conscience that, surprisingly, seems not to have sown doubt in the minds or the very souls of the poor: Will we really be "judged" on one attempt at life? Double or quits? Was reincarnation, even in the shape of an animal, thus inconceivable? I have stated above the position of the Christian Church, that life has no emergency exit. It was only toward the end of the twelfth century that the Church became aware of the frightening "all or nothing" dilemma in which it had placed its faithful. It thus endorsed, but very slowly indeed, the saving idea of a third way: that of Purgatory. The faithful had a simpler way of thinking. Death may not be complete, or at least not immediate. Could life be prolonged a bit by keeping the fingernail cuttings of the deceased or a bit of his blood? Does not a beard continue to grow on the face of a dead man? In this fashion the idea took root that even if death was indisputable, it was not total. *Armiers*, mediums endowed with spiritual powers, could call up the dead to incite them to penitence and encourage their regrets. The Church obviously condemned these evocations, which it qualified as necromancy, almost as sorcery, and pursued as such.

Calling back the dead did not produce any real adepts, and the common people were content with a physical contact with the Beyond through objects that had belonged to the living, and even more, with the remains, or *reliquia*, of a saintly personage, a local bishop or abbot, or, of course, of Jesus. The reverence, even the veneration given to relics is undoubtedly a spiritual phenomenon, but by its material effects on the places of devotion, their profits and their access routes, it went much farther than a simple respect of the dead. This is a question that merits revisiting. Although one could not touch the relics, presented as "authentic," of a saint or even a glorious personage whose support one hoped for, one could at least touch his reliquary or his tomb. After the fourteenth century, the dramatization of death opened the way to some fearful exhibitions of nude *gisants* represented in decomposition on their funerary slabs.

If touching the dead was impossible, at least one could see or, in any event, imagine them. The interpretation of dreams and apparitions of the dead occupies a large place in moralizing literature.

Children in particular were the beneficiaries of these. They heard and saw the ancestors and repeated what they had said in what were known as *miracula*, pious visions destined to inspire an attitude of fear and of devotion, and *mirabilia*, astonishing anecdotes, premonitions, at least worthy of curiosity among the child's entourage. The Scandinavian peoples hold this link between death and the child to be one of the essential inspirations for the sagas.

The case of ghosts is different. Their appearance was of course part of the realm of the supernatural, but in the minds of those who saw them or thought they saw them, ghosts responded to the sentiment that they were a family matter, to be taken care of within the family. More often than not, ghosts originated in an "abnormal" death, one of a person buried without rites and without prayers, even a suicide or someone who had not been baptized. The ghost appeared at night, outside the home, and only to a few people, those who had already had some commerce with the dead. But awareness of them was more tinged with remorse than with a genuine fear of the next world.

Thus passed the various ages of life. From birth to death, man underwent a number of constraints arising from his own body, from his work, and from his environment. Now he was at rest, at peace if possible. What peace? He had simply forgotten all the rest of the living world, in the middle of which he had operated. That world was capable of making its hostile force felt.

3

NATURE

Rain and fine weather, falling leaves and sprouting grass, the time to train horses and the arrival of the swallows: things that men have talked about among themselves since they shared the same cavern. What, after all, is the importance of the existence of God, the most recent electronic gadget, or the soccer championships if the summer is "rotten," straw hard to come by, and the cow sick? Man can flail about and bestir himself, but the world holds him by the throat. Anguish and paralysis reign if the grain does not thrive or the horse dies. Then or now, nature commands man. He can pollute the atmosphere, destroy the vegetation covering the earth, massacre animal species, but he still cannot reroute hurricanes, prevent planetary warming, or defeat an infestation of termites. How did he view the situation, and just how was he subjected to that domination by the environment?

THE WEATHER

In our own day, when we have an unusually hot summer or a stormy winter, people who are impermeable to scientific data declare they have "never seen the like," or comment, "never in the memory of man." Given the capacities of man's memory, this is not a particularly interesting statement. Our contemporaries, incapable of evaluating the rhythms of natural phenomena, are kept in a state of panic by timely but hasty information. Heat waves or typhoons, rises in the sea level and retreating glaciers, higher temperatures and increases or decreases in plant species have been observed for over two centuries, and the scientists, who have the means for measuring these things, know about them and talk about them. But their voices are covered by the frantic clamor of the ignorant, many of whom occupy the centers for the diffusion of news. The men of the medieval centuries, who may have been less sensitive to their immediate environment, did not jump at every caprice of the weather. Did they even notice it, and what do we know about the topic?

The Paleo-Environment

Regular readings of temperature and humidity levels in the various regions of Europe, and scientific observations of vegetation, have been taken since about 1850, but for some time they were considered of interest only for the study of geographical evolution from an ahistorical perspective. Some of course have attempted to apply these findings to such human phenomena as epidemics, even the psychic behavior of men, not to mention the effects of drought, volcanic eruptions, or earthquakes on daily life. The exploitation of these data for a study of the natural environment really began only in the second half of the twentieth century, perhaps when curiosity, or a degree of concern, started to develop outside scientific laboratories, for example, over the preservation of our natural living space.

The study of ecology or the environment has gone beyond the framework of the contemporary age to explore what the situation was before we had dependable statistics—that is, in protohistoric, medieval, or "modern" times. Determining the nature and the extent of the vegetable world, the numbers and the specific details of fauna, or climatic variations allows us to cast light on the place of these components in alimentation, the habitat, and labor—everything that makes up what was long called material culture but is no longer known by that name, for no discernible reason. Nor is it to be excluded that such investigations might illuminate the origins of a good number of mental reactions. The ten or twelve centuries of the Middle Ages offer a sufficiently *longue durée* to permit us to discern, beyond the precise phenomenon mentioned in a text, tendencies that punctuate human life.

An examination of techniques of discovery, their progress and their limitations, lies beyond my scope here; I shall limit myself to stressing what these have contributed to our knowledge of human life. For the last hundred years, it has been the movement of water, an immediately visible phenomenon, that has aroused the curiosity of tourists and the interest of scientists: the interval between high and low tide, variations in the shores of lakes, terraced river banks in which vegetation, remains of aquatic animals, and the soil strata attest to changes in the water level over several centuries. Even more spectacular are the faces of glaciers, where successive cushions of the lateral moraine conserve datable evidence of crushed vegetation or destroyed habitats. In the last fifty years, information on grasslands and forests has increased our documentation, while dendrology, the examination of annual rings in tree trunks (in Europe, certain resinous trees permit us to go back to the eleventh or twelfth centuries) throws light on phases of drought and humidity. Palynology, the study of pollen and spores, is even more ambitious. Overlying layers of pollens, herbaceous species included, laid down on spongy soils years after year, allow us to establish the full range of local vegetable species, both natural and cultivated, in some places going back as far as the Neolithic. Carpology, the study of grains and seeds, in the storage areas attached to habitats, or anthracology, the study of what was burned in domestic fireplaces, all bring us closer to man, to what he gathered, consumed, or utilized in his daily life.

These are exciting possibilities for research in my subject area, but prudence dictates not straying too far afield. Pollens have not been conserved everywhere. The nature of the soil, the plant environment, and prevailing winds falsifies our examination. Tree rings vary according to species, orientation, and the surrounding cover. Dating a beam by its carbon 14 level, which indicates when the tree was cut down, disguises the effects of a later reuse and limits chronological conclusions. And even the twigs, shells, grains, or small animal bones collected are simply raw data that give no notion of volume, provenance, or effects. Where the collection of samples has been systematic—in the United States and in western Europe—these precious data are accumulated carefully, but specialists in these sciences are well aware that what we think we can see in one eighth of the 10 percent of our planet that emerges out of the sea cannot be generalized. We will have to be patient.

Written support documenting these phenomena exists, and the men of those times have indeed left us some indications. Recently efforts have been made to bring together all the information that seems useful in this connection: allusions inserted into annals, chronicles, biographies, account books and *livres de raison*; accounts of harvests and of transhumance; dates of the grape harvest and the *banvin* (the authorization to go into the vineyard and begin picking); and even deliberations among the *échevins* of a city as to what dispositions to take in the face of a calamity. We have some 3,500 notations of references to climate-related events over a period of four centuries, from 1000 to 1425, some 600 of which are genuinely meteorological. Unfortunately, neither this data nor geographical surveys permit us to draw up more than a rough sketch of climate change, and only for the extreme western portion of Europe. From the third to the fifth centuries, the climate was hotter and dryer, although this was more true in the south than in the north, a variation that can be ranged among the possible causes of the "weakening" of the Roman order. Next came a cooling and more humid conditions, this time more in the north than the south, the high point of which is known as the *crue mérovingi-*

enne, just as the plague that struck during the period is dubbed "Justinian." After 900 or 1000, the "optimal" phase (for grain and for men, at least) in the economic progress of the West lasted until around 1200. A change came, in some places before 1140, in others, not before 1260, with the arrival of rain and periods of heat in half-century fluctuations that we understand better, since written evidence was more plentiful by then. Finally—but this goes beyond the "medieval moment"—there came a return to the earlier state that the sixteenth century characterized as *beau*. The causes of these wide fluctuations still remain to be recognized, preferably without place-related preconceived ideas. This has been attempted, and fairly successfully, but these data combining oceanic masses in movement, the accelerated circulation of stratospheric currents, and the solar origin of those currents exceed both my competence and the limits of my field of inquiry.

What Did They See or Feel?

When the "knight-peasants" of Charavines in the Dauphiné evacuated their habitat after only twenty years of occupation, the denizens of Bourbourg in Flanders built their dikes out into the sea and planted crops in the resulting soil; the "pontiffs" of Avignon risked crossing the Rhône; the inhabitants of the lagoons of Languedoc fled the shore to move their houses to higher ground; or the shepherds of the Alps built their *mayens* higher up the slopes than their ancestors had, they were obeying the orders of nature, although without saying so. The waters of the lake were rising, the sea was retreating, the river was running less fast, the mosquitoes had gotten the better of the population, the forest had retreated, leaving cleared-out mountain pasturage. A hundred other examples could be given to show that human groups react to the caprices of nature. Those groups do not write, however, so it is up to the learned to tell us about such things. The latter were at first monks, then preachers, men of a merchant city or the familiars of the powerful. This means that we need to approach what they say with caution.

Given to extraordinary exaggeration, they used general terms and were not interested in looking at events as part of a series. Each phenomenon was deemed a catastrophe because quite often, in the *exempla*, for instance, it was used as an "accident" to touch the soul of the sinner.

Naturally, it was the exceptional phenomena—meteorites, comets, eclipses—that were noted in detail, thanks to their very rarity, but man did not often suffer from their effects. When other infrequent and unexpected events—an invasion of locusts, beetles, or mildew—ravaged the crops, they were recorded. As for more purely chthonic events such as earthquakes, a volcanic eruption, or a landslide, their suddenness and the visible damage they caused defined them as isolated acts of brief duration. We can date the layers of lava extruded by Etna, which the nearby villagers were watching for. When Mont Granier, south of Chambéry, collapsed in 1248, the inhabitants of Savoy were more struck by the event than the Swiss had been, fifty years earlier, when the town of Grindelwald was crushed by fallen glacial ice. In ordinary practice, manifestations of a meteorological nature were grouped, according to men's interest in them, into several general domains, although the frequency of such episodes preoccupied them less than is the case today when we are bombarded by "warnings" and "alerts" of impending bad weather.

One of these domains was temperature, which affected the ripening of grapes, the lactation of cows, and the possibility of doing field work. The vocabulary used was full of stereotypes. Winters were *rudes*, freezing temperatures were *constants*, and summer heat was "torrid" or "stifling." Out of the 3,500 mentions of natural phenomena, 1,560 speak about temperature, but because their proportion in the sources consulted remains nearly stable between the eleventh and the fourteenth centuries (whereas the climate, as we have seen, varied during that same time period), the thought arises that the chroniclers' observations became fixed and less meaningful as time went by. Another domain that received attention lies close to the first, since it concerns rainfall, including heavy down-

pours, hail, and thunderstorms, all of which have similar consequences. These represent a good thousand notations, including
windstorms that were also capable of ravaging planted fields. This
time, however, an increase in the number of items in the fourteenth
and fifteenth centuries conforms better with the overall evolution
of the climate at the time. Froissart describes the wagons stuck in
the mud and knights sliding in the rain at Crécy, but in the same
region and at the same time of year, though 150 years earlier, Guillaume le Breton does not report having seen anything of the sort
at Bouvines. Floods, and much more rarely inundations of sea-
water—the *zeegang* of Flanders—strike the imagination thanks to
their uncontrollable violence, their duration, and the destruction
they leave behind them in terms of houses, crops, and livestock.
Even today, such cataclysms are more feared than a forest fire or a
thunderstorm. There were more than five hundred floods in four
centuries in western Europe, and their number grew through time,
quite possibly in relation to an increase in rainfall. Other calamities of climatic origin such as a mediocre harvest, hay or grapes of
poor quality, the dispersion of swarms of bees, or damage from rodents were undoubtedly due to the same underlying causes.

All of these phenomena set the rhythm of life and work and influenced people's health, but their frequency or their extent were
probably no greater than today. The difference is that we try to explain them as we experience them, whereas men of medieval times
seem to have been resigned to suffering through them without
searching for a cause. As we read the written sources, it is striking
to note something like a characteristic general indifference, interspersed with brief moments of panic, almost as if men resembled
the domestic animals that surrounded them. What good did it do
to be informed on a daily basis or to attempt to predict such events
since they were not viewed as "natural" phenomena that could be
studied or circumvented? Such unexpected and unavoidable "accidents" were part of the unknowable, hence of the Divinity. We
are told by Scripture that God gave man power over nature. If a
"disorder" takes place, it breaks the contract between God and his

creature, in which case it must be the latter who bears the fault and undergoes the punishment. To attempt to furnish an explanation in human terms was thus to defy God and to reject the alliance that he concluded with his creature. There were even some scholars in the early Middle Ages—in the East, it is true—who were condemned for having sought "causes." Only the Devil could have inspired an inquiry into such signs of the emancipation of Nature, just as Lucifer had done before the Lord. Events of the sort were premonitory manifestations of Judgment.

This was the thesis of the theologians, at any event. God punishes the wicked, and many meteorological notations had no other aim than to prove the existence of divine power. Too bad if there was "collateral damage," as is said today of unsuccessful strategies. Still, some minds in the West were not satisfied with that attitude. Even before the end of the thirteenth century in England and then in Paris, thinkers acquainted with ancient culture and with "Arabic" thought merged the rationalist and Thomistic spirit with an attraction to experimentation. They found in Plato an approach to geological time, in Aristotle, an introduction to the idea of a linkage of mechanical causes, and in Seneca and Pliny a sharp curiosity about astronomical phenomena and their causal systems. But it was the human body itself that was the foundation of such studies. Because this microcosm, according to the medicine of Hippocrates and Galen, was subject to the four elements (fire, water, earth, air) and to their relationships and their effects, some sought and found a connection between human life and the weather. The four seasons that succeed one another were patterned on the four elements, a notion that led to particular physiological, alimentary, and even psychic behaviors. The seasons reflected solar rhythms and were subject to astral conjunctions; hence the study of "natural accidents" was a logical next step. There is no point in pausing to review the ancient philosophers' interpretations of these matters—interpretations that diverged, moreover, and that were taken up again by "Arabic" (actually, Persian and Berber) experimentation and science. In the early thirteenth century, after a long period in which the doctrine of the blind omnipotence of the Divinity dominated, physicians, or *physici*, relit the flame of science in the Christian world. If the mechanisms underlying these phenomena were not perceived—for example, those regarding the terrestrial crust, atmospheric pressure, or the movements of the oceans—many phenomena related to climate were explained: Jean Buridan explained the principle of eclipses, Brunetto Latini that of the formation of clouds, Albertus Magnus how air varied according to altitude and humidity, Robert Grosseteste, the connections between temperature and plant cycles. A Frenchman, an Italian, a German, and an Englishman: the very embryo of a "European" science.

But not everyone went to listen to the learned in Oxford, Paris, Montpellier, or Salerno. The good people could not see that far, and the Dominicans' sermons prudently kept the faithful reasoning on the level of the fear of God. It was demons who created tornadoes; comets announced the coming of a miracle; when the sirocco blew in red sand, it announced a bath of blood; if lightning struck the church, Satan prevented it from striking the castle. When they could not explain Nature, since that would be flouting God, at least, and obligatorily, men of the time reacted to her aggressions and caprices. Villages that were left perched above eroded terrain or the consolidation of the *terpen* in Frisia had other causes than social ones. The soil and the water had wanted this to happen. The draining of ponds and salt lagoons did more than gain a few hectares, hence increase income; it also eliminated malaria and limited air pollution. Choosing to create a ford over building a bridge was not only for reasons of its lesser cost as it avoided the dangers of a furious and probable flood. Organizing noisy concerts in the middle of the field was not intended to charm rustic ears, but to set off a hailstorm that would threaten or prevent invasion by a cloud of locusts. Certain categories of the population were more attentive to such matters than others. Merchants' factors brought them back tales of earthquakes and typhoons, the warning signs of which were well known in the East. As for sailors, who were always confronted with the diabolic element that was the sea, they knew perfectly well how to tell a shipwreck caused by an error of navigation from one due to the caprices of the storm.

This is the way the people of those times lived. They were in the hand of God, who had the power to tempt them, then punish them. But were they not on Earth only for a passing moment? What difference did it make, then, if it rained more than one feared or hoped? There may have been a piece of Paradise left on Earth, a place where it never rains, the sun always shines and it is warm, a place where the water flows, fire burns, and the ground flowers for the pleasure of the eyes and the joy of the soul. The problem was that it was far away and in Muslim hands.

FIRE AND WATER

No one can live for very long without water, and it is a harsh punishment to limit the prisoner to extremely short rations of it. Man depends almost as much on fire, but if need be he can do without it. These are banal observations, but they may explain how little reflection there has been on these two "elements," as Hippocrates called them.

Fire, the Symbol of Life and Death

Man's ability to master natural fire and adapt it to his needs is his principal and perhaps only superiority over the rest of the animal kingdom. Fire is, first of all, the very manifestation of the supreme power, the image of the All-Powerful. It is present with Moses on the summit of Mount Sinai and in the burning bush; it is the favorite weapon of Zeus, surrounds the chariot of Elijah, and accompanies Muhammad in his ecstasy on the Rock. For having attempted to gain control of it, Lucifer is precipitated into the flames, and Prometheus' expiation for his folly of having tried to master it is long. Perhaps the Western peasant, who was unaware of all this, was equally unaware that, as both Hindu sages and Greek philosophers asserted, fire is also the symbol of love: Eros inflames bodies and hearts with the arrows forged by Hephaestus, the deceived husband of Aphrodite, and this mythology is reflected in Rome, where Vesta, the goddess of virginity, is also the guardian of fire. Our modern rationalism finds it somewhat astonishing that the Romans did not find it odd to entrust fire, symbol of the sex act, to a goddess responsible for continence!

This pagan bric-a-brac did not trouble the Christian world, and I do not think that the Virgin Mary has ever been represented in the middle of flames. Fire was decidedly present, however, in the subconscious of men of the Middle Ages. It was the symbol of Judgment and final punishment. The Hell into which the rebel archangel was thrown figures in many a tympanum of a church, miniature in a psalm book, and wall fresco. There monstrous demons, with or without pitchforks, emblematic of Evil, pushed the damned into boiling cauldrons surrounded by flames. Like the parishioners of Cucugnan, the faithful, terrorized, recognize kin and friends among the tortured and the flames. Here fire is no longer a symbol of love, but of the vengeance of God. Rejected from the spheres of the blessed, the damned will be annihilated by the fire that has created them. Those who have insulted the Divinity will be burned at the stake, but others will find in the earth the ashes out of which they were made. None of the dogmatic deviations of medieval times and not one of the three religions that share the shores of the Mediterranean—Judaism, Christianity, and Islam—condone the incineration of bodies at the end of life on this earth. The purifying role of fire, although magnified more and more widely as one goes toward the East, is justified only as punishment. Oriental or pagan cremation of the dead disappeared in the West, at least until fairly recent times.

A symbol of life and of love, but also of pain and death, fire thus had two faces. It killed and it resuscitated, like the phoenix, the firebird of Oriental legend. Its ambiguity was certainly not perceived by the commonality in quite such complex terms, but all would have been aware of the two images. Fire was, first, a menace: that of a wildfire set off by lightning, by lava, or by the malignant forces of little "fire genies"—imps, elves, goblins, sprites, and will-o'-the-wisps known as *lutins, farfadets, feux follets,* or *poucets.* In those times wood was not only found in the forest, waiting for the gatherer or the shepherd; it was also the basic raw material for all construction, even the lordly dwelling before the use of stone became prevalent. This means that mercenary soldiers often and easily burned cottages after emptying them of their contents, but the entire town or city might burn if fire broke out in a workshop or an attic or from an unsupervised hearth. Like the ancient city, the medieval city had its watchmen—the *guet* or a *corps de vigiles*—but often there was no well or ditch from which to draw water, so tragedy was inevitable. Fear of fires led to classifying arson, voluntarily setting fire to a mill or a stable, among the "blood crimes" and making it punishable by death.

Fire was a threat and was feared, but it was also a blessing. First, and this is obvious, because it warmed people by the hearth; under a cauldron it cooked the meal; and it lit up the corners of the common room. In the castle or the monastery, a fire was carefully maintained in a special room reserved for children or the sick and for purgation or massages. In the cottage, red cinders were kept going as long as possible. Fire lit up the potter's kiln, the blacksmith's forge, and the goldsmith's workshop, and bystanders, who would have been mostly men, watched in fear and wonder as one of their fellows worked amid sparks to master fire and tame earth and metal.

Men ruled at the forge, but in the home it was women who were the mistresses of fire. Fire was female because it represented the intimacy of the home, because it purified and created, but also because it was inconstant and burning hot. When the custom was abandoned of having a common outdoor fire, and fire entered the house (an important step that archaeology situates as occurring somewhere between 900 and 1100), the woman and wife gained undivided authority over the family nucleus, as we have seen. The familial group, conjugal or broader, was known as a *feu*, or fire, and modern French still speaks of a household as a *foyer*. Fire was at the heart of every human group; it brought men together to eat, women to spin, children to sleep, and the old to tell tales and recite poems. Fire, whether started from a glowing coal or created from striking sparks off a flint or tenaciously rubbing sticks together, became the symbol of life. But it also could be the symbol of death.

Saving and Beneficent Water

Fire was surrounded by fear and respect, but water was man's obliging and familiar companion. It was the source of his life; he could not do without it, and even where the nature of the soil or the climate made it a rare commodity—perhaps especially there—it was the foundation of everything he did. It saved the traveler, the pilgrim, or the merchant on the road by slaking his thirst; when sanctified it welcomed the newborn and the newly dubbed knight and baptized the Christian. Purifying and fresh, it was offered to guests for their ablutions or as a gift; festive, it animated the fountain displays of royal entries; fascinating, its mirrored surfaces brought beauty to the gardens of the wealthy; curative, it relieved the bather and the invalid; hard-working, it turned the wheel of the mill, irrigated the fields, or absorbed dyes. People also drank it, but curiously, this was not its prime function. Its life cycle had been understood since antiquity. The ocean creates clouds, which in turn produce rain to fill the wells and the watercourses that eventually carry it back to the sea. Aristotle explained the process, Hesiod sang of it, and divinities presided over the fecundity of rivers, while in Gaul, Taranis protected and lauded the water that sprang from the ground. Obviously, it might rain more or less than hoped, and there might even be formidable floods. Too bad! That was the price to pay for life, both in the countryside, where the well was a convivial gathering place, and in the city, where water was the "signifier" and its fountains and ditches dictated the city layout and provided security.

There were a number of ways to gain access to water, even when nature was not too generous. Rivers, or perhaps even more easily, streams, provided water, but it had to be fetched, a major activity in a flat landscape, and this was women's responsibility. This might be hard work, for example, when the return trip involved coming back uphill from the river to the plateau with two pails swinging from a carrying pole. A well or a nearby spring eliminated that difficult chore, which is why scholars have often seen rearrangements of the collective habitat as reflecting an interest in gathering around the water much more than as a way to guard the group from threats or search for better soil. The well or the washhouse, when it was nearby, thus became the "parliament of women," just as the forge was the gathering place for men. Documentation is scarce on this essential aspect of daily life; all we have are some hints in law suits on the occasion of an individual appropriation considered to harm the community or a few excavations of public or private cisterns. Exactly how a well was dug and water was captured, and how the structure was consolidated all remain largely unknown, along with the typical depth, input and output of wells. Iconography shows us simple frames or poles with a horizontal arm and (later) a pulley, along with pine buckets and a tub or vat reserved for drinking water or water to wash with. Water that filtered through the soil was often salty; rainwater was softer, if it could be had. If not, the condition of the well had to be checked on a regular basis and running water had to be filtered. An entire army of well-diggers and specialists in making fountains oversaw the various devices for drawing water, along with the gutters, channels, and jointures. This was a difficult and demanding profession, very tightly controlled, and at times hereditary. Finally, it is odd that we know much more about systems for bringing water to the cities in antiquity, perhaps because aqueducts were public works and essentially an urban phenomenon. Without lingering over the topic, which is crammed with trompe-l'oeil details, we can say that the placement of fountains or wells in the city was often a legacy from the ancient world, more or less well adapted to the new aspect of the medieval city. This system has been thoroughly studied for Italian cities and Mediterranean sites in general, often stressing the role, more in the realm of the mystical than of economics, of water in the city, where it incarnated the power of the city or of its master.

The use of domestic water touched all sectors of the human world, but in almost all cases, its purifying role was dominant. Given that it was usually undrinkable, water was used to flush human and animal waste toward the ditches and the moat of the city or, in the country, into a cesspool or to the fields. City wastes included drainage products and bandages from the hospitals (which tended to be built on bridges or on the banks of the river for that very reason) along with waste water emptied into the streets from the latrines and kitchens. This meant that the moat outside the city walls went beyond its role as a defense in time of war to become a rampart of hygiene and a public lavatory. The leaders of the ancient cities, followed by their medieval counterparts, put much effort into containing these waters and their unspeakable contents. After the thirteenth century, municipal bodies reinstated a number of stoned-lined sewers dating from Roman times, some of which were simply natural rivulets that had been captured and channeled. By the end of the Middle Ages, the regular cleaning of these sewers and the opening of peepholes (*regards*) that permitted inspectors—a highly regarded post—to check on the flow appear in the accounts of nearly all the cities of the medieval West. Pollution by dirty waste water was denounced early on as a prime cause for the propagation of epidemics, even when they played no role in contagion, as was true of the plague in the fourteenth century. This is why heretics, marginal individuals, or Jews were often accused of pernicious acts when a well was polluted or a sewer blocked. This resulted in the notion of "private waters": the water in one's dwelling, its courtyard or its gatehouse, at times in its "chapel." Apothecaries prescribed purified water safe from diabolical influence for baths to be taken in previously blessed tubs garnished with balms and heated by hypocausts in the ancient Roman style. "Taking the waters" was more than a Greco-Roman tradition. It was a medieval practice, and I have spoken above at some length on the place of the *étuves*, or public baths, in the life (urban life, at least) of these centuries. It is difficult to measure the "consumption" of water by the public baths: there is some indication that there was one public bathing establishment for every two thousand city dwellers, but the data are too uncertain to be sure. The Church, which tended to be disapproving in this domain, endorsed bathing without showing any sure signs of interest in public hygiene. Perhaps it saw it as a sort of bodily purification, the effects of which were comparable to those of baptism for the soul. Or perhaps it was attempting to discredit Jewish ritual baths, which were celebrated immediately outside the synagogues and often quite close to the baths.

People drank from springs, fished in the rivers or the lakes, and channeled water to the millpond just above the mill wheel. Water was gathered to wash leather skins or soak flax for linen; it was mixed with flour and used to boil foods; it was drunk, drawn from the ground or from water courses. But if we continue to follow its course, we can see it finally tumbling into a hostile and unknowable immensity, the sea.

The Sea, Horrible and a Temptress

Man is a terrestrial mammal. He cannot live in the water, and only with difficulty can he stay afloat in it. That liquid element was thus physically and naturally hostile, dangerous, and repugnant to him. He felt anguish as he neared the sea; its immensity gave him the impression of being besieged by water. Still, neither the Greek, Arabic, nor Indian geographers, nor the travelers and adventurers who crossed the sea or studied it really measured its extent at the time. Theologians, philosophers, and the faithful were persuaded that water completely surrounded the Earth that was inhabited by men. It was centuries before it was known that in reality water covers three-quarters of the planet. For tens of thousands of years, men had seen the sea as the frontier of fear and the world of Evil. Everything in it was uncertain, deceptive, unpredictable, and, in a word, tragic. But how to avoid contact with it when, in a Europe profoundly penetrated by the sea, no one lived more than 350 kilometers—a few days' march— from a coast, and in most cases much less? On the other hand, no sailor ventured farther from a shore or an island than six hours' sail. It was the merit (or the folly) of Christopher Columbus to have thrown himself onto the high seas, with no landmarks to guide him, for more than a month. It is true that he was completely wrong, as were all the geographers of his day, about the actual distance between Europe and Asia, which explains why, after landing in the Americas, he remained convinced until his death that he had attained his goal.

The sea and its currents, its moods, and its dangers were relatively unknown at the time. If it was absolutely necessary to travel by sea, it was by sailing along the coast and heaving to at night. Speed and profit were land ideas; at sea, safety was the prime concern. Shipwreck was generally irremediable, storms were impossible to predict, and hurricanes were a terrifying experience. The only resistance to the "fortune of the seas"—the risks of navigation—was to put one's fate into the hands of divine clemency, those of the Virgin in particular, or to invoke Saint Peter and his miraculous boat. And if that was not enough, a man could be thrown overboard as an expiatory victim in an almost magical sacrifice. All of the civilizations that had had anything to do with the sea's immeasurable forces saw it as maleficent and infernal. This was true of Phoenicians, Greeks, Celts of the islands or of the ocean, and of Scandinavians in particular, those Vikings that panic-stricken Carolingian monks took for demons from Hell. Progress in ship-building techniques and navigational aids limited the sailors' risks. In Nordic lands hulls were built with overlapping sideboards beginning in the ninth century, and the bulging sides of the *hoques* or *kogge* of those waters, along with their "bridge," which kept the sideboards from taking on water, allowed ships to plow through enormous ocean waves. In the Mediterranean the diversification of sails, following Eastern patterns, permitted economizing on at least some of the crews of oarsmen. Around the eighth century, Islam popularized the use of the Chinese compass, then of the Indian sextant, and, in the fourteenth century, portolans—maps showing anchorages, roadsteads, and ports—came into use. It is true that if these inventions helped the merchants, they also helped pirates, who became more numerous and more aggressive. Still, vessels shipwrecked or sunk to the bottom remained to bear witness to divine wrath, and, on the shores, the wreckage belonged to everyone. Only the seagulls, the reincarnation of sailors who had perished at sea, remained to watch over these relics.

In spite of its dangers, the liquid immensity of the ocean fascinated men and inspired wonder. As with nautical sports and oceanic competitions today, people of those centuries saw the sea as fully charged with marvelous and dreamlike qualities. The shore was a line of contact with the unknown and the imaginary; the ocean, and even the more modest bordering sea, were a world of adventure, of the silence of men, and of the perpetual movement of things. The ocean was where the paradisiac worlds or the marvelous islands sung of in Celtic, Scandinavian, and ancient folklore—the myths of Atlantis, Thule, or Greenland—were to be found. It was the thought that by confronting danger one might reach Purgatory, or perhaps even Paradise, that sustained the soul.

The populations crowded to the lands by the sea, which were all the more densely settled when the inland areas were arid, rocky, or swampy. And not all sailors were there to breathe in hope of space or salvation; nor were they all adventurers or even merchants in search of rare products. They were more simply "workers of the sea" who lived by the collection of various sorts of seaweed, by coastal fishing, or by short-range short-term trade. They struggled with technical difficulties, not all of which have been eliminated today. Nets had to be laid down, retrieved, and mended; flotillas of boats had to be organized when men wanted to fish a bit far off the coast; it was unsure whether the sale would be profitable if few fish had been gathered in; and few fishermen had other, land-based resources. This is why sea folk formed a closed social group. Mutual assistance, solidarity, and shared hardships and joys were sealed by a solid scorn for the landsman. The fisherman alone knew how the tides ran or what were the best ways to get through off-shore banks. The jetties, retarring sheds, cauldrons for processing salt, and huts where fisher-folk lived in tightly knit family groups formed a domain that no local peasant could penetrate. What is more, at times—at fish auctions, in the taverns, and during Calvary processions to honor the drowned—these small groups of men who faced danger on a permanent basis were capable of fighting one another in violent brawls.

The sea avidly swallowed up men, but it nourished them generously. The place of fish and shellfish, the "fruits of the sea," in the diet of the time can be measured by glancing over the lists of payments in kind, in particular to the monasteries, the only consumers for whom we have some pertinent archives before the fourteenth century. Such lists include hundreds of thousands of herring caught during their annual autumn passage through the strait of the Pas de Calais (the Strait of Dover) or off the coast of Brittany. As has been said of pork, the herring saved all of Christianity from famine, and not everyone had the good luck to have a whale beach on a local shore and feed a village for an entire winter. Knowledge gained about the seasonal patterns of fish migration and where they reproduced, about how best to capture them, and about the devices best adapted to catch the different species of fish was often a family affair. But whereas the man who fished the rivers or the ponds created upstream of a mill chose between species and kept a careful eye on the fry, the sea fisherman was a predator without complexes who gathered whatever was edible. Attempts have been made (and are still being made) to train dolphins to fish for us, thanks to their seeming interest in our species, but results have been inconclusive.

There is one final aspect to the sea, and not a small one: salt, which was indispensable for the conservation of many foods and for human life in general. Salt could of course be extracted from mines, but it was the works by the sea that produced salt by evaporation that furnished the better part of it. Salt marshes were usually seigneurial possessions, in practice rented out to those who lived nearby and exploited them. Sizable amounts of salt traveled by water or by caravans of animals with loaded saddle packs, starting from the various coasts—those of the Atlantic or the Tyrrhenian Sea, for example—that had rich salt marshes. What the historian of those times finds original in this salt trade is not the method of accumulating the salt, which has changed little since then, in spite of the use of industrialized methods. It is the place given to women. Women did not spend their time mending nets, setting out ex-votos, or watching out, with resignation and anguish, for the return of the sailor; they did hard physical labor, raking the salt pads, tending the drying ovens, and carrying the sacks of salt. This sort of activity was rarely individual, but it took up a large part of women's time and contributed to isolating these sailors' wives while their husbands were at sea.

THE PRODUCTS OF THE EARTH

Medieval historians who specialize in the city obviously attach a great deal of interest to the transformation and exchange of raw materials; they closely investigate the market, the market hall, and coinage; they have a passionate interest in commercial and financial studies; they speak of money, credit, and ships; they busy themselves with merchants and burghers and seek out the structures of exchange as a framework for the medieval economy. To read their works, knowing whether the medieval economy was "capitalist" or not, from the thirteenth century on, is a primordially important topic for reflection and even erudite quarrels. But they do not speak of the soil and what it bears, as if this were not the first, and perhaps the only, preoccupation of eight or nine out of every ten men of the time. And since it is precisely these men I am trying to reach, I shall desert the world of the cities and concentrate on what was essential.

In the West, the medieval world was one of tillers of the soil. By its pedological and geological constitution, western Europe was a land of peasants, not (or no longer) one of nomadic shepherds, and animal-raising had become one element in the overall picture— an important one, to be sure, and one that had become sedentary. Transhumance, or "removes" (*remues*) from the mountains or dry plateaus, was an integral part of this picture. Shepherds and herds- men had their own customs and their mind-set, but their flocks and what they produced were connected with the village, not the steppe or the desert. The population lived essentially on grain, milk products, and meat. The first step was to master the earth.

No countryman, today or yesterday, is incapable of evaluating the soil that he works. He will say that it is "hot" or "cold," "free" or "heavy," "deep" or "light"; he will know that wheat will grow well here and rye will grow better elsewhere; he will note whether water penetrates the soil or runs off. He needs no learned geologi- cal knowledge, or even any pedological knowledge; he will know that the soil is black or yellowish, dry or fertile, but will not know whether the local rock is chalky, clay, sandy, or other. Thus, his evaluation of his environment will be based more on observation of variations in the surrounding terrain, the general orientation of the land, and the flow of water courses than on the earth's chemi- cal, hydrological, or mineralogical components. His knowledge will be experimental and his science empirical. At least this was how it was for the medieval peasant. Today, with the importance of scientific agriculture and agronomic knowledge (for the better or for the worse is not the question here), these simple evaluations have often been abandoned and are thought simplistic. Here and there, however, the experience of the "oldsters" proves superior to the opinions of the engineers.

The centuries of the Middle Ages did not lack practical lessons. The agronomists of Greco-Roman antiquity, experts in botany and familiar with rather poor soils, were sensitive to the smallest positive sign of fertility, and they made many observations and gave much advice. It is interesting to note that the loss of ancient documents, which is calamitous in almost all domains, was relatively light in that of agriculture. I might add that the "Arabs"—who were familiar with an ungrateful environment—preserved and even enriched a large part of the ancient heritage. Hesiod, Cato the Elder, Pliny, Varro, and Columella were known, both within the monasteries and outside their walls, since short didactic poems drawn from those authors works in northern France called *chatonnets* after a quite different Cato were occasionally read in the castles. Moreover, even before the enthusiasm of the fourteenth and fifteenth centuries, the age of Jean de Brie and Pietro dei Crescenzi, people read books of recipes and practical advice. This had been true for some time, since in the ninth century there are echoes of the ancient treatises in the famous capitulary *De villis*, a vast Carolingian compilation that historians who specialize in the period delight over. Later texts came from the Britannic archipelago and Normandy, and, far to the south, Catalonia and Andalusia accumulated practical works at the end of the twelfth century and, in the following century, works like *Housbonderie* (Husbandry), the *Fleta*, and others. Naturally, it might be said that all of these "treatises" were idealized or, in any event, could serve only for the domains of the masters, which were better equipped and supervised. Still, they are a sign of a constant interest in working the soil.

Not all of the peasantry was grouped on the richest lands. There was mediocre, unfertile soil everywhere, as is true in many places outside of Europe today, that supported a meager and wild vegetation with short grasses and small ears of grain. Even if it was worked with care and skill, such soil remained "vain" or "deserted." It needed to be enriched. In this capital sector of agriculture, medieval men accomplished a task whose effects are still visible today, when chemical fertilizers have taken over from empirical practices. I say empirical, because the virtues of such chemical components as potassium, phosphates, nitrates, and mineral salts were unknown. Only a few Latin words, manipulated by clerics who did not understand them, float to the surface in the midst of a deplorable documentary void. *Stercora* obviously refers to animal manure; *marlae* was a mixture of chalk and clay; for the rest fertilization was dependent on such chance events as the movements of herds over "vain" terrains. Perhaps someday, when more work has been done on the deposits or the fields themselves, archaeology will provide us with better information.

I have no intention of presenting an all-inclusive picture of medieval agriculture, and will limit my remarks to an overview, concentrating on the acts and the constraints that a necessary preparation of the soil imposed on all, young and old, men and women, and even children. In this connection, the task of spreading table leftovers or human excrement, animal manure and used animal bedding, and cleaning the cesspools was normally the work of women armed with pitchforks, shovels, and pails. Roughly once every two weeks they carried all such refuse to plots that were relatively close to the home, since there was so much of it that it could not be transported very far. Bone remains, shells, and fireplace ashes may have been taken somewhere else since they were early identified as harmful to cereals. Grains benefited, however, from cow manure with its high nitrate content, and it was mixed into the soil by the animals' hooves. This time it was the children who were charged with moving the *parcs*, or provisory enclosures, as the animals were moved, a practice that has not completely disappeared at the higher altitudes in France. Pigeon droppings, or *la colombine*, were special. They were considered the best fertilizer, hence reserved to needy soils. But there was not much of it, since it had to be collected from under the pigeon coop. The construction of stone coops was costly, and they had to be cleaned and supervised, which meant that they were seigneurial constructions and their fertilizer went to the master's orchard or garden. As for kelp and seaweed, their source limited their use to coastal areas, where they were buried with the help of a pitchfork, a strenuous task reserved to men. The plants that sprang up on fields left fallow—lupine, artemesia, pea and bean vines—were also turned over into the soil for future planting. All these efforts to enrich the soil preceded sowing seeds, hence—except in the vineyards, which were fertilized toward the end of winter—they took place in the autumn.

Treatises on agronomy give a wealth of details about how to fertilize the soil—depth, opportune moments, and working rhythm—but their writers seem primarily sensitive to notions of heat and cold and say nothing about seeking an equilibrium among the fertilizers on the level of the soil itself. There are only rare indications of procedures—always based on local observation—to rectify the quality of the humus or the topsoil. They state that sand should be spread in one place, powdered clay or marl taken from a nearby hillside in another; elsewhere powdered clay is recommended to restore balance to an overly dry humus, or else mud taken from a nearby swamp to bring carbon to a soil deficient in it. All of these tasks were done on a large scale, often by bands of men as a *corvée*, and they left holes or digging pits that are still visible today on the ground or on the sides of valleys. In order to avoid excess, such large jobs were done only every eight or ten years. That rhythm set the pace for country life.

Making the Earth Render

If economic historians determinedly, even aggressively, debate the productivity level of medieval agriculture, its stages, and its regional variants, they all agree that progress was made, at least in terms of volume if not in productivity, in wheat cultivation during the ten centuries of the Middle Ages. The more optimistic among them do not hesitate to estimate wheat production in France in 1300 or 1500 at the same level as in 1789 or even 1900. They differ, however, as to the causes of that "boom": there were undoubtedly more men and more arable lands, but did not the quality of the soil, improved as we have just seen, play a primordial role in this progress? Many scholars believe that the "means"—that is, tools—were of equal importance. The question is not vain, given that it opens the question of the medieval worker's ability to adapt to new ways and new techniques.

For a long time, great importance was attached to the tools used by workers in cereal-producing lands, and an impressive list of medieval "inventions" has even been drawn up, as we have seen. These included shoes for the hooves of horses and other draft animals; devices for hitching up draft animals with a shoulder collar or a frontal yoke, depending on the species; the plow with a coulter and a lateral moldboard, which turned over heavy soils much more deeply than the earlier plowshare could do. Today we are less confident about the efficacy of these "improvements." First, because it is hard to imagine by what channels, intellectual channels in particular, an inventive spirit could have been introduced into western Europe—a spirit that the "ancients" lacked, even though they were credited with a good imagination. Next, because many of those supposed "inventions" existed (in somewhat rudimentary form, it is true) in Asia or in the Greek and Arabic Mediterranean world. Finally, because it is generally accepted that such innovations were quite unequally distributed. Until the sixteenth century and perhaps later, people continued to use the shovel, the hoe, the weeding hoe, and the pitchfork, even on large plots of land. That *jardinage*, although exhausting, was nonetheless efficacious, as shown in country areas in Asia.

Some scholars tend to stress the means by which agricultural work was accomplished, and the diversification of those means, which they credit to the peasant's empirical observations. As land under cultivation was extended and the demand for foodstuffs grew, the men of these times had to adjust their practices in order to increase productivity. They admitted the need for a cycle of cultivation that would let the land rest, when fertility might become exhausted by seeding the land too frequently. It became customary to leave the land fallow every two or three years (sometimes longer), which meant that the soil, left without grain, was available for the fertilizing passage of cattle. Added to this was the principle of closely seeded plots, at least when the soil lent itself to this method and it had been correctly enriched. But the disposition of the plowed ground in closely grouped small parcels or in long narrow strips does seem to have originated in the use of a particular instrument, as Marc Bloch proposed, and not to any great extent in the nature of the soil and the climate. Today such variations are seen as reflecting a system of a familial division of the land into plots of equal size: in some places, in a more individualistic fashion and without collective constrains; in others in open fields divided into long lots; in still others in closed lots, at times surrounded by thick hedges. Thus it would be local tradition and the structure of the family group that determined the agrarian landscape. Similarly, certain practices that seem unusual at first sight were certainly connected with considerations that had nothing to do with technology, but were simply social. Cutting grain very high on the stalk left the straw needed for animals' bedding and for roofing, but it also permitted a few days' worth of gleaning by the poorer members of the community, after which it encouraged the sprouting of pea and bean vines, which attached themselves to the stalks. At times the grain might also be allowed to sprout again as cattle fodder. Controlling the ground water by placing the furrows, the ridges between them, and the furrow drains close together and parallel led to a system of plowing in *planches*, or long parcels. With this system, pushing down on the plow handles required greater physical strength, hence the number of turns (*la tournaille*) of the team at the end of the field had to be reduced. That maneuver, with a team of two animals side by side or one behind the other, required two men per team: one, usually a young *valet*, at times a woman, to guide the horses or oxen and keep up the pace by means of rhythmic chants that had no relation to rural lyricism. If the ground was dry and the plow moved more easily and turned without difficulty at the end of the furrow, or if the family was a closer unit, the square field without drainage ditches would be retained, at times bordered by a hedge of bushes that did not require much water.

It should be obvious by now that I am attempting to give human beings and their personal efforts their full place in these regular and constant practices imposed by the cultivation of grain, which was the environment of almost everyone. Two final observations will take us to the realm of beliefs and the subconscious. As was true of many ancient cultures from Egypt to Mexico, working the soil had a theogonic dimension. The worker labored facing the sun, the emblem of life, and the orientation of the land parcels probably took the sun into account. In the Christian western Middle Ages, there is no trace, however, of any sacred requirement of this sort, perhaps because geographic conditions would have made it impossible. There have been attempts, in England in particular, to investigate the orientation of land parcels to try to discern a relationship between the sun and the crops. If this research direction seems highly hazardous, another is surer: Ethnologists have reminded historians (if ancient mythology had not already suggested it to them) that the Earth, which bears the fruits of life, is usually seen as female. Man penetrates it and fertilizes it with his plow and his seeds. Thus it is quite natural, all technological considerations aside, that it be the male—even a weaker man—who works the soil, and the woman, although she is not alone at the harvest, who gathers the sheaves and carries them to the barn.

Grasses and Vines

Forest, hilly, stony, sun-drenched *garrigue* with little vegetation; and maquis covered with underbrush occupied more of the land than they do today, but less than is often said. Leafy flora, interspersed with lands worked by man, was the rule, and the landscape was a tree-studded savanna with a plant density that varied with altitude, latitude, and humidity or dryness. We need not draw too fine a distinction between a "Mediterranean" landscape and an "oceanic" one. An Asiatic steppe needs to be differentiated from a virgin forest in Africa, but in western Europe it is more a question of nuance. But while the grain that grew in plowed fields, and the flax and hemp, textile plants that grew on slopes and river banks, absorbed most of the peasant's labor, he showed little interest in meadow grasses. Or, rather, they were used, but without any attempt to elicit more than nature provided. The prairie often remained as it was, with its plantain, artemesia, clover, couch grass, lentiscus, cistaceae, and gramineae of all sorts, as well as low plants like rosemary, thyme, thistles, and salads of all varieties. In common language, plants that were picked without working the soil were called *herbes*, a term that included vegetables and fruits, peas, lentils, beans and other starchy plants, and everything that went into the *potage*, as discussed above.

These "grasses" were the very definition of common land, or *vaine pâture*, and an owner might or might not claim payment for its use. Plant material was cut from it to stuff beds, light a fire, or add to manure for fertilizer. Such lands were also used for the collection of medicinal plants whose virtues were undisputed: cabbage for liver complaints, onion for rheumatism, watercress for insect bites, parsley for bad dreams, beans for leprosy, lentils as an aphrodisiac, and more. All of this was the province of women, often with the help of children; men took part only when there were large surfaces to be cut, as in mountain areas to prepare the *alp* for the transhumance. In Mediterranean areas, cattle might have been led to the impenetrable maquis and the sparse vegetation in the low hills to complement what they might have found to eat in the woods. It is not that there were no grasslands or meadows to produce hay for the livestock, but the upkeep of such terrain was costly and had to be carefully supervised to maintain the quality of the grass, which meant that only the wealthier owned such *prés*. As for the scythe, it belonged to the mower. Some parcels of land were enclosed; other plots were plowed from time to time; space was carved out for truck gardening or an orchard for red-fruited trees that might be stifled in the forest and for tender fruits such as peaches and apricots. The "garden" remained part of the lordly landscape, however, as a place for leisure time, relaxation, and to meet friends within the confines of the castle or in the courtyard of the bourgeois *hôtel*. This is hardly surprising, when in our feverish and stress-filled lives we too aspire to the "green" of nature!

The vineyard is a case apart. For a Frenchman, to hoe one's own vineyard or *clos* and to drink one's own wine are still emblems of social dignity. The attention to the minute details of the "art" of grape culture and the very special care that the plant required inclined the vintager to scorn the man with a plow, or the shepherd—both of whom were forbidden to enter the *clos*. In the city, if a man owned land inside or outside the walls, it was a vineyard. Long before Christianity gave wine the dignity of being one of the two species of the Eucharist, it was the symbol of joy, conviviality, and also health; it accompanied sacred dances, festive meals, and pious libations; it welcomed the traveler or the guest; it marked the churching of women and the signing of a contract. Naturally, no one was unaware that excessive consumption risked having disastrous effects. The drunkard is well represented in the *fabliaux*, and many of the great of this world were overly fond of wine, as was Philip Augustus, as we have seen, who was a connoisseur, or Charles the Bold, who was killed in war before he could die of advanced cirrhosis. It is true, as I have noted, that the drinking of wine—nearly two liters a day—must have been compensated for by its low alcohol content. As for the rejection of wine in Islamic lands because it alienated the body and the soul of the faithful, the Christian chronicles written in the East hardly allude to the fact.

A long-standing tradition credits the Romans with having introduced grape cultivation into Gaul. Anthracology has shown that the grapevine was known in these regions well before Caesar, but wine grapes were probably not deliberately exploited. It is true that Latin agronomists described the conditions, the exposure, and the temperature most favorable for grapes and the places where they grew particularly well. But in the Middle Ages grapes were known and raised everywhere from Scotland to Sicily and even in Scandinavia. Some have stated, with a perfectly straight face, that their ubiquity came from the fact that the priest serving at mass drank a goblet of wine at the sacrament of the Eucharist, even though communion under the two species was no longer practiced among the laity. It is wiser to admit that the planting of vineyards far from the terrains in which grapes grow best was due to the bad quality of the unfiltered water almost everywhere, which was reserved for use in the kitchen, even in places where beer, cider, or perry (*poiré*, a drink based on pear juice) competed with wine, as has been noted. Wine became a sign of domination and prestige, first among the wealthy, then everywhere. It was only very slowly that the care taken in the selection of root stock or the evolution of taste brought a reduction in the geographical extension of viticulture. In the fourteenth and fifteenth centuries, tastes shifted to the production of "strong" wines, reds for the most part.

Work in the vineyard mobilized the man and his family throughout the year, even though the current notion of a village dedicated to wine production had not yet been established. From one grape harvest to the next, the stump of the grape stock had to be "booted" (*chaussé*) with mounded-up earth and then fertilized; next came pruning and layering the vines. Stakes had to be prepared for the leafy vine branches, and then there was hoeing and weeding, stripping leaves and cleaning up. When the moment arrived—chosen by nature—to pick the grapes, a *ban* was proclaimed that mobilized the manpower of the entire village. The master's vineyard was picked first, but only after he had used all the wine that remained from the preceding harvest, because wine was not kept from one season to another. We do not know enough about the winemaking process at the time to judge, but we can guess that the workers were less skillful than in our own day. People tried to use up wine as quickly as possible, even the *mère-goutte*, the first juice obtained even before the grapes were trampled, and the *verjus*, the wine made from the first pressing, which was acid and reserved for use as pickling brine. Putting the wine in barrels and sending it to market (when it was not all consumed locally) explains why vineyards were often planted near the shore or by the banks of a river, which facilitated the transport of casks that were considered insufficiently solid to withstand the bumps of dirt roads.

Hence the work demanded by grape plants required a human and material environment of the highest level: Trellises were required if the vines were to be trained onto an arbor, and stakes were needed in all cases. Then there were barrels, casks, and tuns to be provided; terraces to be built up on sloping terrain. In mixed-use planting arrangements, fruit trees had to be found to connect the tendrils; in all cases, solid fences or hedges had to be built to keep rodents out and attentive guards were needed to ward off stray dogs and marauders. All of this cost money, raised prices, and added to seigneurial levies, thus granting wine a place in the medieval economy and in daily life that equaled the place of grain.

THE TREES AND THE FOREST

Was man of early times tree-dwelling, like his "inferior" brothers, the monkeys? Or did he limit himself to using trees for food or as a place to hide? This is something that mattered little to the "people of the Middle Ages" for whom human origins were engulfed in a past ruled by the hand of God. However, a few thousand years of "history" could not have totally effaced the mark of hundreds of thousands of other years. The tree remains the inevitable companion of man. Where it is lacking, there is no more "normal" life, and even the nomadic shepherd goes from oasis to oasis, to find water, to be sure, but also to find trees.

The Forest, Overwhelming and Sacred

Whether it took the form of a forest of evergreens, an oak grove, or thorn-laden scrub growth, the forest was the barrier that marked the horizon for human groups. Even from the walls of the city it could be seen surrounding humans, and before any other form of taking control, seigneury in the Middle Ages meant primarily clearing woods. The nearby forest weighed on the minds of the living; it was the indomitable domain of Nature, regenerated with every springtime, a place where certain trees grew whose life span was much longer than humans'. It was the sacred part of Creation, the part that could not be approached without a religious shudder because everything in it was strange and unknowable: its perfumes, its noises, the beasts who lived in it or who were thought to live in it. Along uncertain paths, thorns and barbs caught the traveler; fallen tree trunks hindered his progress; hidden quagmires lay in wait for him. These were the snares of the Evil One. He was the master of these shadows, he and all his loyal devotees: elves, goblins, trolls—or Kobolds in Germanic lands, with their king the Erlkönig or Harlequin. More to the south, they were called fairies, dragons, *tarasques,* and troops of fauns, sprites, and green dwarfs served Pan. All these were in league to bewitch and deceive credulous and fearful humans. One might stay in the forest for several days shaking with terror, as did a German emperor of the eleventh century, without finding a way out; the forest was where hated princes or lords were assassinated, where bandits lurked, and where one encountered such strange phenomena as pierced rocks, the remains of megaliths, and fairy circles. The Bible had already sent Absalom into the forest to die, and the Christian Church, forgetting the sacred fountains (although they were more attractive), insisted on cutting down the trees that had been venerated by the Celts, and it charged saints like Michael, Hubert, George, and Marcel to penetrate the forest and conquer the spirit of Evil.

The forest, like the sea, both terrified and attracted. First, as we shall see, because it was basic to the material life of man. But also because it incarnated eternity and renewal. The mistletoe of the Gallic druids announced the new year; laurel crowned the glories of this world; myrtle and other wild plants cured many ills; the pine tree, ever green, signaled the birth of the Child God. Chapels and wayside altars were constructed at the edges of woods or in a grove of trees, and hermits chose such spots as their "desert." Moreover, in the Gothic age relations between men and trees gradually lightened. Saint Bernard insisted that one could learn a good deal more from trees than from books, and Saint Francis went into the forest to preach to the wolf and the birds. Toward the end of the Middle Ages a new veil of fear fell over the forest as the haunt of miscreants, but in the meantime, during the four centuries from the eleventh to the fourteenth, people penetrated the forest, dominated it, and subjected it to rules.

Greco-Roman authors such as Julius Caesar, Tacitus, and Strabo, who were accustomed to the more open landscapes of Mediterranean zones, successfully propagated the idea of an almost unbroken forest cover that thickened as one went north or east. This was the "thick-haired Gaul" of Caesar's *Gallic Wars* and Tacitus's "black Germany." But they were clearly mistaken. Extremely ancient archaeological evidence of habitation in those regions points instead to a landscape of dense but largely wooded savanna; the scrubby maquis and *garrigue* of southern European regions were probably what remained of a vegetation that had been much more ample in Neolithic times. Without embarking on a botanical study that would exceed my competence, I might say that there is no serious proof of a modification of tree species due to the hand of man. Palynological studies show that in western Europe various species of oak held steady, beeches gradually declined, birches increased notably between the fourteenth and the seventeenth centuries, conifers increased in the modern age, and chestnuts shifted from the north to the south, with the inverse occurring today. A rivalry persists between bushy growth (beeches and conifers), on the one hand, and oaks and chestnut trees, on the other. But neither stringent medieval legislation prohibiting the cutting down of oaks nor the development of the use of chestnut wood to frame buildings in the towns played the least role in these broad natural movements. Climatic variations seem to have dictated an evolution that stretched over a number of centuries.

This observation requires a slight correction. Although tree pollens give no evidence of any perceptible action on the part of man, cereal and grain pollens do show evidence of his passage given that they are tied to agriculture or animal husbandry. The medieval peasant used the undergrowth of forests to satisfy his needs. Little grows under evergreens, which pump quantities of nitrogen out of the soil and isolate the ground under a carpet of sterile needles, but a modest amount of undergrowth lies at the foot of beech trees, thick with ferns and heathers that in the Middle Ages could be used for bedding. And the growth under oak and chestnut trees was excellent for getting mushrooms, tubers, and edible plants of all sorts. Man discovered how to exploit or develop all this wealth. As for the olive tree, although it typically grows in a fairly poor environment, its role as an oil reserve assured it the sympathy and favor of men.

Another obvious minor correction: forests retreated during and after the medieval age, and we have a number of written documents and painstaking pedologic observations that inform us about surfaces and soils in formerly wooded areas. Here again, however, exaggeration twists the facts. The image, ceaselessly repeated, of the *moine défricheur* clearing forests is a patent falsehood, first, because the monks who are usually gratuitously credited with this role, the Cistercians at the head of the list, were, to the contrary and by an imperious rule, isolated in the middle of forests, and their specialization was much more in skillful management of their forest patrimony than in its destruction. Second, the total number of monks working in the woods would never have sufficed to modify the range of the forests. It was not the monks but the peasants who worked there, often, it is true, at the request of the monks and on the property of the monasteries. All in all, and including zones of discontinuous vegetal cover such as mountains and certain regions of southern Europe, it is quite probably closer to the truth to estimate that the forests of western Europe lost 10 percent of their surface area. This is nothing like the frightening destruction of forests that has been going on inside and outside Europe since 1900 or 1950 and that has reached insane proportions today. Our descendants will pay the price for it in a century or two.

Concerning these *défrichements* (a term that refers much more to clearing brush and shrubs than to felling oaks), I will limit myself to citing figures. First, the vocabulary used in contracts for cutting a forest area mentions a number of clearly defined stages and objectives: *rumpere* and *ruptura* speak of penetration, making a hole; *sartare, exsartare, exarare* refer to digging out and pulling up, as does *artigue* in southern France; *adalere* or *exardare* means simply "to put into a condition to produce foodstuffs" or to burn. Burning was probably the most widespread method for clearing wooded areas. Cleared terrain was simply burned over or subjected to *écobuage*, or burn-beating, a process of digging up clumps of earth with grass and plants attached, burning them, and reincorporating them into the soil so that the chemically basic ash enriches the humus. We have the impression that the axe, hatchet, or saw were used less than the billhook for cutting branches and the hoe for breaking up the soil. This work preceded cutting down tree trunks, and several years might go by before oxen (the only animals dependable enough and powerful enough to do such a task) could tear out the stumps with pull chains—roots and all. Even then, for some time only a light plow could be used on cleared terrains, where small roots still impeded the progress of a heavier plow. Such *gagnages*, lands gained from the forest, were better suited for the cultivation of cereals than burned lands, and aeration of the humus increased the levels of nitrogen, phosphates, and potassium. Medieval man did not know these words, but he was well aware of the effect of such substances, and landowners jealously—even severely—guarded and preserved new terrains, a source of foodstuffs and wealth, by regulating their use, enclosing them, and keeping watch over them.

Because they understood the role of the forest, both the powerful and the humble came to accept the notion of its rational management. Surveillance of the forest's health, assuring reforestation, and organizing its exploitation were three obvious duties that came well before the unrestrained profit seeking that dominates public or private owners blinded by immediate profitability today. Although the Cistercians played an important role here, lay authorities joined them in developing an entire personnel of foresters, *verdiers* or *gruyers* (terms derived from *vert* and from *grün*, or green), as they were called in northern France. Legal documents and *chartes coutumières* fixed the conditions for access to the woods by men and beasts, forbade the use of harmful tools, and prohibited the clandestine felling of certain species such as fruit trees and oaks. In France around 1280 or 1300, the king moved to create a body of *maîtres des eaux et forêts* and in the fourteenth century to regulate the pace at which trees would be harvested, the conversion of logs into timber, the marking of trees destined to be cut, and the supervision of log removal, usually by floating logs down a stream. Particularly detailed prescriptions were drawn up in Italy. The treatise of Pietro dei Crescenzi displays such great awareness and expertise in these matters that the sweeping laws of the sixteenth or the eighteenth century could do no better than copy him regarding the parceling of forest lands, the renewal span for various species of trees (from three to twelve years), and the growth of young trees and saplings. At the end of the medieval period, the forest was no longer either wild (*wald* in German) or cut off from the world of men (*foris*, "outside of" in Latin). Its domestication was one of the essential accomplishments of that age.

The Forest, Necessary and Nourishing

Wood came first, and since iron—no matter what is claimed for it—was too scarce to be used in anything but modest craft operations, and it can be said that the Middle Ages was the "age of wood," wood was the essential raw material in these centuries. People went into the forest to seek primarily lumber, wood to build with, or *ad aedificandum*, as the rights documents proclaim. Logs from oak or chestnut trunks provided framing timber (and, if we can believe Suger, it was genuinely difficult to find enough timber in his forests to roof Saint-Denis); beams were used to support fortified towers before stone was used; lath boards were needed for pisé framework; posts reinforced palisades or supported the town's pigeon coops. Hard woods—chestnut, walnut, oak, olive—were used for furniture, which was spare but sturdy; for door and window frames; and for almost all tools and instruments of daily use in agriculture and viticulture, including containers, bowls, barrels, and even working tools subjected to hard use. Moreover, protection was necessary against thieves, carnivorous animals, and rodents, and perhaps even more against indiscrete neighbors and all who operated outside of the law: malefactors (*male factum*) and *forfaiteurs* (*foris factum*). People of the Middle Ages ceaselessly erected palisades of "dead wood" to protect their rights: hedges of bushy plants such as alders or *mort bois* barriers of heaped-up willow, birch, or hornbeam branches. A portion of the forest might be set aside *en défens* or *en devèze*, and small forts were built at sensitive points, along with *plessis*, from the Old Gallic *ploïcum* (which indicated a terrain fenced in with interlaced tree branches), a term that has left its trace on French toponymy.

Then there was wood *ad comburendum*, for burning, as all fires burned wood. This was another domain of severe regulation. No one could simply suit himself and go out to any place at any time to cut wood for cooking or heating the house. The nature, volume, procedures, and moments for cutting wood were fixed by law, as were fines for infractions, and the master's agents patrolled constantly. Anthracology, the science of combustible fuels, has shown that the traditional picture of an enormous oak log burning brightly in the lord's hooded fireplace under a roasting boar is, once again, totally false, or at best reserved to a truly exceptional festive occasion. In reality, what burned in both the castle's large fireplace and the modest cottage hearth was branches and twigs of non-fruit-bearing trees; armfuls of ferns, broom, gorse, and heather; resinous "white woods" like poplar that sooted up the chimneys and stuck to the andirons, or else windfalls of good wood gleaned in clearings. As for the charcoal that specialized workers prepared in the forest in covered huts, it took more than ten kilos of green wood to produce one kilo of charcoal, which reduced the use of charcoal to exceptional occasions, in forges, for example, or in towns and cities, where it cut down the risk of fire. Bark, picked up off the ground or stripped off trees, went to the tanner for his dye baths.

In a world in which grain dominated but market gardening seems to have been rare, people were tempted to seek out places to find edible plants. As it happens, the *herbes et potages*—greens and legumes—that we have already encountered were present on all tables. When some impending danger sent people fleeing to the woods, the villagers could hold off for several months without dying. In the fourteenth century, the Tuchins of Languedoc (who took to the brush country, the *tosca*, or *touche*, like the *maquis* of more recent times) resisted for years all public or military control. This was because the forest supplied foodstuffs, and today scholars tend to agree that an economy of gathering and small-scale animal-raising, providing the main sources of food, was typical of the Middle Ages, as had been true since Neolithic times. In the coppices, people found not only various red berries but hazelnuts, almonds, walnuts, and olives (which also provided oil) as well as mushrooms, chestnuts, medlars, acorns, squash, and pumpkins. They could plant and pick asparagus, leeks, chard, cabbage, rhubarb, artichokes, carrots, parsnips, and beets, and there have been interminable discussions among the "experts" on the place of the tubers that preceded potatoes and on the date of the introduction of spinach and salsify into western Europe. If we add to all this cherries, apples, quinces, figs, and pears, the basket is full, leaving just enough room for garlic, onion, mint, and oregano and for herbs to prepare useful infusions: of linden leaves for insomnia, elderberry for purges, myrtle for bathing the eyes, and coriander as a sexual stimulant. A final gift of the woods was as valuable as all the rest. Bees provided light and sweetness—candle wax and honey—and the willingness of these insects to let man or some other gluttonous animal rob them of the results of their labors won them an excellent reputation. If "raising" bees in a hive was usually carried on outside of the woods, the forest remained the place to find wild swarms, a form of "the hunt" so gratifying that laws had to be passed to prevent the greedy from sawing down trees that hosted out-of-reach hives.

It was not only man who frequented the forest. Though berries and herbs did not attract the carnivores who peopled wooded areas, and held little charm for rodents, certain parts of the forest could be set aside *ad pascendum*—for pasturage. We find it difficult to imagine horses and mules or bovines pastured, either freely or under supervision, in the forest, in particular because of the obvious limits to free circulation, but areas cleared of undergrowth could provide forage for herds, provided the animals were not of the sort that stripped plants of their young shoots, which meant that sheep and goats were prohibited. But in September, when acorns were plentiful, pigs were let loose in the forest. They might even live in the woods all year long, with the result that until at least the tenth century, a forested stretch was measured "in pigs," or the "surface necessary to nourish one pig for one year," estimated to be about one hectare. Peasants did not always practice this sort of free pasturage, as the animals might hurt themselves; they could be attacked by carnivores; it was difficult to gather them for milking or breeding. Sows were often mounted by boars, which led to a change in the behavior and, above all, the exterior appearance of their progeny. It is thus thought that when crop rotation began to spread, in general after the thirteenth century, and animals began to be housed in more or less permanent stables, this facet of the role of the woods declined somewhat to the profit of pasturage on fallow land. This is a question to which I shall return.

And the People of the Forest?

Today the forest is still a reserve source of wood—which we waste without thinking twice—but also a terrain for walking, a place of relaxation, a bath of clean air for the city dweller. Those whom we meet in it are no longer restricted to woodsmen, forest guards, and hunters in search of game; we do not encounter horses, cattle, or pigs, but only an occasional person hoping to find lily-of-the-valley, mushrooms, or chestnuts. In the Middle Ages, and especially toward the end of that period, the forest was teeming with people. First, there were all those whose labors we have just been examining: shepherds, berry pickers, root diggers, teams of woodsmen making a clearing or an isolated man cutting down a tree;

but also a second stratum of gleaners, people who picked up bark or ashes, and charcoal burners installed in their huts. Before they moved their forges into the village, probably in the eleventh century, various sorts of ironworkers, *férons*, *fèvres*, and *ferrari* worked near the charcoal burners in places where iron could be gathered at the surface of the ground. All these people lived apart, away from the village, and the villagers soon suspected them of being marauders, poachers, and marginals, not to mention followers of all the sorcerers and demons who were thought to be found in the forest. And this is without counting the fugitives, the banished, and those avoiding justice, who held it certain that no one would come looking for them in the brush. In times of war, soldiers and mercenaries would regroup in the forests, and in the fifteenth century their presence was so closely connected with the forest that the good people of France, noting both a slow-down in clearing projects and the importance of the forest in warfare, said, "In France, the woods came with the English." They called the English *les godins*, although historians disagree as to whether the term comes from *gawaldi*, or people of the forest (*wald*), or from "Goddamn," an oath that the enemies of the king of France supposedly repeated ceaselessly.

To end the list, there were two other highly interesting groups in the forests: hermits, who dispensed consolations and remedies to all whose soul or body was in a desperate situation; and adventuring knights, whose fantastic exploits were enhanced by the somber glory of having gotten the better of the forest—Lancelot and Arthur's knights as masked avengers, and Percival, Galahad, and other seekers of the Holy Grail, the vessel that collected the blood of Christ on the Cross.

For the convenience of my narration, I have ignored the nuances made clear by scribes in their choice of terms, and by nature in its dispositions. They are not negligible, however. If the *saltus*, a quasi-juridical term, and the *foresta* were indeed zones that were "outside of"—that is, outside of the *ager* that was cultivated, and outside of common law—no one would confuse the *mescla*, a nearly sterile land with scrub growth and spiny plants, with the *silva* of oaks and beeches, and even less with a sandy *garenne* or a nearly plant-free dune. Man had done his best, at times even with success, to outwit these varying terrains and to shape them to his purposes. Animals had done so for some time. Where are they?

AND THE ANIMALS?

For the millions of years that followed the consolidation of our planet into a compact sphere (and whether this was a process of the concretion of debris torn from the sun or had some other origin hardly matters for our purposes), a prodigious parade of living beings succeeded one other, of which man seems—at least to this date—the most recent. Naturally, I am interested only in those beings who still surround us in this infinitely thin film of time that we call history. I shall thus leave it to the paleontologists and the children to speak of disappeared species that are inconceivable, usually frightening to the point of ridicule, and are illustrated today by puerile simulacra.

Let us return to the situation at the end of the Holocene after the last observed glaciation some thirty thousand years ago. Most of the animated beings of these few thousand years are the ones that we see around us now, or rather, in the midst of which we are engulfed. I say engulfed because for one *Homo sapiens sapiens* (what a grotesque name!) there are more than one hundred other species of terrestrial mammals, thousands of birds, countless fish and insects. What is more, out of these hundred mammals, man has some real familiarity with only half of them, and has exercised his talents on only some dozen or so species. This is a ridiculously small proportion, but it is useful to recall that although man is immersed in the animal world, he has persuaded himself that he dominates it because God supposedly gave him that responsibility. As for the animals in question, aside from the dog or the horse, they have never noticed a thing. But let us put aside this debilitating fact, which did not trouble people of the Middle Ages, and see what their attitudes were.

MAN AND BEAST

In the Garden of Eden men and beasts lived in mutual understanding and respect; they all drank at the Fountain of Life, and the love of God extended to all of his creatures. It was nevertheless one of those creatures that precipitated the Temptation and the Fall. This introduced the germ of a "distancing," as the psychologists would say, between the world of men and that of the beasts. Whether that negative role fell to the serpent, as in the first credible redactions of the Bible, or to the wolf, as many medieval authors suggest, the fact remains that fear of the dangerous animal was the first reaction of man to the animal world.

Fear and Disgust

Aristotle spoke in vain of the community of all living beings, which the Christian world saw as a fiction. Saint Paul said as much: animals are the creatures of God, but they have no soul; at most, they possess enough instinct and sense to be of service to man. Saint Francis himself spoke to the wolf of Gubbio like a brother, but an inferior brother who needs to be taught, because God gave man full power over his creation. To be sure, medieval literature contains many "humanized" animals, but it describes them either by displaying a somewhat bland complacency, as with the warhorse

Bayard, who taps his foot when his master appears, or by endowing them with a disturbing malignity, as with Renard the Fox or Fauvel, a horse. To be sure, these animal disguises serve to satirize human society; still, a scorn of animals underlies the tales. This state of mind is still so much that of all humanity that I hardly need recall the list of insults involving animals that men fling at one another, or the traditional but usually unthinking way that we describe beasts. The goose is stupid, the cock pretentious, the pig dirty, the he-goat lecherous, the boar brutal, the wolf cruel, the cat a thief, and I shall skip over many others to arrive at the condensation of all such insults. The donkey, that solid, indispensable, and hardworking friend of man, is judged stubborn, lazy, a gourmand, ugly, noisy, and stupid. Historically, lovers surprised in sin have been exhibited naked, riding a donkey, forgetting that the donkey also bore the Infant Jesus to Egypt and Christ at his entry into Jerusalem.

Scorn is a palliative for fear. And man, refusing to recognize his own weakness, is fearful. He is afraid of being attacked by things and beings stronger than he is. This means that from prehistoric times, and because he is the only creature who has learned to dominate fire, he has used it to light up a night filled with dangers and to keep away carnivores who can see in the dark. Defenseless, he sleeps with his head to the wall, as we have seen, to avoid being attacked from behind. His fear was far from irrational. First, because there were a number of animals who caused indirect harm to men. The wolf attacked his cattle, the boar gored his horses, locusts ravaged his fields, the rat devoured his food reserves. There were also direct attacks to fear. Insect bites could be cruel; a wounded bear or boar was a danger to the hunter; silent and swift reptiles bit the inattentive peasant; the gray rat or, even worse, the black rat propagated mortal illnesses. Even "domestic" animals presented a danger. A dog who is afraid bites, an irritated horse can kick hard. As for the cat—which the Church as early as the late eleventh century and public opinion after that connected with witches' sabbaths, magic, and the Devil—he scratched, he stole, he set off allergic reactions, and his lecherous nature made him odious to men (though much less so to women, as our modern advertising shows). But during the Middle Ages (and at other times as well), of all the animals, it was the wolf who concentrated men's terror and hatred. The wolf was courageous, tricky, able to think ahead, and ambiguous. As the "tiger of the West," he was the only mammal capable, when hungry, of directly attacking humans—the traveler who had lost his way, the defenseless shepherd, the wounded soldier, the child, or the old man. His misdeeds, exaggerated by human fear, were told from village to village, even if he did not penetrate the city when hunger gnawed at him, for instance in Paris in the early fifteenth century. Wolves encumbered childhood memory, inundated literature, fed scary tales. The extermination of wolves, which was encouraged by a spate of laws calling for drives and offering rewards, was not pursued (in France, at any event) until the eighteenth century. Although today the wolf constitutes a danger only for poorly supervised sheep, his return, even under strict laws, infuriates villagers and raises new fears.

All such animals inspired fear, to be sure, but in general they did not inspire disgust, because in different degrees they belong to the anthropic world. They have blood, fur, or feathers; they appear in the daytime and most sleep at night; they copulate and defecate like humans. But other beings, viscous, sticky, cold, and soft ones like fish and reptiles; elusive, black, invertebrate, and often malodorous creatures like spiders, ants, cockroaches, and all insects from mosquito to flea were repugnant and the source of disease. Before scientific progress threw light on the role of microbes or bacteria in setting off pandemics, the vast human hecatombs that devastated humanity over the centuries—dysentery, cholera, malaria, and of course the plague—were all blamed on insect bites.

Respect and Affection

There have been cultures that were perhaps less persuaded of the superiority of man than Judeo-Christian society and that have held the animal—or certain animals—man's equal or even his god. Some of these cultures seem to us exotic—pre-Columbian America or ancient China—or self-centered, like Egypt of the pharaohs, where the gods appear as beasts. Closer to us, and perhaps not without influence on us, Indian or Iranian beliefs include reincarnation in an animal body or hold certain animals as sacred: the Persian eagle and falcon, the cow in India. The cult of the bull, the emblem of virility, may have come down to us from Crete and through the Mithra sect, and it still inspires bloody and brutal ritual festivities in Spain, the Basque lands, and Provence. The supercharged *aficionados* of today's *corridas* are undoubtedly unaware that they are imitating the adepts of an Eastern cult. The goddess Hathor, Minos the king of Crete, the nymph Io, or the god Mithra are names that probably mean nothing to them. Christianity, at least in its early centuries, made no brutal break with such zoomorphic practices. It gave glorious animals to three out of the four evangelists: the eagle, the lion, and (once more) the bull. Although the veneration of such animals has gradually disappeared, hagiography conserves their memory. God can take on the traits of the royal stag, the dove, or the lamb as a symbol of peace or clemency. As late as the mid-thirteenth century, the Church admitted (somewhat unwillingly, to be sure) the cult of Saint Guinefort, a greyhound that saved a child from being bitten by a venomous snake, an obvious emblem of the Devil.

The Celtic or Germanic contribution dissolved only slowly within the Greco-Roman and Eastern legacy. Like peoples of all times in search of virtues they do not possess (courage, loyalty, and strength in particular), human groups gave themselves animal totems, usually connected with the demands of hunting: the wolf, the bear, the boar, the eagle. A driver in France who consults the Web for advice on which route to take may smile at the name "Bison Futé" (in English, Canny Buffalo), but not at the name "Bernard," which means "courageous bear." It has long been thought that the refusal to eat the flesh of dogs and cats came from affection toward those animals and, inversely, that eating horsemeat or drinking the blood of horses filled the warrior with the "heroic" virtues attributed to that animal, and that the Church had forbidden these "barbaric" practices. Unfortunately, archaeology offers evidence of horse bones that bear traces of butchering, and we are told that dog meat, like wolf meat, is nauseating and indigestible, which does not seem to stop Asiatic consumers from enjoying them.

Men's interest in the animal world did not necessarily reach the level of veneration, however. It often stopped at admiration of the suppleness of felines, the grace of birds, and the elegance of the swan, and the steady gaze of dogs moved men and artists who expressed the subconscious of their age in their works. We can see this in Egyptian or Persian bas-reliefs, Germanic jewels, or medieval miniatures, but only to a lesser degree in the Greco-Roman culture and legacy. Naturally, the less well known the animal was, the more virtues were lent to it. The elephant, which was quite rare in Europe, headed the list. He was seen as powerful and docile, loyal and chaste, timid and generous, full of wisdom and knowledge. Similarly, the dromedary, the "ship of the desert," was seen as sober, extraordinarily resistant, and affectionate; the lion was majestic, filled with courage and magnanimity. The ideal was the unicorn, which no one had ever seen, the symbol of Marian chastity and the purity of the world. We can of course suppose that men of learning knew that the elephant was capricious, the "camel," as they said, had an odious disposition, the lion was faint-hearted, and the unicorn was reputed to be of loose morals.

What man sought in the animal was the symbol, and it did not matter whether or not that symbol was supported by social or even economic contingencies. The donkey that the Lord chose as his mount was the symbol of holy humility; the dove with the olive branch in its beak was the sign of the lessening of divine wrath; the fish, the Greek name for which (*ichthys*), was the symbol of Christ, the fisher of souls, as we have seen. The bee who gave honey, just as Mary gave milk, was the symbol of the family, and even the humble pig, whose sacrifice on the night before Christmas inaugurated the festivities, appeared as an almost mystical "signifier." As for the bear who inhabited the mountains and the forests of western Europe, he was the food-loving companion of the hermit, a good-humored and basically not dangerous creature endowed with virtues that made him, for a long time and well before the lion, the king of the beasts.

In reality, of all these mammals nourished, sheltered, and used by man, there were two species, and only two, that established genuine ties of affection with him: the horse and the dog. The cat, who invades our lives today, continued to live its life in independence (some would say egoistically), sure of the favors it deserved, thanks to its grace, beauty, and the almost therapeutic calm that emanated from its attitudes and from the soothing and serene contact it offered. Since the seventeenth and especially the nineteenth century, when its somberly demonic reputation faded, the cat has become a sought-after comfort for man—and especially for woman—but it has never been in the service of either.

This is clearly not true of the horse, that "noble conquest," as popular wisdom puts it. This was a recent conquest, dating back from five to ten thousand years, that is incomplete, given that there are still many wild horses in the world. What man hoped for, sought, and found in that elegant and loyal but nervous and fragile animal was a companion for relaxation and for work, a mount that would abolish distances, and that has an intelligence and sensitive strength. Capturing and training this capricious beast is a difficult task, a topic to which I shall soon return. The result is certain, however. A horse, broken and trained, recognizes his master and is attached to him; he might even exceed his master's expectations in the hunt, as was true of his ardor and courage in war. Medieval literature is full of tales of equine companions who were given human names, and the period has left us more treatises on the care of horses than manuals for bringing up children.

And finally we arrive at the over 150 varieties of dog, the oldest and the surest companion of our species. Dogs have been at men's heels or running ahead for over thirty thousand years, and they have become nearly incapable of living without us, the only animal to have reached such a state of dependency. In one era and another, dogs have been expected to guard the house, aid in the hunt, make their presence felt accompanying herd animals, and provide companionship for solitary or afflicted humans. Antiquity was less favorably disposed to dogs, the Middle Ages protected them, and our century is infatuated with them. Dogs are the very symbol of obedience, affection, and devotion, and the death of a dog's master often brings on his own. In spite of a degree of scorn, following the example of the ancient world, reflected in our use of the term "dog" as an epithet, the dog watches over us like a sure aid. The dog may be an exceptional case, but it is thanks to him that the animal species (mammals at least, the only animals with which the Middle Ages were truly familiar) were perceived as examples to follow. In a world in which God may have deposited a portion of his good will in his creatures, the dog was the very image of that good will. He was neither scheming nor faithless, not cowardly, inconstant, egoistic, or deliberately cruel.

Given that today we have ambiguous feelings about the animal world, is there any way that we can know how animals were perceived in medieval times? Animal behavior still eludes the reach of our scientists, and this was probably even more true in the centuries of the Middle Ages. The one thing that men of that time were sure of (as we are today) was that all the animals that have taken notice of our own species (which excludes the water world and insects) were afraid of those who possessed fire and tools and fled from them. The medieval mind saw divine wrath in such fear, extending out from the serpent, punished for the Fall, to all the other beasts. Today we admit that man is the most brutal of all predators, the most egoistic, the cruelest, almost "bestial," as we might say with a certain audacity. Even the species that band together to defend themselves against man, as did wolves in the Middle Ages, that use craft, set traps for their aggressor, and help one another in hunting him down, inevitably succumbed. How can we discern the hatred in the eyes of the stag at bay, the wounded bear, or the bull stuck with banderilias? And, from another perspective, can we perceive signs of interest, curiosity, perhaps affection, in animals who live outside of our immediate control? The parasites who assail us and the birds who come to pose on our balconies are attracted only by a desire to feed on our blood or our food. Zoophilia leads us to thinking that a cow is sensitive to the presence of a certain cowherd or that a she-goat will permit only known persons to milk her, but these are animals who have already been subjected to human care. It has also been said, perhaps more scientifically, that man's odor, which is thought to be as acid as that of urine, or his extremely salty sweat arouse covetousness or interest in certain species. But does this imply any affection? Monkeys are a case apart. The Western Middle Ages had little acquaintance with them, but, as good brothers from our origins, if they do not "like" us, they nonetheless seem close to us, accessible to us, and curious about us. It might seem more surprising, because there is a less obvious link between our species and theirs, that it is marine mammals who give the impression of appreciating our company and even seeking it. This has been observed in the seals and walruses who used to haunt our shores until recent centuries and are still seen there occasionally, or whales of all sizes, which cannot be accused of beaching on our coasts in the unique desire to be cut up and eaten by lucky villagers. The champion in this category is of course the dolphin, which has been amply described, painted, and sung of since antiquity; which continues to charm children with his aquatic play; and which seems to take pleasure in our company. Dolphins might be of some service to us in fishing, but no attempts have been made in that direction. Perhaps a new "conquest" for man awaits.

All of the preceding remarks are universal in nature and pertain to all periods. It is time to turn to the centuries of the Middle Ages to see what was known and done.

KNOWING AND UNDERSTANDING

Immersed in the terrestrial and even the aerial animal worlds, man of the Middle Ages could not be content with being subjected to contact with the beasts. Fearing them and admiring them are passive attitudes. If only in order to limit their actions and attempt to dominate them, he had to study them and grasp their weaknesses.

What Are the Beasts?

The Church insisted that since animals had no soul and were simply a reflection of the power of God, studying them was neither useful nor desirable for salvation. Too much interest in them was close to idolatry. If sexual contact with animals could be proven among the groups of men who lived in isolation, as it was with shepherds in the mountains, the guilty party was charged with "bestiality" and burned at the stake for having insulted the Creator in his work. Thirteenth-century Scholasticism pointed to the dangers of totemization, the likening (in intellectual terms at least) of the beast, normally subject to man, and man himself, the only worthy object of study. Even the few who thought in zoological terms had an anthropological viewpoint, whether they were Isidore of Seville in the seventh century, Hildegard of Bingen in the eleventh century, or Brunetto Latini in the thirteenth century. Their thoughts about the animal world all followed the same schema. There are some animals who "serve" and others who "threaten"; the virtues that they display are of interest only if they contribute to the animal's state of dependency and submission to man. This view did not change before the fourteenth century, when some began to take an interest in the animal world (or at least in looking at it), although without any change in the attitude of self-satisfaction with our own species and scorn for other species (a vanity that remains solid among our contemporaries). That slight change in evaluation was perhaps due to the development of a sense of the real that began to affect other areas as well and that was displayed in a curiosity about appearances, movements, and even mores. This was the epoch in which princes demanded menageries to amuse their guests and in which artists of the pen and the chisel perfected animal forms. King René amused himself drawing rabbits; Gaston

Phoebus, the count of Foix, may have illustrated his hunting manuals himself. Still, Buffon was far in the future.

These concerns were matters for clerics, the learned, and the powerful. But what about the common people, the overwhelming majority of those who were in daily, physical, and natural contact with the world of beasts? In fact, if we can believe what we read in works about saints' lives (which were written by learned men, however), or the romances and the *fabliaux*, we see that they knew as much, if not more, than the guardians of the Truth. The knowledge displayed in such works was direct and the observations visual; their authors remarked, registered in the minds, and at times cared for a horse's maladies; they knew its fits of humor. They had adapted certain types of dogs to the services that were expected of them; they understood how to make it easier for an ox to work the soil according to the grain he ate or the ground he was to plow; they had drawn up rules for the life of the sheep, their movements, shearing, and lambing time; they made the best use they could of the pig. The cat was the only "domestic" animal whose caprices they failed to investigate. To be sure, such writers hardly ever went beyond the level of external observation, but the use they made of animals to "ape" humans shows clearly that they had a clear perception of animal behavior. The *Roman de Renart* and other such tales after 1175, as well as the *ysopets*, brief popular fables of the same age, are not just stories about men. Animal behavior shows through in them as well. What is more, knowledge on that level was not inaccessible. To be sure, the *Physiologus* of late antiquity and the compilations made of that work until the thirteenth century were in Latin, hence had little hearing among humble folk. In the late twelfth century and throughout the thirteenth century, encyclopedists like Bartholomaeus Anglicus (Bartholomew the Englishman), Peter and Vincent of Beauvais, or Hugh of Saint Victor kept to scholarly language, but they inspired a literary genre capable of touching the "little people" in bestiaries, often illustrated, that they could see or have explained to them by the village curé.

That "popular" approach to the animal world was obviously un-
scientific. First, because of the weight of the anthropological slant
I have just spoken of, which limited reflection. And next, because
a screen of symbols veiled comprehension. How could anyone explain the growth of ten-pronged antlers when they were consistently viewed as a reflection of the Ten Commandments? This explains the continued popularity of a good many false ideas, some
of which are still held. The salmon is the male of the trout because
the two resemble each other and the salmon swims upriver to lay
its eggs; dogs are the sworn enemies of cats because they are emblems for man and woman, in constant competition; the bear is
good-humored and approachable because he likes to eat honey,
the symbol of Mary's milk; the bee is the very emblem of the family because, from dawn to dusk, it works for the entire hive. One
could add to this list the strange descriptions of travelers such as
Marco Polo and many other merchants in exotic lands, or those of
the Franciscans, itinerant evangelists who claimed to have seen in
distant lands extraordinary animals that were deformed versions
of those at home. Such tales fed the imagination. The cobra, and
hence other snakes, became dragons; the horned rhinoceros was a
male unicorn; the female seal was a temptress siren; felines such as
the ocelot, the leopard, or the panther were the reincarnated souls
of sinners that bore the signs of their sins. And the sorcerer dressed
in animal skins who frequented the woods at night was the man-
eating wolf, the werewolf, *loup-garou*, or Germanic *wehrwolf.*

That ambivalence regarding animals during the medieval centuries explains some strange practices that make us smile, such as
the trials of animals. These involved public arrest, formal accusation, defense of the assumed guilty party, and punishment, which
was usually hanging. This is what happened to the pig that wounded
a child, the badger that devastated a vineyard, the wolf that had
killed and been killed but was hanged anyway, or even insects such
as June bugs. These mock trials, which were serious enough at the
time for the jurist Beaumanoir to set down rules for them, throw
light on the vague zone separating man, who is at the right hand

of God, from the beast, who is a disobedient creature. We would be wrong to laugh. Our nervous equilibrium is strictly dependent on the dangers that threaten it. More than the tooth of the wolf or the dog, it was the wolf's sinister nocturnal howling or the ceaseless barking of the dog that created a state of tension (today we would call it stress) that was judged harmful to man's activity as an exceptional being.

Penetrating This World

Dangers fade when they become familiar. From the time that he began to live in a group, man has tried to extend his authority over the other species—to force them into his service and even to attach them to him, to "domesticate" them. But the latter implies a reciprocal contact, almost an affective one, if the word is taken in its full sense. But man has never truly domesticated any animal except the dog, perhaps the horse, about which I have spoken above. For tens of thousands of years no species has consciously subjected itself to his control, not even the cat, as I have said. For the first two, we can still find stray dogs that have become wild and horses that run free. No other branch of the animal kingdom has been "conquered." To be sure, cattle, sheep, and others are commanded, supervised, milked, and shorn, and pigs are led to gather acorns in September. But if we can admit that the attraction of nourishment or the feeling of security can suffice to make them docile, we cannot say as much for the aurochs, bison, or boars who are their wild brothers. As for pigeons, bees, or silkworms, we are fooling ourselves if we call them "trained" or even "raised," and the same is true of the beavers, swans, and falcons that were so highly appreciated in the Middle Ages.

It is hard to know whether the men of those times thought it possible to increase their control over the animal world that lay within their reach. At least it seems that they were attentive to ways to improve the capture and training of such animals. Reproduction is obviously an essential aspect of raising animals, and it is subject to human control. The breeding of horses and cattle was supervised, even subject to regulations in the village, and it was conducted under the eye of a sergeant of the master; the bull, the stallion, and the boar were called *banaux* as early as the thirteenth century, for their services were quasi public, given that the composition and the condition of the herds and flocks could not be left to chance. Owners of pigs took precautions (probably in vain) to prevent their sows from being impregnated in the forest by male wild boars. Inversely, the castration of excessive numbers of male animals was a necessity, but we know little about it. The only animal for which we have something like accurate information is the horse, because that pearl of military equipment demanded the entire attention of the mounted aristocracy. Given one stallion for every seven mares who foaled once a year, that left a large number of stallions for the cavalry. Both iconography and narratives of the hunt or of combat clearly show that the mounts were "entire," at least to around the end of the thirteenth century. At that moment the practice of castrating male horses, which was old, if not ancient, spread. There is no proof of a systematic use of castration before 1300, however, nor is it known whether the expression, *cheval hongre* to designate a castrated horse has any real connection with Hungarians, who were indeed horsemen.

Although we know little concerning other species, we do know about horses that a search for improving the stock by cross-breeding or the importation of exotic sires occupies a notable place in veterinarians' treatises. It is known, for example, that the diversification of races of horses comes largely from contacts with "Arabic" Spain in the twelfth century or with the Near East at the time of the crusades. The original horses established in western Europe at the dawn of the Middle Ages, which were heavy and powerful animals, were joined by *genets* (genets, or jennets, a name deriving from the Zenata Berbers), animals that were light, rapid, adaptable to the saddle, and that supported climatic variations well. Such differences in weight and size have been demonstrated by archaeozoology. Bovines, too, which are usually less studied, were also affected by an interest in improving their services. The Cistercians, who, as usual, were more interested in cultivating their own wealth than in general considerations, encouraged the implantation into Aquitaine of Norman milking stock, thanks to "visits" of herds under the order's command; and we are told that Saint Bernard himself sent off a brother to ask for *bufali* from the Tuscan Maremma for his herd in Champagne. We know more about merino sheep (and "merino" is another word that probably originated in the Maghreb, but scholars hesitate between several possibilities), thanks to the importance of trade in wool and wool products. Introduced into Spain in the mid-fourteenth century, merino wool was traded even in England, where it competed with Sheffield and Yorkshire wools. In this case, study of sheep skeletons has clearly shown an evolution in which man had a part.

There remains one isolated corner of the "domestic" world to be investigated, which is the *basse-cour* and its fowl. Here we are completely in the dark about possible changes over the course of ten centuries. Were these birds subjected to the wishes of man, or did they simply react to the constraints of the environment? Complete silence, or, rather, we have nothing but words, which are always the same: chicken, pullet, egg, duck, cock or rooster, capon, goose, but nary a bone or an accurate image.

If there were some animals—the majority—who were asked only to serve man without really wanting to, there were others who were trained and from whom men demanded a more personal participation in their service. If we are well informed about this topic, it is because manuals for the hunt, for veterinary care, and for the care of horses, and encyclopedias in the style of Bartholomew the Englishman, teem with practical advice and examples. One thing stands out and justifies the consultation of monastic and seigneurial account books in addition to the theoretical works after the fourteenth century. "Training" an animal was extremely costly, as it required specialized personnel, time, and space. Even pigeons had to be collected in constructions that had to be kept clean. Several thousand of them lodged in pigeons' cotes were a sign of the lord's high rank. Pigeons had to be attracted with decoys or bait, and it was perhaps easier to collect swarms of bees, build hives for them far from predators and from winds and other effluvia that might upset them. Above all, bees required supervision and, in particular, an *apicularius* whose tasks included collecting and working the wax even more than gathering the honey. Training a ferret for hunting, or a falcon (and I shall have more to say about falcons), was also a job for a technician. These animals could only be attracted by meat as a bait, but one also had to know how to release them, hold them back, and get them to return to the cage or the fist.

Obviously, the horse and the dog were subjected to strict surveillance. Breaking in a horse, given its natural disinclination to reins and a saddle, could be dangerous and require much patience and many precautions. Breeding stations, known since the tenth century, were placed in the forest to facilitate capture with a lasso and early training. Certain lordly families such as the Rohans in Brittany even made a specialty of such stables in the wold, and in France they existed in the forests of the Île de France, on the banks of the Loire, and in Roussillon. Various stable personnel—*palefreniers* (from *poledarii* in bas-Latin)—were set to the task before the animal, judged to be sufficiently docile, was trained for combat or for draft work by a stable boy or an elderly valet or *sénéchal* (from *senex schalk*, former valet). The vocabulary of the romance tells us much more about the nomenclature of the various types of mounts than about their intrinsic qualities. We have the palfrey or *palefroi* (from the *paraveredus* of the Roman postal system and the Germanic *Pferd*, who carried messages), which was a saddle horse; the hackney, named for the English village of the same name, was a trotter used for travel and for the most part reserved for lady riders; the bidet was a small horse and good runner; the *sommier* was a workhorse named for the packs he carried. The destrier or warhorse, the origin of whose name continues to divide historians. As for the old nag, the *roncin* or *rosse*, it might be of any variety. After 1100 or 1150, the problem arose of shoeing horses, which was the work of the *maréchal*, or farrier, both in the castle and in the village. Shoeing horses was nearly unknown in the ancient world; it may have come from Asia; its use spread only slowly, and its obvious advantages for the strengthening of horses' hooves was long neglected.

The dog, for thousands of years attached to man, presented a simpler challenge, since dogs had been accustomed for generations to the notion of docility toward humans. Still, there were lead dogs, *maîtres-chiens*, who were responsible for the hunting pack and required a training appropriate to their particular breed and the task at hand; the mastiff for attacking the wild boar or the wolf; the *dogue*, who also guarded the herds and flocks or the farm; the greyhound used for coursing deer; the *braque* or hound used as a field dog; the spaniel or the barbet to hunt burrowing prey.

This training rarely involved any effort on the part of the master to work for complicity between man and beast. Still, a number of these "domestic" (or almost domestic) animals seem to have enjoyed attempts to improve their performance by encouraging almost conscious appetites or tendencies. The horse enjoys races and jumping contests in competition with other horses; the donkey seems happy to have pompoms on his harness; the ox seems to like it when his yoke is decorated with flowers, as does the cow wearing a bell or the dog commanded to sit up and beg. That appeal to something basic in the inner consciousness of an animal cannot be called "instinctive," even for commodity's sake. A taste for the "beautiful" is not an instinct.

UTILIZE AND DESTROY

It should be clear by now that in my approach to the animal world, man—be he "ancient," "medieval," or "modern"— thinks above all of himself. His will for power and the means that he has to exert it open a dual road for him. In a natural environment that he has "anthropized" and modeled to his use, how, and to what point, does he exploit the animal? And how does he eliminate animals when they no longer are of use to him or when he fears them?

The Services of the Beast

One can reasonably acknowledge that the first men who looked at the animal universe saw it as a source of nourishment. As a carnivore—but since when?—the human being needs animal protein, the flesh of mammals, fowl, or fish, for his physical and mental equilibrium. We have already seen their part in medieval alimentation. Although raising animals can have other goals than furnishing things to eat, fishing and courtyard animals served that purpose. It is not excessive to say that without the pig, the herring, and the pullet, the Christian world would have perished. But I have also stressed that despite beliefs that were vague until the eighteenth and nineteenth centuries and that last to today, a certain indifference runs through this domain of alimentation. We are still unsure about exactly what cheeses or what species of fish were consumed; we have to admit, citing archaeological findings, that the traces of bones in the trash heaps vary little from the castle to the cottage, and that the variations from meal to meal often seem determined by taste, which is undefinable, or by aleatory economic contingencies. The notion of regional dishes, like that of a social hierarchy of foods, is imaginary. At best, there is a difference in amount. Moreover, all Christians found themselves equal on "fast days" and during Lent. To be sure, Lent occupies a spot on the calendar when the grain lofts were empty, but it was respected even where there were appetizing reserves. Even the brigands and mercenaries who lived on pillage respected Lent by not killing the livestock and contenting themselves with chickens and eggs. That ritual observance was a basic requirement for salvation. God had created the *espèces maigres*—animals that could be eaten on abstinence days—on the same day of Creation as the others, and his works must be respected.

Only fish seem to have had a purely alimentary role, and fish required seashores, plus salting or smoking. The secondary products that we get from fish today seem unknown. It is not at all sure that such ancient practices as making glue from fish fat or using it to oil amphoras survived the decline of Mediterranean commerce. On the other hand, the exploitation of fowl and captured birds eventually surpassed use of their flesh and their eggs. Feathers and down were used in the home to stuff a pillow, a mattress, or a bedcover, and feathers furnished the scribe and the miniaturist with a pen to write with and a brush to paint with, replacing the reed calamus that had been used throughout the early Middle Ages and even up to the fourteenth century. These aspects of technological change, which at first sight seem small indeed, should not be neglected. The feather, goose feathers in particular, had a strong influence on handwriting, rendering the tracing of letters more supple, the ligatures thinner, even (and perhaps especially) on paper, when it began to replace parchment in the thirteenth century.

Mammals, too, furnished useful things to the household and even to the artisan, such as badger hair for brushes or hog bristles. Obviously skins and furs came first. This time we know much about obtaining and using such items in medieval times. Our symbolic and vaguely Germanic image is that of a man dressed in leather, iron, and fur: a romantic image, to be sure, but not totally unreal. Leaving the iron aside, fur was indeed an important element in both clothing and decor: squirrel, sable, rabbit for cuffs and facings and headgear, while bear, reindeer, and wolf provided "clothing skins" (*peaux vêtues*) for cloaks and blankets. The prices that furs and fur products commanded in the markets of central Europe and the ways in which they were used compete in the account books with those of rare stuffs and jewels. In all centuries, and with the aid of fashion, an "aristocracy of furs " distinguished the wealthy man or the courtier from the common man with his leather vest or the peasant in rough woolens.

That same leather, however, played a role that was both modest and immense, since it was used for gloves, belts, hats, shoes, vests, and shoes; and also for saddles, harnesses, scabbards, water-skins, and purses. Whether as raw hides of tanned leather, the skins of all sorts of animals were used—bovines, sheep, goats, donkeys, and even horses—addition to skins from the hunt or the chase, such as those of deer, wild boars, badgers, otters, beavers, wolves, and foxes. For those of original tastes, there were even exotic skins brought from Africa and Asia such as those of camels and leopards. Tanners and curriers had their workshops at the water's edge so they could clean the skins easily, but also near the *hôtels* of the wealthy, where they could sell their high-quality products, the lightest-colored and most supple leathers. The elite in a ·smelly and unhealthy trade with a generally poor reputation were the parchment workers because the demand for skins to write on grew ceaselessly. It has been suggested that sheep, whose flesh was not held in high esteem, were in great part raised for their skins as well as their wool.

The Middle Ages had no elastics and of course no plastics; cotton appears only near the Mediterranean and not before the late thirteenth century; jute was ignored and linen rare; hemp was rough and silk costly. That left woolens as the basic medieval textiles. This is not the place for a complete exposé on working the fleece of sheep or the organization of the wool trade. It was, to be sure, the only "trade" that was organized and regulated vertically, from the shepherd shearing his flocks to the worker who affixed a seal to the cloth sold in the market hall. Nor is it the place to examine the destiny of the balls of fluff according to whether they came from the *churro* of the Iberian Peninsula or the sheep of the Cotswolds, or to whether they were taken from the legs or the back of the animal. I am not about to offer an economic history of the textile industry. But since relations between man and beast are among my interests, I might recall that wool occupied as great a place in medieval life as wood. The Middle Ages was thus not only the "age" of leather and iron, but also that of wood and wool. Wool was omnipresent in daily life. As the day went by it was worn and mended; the housewife spun it without stopping, even with a child at her breast; it was used to stop up holes in the roof, to cover sleeping family members, and, among the rich, it was hung on the walls as tapestries to conserve heat.

Whether man captured, trained, or raised animals, he removed their flesh, their enveloping skin, their fat, and the various products of their bodies. There were some creatures that may seem modest but were essential—bees—from which he took the fruit of their labors. As we have already seen, although men built bee hives, regulated the bees' production, and respected bees, he did not "raise" them, but rather exploited them. The importance accorded to bees can be seen in the high fines in the early Middle Ages for being caught stealing or destroying a swarm of bees: several thousand derniers, a sum equal to the punishment for the abduction or theft of an ox. The rules (verbal ones, at least) that applied to those who perturbed the peace of God in the eleventh century included the obligation to spare beehives from their violence. Moreover, owners of hives considered it a seigneurial right to levy a tax on the products of the hive. It has long been thought (and some still think) that it was essentially honey that man wanted from the hives, as honey remained the most abundant and the most sought-after source of sugar. Neither sugarcane—which people attempted to adapt and raise on the shores of the Mediterranean in Spain, Sicily, and Italy and managed to do somewhat late and quite modestly, even after the eleventh century—nor the sugar beet and other sweet roots that remained almost unknown, nor the very costly spices such as cinnamon and vanilla, carried to Europe by trade with the East, could satisfy man's need for sweetners. Honey, gathered with the use of techniques that have hardly varied since then, could fill that void. It was consumed in liquid form or hardened into blocks, mixed with wine to produce "divine" but rather bland drinks such as hydromel or hippocras (with the addition of perfumed herbs), or else into a finely strained jelly, *gelée royale*, which was credited with medicinal or aphrodisiac virtues. The court world was so fond of the latter that in the fifteenth century its sale had to be restricted. Thus there has been a tendency to minimize what was, in the final analysis, the base product and the most precious product of the bee's labors: wax. A swarm of ten thousand bees could produce a kilo of wax in a year, or ten times more than the honey it produced. Wax, the "plastic" of the Middle Ages, had a basic use that explains its popularity. It chased away the dark without the smoke of the resin torch, the flickering of logs in the hearth, or the feeble lighting power of the oil lamp. No matter the type of candle—*cierges* for church services or *chandelles* and *luminaires*; *bougies* for everyday use—wax drove away the shadows freighted with fears and the perils that were hidden by the night. Wax accompanied man in his nocturnal anguish and in the joys of festive occasions and processions. It was invaluable when used for waxed writing tablets and for the seals that validated a written act.

All of this exploitation of the animal world cannot be taken for granted, and we do not know whether, in the earliest times of human history, man's first thought was to use dogs to guard cattle, horses for riding, and sheep for shearing. All these animals offer several possibilities. A dog catches game, the horse can pull a weight, and the sheep gives milk. The services rendered by these animals were thus many. It is banal to recall this, for those services remain the same today, but of course with the use of machines. The first of these services was pulling and carrying, which lay in the domain of the "domestic" portion of the animal environment. The horse, the mule, the ox, and the donkey enabled men and things to be moved from one place to another, and they pulled loads or agricultural devices. Each animal, according to its aptitudes, was turned to what it did best. The sure-footed mule was used in difficult terrain; the slow-moving donkey worked the vineyards or carried produce to market; the ox was unrivaled in the fields or for grubbing up trees and roots to make a clearing; the horse was good for all work. The choice was a matter of physical structure; for example, the horse offered steadiness and strength for pulling a cart out of the mud, rapidity when it came to carrying a message, or resistance in combat. When there was a tree stump to be pulled up or a heavy wagon to be moved, it was a job for an ox. If there was a pack to be carried, the donkey would carry it; if a saddle was needed, it would be the mule. This was a question of equipment, and it depended on the bone structure and the nature of the animal, as we have seen. Dogs would be trained for the hunt, as we shall see. Other essential tasks were assigned to the dog: keeping guard, smelling out things, or—a more difficult task—turning the team at the end of the furrow traced by a plow, or guiding a pig as he cleaned up refuse in the courtyard. Finally, and this was true of all domestic animals, their excrement went to fertilize the fields, whether it was cow dung (*bouse*), horse manure, sheep droppings (*crottin*), or *columbine* from the pigeon coop.

Thus quite a few services were demanded of animals. For most of them, this was what they paid for human protection and the fodder that man provided. But man was conscious that these services were not equal in value. In the early centuries of the Middle Ages at least, we can evaluate the relative importance of animals by a hierarchy in the fines levied for harming them (a scale of values that would be quite different today). Harming a pregnant mare cost 1,600 deniers, a stallion a bit less, and a gelding half of that amount. The fine for hurting an ox was set at 2,000 deniers, but a milking cow only one-fourth of that and a sheep one-twentieth. The fine for a pig might be 500 deniers, but harming a cat brought no fine. To be sure, these are only regulatory texts capable of alteration by contingency and custom, but they may offer an indication that throws some light on the last aspect of man's relations with animals that I want to present.

Killing: Man's Job

This heading is deliberately provocative, but I will try to justify it. A skin or meat can only come from a dead animal, and it must die a violent death so that neither is spoiled by disease or time. Must we not also destroy what threatens or merely bothers us, nuisances such as insects, rodents, and carnivorous animals from which man himself, his "domestic" animals, or his goods must be protected? Obviously, one could wait for nature to do the job and help her if need be. In the universe, equilibrium is the rule. When one thing swells up, another immediately destroys it, and the animals do not escape this rule. Men of the Middle Ages noted this daily struggle. The fly eats the plant louse, but the spider kills the fly and will in turn be swallowed by the small rodent, just before a duck snaps it up and then a predator does away with the bird. This "law" of strength led men to amuse themselves with animal combats, a source of gaming spectacles and advantageous bets, and today there are competitions between "queer" cows to see which one will lead the others to alpine pastures, cocks in the village, and even dogs or cats. This is where the trouble lay. To kill a beast in order to eat it might in fact be a necessity, as is true for all living beings, but this need and the act that follows it are not, in principle, imbued with any enjoyment except perhaps that of fulfilling a requirement for survival. This is how beasts behave. But attending a combat between fighting cocks or a repugnant *corrida* involves an undercurrent of cruelty, even of sadism, that it would be difficult, even among avid fans, to cover with the veil of "tradition" (just what tradition?), of "sport" (a rather mortal one), or with the hypocritical pretext that the beast can "defend itself" (which is an ignoble joke). The Church hesitated for a long time. Not killing one's neighbor was a divine injunction or an obvious precaution, but killing another of God's creatures? Probably following ancient custom, the Church remained silent about hunting or capturing wild animals; at the most it used hagiographic tales to contrast Saint Hubert and the stag that was his victim and may have been an incarnation of Jesus, a confrontation that led Hubert to convert. In the Carolingian age, however, some voices were raised—that of Jonas of Orléans, for example—to criticize the pleasures of the hunt, a source of pride and quasi-sexual gratification. But the traditional comparison between force or the royal and seigneurial mission and the imaginary of the hunt limits the effect of such criticism. We also see here evidence of the aristocratic equilibrium that backed up the Church and the Church's care for the comfort of the peasant, to be supported in his progress toward salvation. Besides, the beasts, and in particular the "wild beasts" that were surely inhabited by Satan, had no need to be saved. Bishops hunted, and in the fourteenth century there were manuals of venery in monastic libraries. Moreover, there were so many men who killed one another meaninglessly throughout the centuries that the priests had enough to do trying to stop such floods of blood without worrying about shedding wolves' blood! This was an attitude that hardly varied. If one considers the animal an inferior being, fated to be sacrificed by a human hand, it is not all that wicked to kill it, even when it cannot defend itself. Some went so far as to enjoy doing so, something that an animal never does, as far as we can see. It is true that certain meditative individuals (for example, Albertus Magnus in the early thirteenth century) represent a deep current in medieval thought that held that killing for pleasure is not "noble." The proof of this was that the king of the animals, the "noble" lion in the *Roman de Renart*, spares his victims, in a sign of a magnanimity that places him above the other animals.

Obviously, the destruction of an entire animal species does not necessarily involve hatred and violence. Bouts of malaria such as the ones that carried away Emperor Otto III, King Philip Augustus, and the poet Dante were underhanded attacks that it was considered perfectly acceptable to turn aside or combat. Swamps and marshes were drained, and at times the anopheles mosquito was also smoked out. Protection against fleas involved washing the skin with an herbal decoction, and ships were required to wait for forty days offshore so that vermin would die. Locusts were more formidable. If a cloud of them landed on a field or covered an entire terrain (they could be in the millions, enough to blot out the sun), it was a total disaster, and eating them would be only a meager consolation. They had to be chased away by making an enormous amount of rhythmic noise, whether the neighbors liked it or not. In reality, the last massive attack of locusts in western Europe was noted in 873. Though there have been none since then—perhaps because climatic or biotic conditions have moved them farther to the south, toward the subtropical zones where they are still a problem in spite of our modern defenses—it is still said that they tend to move north.

And then there is the hunt. The passions that hunting arouses in our own times justify looking at the situation in the centuries of the Middle Ages. I shall leave aside the beats that were organized after wild boars or wolves had attacked flocks and herds or damaged cultivated fields. As is true in all times, these required public intervention: a sizable gathering of men, dogs, and horses; the establishment of a plan for how to conduct the beat; and a technique for killing the prey, a delicate question because, except for the bear, who lived in isolation, the predators might be present in large numbers. This task was related to the general interest, and it involved neither joy nor hatred. It was a simple question of cleaning out an uncultivated area. Man came first; too bad for the beasts. In this manner a number of species were nearly eliminated between the twelfth and the eighteenth centuries—wolves, lynx, bears, aurochs, and European bison—but foxes, rodents, and cervidae are still holding their own.

Hunting by an individual or a small group is another story. Today our contemporaries who hunt do not expect to complement their diet; they are not attracted by the risk; they do not think they are carrying out an "ecological" good deed. In France, at any rate, hunters often (quite wrongly) invoke "tradition" or a "revolutionary conquest," referring to the abolition of a seigneurial monopoly that dated from 1533, but they forget that in the Middle Ages there was no such thing. Or else they talk (with more justification) of the conviviality of the sport of hunting, omitting to mention, either sincerely or deliberately, a taste for killing that inhabits the soul of man—unfortunately, and as I have said some twenty times. In the centuries of the Middle Ages the situation was completely different, even if we find the same appetite for gratuitous violence. At that time the hunt was a pillar of society, and literature staggers under the weight of the miracle tales, romances, poems, chronicles, manuals—and trials—in which hunting is prominently featured. Thanks also to iconography and archaeology, we know almost more about the hunt than we do about commerce. A veritable passion among the aristocracy but also among the common run of men, hunting had causes that remained invariable for the span of a thousand years. The first thing to be said about it is that a search for meat, which probably lies at the origin of the hunt, does not seem to have been a prime motivation. Excavations have shown that the bones of wild animals—deer or birds—account for less than 8 percent of the meat consumed, a figure that hardly varies from the castle to the cottage. Most of these bones point to birds, cervidae, rodents, omnivores in particular, as carnivores were thought to be inedible. We have long heard that the hunt was a sporting exercise that prepared men for war, and riding over difficult terrain, dispatching a wild boar with a knife or a bear with a spear might in fact seem a test of endurance, courage, and skill. But this pertained only to the fighting aristocracy, and there is quite a distance between encircling a pack of wolves and a heavy cavalry charge. The result is that today's scholars emphasize the "relaxation" and the "sporting" nature of the hunt, which permitted even the presence of women. Hunting was thus a way to flee, collectively, the boredom of the rooms of the castle or the cramped confines of the cottage to inhale the odors of the beasts and of the woods; to get free of the constraints and tasks of daily life; and to frequent, in good company, the unknown or the unexpected—all of which, and to our own day, gives hunting its role as a sporting pastime.

This is not all, however. It does not explain either the warlike equipment of our modern hunters or the determination shown by the villagers of those days to drag the corpses of their prey through the village. There is in hunting a dimension of violence satisfied, of the realization of domination over wild nature and over the animal. Hunting is a mark of superiority that distinguishes the chief: the head of the family, the clan, or the state. All the kings hunted and had to hunt. Those who refused to do so, as did Charles V and Louis XI in France, got bad press. Domination and, even beyond that, the ceremonial rite of virility find expression in the hunt. And when this psychological pleasure was reserved (in principle) to those who paid for it—the rich and noble, by the grace of Louis XI in 1468, then of Francis I in 1533—the peasant remained determinedly faithful to the joys of poaching.

Hunting techniques do not interest us here except for the ways in which they were profoundly different from our own, where the use of firearms has eliminated the need for tracking skills, along with any risk. Medieval texts speak of two sorts of hunt, each with categories that regard men, beasts, and equipment. First came the hunt for *la grosse bête*: meat-eaters, wild boars, bear, large cervidae, which were hunted by lords and by teams with side arms, chiefly knives and swords. Next came hunting *la petite bête*: rabbits, small birds, lesser meat-eaters, or roe deer, for which the peasant used ruses and bait. The animals could also be induced to move into the sandy *garenne* or into bushy areas, where hunters waited with nets, snares, or traps containing bird lime, possibly with small bows capable of shooting some twenty meters at the most. Or else one could hunt cervidae or wild boars in a more "noble" fashion, *à force* or *à courre*, with the aid of dogs, knives, and swords. This was a tiring and problematic sort of hunt but it was held in high esteem. There was also a third type of hunt, which hardly exists today, but that was considered the most distinguished and "noble": hawking, or *la chasse au vol*, in which women participated. It was probably a practice imported from the East in which small birds of prey—falcons, sparrow hawks, gerfalcons, and vultures—were trained to locate prey and pin it to the ground until the dogs or men arrived. Hunting manuals, such as those redacted in the mid-thirteenth century by Emperor Frederick II or, a hundred years later, by Gaston Phoebus, the count of Foix, make much of this form of hunting. It was very costly, as the birds of prey were rare and commanded high prices; very difficult, as training could only be done by tested specialists who acquired renown and power; very convivial as well, for the bird of prey was carried to the hunt by the women; and very relaxing, as the bird obeyed voice commands and gestures and responded to the bait prepared to keep him from tearing his victim to pieces.

Hunting was thus an essential element in medieval life in all periods. The notion, so familiar to us, of the opening of the hunting season appeared only after the surfaces large enough to support the hunt—dunes, woods, or maquis—had been reduced, hence in the early fifteenth century in France and Spain, by royal order, by municipal decision in Italy, and much later in Germanic lands, where the ritual dimension of the hunt was stronger. This occurred at the same time that the king, the Church, and the lords, who were the owners of the forests and were already concerned with the diminution of woods cleared to grow grain or by the strong increase in privileges of access to the woods accorded to or sold to villagers, moved to close off wooded areas in order to reserve both hunting and cutting trees to themselves. Wooded areas, which had been *saltus* open to all, *res nullius* belonging to no one, and *foresta* beyond all laws, then became prohibited and fenced in. We have difficulty perceiving the effect this had on the fauna, however.

We cannot leave the domain of animal death without stopping briefly at fish and fishing. It will be brief as we know little or nothing about the subject. I have spoken above of the sea as a world of merchants more than of fishermen, who formed an original human group as closed off from others as they are from historians. There are allusions to Frisian ships in the early Middle Ages and to the sale of smoked or salted herring, even far inland, but this is all. In reality, it was freshwater fishing for carp, pike, and gudgeon in lakes, rivers, and mill ponds that accounted for most fishing. Iconography is fairly rich in depictions of nets, bow nets, and fixed or mobile fishing poles. Documentation is superabundant, however, in the domain of legal procedures involving interminable quarrels over fishing spots, the nature of the equipment used, and the sums involved in seigneurial taxes. As the monastic communities consumed no meat, it was the monks, fish eaters and distributors of alms, who reigned over fishing rights in fishing preserves, millponds, and streams. This means that monastic archives abound in quarrels between one abbey and another, but also in information about peasant communities suspected (often with reason) of troubling the raising of fry, fishing out a pond, or using nets with too fine a web. In France, Saint Louis was moved to fix rules for fishing seasons and equipment in a decree of 1259. With what success? Is the absence of documentation a sign of an existential void? Or did this type of activity produce nothing but appeals to tradition and oral arguments? Fish play hardly any role in medieval literature, and there seems to have been general indifference regarding aquatic species and their behavior. Are we the ones who are wrong?

A Contrasting Balance Sheet

At the end of this long consideration of the animal world that surrounds that of man, can we draw up a balance sheet of the contacts between the two? For obvious reasons, it would have to be based on the observations made by man himself, about what he has perceived as an effect of animal activity on himself or, and especially, about what he has noticed as the result of his own activities regarding the beasts. Unfortunately, the latter domain has left only passive evidence; moreover, the judgment of men in the Middle Ages was blinded by their belief in the full will and the essential knowledge that the Divinity has of his Creation. This means that we have to rely on deduction rather than reason.

Permanent contact with the world that man exploits for what it gives him or for what he takes from it, in materials or in services, has contributed to shaping (or at least reinforcing) within human society two traits that are regularly attributed to the Middle Ages. The first of these is the asserted superiority of the male sex. Because it is he who hunts, fishes, works the soil, trains the animals, and defends the home site, the male found domination in his contact with beasts. Reputed (probably wrongly) to be more fearful and weaker, the woman placed herself under his control, to the point of passing, here and there, for yet another inferior creature, hence for a "beast." The Church is silent on the question. Did it not exclude woman, since the Fall reputed to be accessible to temptation by the animal, from the service of God? In the extreme case of crimes of sexual bestiality, only men were charged. Women may have succumbed as well, but the very thought was so monstrous and stupefying that it could only be taken as an animal act, which, precisely, was not to be talked about. Would it not be useful, today when we have gone so far along many roads, to observe the behavior of animals, male and female, especially the "companion" animals: the dog, the cat, the horse, or, rather, the bitch, the female cat, and the mare? It is a question to be thought about, even if it is not within my purview. Still, if the texts have little to offer, iconography deserves more attention than it has been accorded. Might not how an animal is looked at or placed at the side of the master or mistress give some indication that the painter or the miniaturist perceived something?

The second effect regards human society as a whole, in particular in its hierarchical social structure. Control over animals indicated rank and placed the individual. The horseman physically dominated the pedestrian, not only in combat, but also on the roads for commerce or pilgrimage. A man who hunted with a pack of dogs, beaters, and huntsmen was normally the master, at least of the forest, for the abundance or the sort of his quarry was not directly involved. The owner of a costly pigeon coop would be alone among his fellow peasants in having access to the fine fertilizer that allowed him to load his table with the fruits or choice vegetables that the others could not obtain from poorer soil. And wealth was quite naturally counted in falcons, in horses, or in plowing teams. As for the economic advantage for those who exploited the animal world, it is useless to reiterate the place that animals procured for their owners in daily life.

The other side of the mirror is duller. Has man marked the animal world with his authority? Yes, certainly, but rather over the long time span than during the relatively brief thousand years of the Middle Ages. To be sure, some species disappeared, the victims of hunters or of the elimination of their habitats. It can be claimed, however, that this was actually the result of changes in the zoological equilibrium of the world. At times man's actions might even be considered positive. The draining of marshlands and the retreat of the woods were a rude blow to blood-sucking mosquitos; improved plowing practices deeply aerated the soil, thus lowering the number of earthworms and June bug larvae; control of bee swarms deprived the bears of their favorite food; moving swine from the woods back to the barn broke their physiological connections with wild boars. But natural compensations usually followed such actions, and not always in a positive direction. The struggle against rapacious birds profited the rodents; the withdrawal of the bear and the wolf benefited wild boars, and the disappearance of the heron encouraged a growth in the river insect population; the war declared against snakes opened the way for rats to invade grain storage areas. On the whole, the taste for gain and pillage that resulted from these changes perturbed the division of the animals' alimentary reserves, thus modifying the ecosystem. Among many cases, one of the most studied (if not the most important one) is that of sheep. Observations founded on written documentation or on archaeology are clear. Speculation in wool set off, in 1250 in England and a bit later on the continent, an irresistible increase in flocks. The lords and the monasteries gave up growing grains to turn to raising sheep "whose feet change the sand into gold," as it was said at the time, and they set up barriers around the abandoned plowed fields, given over to grass, thus forming the typical "English countryside." The time of the "enclosure" movement in England corresponded to the fourteenth-century conversion of the Spanish meseta into vast domains of the "great" and the military orders, united in an association, the Mesta, so as to extract maximum profits. In both cases, the systems for collective efforts to improve the soil and the customary law that formed the economic base of village groups and the cement to hold them together were destroyed. In Spain this was the beginning of a ruin that is still unremedied; in England the peasants, divided and impoverished, flocked to the cities as cheap manpower, which helped to create the nascent industrial enterprises of the British Isles. The economic and commercial superiority of England of the eighteenth and nineteenth centuries over the rest of Europe has few other explanations.

It remains to be seen whether, beyond these staggering blows to animal behavior, man also managed to modify animal physiology. I have already alluded to cross-breeding among bovine species, the introduction of exotic breeds of horses, and a notable change in the external appearance in swine, but we have no scientific certitude that there was any sort of policy for the improvement of strains of livestock or animal behavior. In contrast, archaeozoology poses new problems, which remain open. For example, excavations have produced many bone samples that show that the height at shoulder level of horses, cattle, and even sheep underwent astonishing variations. These measurements, comparable to their modern equivalents at the end of antiquity, brusquely declined between the third and the ninth centuries and seem to show a clear return to earlier figures only after then. Was this a question of the biotic environment in general? Of differences in types of fodder or of the use of such animals? Of the introduction of new species? The importance, but also the contradictions, of these data are obvious, but researchers have not yet come to a conclusion about them.

It is time to summarize, and it will be a pessimistic assessment, as can be suspected. As long as man has left traces of his activity, beginning 15,000 or 29,000 years ago and most notably during the thousand years of the Middle Ages, he has not been able to domesticate or even reduce to his mercy any more animal species than his Neolithic ancestors. It has even been suggested, in jest, that it was the cat who domesticated man. Indisputably, human beings have penetrated animal groups and have utilized, at times even altered or modified, certain fauna. But which? Only the fauna that frequented the spaces where man's life unfolded, and no others. Fish are better left undiscussed; of the insects who ignore man or live at his expense, there was only the bee; for the world of the air, the sparrow hawk and his like. This leaves a handful of mammals—ten or so—that man exploited, a hundred others that escaped his control, many of which lived close to him and laughed at his pretensions, like the rats who reigned under his feet.

In the face of the vegetable world, the powerful indifference of which continues to dominate man, and in the face of the animal world, which ignores him, man is actually a powerless and marginal being. I have stressed his weaknesses from the start. The doctors of law and the supporters of Faith indeed declared that God had made man the master of Creation. This may have to be understood in a figurative sense. Lamentably weak in his dealings with the other living beings, does man perhaps dominate them by his soul and his mind? Perhaps. This remains to be seen.

— PART TWO —

MAN IN HIMSELF

Up to this point it is the bodies and the actions of the people of the Middle Ages that I have attempted to depict, their daily life and their attitudes in the face of a nature that dominated them or trifled with them. I have sought out the purely material—some would even say "materialistic"—aspects in all of this. I know just as well as anyone how biased this approach is. My sources of information are profoundly marked by their "aristocratic" origin—even those that come from archaeology—which means that more often than I would have liked, I have had to extend to the "common people" what is known of the "higher" echelons of society: the monks, the nobles, the bourgeoisie, and the merchants whom I did not want to talk about so as to avoid the snags of "social and economic" history. Within the modest jousting ground that I have occupied, I am also aware of how much of our own twenty-first-century vision I have had to include. Our conception of passing time; the space we abandon to the machine that alienates us; and even our vital needs are not, or are no longer, those of a peasant of the thirteenth century. If the human being remains the same, his mental attitude has changed since those distant times, and I have often had to appeal to the unknowable to define a rite or an "irrational" act.

Here I stand, in fact, at the edge of another poorly illuminated and vast domain, that of mental "superstructures," as the aging Marx would have said. I feel ill at ease here, and intend to advance only with prudence. First, because I remain more persuaded of the role of horseshoes than of that of the *Summa* of Thomas Aquinas in the march of humanity; next, because, competent or not, I am now confronted with the enigma that I sketched—or perhaps that I eluded—in introducing my remarks to the first half of this volume. Man is certainly not the most beautiful success of Creation, as I hope the first flower the skeptic encounters will persuade him. Still, man thinks, he projects his thoughts into the future, and he expresses himself certainly much better than any other animated being. In our age of moral contestation, this problem of human "superiority" divides the thinkers, and even goes so far as to set them against one another in partisan ranks. The "creationists," as they are called in America, permit no discussion that might offer the slightest challenge to the idea of a unique will, an "intelligent design" originating in the Supreme Being. This view was nearly undisputed in the Middle Ages, and Saint Paul, his standard held aloft by the divine Word, implanted it in Christians. For the modern-day "evolutionists," man is, to the contrary, the result of successive modifications, some would say "improvements" taking place from the jellyfish to the illustrious Darwin, the august father of this long-range overall view, which quite obviously would have been incomprehensible to anyone in the Middle Ages. And now the ethnologists and the paleontologists have shaken up these evolutionary theories. For them, man has only recently detached himself, perhaps as a result of some happy chance, from the main line of the hominids, and the larger primates—chimpanzees, bonobos, orangutans, and others—display our physiological characteristics nearly intact. They are not our ancestors but our brothers.

I claim no competence that would permit me to raise my voice in this concert. What I have had to say thus far leaves the reader the choice between the finger of God as he is depicted on the ceiling of the Sistine Chapel and the DNA of a Gabon gorilla. Let us attempt, however, to approach that other face of humanity, without letting ourselves be discouraged by the thick cloud of a priori statements, stereotypes, and things left unsaid that dogmas and habits, the law and custom, have thrown over the souls and the brains of those times.

5

MAN IN HIMSELF

"Man is a sociable animal," Seneca states, with little regard for his own application of this postulate. All friends of man attempted to go him one better. Mutual aid, common thoughts, polite gestures, friendships, and groups, everything in daily life throughout the world, it seems, bears witness to the force of group sentiments, even to "gregarious" and docile sentiments. Only "it seems," however. There are many regions of the globe—and this may be even more true of the so-called developed ones like our own—in which people do not salute the passerby or "hold the door" for him; where an accident in the street arouses only short-lived curiosity; where an apartment dweller knows nothing about his neighbor; where calumny is accompanied by servility—without saying more than is necessary about the strange alliance of a "like everyone else" spirit and a fierce individualism channeled today by the two most widespread media, television and the portable telephone! Besides, defending his territory is not a behavior exclusive to man. All we need do is watch the behavior of two dogs who find themselves suddenly face-to-face. First there is a spontaneous show of aggression, then a careful approach and a sexual reconnaissance, two preliminary steps that we pretend to have surpassed or have become accustomed to ignoring. The schema is the same, however. Let us search for it in the age that interests us here.

LIVING IN A GROUP

The vocabulary of our own century teems with "collective" terms. We have sects, parties, societies, syndicates, clubs, and so forth. Our vocabulary is almost as rich when it comes to describing isolation, marginalization, exclusion, and solitude. The linguistic situation was totally different in the Middle Ages. A man alone was a lost man. There was no word to designate him, or else such words have changed meaning. The Greek *monos* (alone) gave us "monk," but monks lived with other monks; the Latin *solus* appears only as a qualifier applied to many nouns; the "hermit" (Greek: *eremos*) in the "desert" or the voluntary recluse in his urban cell are but pious examples of the dispossession of the self in prayers. There was no word but *homo* to bring the isolated individual out of his nothingness, and without an adjective, that word meant nothing. Naturally, the old maid, the exile, the leper, and the dying were alone, but that was because they were or were about to be excluded from the social group. They did not choose to live without support, and that support—moral or otherwise—and that consolation in misfortune would come to them only in good time, for God is watching even if men fail to act. In the secular world, those who chose the narrow path of voluntary isolation were only a handful of individuals who were proud, disgusted with a hateful present, and adept at scorning the world (*contemptus mundi*). The road they followed normally led them to suicide or at least to ignominy. They were the "desperate." How many of them were there? The Church refused to count them and even to speak about them: they were considered no longer in the ranks of the Lord; they had abandoned their souls to Satan; they were no longer human. But the others? All those who lived in a group? First we need to know why and how.

Why Come Together?

There are many reasons for coming together to live, even above and beyond that of the "fire," the "hearth," of which I have already spoken. Such reasons are not "natural" but were acquired in the course of all the accumulated centuries, those of the Middle Ages and our own. I shall enumerate the ones that were surest at that time, but first I need to define a focus. The medieval world was dominated, in all of its attitudes, by a state of mind of which we know only snatches. In the first place, people were acutely aware of duration, of the inevitable accumulation of the centuries, of a linear and implacable march toward the "end of time" and toward Judgment. This may have been the basis for the age's lively interest in works of "history." That eschatological expectation ruled out any rupture of destiny. Parables and even representations of the wheel of Fortune, turning perpetually, showed the powerful being thrown down, then raised back up to honors. That turning wheel was the symbol of the uselessness of man's hope to liberate himself from his destiny. Second, the people of modest fortune who interest us here would not have dreamed of combating the divine plan, denying the past, or puffing themselves up with vain pride. In the twelfth century Bernard of Chartres stated: "We are like dwarfs upon the shoulders of giants; and so able to see more and see farther than the ancients." That homage to the "ancients" is far from our own puerile self-satisfaction. The two veils with which altruism covered itself were thicker than they are today, but they permit a glimpse of why medieval people had to cling to one another in the face of nature or chance.

None of those motivations is exceptional. Only their color or intensity varies from those centuries to our own. The first of them belongs to the domain of the heart and the mind. It is mutual aid, the charitable impulse, and generosity that push men into one another's arms. We see this as a "gratuitous" gesture, simple evidence of our idea of the good. I fear that such an impulse was more constraining in the Middle Ages. Failing to act in accordance with it would, in fact, seriously alter the spirit of the Creator's salvation and his good will. Of the seven "capital sins" with which preachers ceaselessly threatened the fearful faithful after 1250 or 1270, four—envy, sloth, greed, and pride—were considered insuperable barriers to charity, and "giving alms" (more often to monks rather than to a poor person or a neighbor) was, it seems to me, both in the abstract and in the spirit of the times, much more an insurance payment than a gift from the heart. We will find impulses closer to our own in forms of cohesion that imply consideration of others. Medieval terms in this domain were freighted with precise meanings. Politesse, civility, and urbanity are words constructed on and for the city, the Greek *polis* and the Roman *civitas* and *urbs*. As for courtesy, which has more of a country air about it, the *curtis* that underlies it is uniquely that of the great and the wealthy. Did the common run of people not practice such virtues in the fields? Did the peasant, indifferent to the city, know only rusticity, paganism, and *vilenie* (which means meanness but derives from "villein"), all three of them words attached to the soil? Yes, if we believe the portraits that the writers and swordsmen made of the country people; no, if we take the trouble to scrutinize the accounts of the learned for acts benefiting others, even if they limit themselves to a devouring curiosity for everything that the neighbor, the pilgrim, or even the Jew passing through might say or invent.

The contacts established by a common progress on the road to salvation, by a faith shared by all, and by beliefs or myths that the parish priest did not even have to comment on in his sermons produced a unity of the faithful that went far beyond strictly Christian values and led to (or came from—one might dispute the matter) a spirit of conservatism, one might even say immobilism, that corresponds to nothing we know today. Because the "common good" was supposed to carry the day over private interests, because that faith was not debatable, because the order of the world was subject to the will of God, any change would alter that equilibrium. *Malae sunt novae consuetudines*, all novelties are the symbols of Evil, every chosen thought (Greek: *heresis*) inspired by Satan. *Quieta non overe*: "Do not touch what has been established," Sallust admonished. This explains why, given this ultrasensitive consensus, the effects of a technological or economic evolution, the audacities of a free thought, or the brutal measures of an "enlightened" ruler were systematically condemned, even if they eventually were accepted. After 1220 or 1270, entire segments of that armor of common "certitudes" were swept away, but even at that moment, Frederick II was excommunicated, Thomas Aquinas was disavowed, and Saint Francis barely escaped being burned at the stake. As for the avowed "heretics" or the discovered sorcerers, their chances were slim. Naturally, in the fourteenth century, the *via moderna* opened up new horizons, and soon those who clung to the old customs were thought "gothic" or "barbarous," as some petulant Italians of the pre-Renaissance stated.

Less persuasive zeal is needed if we pass to the material domain, for in that context, life in a group is an evidence and a necessity. Even if I avoid painting a picture of the economy in general, as I have done thus far, it is a simple banality to recall the point at which working the land, organizing exchanges, the various stages of artisan work, and even the activities connected with war or with thought can be conceived of only as a team effort including family members, neighbors, or people of the same level of society. The use of tools in common, mutual aid in the face of nature or the animal world, agreement among men for guarding the herds and flocks or for assuring the watch in the city were imperious necessities. Naturally, a great gulf would open up before me if I took on the task of distinguishing between nuances. Working the fields implied more work in common than a vineyard; wool demanded different efforts in its various stages of preparation; and the same could be said of commerce, the school, or the veterinarian's job. At this point all the effects of a hierarchy of work make their appearance, up to the highest levels of power. This is not my intent. I shall limit myself to repeating that all these men and women were linked by work, just as they were by faith. Moreover, there was no plot of land in which man had no interest, no ground was *res nulla* or *res nullius*.

All land was claimed, if only by the tax man; all land had a purpose, even just that of free pasturage. Historians devote more and more attention to studying problems of the habitat, in the city or in the country, and I shall return to the topic. But all agree that taking possession of the soil, establishing or redistributing parcels of land or urban blocks were tasks for a group, which might be familial or clan-based, spontaneous or directed. In all instances, this implantation led to common residence, that of *manants* (from the Latin *manere*, to live, stay), and included pastoral forms as well.

All of the elements I have just evoked are active and more or less voluntary manifestations of grouping together. Its other face is passive, even negative, and may creep in under the guise of a positive act: fear. People were afraid, and they gathered together to conjure away that fear. All culture, even all civilization, is a struggle against fear—a struggle to guard oneself from danger from any quarter, from hunger, and from pain—and against dread of the night, which was "horrific" and the lair of treason or violence. These sentiments belong to prehistory, but the animal world knows them too. The human species is different from other species in that only among humans does fear take on a metaphysical dimension. Fear is more than a sudden fright or rush of adrenaline; it is an anguish in the soul, and medieval times went through a good deal of it. The fear of death was not only an apprehension of the end of life; for man, it was also fear that salvation was compromised. Sins committed—those of sex, of blood, or of money—were not just inconvenient strayings that could be corrected; they were an unredeemable insult to the work of the Creator; the night was not just a dangerous moment to get through, it was when God and the chthonian forces manifested themselves and fought. In a heavy atmosphere inhabited by both the good will and the wrath of the Supreme Being, there were some defensive attitudes, however. No "freethinkers," to be sure, and hardly any sceptics, but many grimaces that hid fear under the cover of irony, and some provocative prowess, laughter, or exaggerated tears. It was this mixture of fears and unthinking joys, those reactions "like those of a child," as Huizinga said, that gave the medieval age its "freshness" and its "natural" quality. Over a span of a thousand years there were obviously nuances that marked the passing centuries according to the clemency of the times, physiological factors, and the religious or political climate. Here iconography is queen, and we can see the contrast between the fearful faces with bulging eyes of the Roman age to the smile of Reims, before returning to the terror-stricken grimaces and deathly grins of the fifteenth century.

How to Assemble?

Imagine a group of men searching for a place to settle durably. They come from an unfertile land or an overpeopled city, or else they are abandoning nomadism or perhaps want to extend the space under their control. We are in Europe in the Neolithic age, during "ancient" times, in the Middle Ages, or even in our own day. The image is always the same, and the first acts are always identical. The ground in the chosen area is freed of brush, which is burned; large stones are removed; and the rodents and especially the reptiles are chased away. When today's colonist does this, he thinks he is simply accomplishing a useful piece of work. He no longer knows that he has put his mark on the forces of nature that formerly dominated that land, erased any eventual traces of an earlier occupation by others, and conquered the forces of Evil of which the serpent is the emblem. The spirit, the "genius" of the place, is thus appeased and conquered. All that is left to do is to render to that spirit the homage that is its due. Among the Celts and the Germans, this meant raising up a stone, a *pierre levée*; in Greco-Roman lands, it meant tracing a ditch bordered by a slope; Christians raised a cross; today it might be putting up a radio tower.

Unless there was an arbitrary plan backed by some powerful person, for example to create a "reserve" for a vanquished population or for prisoners (the Romans were past masters at this), the choice of the place to live responded to very simple requirements: land that was known to be good and healthy, such as the *curtes* of the deserted Greco-Roman domains; a site that provided the possibility of refuge, such as the "perched villages" of southern France; a crossroads of frequented and useful itineraries, for example, at the confluence of rivers; a favorable microclimate such as a sunny slope in the Alps or on the back side of ocean dunes. The initial structure of country agglomerations was strongly marked by the initial choice of a locality. The *castro* in Provence or Italy, the Gascon *castelnau*, the *puech* in Auvergne, the Frisian *terpen*, the *bourgs* of Charente were huddled on a hill; the *rupts* in Lorraine and the *villers* of Picardie were clustered buildings in the middle of a flat plain; the *longue rue* and the *ville neuve*, as their names indicate, were new towns set out along a main street with branching, sometimes perpendicular side streets bearing the mark of conquest or an authoritarian creation. All settlements conserved the mark of a gathering of men, spontaneous or not, and formed an important link in the history of country areas in Europe. Rather than the Italian term *incastellamento*, which insists too strongly on the place and the role of the castle, or *castellum*, in this movement, I prefer the term "encellment," which is not particularly euphonic, but has the advantage of insisting on the creation of central organs for grouping people into a whole. That "whole" could be dispersed in hamlets, but these remained included within a group of lands and an ensemble of common rights and obligations. This is why I think that at this point, but only at this point, we can speak of a "village" in the full sense of the term, either tightly unified, distended, or "broken apart." This problem quite rightly concerns medieval historians, because it involves trying to discern the origins of the various aspects of the phenomenon. Is what we see the result of the will of a master, the effect of new clan or even conjugal structures, or interests of the moment within a shifting demographic or economic conjuncture? The successive phases of this morphogenesis are also important. Into what slice of time should that *congregatio hominum*, that grouping of men that remained valid until the late nineteenth century, be fitted? In my opinion, there was a fairly brutal shift in the decades surrounding the famous "year one thousand"—say, in 925–1075—and to which that event contributed. Others have other opinions, but this is a question for specialists.

If I have not spoken of the cities in this connection, even though they have been an object of admiration for our contemporaries since Augustin Thierry, especially in light of the striking desertion of rural areas in our own time, it is, first, because I maintain that, in the time period that I am surveying (but less and less, I admit), cities were secondary, and the time of the priors of Florence or elsewhere was only occasionally that of "people of the Middle Ages." We are victims of our sources! Next because, in the domain about which I am speaking at the moment, I think that the "city" was born and grew in exactly the same ways as the ones that the village followed. Even in the Mediterranean zones known for their urban density and the importance of citizen power, the phenomenon was the same. Athens was a defensive acropolis, like Rome with its Palatine of Romulus's day; Marseille was nothing but a good harbor in which to anchor, Lyon a remarkable site of the confluence two rivers. Later or farther to the north, Venice was simply a survival archipelago, Madrid and Aigues-Mortes were artificial creations, and even Paris was only a basin of river confluences. Later development had many causes, but these are outside of my purview and were the same as the ones that changed villages.

Let us return, then, to the founders or the new occupants. The site, chosen and marked with a sign of appropriation, took on life only at the end of several stages, about which historians quarrel. In my eyes their order is a matter of simple logic and can be easily grasped, but counterexamples are many. The first step was enclosure, not only for defense, but perhaps even more to assert a right over what would be built or what the agglomeration would depend on, locations of exchange to be defended, or nearby lands to be isolated. Walls with watchtowers and guarded gates would be built, made of tree trunks, rubble stones, or cut quarry stone, depending on the materials available and local techniques. This was of course the case of habitats raised to the dignity of "city," but in the countryside there are many similar examples, both toward the south of Europe and in its Slavic center. How many "cyclopean" walls there are, "Roman" gates, and "feudal" towers to arouse the fervor of tourists! If there were no walls, the village would be surrounded by a palissade, a *tour de ville* or a Germanic *Etter* decorated with crosses, a custom revitalized by the Catholic reconquest of the nineteenth century. The most important element was the ditch or moat, or a series of them if the city had grown in size at a later time. When the village "exploded" or when the city developed what lay "outside" the fortified center, there were *faubourgs* (from the Latin *foris*, "outside"), and the city officials drew marks on the ground or set out stones or crosses to mark the limits of the zone over which the city's justice and law extended—the *ban* of the built-up community. There is a rich vocabulary pertaining to the areas near cities. Romance languages spoke of the *pourpris* (from the Latin, *porprendere*, "to occupy), *plessis* or *plouy* (from a probable Celtic word, *ploicum*, which meant "enclosure"), *pourchainte* (the space on which one could still pursue and seize a criminal), or, more simply, a *banlieu*, the zone of one or more leagues from the walls (usually five or seven) in which local law pertained. All of this obviously implies, as does the division of land plots, houses, and farmlands, a mastery of surveying procedures, to which I shall return. We have a number of ancient treatises and later copies regarding the tools necessary for such operations, and here archaeology and iconography are sure aids.

After the walls came the name. What may seem to us obvious thanks to daily acquaintance was not quite so clear in medieval times. The provenance of a toponym, or a later substitute for it, reveals notions of capital importance, in particular regarding the founders' motivations. The founders might have been content with a chance occurrence and named their settlement "there, where there is" a bridge, a ford, or a hill (*briva*, *rito*, *dunum* in the Celtic world), or even for some vague indication of topography. It has been said that, farther to the east, "Istanbul" is not a deformation of the ancient "Constantinople," but simply a contraction of the Greek phrase *eis ten polin*, or "toward the city." How many localities in France are named "Longueville," "Pierrepont," "Chaumont" and the like! At the level of more populated centers, the cities in particular, founders opted for the name of the people or the tribe for which it served as a center; at times the Romans added to these the name of the military unit garrisoned there. In France many cities recall this origin: Limoges, Arras, Metz, and a hundred others, of which Paris is the prime example. The search is even more fertile regarding place names that reflect the name of the master of the territory, perhaps the founder or the group that lived under his wing. Thus we have many places in ancient Gaul in which the -iacum that indicates appropriation is combined with the name of a man, giving the locality a name ending in "-y," "-ac," "-ieu," and more. Moreover, the centuries of the Middle Ages saw the rise of original appellations or changes of name to toponyms that placed the locality under the patronage of a saintly personage (called "Dom" or dominus until the eighth century rather than "Saint," sanctus, which came later). If I were to yield to a more detailed approach, I would have to pause over this sometimes deceptive access road, which would take me away from my topic. Let me just say that all of these names—geographic, anthroponymical, and collective—exemplify men's most powerful attachments to their habitat.

That attachment was also sacred, the third stage in bringing a life environment into being. Whether it was the initial enclosure around which the founding group settled or a creation imposed by contact with the unknowable, a spiritual element was needed at the center of the human group, even if it was a simple storage place for goods, a merchant portus, for example. This enclosure was the place in which the divine found expression. It could be no more than the cemetery, the atrium that offered asylum and peace and about which I have already spoken. In this case it was the dead who fixed the living in one place. But the sacred enclosure sheltered the images of the gods (or of the emperor), and later that of the one God. When that happened the Greco-Latin naos and the nemeto of the Celts became the Christian sacrarium where relics were kept and where the principal sanctuary of the group of the faithful would be built. This was where pilgrimage roads ended and where processions or stations of the cross began. A patron saint kept watch over it and gave his (or her) name to the parish center, though not necessarily to the habitat as a whole. These patron saints were Christ, the Virgin Mary, an apostle, a martyr, a propagator of the faith, or any other personage, even a pagan whitewashed as a venerable saint by popular acclaim. This often had a curious effect, the pursuit of which would take us too far astray. The patron saint reached beyond the city walls, his name winning over the nearby villages or suburbs, at times as simple fragments of a larger group of dispersed men. This created networks and upheld connections that were no longer sacred but economic. This phenomenon, called centrality, is always late and at times artificial, but it interests today's medievalists who are fond of "systems."

Since we have arrived at this point, I might launch into a history of the evolution of the habitat, if only to destroy the idea of the "immutable serenity of the countryside," the "eternal village," or the "primacy of the city," foolish statements often sagely repeated, but the insanity of which shines before our eyes. But this would be, once again, to be tempted by a socioeconomic exposition that lies beyond the scope of the present book. I shall keep to a few observations that seem to me sufficient to light the way. In the first place, these men did not stay in one place. Archaeology (and not only archaeology) shows that throughout the first five centuries of the Middle Ages, say, through the Carolingian age, the inhabited sites, necropoli, and routes were utilized only from one hundred to two hundred years in the same locations, and when, around 1200 or 1250, we can compare fragmentary lists of men from one generation to another, we see a veritable "brownian movement," as Marc Bloch put it, in both the city and the countryside. People and artisans listed in a census stay put for only ten or fifteen years, then go elsewhere. This phenomenon can be ascertained quite early in regions that have an abundant and early documentation: Catalonia, Italy, the Low Countries, London and environs. As for the osmosis between city and country, it seems to have been much more lively than was imagined. Cities swelled in the twelfth and thirteenth centuries with a flood of unskilled peasant labor, only to empty out in the fourteenth and fifteenth centuries, the result of an effort to control the country areas, now better equipped and more productive. The villagers took refuge in "safe places" in times of political crisis, but they opened up *bastides* and "new towns" when faced with a rise in population or production. Cities expanded beyond their old walls, where newcomers settled around new religious or commercial centers. Within the walls, a specialization among human activities and among city dwellers in general followed local patterns, thus enchanting historians of urban society or preaching in the cities, who contrast the *cité* of the bishop and the *bourg* of the merchants; the "trades" and "men in high places"; the "commonality" and the "bourgeoisie." As soon as you pull this thread, there follows a perfect waterfall of problems concerning rights and charters, wealth and power, coinage and exchanges, appropriation and "capitalism," and—why not?—monarchy and the "modern state." I am no longer on my canvas and I shall stop.

Where to Gather?

Thus both villagers and city dwellers formed a dense population. As I have said above, it is difficult for us to advance global figures and to sketch out a curve of population shifts. It is relatively easier to look more closely at the various threads in this fabric. We have lists of property holders, taxpayers, and conscripts, at times listed by name and with economic or professional information, but we have to remain on the level of evaluations and averages. The traps include the reasons for taking the survey, the competence of the scribes, the void when it comes to children and females, the territorial area of the inquiry, and the value of the "fire" or "hearth" that the accountant adopts. And, naturally, a late chronological setting—in general, the thirteenth century—adds to the difficulty of finding other comparable examples. All of this leads me to simplify. Attempts have been made to count populations in zones of grouped villages—in France, for example, in Picardy, Normandy, Flanders, Auvergne, Savoy, and Provence—and archaeology has furnished data on inhabited structures. Averages ranging from fifty to two hundred souls for areas of two to four hectares give plausible densities, taking into account spaces that remained "rural." In contrast, figures for urban areas are surprising. For one thing, the area occupied by buildings and adjacent gardens or *courtils* is derisory, at least as we view things today, and the biggest of the cities on flat terrain, such as Paris, Milan, or Cologne, do not surpass from five hundred to six hundred hectares. Thanks to crowding in multistory houses with little empty space between them, the population was proportionally enormous: around 1300, a minimum of from four thousand to six thousand inhabitants for "midsized" cities; from fifteen thousand to thirty thousand for most of the fifty or so dominant cities in western Europe; while a metropolis such as London, Milan, Cologne, Toulouse, Ghent, Florence, and perhaps Barcelona and Venice might contain between fifty thousand and a hundred thousand souls; and there was one monster city of over two hundred thousand: Paris. On average, this works out to some six hundred to two thousand individuals per hectare. In the conditions of hygiene, security, circulation, and alimentation that pertained in the cities of the time, it is difficult to imagine a tolerable life in a city. Even before Villon or Rutebeuf, tales, *fabliaux*, and even iconography offer many examples of the "cries and confusion" of Paris. Given that tumult and those crowds, where did people gather if they were neither a monk in his cloister, a demoiselle in her orchard, a knight in a room in a castle, or a hooded magistrate in his *hôtel?*

They gathered primarily in the street, because the houses, which were subdivided, as we have seen, into modest narrow and airless lodgings, were practically nothing but shelters for the night, even in cold climates. Specialists in urban history go into ecstasies over the *piazza* of the Italian seigneurial government; the cathedral parvis bordered by municipal palaces, and the imposing city halls (*hô-*

tels de ville) in France and elsewhere; over the belfries with their balconies from which the city fathers gave their harangues and over the crossroads where the friars minor, perched on the footing of a cross or a pillory, stirred up the housewives. What remains today of this urban decor of "noble" palaces, *hôtels*, and fountains always inspires the trusting admiration of tourists and sets lovers of a gilded Middle Ages to dreaming. If they should venture behind these monuments, to where the "little people," the *popolo minuto*, the "common" folk, the *armen Leute*, the "poor," and the *simplices*—that is, all the others—lived, they would find narrow streets at best six to ten meters wide and, in northern Europe, rarely paved, with a central gutter to collect rainwater and household debris. All French schoolchildren know the anecdote about King Philip Augustus bothered by the stink of the gutters of the Cité in Paris. Debris and dirty water fell out of gabled windows into the middle of these running sewers, leaving for the ladies (when there were any) only the higher portion of the street under the arcades, the *haut du pavé*, that was free of garbage. Dogs and even wandering pigs took care of the debris; if we can believe Abbé Suger, a man not given to joking, it was not until the fourteenth century that street sweepers (known as *éboueurs*) were hired to remove detritus. The street was a place for casks, heaps of wood, obstructions created by those who dwelled in the houses, donkey carts or tip carts pushed by hand, a horseman or two, chains that were stretched from one side to the other at night in a vain hope of protection, feeble lights trembling in a niche in a facade, pollution, smells—all of which were covered by a blanket of useless regulations meant to assure the repose and the comfort of the city dweller. This "romantic" picture is doubtless exaggerated, I admit. First because here and there urbanism in the ancient style remained or was gradually reborn, next because that portrait applies above all to the quarters in the city where the "mechanicals" lived—men engaged in intense artisan work, valets and masters of the "ignoble" occupations such as butchers, curriers, cobblers, tanners, metal- and woodworkers—as reflected in a number of street names in French cities. Still, despite their arrogance, the people of the cities could not shake off the idea that one lived better, day by day, in the village.

Meeting in the street to chat was thus a risky activity. A better idea was to seek out a less encumbered space. Antiquity had evidently understood that. Vast "baths" were as much sporting grounds as they were actual baths, as well as places for an exchange of ideas or of money. In Gaul, in Spain, and in Britain, when the Romans attempted to urbanize a conquered land that they judged too rural, hence poorly controlled, they began by setting up a military camp, then a place for spectacles, and then baths to attract the subjected people. Archaeology has often brought to light "agrotowns" of the sort; many of these were stillborn, but others, perhaps with better locations or ancient cult sites, prospered as "colonies" and even as "cities." If the medieval powers attempted nothing of the sort, they allowed *non aedificandi* zones, as our aediles are fond of saying, to develop, sometimes going so far as to create them. As for the fountain, often of royal or municipal origin, it was a symbol of urban, even royal, power, and it was around its basin that the "parliament of women" could be found, just as they gathered at the spring or the well in the village. The market hall, which might be gigantic in Italy or the Low Countries, was another monumental place for exchanges of all sorts. It was where, under the eye of sworn officials, standard weights and measures were available, calibrated for liquids, for grains, or for anything one might want to measure, weigh, and of course tax. Nearby there were moorings for barges (when needed), and taverns where contracts could be drawn up and violence might break out. There were also podiums or platforms for the public crier, the Franciscan in a revolutionary trance, or the Dominican preaching concord and condemning commerce—*inhonesta mercimonia*, Thomas Aquinas called it. If the city had reached the point of holding an international fair, as in Champagne, Lombardy, Brabant, England, or near the Rhine, the market hall became its heart, even if buying and selling also took place outside its walls. In the village the setting would be more modest: an open and perhaps grassy space, in England the "green," in Aquitaine the *couderc*, the Norman *baile*, originally a space for gathering the village herd, then the villagers, who preferred it to the parish church or the nearby atrium. The green also contained a cross and, at its foot or next to it, the *perron*, or stone bench from which the local lord rendered his judgments.

These aggressive and boisterous cities and these slow and simplistic villages were not just sailing about at will on a limitless ocean. All of them were solidly bound within a network of community ties that revealed their meaning in encounters or common aspirations. The first of these ties was the parish. I have no intention of embarking here on a history of the parish, and even less on a study of its religious function. I do want to recall that in France, as in most Christian lands, the territorial area of the parish became the first cell of life in a group, both in the city and in the village, and what was so aptly named the "commune" was the day-by-day framework not only for religious practices but for all social occasions. The jurists may squirm and protest, citing in particular the urban tissue that has been reworked so many times and is still being reworked today, but all that is trifles. From the moment that Christianity emerged out of the "cities" that welcomed it for centuries, it became rural. This occurred fairly early on the shores of the Latin sea, but hardly before the seventh and eighth centuries more to the north, and even later toward the Baltic or Slavic regions. I shall return to the topic. When men were asked where they were from, the faithful (who alone counted and recognized one another) stated that they were men of a certain parish rather than a certain seigneury, village, or city neighborhood. When, in 1215, the Fourth Lateran Council decreed that every believer must account himself from only one parish, it was by no means a novelty, but a means for avoiding the possibility that "oblations," that is, the revenues drawn by the priest who dispensed the sacraments, not remain in the purse of the faithful under the pretext of not being "of that parish." The *dîmes*, or taxes levied on the faithful, served for the upkeep of the priest who had the charge and the care (*cura*) of souls, or of his replacement, the *vicarius*. The *dîme*, entire or in part, could be sold, given, or bought, and it played an essential role in establishing the authority of the Church in those ages. All such rights and goods were a common concern. They made up the "work" of the Church, and all of the faithful were responsible for its smooth operation. They supervised the bookkeeping, designated sure men to form the organization—here and there called the *fabrique*—charged with its supervision. These men "of the register" (*matricularii*) were the churchwardens, and since the parish also covered the entire territory inhabited by the people of the village or the city neighborhood, it was the church building itself or the nearby atrium that served as a place to meet, a place of refuge, and a place for contacts. It was there that emotions were collective, even when the structure of the habitat might tend to disperse common efforts.

If they did not find one another in the church, the most pious, and initially perhaps also the most disinherited of men could hope for a gesture of fraternity, charity, and aid from the others. But individual, occasional, and even furtive alms-giving was not enough. In all ages, pious groups have brought together men with warm hearts who formed "confraternities" and "charities" and, since at times money had to be gathered for the poor, "guilds" (from "gold" or *Geld*, money). These groups, which were secular and spontaneous, grew in number in the eighth century, when we have word of many of them, especially in cities. The Church became concerned because it attributed to itself a monopoly of charity, because it had "its" poor, who were sometimes inscribed in registers carefully kept up to date, and because it viewed such groups as close to being sects. Thus Carolingian legislation condemned what Archbishop Hincmar himself called "disorders." Such precautions were vain. The confraternities became camouflaged as simple pious works in favor of lepers and hospitals. Beginning in the twelfth century, many of these, transformed into groups of workers of the same trade or craft, served as a framework for the working world in cities; others, become penitential fraternities, were taken in hand by the mendicant orders, the Franciscans in particular, and regrouped to participate in sessions of songs and chants, prayers and music. In the fourteenth century, there were seventy-five of these groups in Florence, ninety-five in Avignon, or one for every three hundred or five hundred inhabitants. Certain of these groups, which had fallen into quasi-insurrectional deviations under the pressure of the calamities of the age, indulged in mystical and exuberant processions in the fifteenth century, as did the bands of "flagellants" who stirred up the cities of the Rhine and the Rhone.

These remained essentially urban phenomena. In the countryside the authority of the Church continued to be rigorous, and such deviations were quickly disciplined by religious sanctions that equated the penitent with the heretic and the deviant with the sorcerer and held out the threat of burning at the stake. In contrast (and this time more in the countryside than in the city), the devout hoped to find salvation in a pilgrimage. The spiritual dimension was all-important. Not that there were not some embarrassing exaggerations: in the eleventh century, for example, during the troubles brought on by the introduction of the peace of God, or in the twelfth century, with the excesses of armed bands such as the *paziers* of Berry or the hood-wearing *encapuchonnés* of Velay, or, at a later date, the *laudesi* in Italy, who called themselves disciples of Saint Francis. Members of these disorderly movements dressed as pilgrims. But these were exceptions to the personage of the "normal" pilgrim. These *peregrini* were "foreigners who march." Alone or in a troupe, some obeyed a vow of expiation; others had been condemned to their wanderings by a court sentence. They had a recognized juridical status, reinforced by their clothing and by signs that they wore, such as a pilgrim's safe-conduct pass from some religious or secular source. Their aim was to travel to a saintly relic in order to see it and touch it, thus obtaining an "insurance" on the Beyond. In spite of their indisputable religious purpose, public opinion, alerted by the established Church, was not favorable to them. First, itinerant wandering, at times with no precise destination, was not in conformity with the notion of order that God desired. Rome had retained bad memories and a large store of mistrust regarding the itinerant Irish and Saxons of the first centuries of Christianity and unattached priests—*Wanderprä-diger*—who went along the routes preaching as they pleased. The "Gregorian" reform soon brought them back into line. But also, the faithful were encouraged to be suspicious of these unusual voyagers. Who had sent them, God or Satan?

By following these wanderers I am obviously straying from the topic of groups, lay groups this time. Two others were essential, and they are well known and amply studied: the "trades" and the lords. These were even the economic or social entities that were the most certain in that age, which means so much has been said about them that I need only add a few words. The "trades" first. Whether peasants who had migrated to the city or born city dwellers, men sought each other out to practice an activity "of the secondary sector," as our economists would say—that is, the transformation of raw materials. They were connected by family ties or a common origin, and might also belong to the same confraternity. They worked with their hands in a specialized workshop, where they were known as *valets*, *Knechten*, or *operai*, and were paid a wage by a "master" craftsman. All of these "mechanicals" were linked by working in close proximity on a certain street or in a quarter where others in the same trade congregated; by connections of *compagnnage* after their apprenticeship; by sharing bread at the workplace; and by their strict subjection to statutes and regulations covering engagement, salaries, hours, and sales. We can omit much of the rest: rivalries between masters and within the workplace; struggles with the municipal authorities; opposition between city workers and country workers; hostility between masters and workmen; the case of workers who were not inscribed in any trade organization; "scares," "commotions," or strikes in the city; the ups and downs of wages or prices; as well as unemployment, itinerant workers, and exclusion. What pertains to my subject in this is that all of these men, whether because of the Church's teachings or because they took a dim view of the economy, were persuaded that the indisputable objective of their efforts was the "common good" and the production of "good merchandise," and that all competition was nothing but a source of violence and a denial of the divine will.

Today anyone you question on what everyday life in the Middle Ages suggests will answer, "the lords," and they will be right. If you ask for more, he will add, "feudalism," and this time he will be wrong. I will say nothing about the latter, or about the exogenic excrescences—nobility, chivalry, vassals, and more—that are grafted onto it. Whatever one might think about the reality, importance, and mutations of those notions, they are merely epiphenomena on the terrain that I am investigating. I shall deal with them by saying that the rich and the powerful who hunted or went to war together or who fought off boredom together in the uncomfortable halls of the castle also experienced a type of group feeling that displayed profound social markings in "castle life," which concerned only one man out of twenty. It is of no interest to know whether, in addition, such a man—this time, one out of thirty—had been given a "feudal" tenure. As for the sentiments of a "vassal," they resemble the common profile. In contrast, seigneury itself was unavoidable, and it constituted the framework of daily life. Modeled on the parish or not, urban as much as rural, in southern Europe in the final centuries of the Middle Ages, seigneury was the city itself. This time, the problem cannot be eluded. Medieval society was indeed seigneurial. It is an abuse of language, unfortunately endorsed since Marx by such illustrious historians as Marc Bloch, to speak of "feudal society." I hope that I have said enough to condemn a useless inflation of a phenomenon that was, in the final analysis, marginal, in the minority, superficial, and determined by the provenance of our documents, which are almost exclusively aristocratic in origin.

That said, the question of lordship, like the topic of trades and crafts, cannot be treated fully here. Thus I shall leave aside certain basic aspects that seem not to fit into my "human" framework. These include the origin, pre- or post-Carolingian, of the seigneurial system; its private or public nature; the territorial dimensions and hierarchic structure of its command cells and, for even greater reason, their evolution between the year 1000 and the fourteenth century, when they tend to blend into the framework of royal politics. Similarly, I shall not treat the specificity of the seigneurial powers of the Church (in particular, over the monasteries); seigneurial power in an urban context; the role of the agents of the seigneurial system, including the parish priest, among those subjected to it; or economic levies on men's labor. I shall not go into detail about the *ban* that granted the power to judge, pursue, and tax men in a state that had long been weak. I shall, however, pause over the role of the seigneurial system and of the lord himself in how men grouped together and their feeling of commonality, which is my subject. The first thing that comes into sight is constraint, which is, incidentally, the source of cohesion among "subjects" as well. It is constraint, sometimes referred to as lordly "terrorism," that has earned the Middle Ages its bad reputation. That reputation is accompanied by a flotilla of absurd legends of "romantic" origin in which we see masters on horseback trampling their own grain, raping girls, throwing men into the darkest dungeons or *oubliettes* when they do not simply slit their throats, and letting beggars die of hunger. It should be remembered that the taxes paid to the lord's sergeant were much lower than what the tax man demands today; that justice rendered at the foot of the castle walls was much more rapid and clement than our interminable and dubious trials; that the security assured by a troupe of sergeants at arms or professional warriors housed in the castle was no less efficacious than the protection that either innumerable or insufficient squadrons of police personnel try to maintain today; and that so-called feudal anarchy is a myth, because perhaps never have men been better disciplined than then. Military constraints? None, for men of low estate were reputed unfit for combat; a tax or a few days digging defenses substituted for it. "Banal" payments for the use of a mill or a wine press that belonged to the lord? The fees for those conveniences, which also provided an occasion to encounter others, fell well below our "property taxes." I could go on to compare the levies on the product of labor, the merchant taxes at weighing stations or "value-added" taxes, or even limitations on personal rights. Besides, peasant revolts, and even revolts in the cities, were not aimed at overthrowing the "seigneurial system," or at least not before the fourteenth century. It was deviations from it or else miserable poverty that prompted such uprisings.

Waiting in line at the mill, working together to clean the castle moat, coming to work as a team for several days to take in the harvest on the master's land were all ways to assemble, but the essential cement of seigneury resided in the "customs" and "franchises" obtained from the master. At times he had to be paid to cede or share a right, but he usually did so, because his own interest was involved in such matters as gathering workers; strengthening his own authority with a few minor concessions; or transforming into common "usage" a wood, a pond, or a *garenne* that could not profitably be exploited alone. Most of these "abandonments" were the result of an understanding, but our knowledge of how that understanding was reached is sketchy. The master could afford to be supple if a request did not involve his rights of justice and of war, but he would have to be paid to grant rights of access to empty "vain" terrains, scrub, fallow land, even forest clearings that became "communal." A written act might be drawn up at the end of mutual concessions of the sort. Masses of these have been conserved for the tenth century in Spain, the eleventh and twelfth centuries in northern France, and the thirteenth century in Germany and Italy. Such arrangements brought productive land to a peasantry growing in numbers and money to the lords, whose needs for military equipment and prestige expenditures were growing, and the many "charters," *assises*, "reports of rights," or *fueros* give material evidence of peasant "conquests."

We should not succumb to the idea of a "golden age," even if something of the sort can be discerned between 1180 and 1240 in Christianity as a whole. There were bad masters whose sense of their own interest was obscured by mutual discord or who were animated by a "class spirit" echoed in the literature of the time. The worst of these were apt to be men of the Church, the Cistercians in particular, who were adept at "direct development" and had no interest in the peasants around them. As for the villagers themselves, it would be an irenic dream to believe that they all benefited from or were delighted by the privileges accorded. It could even be suggested that an increasing social gulf was created between those who were able to pay a tax that covered all the advantages gained and the others who remained "at the mercy" of the restrictions. In the cities, so often brandished as an example, that internal fracture was even clearer because those who led the struggle for emancipation were already privileged persons, masters of the trades, urban aristocrats, merchants or arms dealers who did not forget their own interests in the advantages they won. Such men praised but also scrutinized the texts delivered by the local authority; they might—in the late eleventh and twelfth centuries in the Low Countries and in Italy—have gained self-administration, the constitution of armed militias, and an oath of "communality," that is, spontaneous mutual aid. But different social conditions and individualized chronological frames forbid me from stating what the historiographic vulgate constantly repeats about the primacy of the urban movement over the villages. Arguments in either sense are of little importance. What is essential is that men assembled.

Laughter and Games

All cultures possess a large range of games; some of them, among the simplest, such as throwing an object or displaying strength, occur in all times and all lands. Rabelais quite seriously said of laughter "le rire est le propre de l'homme," and even when it does not go much beyond self-satisfaction, laughter belongs to all centuries, although some epochs seem less prone to it. Although there are individual games and one can laugh alone, both games and laughter are of the body and the soul and seem to be largely collective in nature.

Defining laughter might seem an idle quest. It is, however, the discernible expression of a natural disposition to enjoy oneself, just as tears express affliction. It can be true that gaiety or sorrow is not translated by muscular or glandular movements visible to others, and reactions can be limited to a slight rictus or an increased humidity in the eyes. But the centuries of the Middle Ages did not have that much reserve. Characteristic manifestations were brutal and intense, juxtaposing, as we have seen, good will and cruelty, furor and charity, laughter and tears—and the latter were unceasing, loud, and disorderly. The smile or a contained sadness were artificial attitudes, willed, and, what is more, reserved to "courtly" manners in which hypocrisy reigned; hence they are almost always the affair of the poet or the author of romances, and almost never of the painter or the chronicler. But when we leave the space confined to "high class" sentiments, we see nothing but impetuous and noisy outbreaks of laughter or torrents of cries and tears; gestures and grimaces are excessive, bodily members are twisted, mouths are wide open, and gesticulations are exaggerated. Common literature such as the *dits*, novellas, and *fabliaux* and at times an isolated piece of sculpture furnish a thousand examples of laughter at unexpected and comic spectacles such as a ridiculous fall, a calamitous blunder, a good trick played on a wealthy man, a *bon mot* reported by a choirboy, and, of course, the inexhaustible repertory of tricks played on people or plays on words—usually involving sex among men and scatological matters among women. Laughter exploded in the tavern, in the street, at the market. The Church frowned on all this. It had no difficulty perceiving, behind this gaiety, the temptations of calumny and envy, the sources of disorder. The Church quite seriously posed an insoluble question: did Jesus laugh?

Joy, and collective joy in particular, was externalized in festive behavior. The medieval centuries much enjoyed festivities, and the same events continue to capture the interest of municipalities more in search of turning a profit than in historical authenticity. Occasions for festivities were innumerable. They were sometimes connected with circumstances, as in a royal "entry" into a city or, on a more modest scale, the return to normal life of a village mother after childbirth. Festivities that might be pagan in origin, although repainted as Christian, were spread throughout the year. There was Christmas, of course; Epiphany (*la typhaine*), celebrating the Three Magi; Candlemas, the feast of Mary's recovery from childbirth; Easter, preceded by Palm Sunday, which celebrates Christ's entry into Jerusalem; then Pentecost; Rogation Days; Ascension; Saint John's Day; and more. All of these, or almost all, are of secular origin and have sexual or chthonian connotations. All were accompanied by alimentary rites—the roast pig, the *galette des rois*, pancakes, lamb—or were connected to some rustic concern such as burning weeds, chasing away insects, or gathering livestock. This pagan dimension was well understood, captured, and assimilated by the Church, which, after having stormed between the fifth and the ninth centuries against these *simulacra*, from the Orient or the extreme West, ended up admitting that invocations to the Moon or sprinkling dry fields with holy water could be revived for the greater glory of God. In contrast, the Church failed to stamp out feasts of subversion that, by their very essence, were contrary to order. These included the "Feast of Fools" on January 1, where everything was turned upside down, a souvenir of the day on which the people took over command from the Roman magistrates; Carnival (probably from *carnem levare*: remove meat); and Mardi Gras, a satanic protest against the imminent Lent and its privations. I might add to these the *charivari* in which youth groups harassed a newly married couple and made fun of matrimonial hypocrisy.

All of these feast days astonish us by their variety, their abundance, and their color. In order to understand them better we have to remember that in those centuries work was seen as a constraint, and *otium*, leisure, was an ideal that everyone attempted to reach. It has been calculated that, leaving aside nuances of place and time, in the city as in the village a good third of the days were *chômé*—nonwork days—whether this was a cause or an effect of popular celebration. Naturally, the processions that formed on these occasions, the cross and banners at their head, did not limit themselves to laughter and shouting; people also sang in chorus. This is a domain about which we know practically nothing. We can find painted or sculpted representations of two-stringed vielles, trombones, flutes, and drums, and, inside a house, a psaltery with thirty-two strings, the ancestor of our piano. Since Guido of Arezzo first imagined them in the mid-eleventh century, we also find manuscripts with staves permitting the placement of notes on a scale rather than using simple signs of relative pitch (higher or lower notes) by the use of neumes (from *pneuma*, breath). These rudiments of solfeggio were only used in liturgical music or plainsong, where they continued unchanged. This means that we know nothing about popular melodies, the *chansons de toile* that ladies sang or recited while spinning or weaving, drinking songs, or songs to dance to. For dancing accompanied the festivities. It, too, is often evoked in depictions of city dwellers or peasants, men and women forming a circle, stamping their wooden clogs in rhythm, and changing the positions of their arms or their bodies. And if the dance seems rarer in the higher social milieus of the city, it was there, but not before the fifteenth century, that a two-person dance in which the bodies touched, *la carole*, was first seen. This was a horror and a depravity that made men of the Church hide their faces, and if the canons also danced in front of the altar of their church on certain feast days, it was by holding one another by one finger in an utterly chaste manner.

Festivities led to drinking, hence to the tavern, hence to brawls, which meant useless disorder. Could that appetite for diversion be oriented toward some more moral form, or in any event, something more peaceful? As early as the tenth century, singers, buffoons, and wandering musicians frequented the great halls of the castle, miming for dazzled youthful warriors the amorous or violent exploits of heroes and performing *canzoni* from Italy and the *pays d'oc* or the *chansons de geste* of France and the *pays d'oïl*. This was an affair of the privileged, however, even if some of the oldest texts in the vernacular of French literature, dating from the eleventh century, are of this sort. The "common people" very probably had no access to such activities, hence they were offered (perhaps as a resurgence of antiquity) spectacles that were already "staged." There were no gladiatorial combats or combats with wild beasts of the sort that the people of Rome adored, or at least there are no serious traces of them in the Middle Ages. Instead, crowds gathered around enclosed fields in which the champions of "judiciary duels" fought it out, or else at the foot of the pillory where a beggar or a tramp was being whipped. What could be jollier than a hanging or, even better, a decapitation? Are there not still lands that call themselves Christian where crowds gather to watch the execution of a condemned criminal presumed guilty? We can turn our eyes away from these and look instead at the renascence of the popular theater. It was in Italy and in northern France that the collective festivity of the spectacle "with personages" that enchanted antiquity was revived. It may have originated, in the twelfth century, from the grimaces of the wandering bands of *jongleurs* (*joculator*, he who amuses) and of *trouvères* (*trobador*, he who finds and imagines) who put on a show in the squares of the city by interpreting "farces" and *sotties* of their own composition, while a more "professional" troop might put up a platform with scenery on which they presented works *de métier* (*ministerium*, which leads to the misleading translation, "mystery" plays). After the fourteenth century, these spectacles were taken in hand by the municipal powers as a way to avoid disorders set off by overenthusiastic spectators, and by the Church, which found in such productions a field of action more dependable than the uncontrollable sermons of the Franciscan Little Brothers. The spectacle was free, with the players moving from one place to another in the city, and it lasted several days, changing its subject matter according to changes in the cast. The point was to mock authority, but also to highlight society's moral virtues. This was theater for everybody, although there were no women on the platforms, not even to interpret the role of the Virgin. This exclusion should not be interpreted as "machismo" or as scorn of women. Quite simply, it was not considered decent to subject one's wife, sister, or daughter to the public gaze. On the other hand, the success of such performances was so great that we have *suppliques* (requests) addressed to the authorities for permission to take the day off in order to attend the show.

Parading through the streets shouting, group dancing, clapping at the theater to show joy are collective and convivial activities, but they imply no personal initiative; people behaving this way are engulfed in the anonymous mass. This was not the case with games, even with team games. Here we find complete personal investment, given that games have an objective—winning glory or money—and for the loser, they bring shame and anger and encourage a need to cheat. Such sentiments are quite evidently connected with pride, envy, wrath, and even a rejection of divine intervention. Beginning in Carolingian times, the Church condemned games and gaming as an immorality and a deviation from the notion of leisure, which should be devoted uniquely to God. We have fairly clear ideas about games and sports, at least in France, from the middle to the end of the medieval period. More often than not, a game was played by rival teams, and these were usually games played with a small ball, like the *jeu de paume*, or a bigger *ballon* for *soule*. The *jeu de paume* was an urban pastime; it was sometimes played indoors and did not involve much running about. The players used a racquet to strike the *éteuf*, the ancestor of our tennis balls, and send it toward the adversary over a net or hit it against a wall, which was usually made of wood. The game of *soule* was more "popular" and was played by larger numbers, which meant that it often pitted families, clans, or city neighborhoods against one another. Whereas the ball used in *paume* was made of wool or straw packed into a cover, in *soule* a hard ball was used, even a wooden one, that was kicked or hit with the hand or with a bat; hence it is difficult to pick the modern sport—soccer, rugby, baseball, or cricket—that most resembles it.

Such games required space, spectators, and arbitrators. This was not true of dice, which was a game of chance and put it in first place in the domain of cheating, contestation, and violence. It was universal, constant, and goes back almost to Neolithic times. And as considerable sums of money were sometimes involved when the great of this world played, the Church condemned it over all other games. The situation was different with cards, which were introduced only a little before the end of the fifteenth century. It is said that they came from the Indies and that Rabelais knew the rules for thirty-five card games. But although chance remained present, if only in regard to which cards were dealt out to the players, the role of tactics gave card games a luster that dice did not have. Still, ball games, dice, and cards all ceded before the "king of games" and the "game of kings," chess. This time there were two players, but expert ones, supported by devoted lovers of the game who were ready for anything. Chess is like a mirror of life on this Earth, with the symbolism of its pieces; its pseudowarlike tactics require audacity and prudence, a good memory and a good eye, all of which were qualities primarily accessible to men of a certain age and experience. In the West, chess is known from the eighth century, and it probably came from the Indies via Scandinavia or Spain. Since chess was a combat, there could be no cheating, though the loser might become angry and be capable of violent outbursts; when Robert, the son of William the Conqueror, lost at chess to his father, he is said to have broken the chessboard over his father's head.

And there were other activities than *soule*, dice, or chess: archery, then skittles, knucklebones, hopscotch, backgammon, and many others. They elicited laughter or tears, depending on the outcome of the match and people's sense of humor. Like festive gatherings, dancing, and theater, these activities inspired passions that could bring people together, but that might also set them apart. So it was a good idea to discourage them or contain them.

PRECAUTIONS AND DEVIATIONS

In order for a society to have some cohesion—for example, in order for it to resist violent blows from another social group or even from nature—it was not enough that men be brought together, more or less willingly, within the usual frameworks of life: a parish, a seigneury, a "trade," or even within certain "frontiers." Other connections were needed; at times these might be of ethnic or linguistic origin, at other times they were moral or religious concepts. If this basic identity should come undone, and another not yet substitute for it, a crisis of self-consciousness might shake men's spirits and set off both material and moral confusion. Since human history began, there has been no lack of such crises. In the case of Europe, this occurred from the third to the eighth centuries, at the time of first contact between the Mediterranean and Germano-Celtic cultures, and at the moment of Europe's sudden opening toward the external world of America and the colonial empires in the fifteenth to the eighteenth centuries. Events in our own time lead us to think that we have been living for the last fifty years or so at the dawn of a similar upheaval. The base of our communication structures is disintegrating; our heritage of political or "national" units is dissolving; our ethical foundations have been shaken. These phenomena are slow, however. As is true of the warming global climate, we are enormously naive if we think ourselves capable of slowing them down or hastening them, and it will probably take one or two centuries before something new emerges.

Hence it is not useless to raise the question of the solidity of the cement that held medieval society together, in particular between the two limits that I have just recalled, the seventh and the fifteenth centuries. Today, in Europe at least, what gives an original group its specificity is a relatively homogeneous ethnic background, a common language and uniform culture, a history that is old and shared, deeply rooted attitudes and habits, and clearly defined administrative and political boundaries. These are what enable us to speak of "Englishmen," "Frenchmen," or "Italians." The medieval situation was completely different. In France, for example, there was neither unity of population, nor awareness of a "homeland" and even less a "nation"; there was no common language, no well-defined frontiers, no indisputable destiny. In contrast, there was a solid mold for beliefs: Christianity. Everyone believed himself and declared himself a Christian. There were of course a few rebels and sizable knots of

Jews and Muslims here and there, but they were just isolated groups and, in principle, exceptions. In the eyes of others, Muslims for example, the people of Europe were "Franks." This was clearly wrong, but the error came from the fact that in those times the profane and the sacred were merged, and power was theocratic. It was *dominium*, that of the faith and that of the "dominant" people. That type of society is today at our doors, and André Malraux was probably right when he predicted a "religious century" to come. But let us return to medieval times.

Order and the "Orders"

Celestial order dominated the world; it was founded on a cosmic harmony established in and for eternity. In a universal schema, man can only be an element without free will: such as he is, such he will be. In the most ancient societies, such as Egypt, the Indian subcontinent, and perhaps amid the Neolithic groups of which we have only infinitely few relics (and here I omit the Far East, about which I know nothing), men became aware that the equilibrium of their societies and the superior Order that ruled them imposed roles and distinct internal "functions." It was appropriate that certain people act as intermediaries between humans and divine forces; that others take on the support—armed if need be—of the entire group; and that the least inherit the function of producing both new men and foodstuffs. There is nothing surprising in this tripartite division, but Georges Dumézil and other ethnologists have thought it unique to early Indo-European culture. What can be found in Europe of that vision of the world among the Greco-Romans, the Celts, or the Germans, however, does not seem to include a spiritual content. Artistic representations of human activities give us the impression that the juridical and the economic predominated over men's moral or religious responsibilities. Moreover, neither the Neoplatonic philosophers of the Imperial age nor the Fathers of the Church at the moment of the flowering of Christianity bothered their minds with that sort of division of humanity.

Men were free or slave, Christian or "Gentile," monks or laymen, virgins or married. But these evaluations either have little to do with the will of the Creator, or they touch only a secondary aspect of the life of the group.

The essential mutation came at the end of the ninth century, in the Carolingian age, when the works of John Scotus Erigena and Heiric of Auxerre give no hint that the Order of God rests on the three functions or three "orders" mentioned above, or that each order was conceived for a specific mission that corresponded to an equally specific social status. The formulation of this "schema" by Adalbero of Laon around 1020 or 1030 became the untouchable rule, adopted by the learned. There were *oratores, bellatores,* and *laboratores,* a triad that has been translated (rather poorly) as "those who pray," "those who fight," and "those who labor," or, in other words, the clerics, the warriors, and the others, or, to put it differently, the Church, the nobility, and the people. Not many years later, in the time of Abelard and Saint Bernard, a hierarchy was even drawn up among these orders. The highest rank went to the clerics, for they were dependent on the pontifical authority, the depositary of the divine will in the here below; the second went to the combatants, the knights and the *armati* who were of course the strongest; the third (or the *tiers,* as they were called later) were all the rest, the confused mass of the others, who were the majority in terms of number, to be sure, but were the simple flock of the faithful, the *grex fidelium.* Thus we see a mixture of the religious and the social, the sacred and the profane, as the general climate of those centuries dictated. Moreover, every man is placed by God within one order and not another and cannot change place. Attempting to do so would be to make a choice of life (*haeresis*) that was clearly to be condemned, and I have stressed this flagrant social immobilism above.

Our rationalism, which we inherit from the Enlightenment, is quick to stigmatize an Order that establishes a blatant social inequality in which clerics and nobles carouse in leisure on the sweat and tears of the "little people." This is a gross error of evaluation, fed by the unfortunate notion of a "feudalism" founded on lordly violence and the subjection of the "serfs" (from *servi*, or "slaves" in the Latin vocabulary). This completely ignores the fact that the "trifunctional schema" was the image of what God wanted, which is that humanity achieve salvation, the first goal of our life on this Earth. As it happens, in that universal quest for eternal salvation, which was already enough to inspire resignation in the weaker, the mind-set is nothing like our own. For God and his will, there are no rich or poor, no masters and subjects, but only Christians awaiting Judgment. When that day comes, the priest who has failed in his pastoral mission or the warrior who has engaged in violence, lechery, or acquiring money has a much worse chance of obtaining salvation than those who wore themselves out working with their hands. In reality, people did not become aware of divine injustice until the fourteenth century or even later, when the ministry of the Church weakened or the warrior order permitted itself to slide gradually into sin.

In fact, even before William of Ockham and other Doctors of the Church began, around 1350, to raise doubts regarding the excellence of the divine choice, or rebellious peasants in England in 1381 demanded, "When Adam delved and Eve span, who was then the gentleman": fissures were visible in the schema taught by those who held knowledge. It was the Church itself that first contributed to the disorganization of the life framework that underlay its own power, and it laid itself open to suspicions that it was moving far from its prime mission. It did so by granting increasing importance to the role and the place of the hierarchical principle within its own ranks, notably in boasting of the superiority of the pope over all Christians, even those of the second order. It did its best to obtain material goods for itself (often acquired by more than dubious means); and it taxed with simony—that is, with profane materialism—all those who threatened its fortune, or charged with Nicolaism those within its ranks who displayed moral failures. In the vocabulary used within its own social group, the word *ordonner*—to order—shifted toward meaning entering into its ranks (by "ordination" or "taking orders"), as if its people alone were loved by God, while the term *état*—"estate"—came to designate the two other parties to the divine schema, brought down to the level of the profane.

I could pause over the order of the warriors because the problems posed by its internal divisions, its varying types of status, and its material activities in political and economic life encumber our paths of inquiry. I shall limit myself to one consideration, but one that I think is significant. Whereas the order of the *oratores* failed without remission, and that of the *laboratores* broke apart, as we shall see, the *bellatores* conserved an indisputable homogeneity, at least on the surface. To be sure, there were elements from the *tiers*, the third estate, who nibbled at their edges, and family customs and material interests eroded the strength of the order or moved it in the direction of a caste structure. But in that very evolution, the role of the sword of God survived; "honor" and glory were more talked about than religion and Christian defense, though the "nobility" did not fail in its task.

In this history of the spiritual ties that united men, the case of the *tiers état* is much more complex. It is not my intention, however, to enter into a study of the evolution of religious sentiment among humble folk—that is, among all those who did not belong to the two "dominant" orders. I shall limit myself to widening the three breaches that the centuries have shown to exist in the trifunctional schema and that gradually took away its role as a social cement. In the first place, dissolution came from a lack of perception on the part of clerics who claimed to provide a framework for the material status of men. When, as late as the eleventh century and for even greater reason before then, the thinkers classified the faithful, the *laboratores* were for them manual laborers, and work was elevated to the level of a moral value. But those laborers, whose task it was to nourish others, were, obviously, the peasants, the overwhelming majority of the "third" classification. As it happens, all over Europe, although with local forms and different rhythms, urban expansion, beginning in the late eleventh century, swelled to inundate Christianity and triumph everywhere.

In the twelfth and thirteenth centuries, the city world accounted for four or five men out of every ten in Italy, three or four out of ten in France, and almost as many in Germany or England. These people fit poorly or not at all within the ideal framework. The forces that animated them were closer to individual interest and the local reality; their culture tended to personalize the individual and to weave exclusively secular connections. Moreover, their relationship with money was constant; at times, as wages or in the form of sales, it was the foundation of their economic system. Naturally, not all of these men were cloth sellers, usurers, or master craftsmen, and no one is unaware of the strength of the confraternities or the Marial cult. But the "profile" of these workers was not that of the *laborator* in the fields. How could those who practiced a "dishonest" commerce, who were not "workers with their hands," as Rutebeuf boasted of himself, or who consoled themselves "with living poor, far from a wealthy lord of the land," as Villon declared, be inserted into the old tripartite world? Some attempt was made to adapt the genre of the pastoral, to stuff the *dits* and the *fabliaux* with moral precepts, and the "mystery plays" with pious thoughts. It was for the most part a waste of time. The "birth of the lay spirit," as has been said with some bombast, nibbled away at the spirituality of the third estate.

The second attack was more hidden. The tripartite schema had simply forgotten liberty. It had been forgotten not because it was held to be without importance, but because in the eyes of God all the faithful are souls of the same weight. Even the rigorous Roman law admitted that a slave was not just a body. Thus Christian thinkers did not think that a human group of that sort could bring any change to the established schema. In Carolingian times the notion that "there are only two sorts of men, the free and the slave" was a purely secular observation that had nothing to do with the notion of salvation. The Christian Church had recruited many of its first adepts from the nonfree, thus it did not judge it scandalous to have abundant troops of slaves itself, even in the mid-tenth century. To be sure, it condemned the traffic in slaves in theory and even the use of human flesh, but only in the name of charity, not in that of salvation. It pitied the "sons of Ham," the son of Noah whose descendants, the black race, were condemned by God. But there was no question of anyone entering into the world of the clerics without first having redeemed his nonfree condition. This is why a division among men was not founded on the idea of liberty or servitude in any of the writings of the learned. It is our reasoning minds that condemn that repugnant blindness. Even after slavery in the ancient style—or the Merovingian style—had disappeared (for an entire series of reasons that I will not go into here), the category of the subjected, the "attached," the *servi* in the ancient vocabulary and the "serfs," as the historians call them, still seemed to the clerics unrelated to the "function" of the third order. We might debate the stages and the content of servitude, or emphasize the Church's incontestable efforts to free slaves after the year 1000, but the stain of servitude remained indelible. One can only be surprised that the Church tolerated, and even itself enforced, such persistent barriers to the liberty of certain believers as not being able to marry, move from one place to another, or dispose of the fruits of their labor (even though these were blessed, in principle) without the authorization of a master who called himself Christian, and who was at times even a member of the Church. If the "schema" had already been rendered inoperative by the irruption of city dwellers, this time it was threatened in its principle of equality in the face of salvation.

This schema was also threatened, and perhaps more seriously, by an internal breakdown of the notion that the orders maintained peace in society thanks to their precise, unchanging functions. A stratification of superimposed layers within each of these groups evolved through the centuries, but for the two higher orders this was not too damaging. After all, the fact that some clerics took "minor orders" and others "major orders," that some monks were "ordained" as priests and others not, or that there was a hierarchy in the right accorded only to certain of them to give one sacrament or another did not alter their mission to act as intermediaries between the laity and God. Similarly, whether the *bel-*

latores were feudal or not, knightly or noble, elder sons or younger sons, they retained their role as combatants. It was within the third estate that the germ of decomposition had been introduced. It already contained both freemen and serfs. Economic evolution was the most powerful motive force for internal dissolution. The "commons" included a mass of "the poor," known as *vilissimi*, the *menus*, the *armen Leute*, or the *popolo minuto*. These were all those who had no land, no tools, no trade, no money, at times no dwelling, who could not only be referred to as having neither hearth nor home (*ni feu ni lieu*) but soon as having neither faith nor law (*ni foi ni loi*). Their numbers grew, in the cities especially, for out in the countryside nature kept their numbers to a minimum. The Church was aware that this deplorable state of affairs necessarily altered the faith of these forgotten Christians and led them to contest a schema that claimed the right to stifle them. By using preaching from the twelfth century on, then by *exempla* with commentary, the Church attempted to praise Lady Poverty as a passport for Heaven. Jean Gobi went so far as to draw up a scale of poverty to unmask the "false poor" or, even worse, the "bad poor." It seems a joke! In spite of some rear-guard battles to combat the seigneurial economy in the fourteenth and fifteenth centuries, the abandonment of hope on this earth brought on a fatal break within an "order" that claimed to contain only "worker" Christians all marching together toward salvation.

Peace and Honor

In "modern times" and even more so in contemporary times, an endless stream of disorders, at times bloody ones, disturbed the life of peoples (or at least of "nations"). Not that the centuries of the Middle Ages offer a more harmonious visage, but war (about which I shall have more to say) and the periodic *effrois*, or terrors (about which I will not) were both more limited in scope and more dependent on circumstance. These were troubles that originated within a family or that had relatively modest territorial aims;

no one invoked people's rights, the foundations of society, or "nations," which did not yet exist. This increased the importance of brief "encounters" between princes with the aim of concluding a compromise agreement. These purely formal interviews were aimed at stopping conflict for a certain time, and the list of them is long, beginning in the early Middle Ages: Strasbourg (842), Saint-Clair-sur-Epte (911), Yvois (1022), and more. With the passage of time and the emergence of problems of greater amplitude, the later Middle Ages used "conferences": Montereau (1419), Arras (1435), Bruges (1472), which brought together an emperor, two kings, and a "grand duke of the West," and Venice. Later, in the nineteenth century for example, from Vienna to Versailles, history teems with "congresses" of the sort. And the famous "meetings" that claimed to regulate the effects of the last world war are of much the same ilk. None of these included any consultation with individuals; the powerful disposed of the mass of humanity to foster their own interests. As for the international attempts that are more popular today, they are just as necessary and desirable as they are on the whole inefficacious.

My purpose is not to measure the effect of the "resolutions" of the United Nations, but rather to search for the beginnings of a quest for Peace—with a capital letter and embracing all men—in the Middle Ages. That attempt did take place, and it has quite justly remained one of the symbols of the Middle Ages, even though its efficacy has slowly subsided. Traditional historiography is fond of stressing the gradual decline, around 880 or 950, of public authority, which had for a time been revived by the Carolingians. It is equally likely to contrast the éclat of the warriors of Austrasia and the disorder, violence, and "terrorism" of "feudal anarchy." In order to justify the ardent desire for peace on the part of the victims of a disorder of this sort, who were clerics filled with virtue and poor peasants crushed under their burdens, such historians call on the "terrors of the year 1000," which are supposed to have haunted the minds of people of the time. After some rough quarrels between the admirers of Michelet and the devotees of positivism in the nineteenth century, historians today are roughly in agreement. The "terrors" of the year 1000 never existed; at the most one can find a stifled unease before a social change that is perceived but not understood. Anarchy is a vision of the learned. What was occurring was a slow shift, over one or two centuries, from the public toward the private, with inevitable adjustments in men's environments. As for "terrorism," it was no more than the sign of the return to the village of mounted warriors left with no organized activity after the cessation of slave raids beyond the Elbe. Questions of the degree of violence or the timing of these phenomena are matters for erudite quarrels, where I shall leave them. It is always adventurous, and sometimes false, to project the contingencies of the moment of one period onto another, though I have to say that I find a similar resonance in the year 1000 and the year 2000!

But let us not stray from the tenth century, a century that could hardly be qualified as either a "somber night" or a "smiling dawn," as the Burgundian Raoul le Glabre put it toward the end of that century in his famous phrase speaking about *la blanche robe d'églises dont se revêtait le monde fatigué* (the white robe of churches in which the weary world dressed itself). What caused this gradually sunnier world? Was it the end of the Carolingians? This was a detail. Demographic rise? Yes, but was this a cause or an effect? And where did the population increase come from? Was it of extrahuman origin, a gift of God, or an oceanic mass movement? We are standing on shaky ground, and our only foothold—a rise in faith—is sure but hard to define accurately. Here we leave the mists of learned theory for a more terrestrial development and a more human form. Within its own ranks the Church opened the way to purity and to military actions ranging from building up the monastery of Cluny (910) to the "Gregorian" reform of the late eleventh century. Between those two dates men regrouped, the seigneurial system was put in place, parishes took root, and the dead no longer inspired fear. But one more stage was necessary in order to consolidate Christianity in its first steps in this direction.

This stage was a sworn peace among men. Even if the inspiration for this desire was largely popular, the "little people" and the weak had no real ability to obtain it. It was the Church that took the initiative; its authority, its wealth, and its hierarchy called for calm and submission. Bishops (and, less frequently, monks) organized councils—which remained juridical, hence theoretical—in which both advice and threats were offered in profusion, then assemblies attended (willingly or not so willingly) by lords, men of arms, and at times even representatives of the city. As the spoken word expressed authority in that nonwriting society, the armed men were made to solemnly swear to keep the peace on their lands, between one another, and where the weak, the clerics, and the humble were concerned. This was the Peace of God or, in a more modest form, the Truce of God. The oath was a public one, sworn on a relic or on the cross; it engaged the swearer's honor and, above all, his salvation. Those who to refused to take it were condemned to eternal damnation. The movement began in central France around 990, reached northern France around 1020, eastern France and then Germany in 1050, and the Mediterranean before 1100. Not only were those who refused to swear the oath threatened with Hell; they were constrained to take it, whether they liked it or not. The Church did not hesitate, for the "common good," to arm peasant bands to back up the soldiers of Peace.

In principle, the notion of public order and a cordon of security around society was thus attained. This is not an invitation to unrestrained optimism, however. It is true that for a long time people invoked the peace in the name of the common good, but deviations soon appeared. First, authority within the ecclesial body tended to become concentrated in the secular hierarchy, the pope included, after 1050 or 1070. This meant that the monastic orders, around these dates or slightly later, launched very active movements to return to a more austere piety, more clearly separated from the common people, and often standing in opposition to the secular arm of the clergy. Next, it soon appeared that recourse to a sort of peasant "popular force" to keep rebel lords in line risked breaking up the traditional tripartite schema. The third estate could not be substituted for the order of warriors. This means that as time went by, the "institutions of peace" tended to creep toward a rapprochement between the two higher orders in order to control the third. Moreover, those among the *bellatores* who had few or no lands to manage found it difficult to leave off combat and pillage. The Church, relying on the militant nature of renewed faith, had no great difficulty in orienting the bellicose zeal of the *armati* toward the holy war. The "pre-crusades," as they are known, began in Spain and in Sicily as early as 1040 or 1060, and this movement of the "regurgitation" of the armed forces lasted two and a half centuries, or as long as the Peace of God.

Two moral elements emerged reinforced by this effort for peace. The first is the place of the oath in relations among men. I have stressed its role as a substitute for a written contract, a commercial procedure that eventually dominated in the city. The common folk and most of the warriors were *illiterati*, which meant that they knew no Latin, but they felt themselves to be under the eyes of God when they pronounced an oath. Used to establish an agreement, a promise, a compromise, or an arbitrage, the oath was not the mechanical formula demanded in our courts today. Besides salvation, it engaged one's honor. That notion is, quite naturally, innate in man; touched in his sentiments of wounded pride, or by having goods taken away, or by simple humiliation, the man of those times accorded no attenuating argument to the circumstances of the injury he had received, and his vengeance had to be total, without any condition of "peace," even when suggested by "friends." This sentiment, almost animal in its manifestations of violence, seems not to have been affected by the Peace of God.

So if peace could not resolve differences between individuals or social groups, there might be something else that could. Did the formula of the Roman jurists, *pax est lex et lex est pax*, still remain true?

Law and Power

"Custom" is one of the key words of medieval times: *consuetudo*, *usus*, *habitus*, "what is done," "what has always been done." Custom was called "ancient" if it had been attested for at least ten years, according to the old men who were quite officially consulted in the village; it was "from all antiquity," if it went beyond that limit. It was thus a jurisprudence that was renewed as more cases were registered and that was perpetuated by memory from one generation to another. It touched on everything that the Church did not have the power to decide in case of litigation—problems of inheritance and of fiscal management, and conflicts of interest—for peace was only a principle, a theory accompanied by purely spiritual sanctions. This means that the diversity of local practices or "ancestral" traditions produced a wide scattering of cases and resolutions according to place and person. The Word reigned.

On reading these lines one might think that the judge, whoever he was, the notary, or the scribe were wandering about in the dark with no signposts. This is totally untrue. The written word existed; the law was there, and on occasion the notary, in northern Europe in any event, might happen to qualify a simple *usus* as a *lex*. As is my wont, I will not venture into a technical area that is among the most encumbered, and rather than sketch out a history of the law, I will retain from it only what serves my purpose. Regarding the point of departure to begin with, Mediterranean antiquity, which was highly juridical in spirit, bequeathed to the medieval centuries an enormous baggage of written civil and penal law, the "codes." It did so in two successive waves. The first of these occurred in the fifth century with the condensation known as the "Theodosian code," from the name of the emperor who reigned at the time. The second, which developed that inheritance, was called the "Justinian code" because it was compiled during the reign of that emperor at Byzantium, but it reached the West, through the interposition of Italian jurists, only after 1010 or 1020. This was the *Corpus juris ci-*

vilis, which still finds echoes in the laws of France. We know little about Celtic traditions, but German traditions of several sorts contributed an arsenal of "laws," especially penal ones, orally transmitted. The phase of contacts between these cultures, partial syntheses, and the writing down of all this baggage, enriched by lessons from the daily life of the population, especially among those responsible for wielding power, required almost six centuries to develop, and it did so to the benefit of territorial law rather than personal law. In this regard, the law, written or not, contributed to consolidating connections among men, at least on the local level.

Precisely because of its territoriality, the law offered quite different overall aspects, which the historian has great difficulty classifying. To sketch the situation extremely roughly, I could say that "Roman" written law was predominant in Italy; that in Spain it was strongly contaminated by local usages, as was also true in France south of a line from La Rochelle to Lyon; more to the north, only bits of Roman law appear in the various "customs." But how many shades of difference there are! In Spain, the conditions of Christian survival in mountainous areas in the face of the Muslim invasion stressed defensive dispositions by consolidating the military-pastoral communities known as *concejos* and the predominantly religious fortified enclosures known as *sagreras*; even in Catalonia, which remained more "Roman," that same situation strongly changed the ancient heritage. In Italy, the principal center for the diffusion of Roman law, it was the growth of cities that gave juridical practice an authoritarian shade when city dwellers were obliged to subject the villagers and the lords of the *contado* to their control. The subtlety of mind that was traditional in Italy did marvels to adjust all legal obligations to that purpose. In the age of the descent of Frederick Barbarossa into the Italian peninsula, Otto, the bishop of Freising, was astonished that Italy was the homeland of the law but a place where it was not applied, and he attributed this anomaly, which revolted his good German sensibilities, to such a subtle knowledge of the law that it permitted discovery of its lacunae and weaknesses.

In lands of customary law the same diversity pertained. Still, the case of England remains particular in this connection. Because of the overwhelming preponderance of the large domains known as "manors" and a strong royal control over the townships, custom developed either in the manorial form or under a form proper to free men (*franci plegii*). The fusion of the two came quite early and quite vigorously, resulting in English common law at a time when local usages still triumphed on the continent.

It is the nature of juridical procedures to register the novelties of the moment in a text, often in a particular conjuncture; this means that the time needed to assimilate those *novae consuetudines* and put them into practice had the effect of setting up a gap between reality and a text that was already out of date at the time one might want to use it. Jurists were quite clearly aware of this curse. Hence they thought above all of putting into fixed form in customary law things that were permanent and valid and occurred commonly. Examples include the nature of family relations, which were predominantly agnatic in the south but cognatic in the north, or inheritance, in equal or unequal parts. Where the Romans had left their mark, this might be a matter of dusting off old laws; elsewhere usages had to be "redacted," at the risk of immobilizing them. Jurists on both sides of the Channel worked to accomplish this toward the end of the twelfth century. It is unclear where this movement began, but in both the city and the country *franchises, lois, assises, keures, Landfrieden,* and others were written down between 1180 and 1260. In England, thanks to the revived common law, and in France with the encouragement of Saint Louis, attempts were made to bring greater clarity to usages. Further proof of this desire to clarify the law can be seen in the kingdom of France with Philippe de Beaumanoir, Pierre Flote, and Guillaume Durand, and, slightly later, Guillaume de Nogaret in the *pays d'oc.* Similarly, "Mirrors" such as that of Eike von Repgau were redacted in Germany. Still, we would have to wait for a long time—in France until 1454 or the time of Francis I—to see the royal power order the clarification of all the accumulated jurisprudence on the basis of earlier local practices.

Naturally, it would be enormously naive to suppose that a "redacted" law could bring any benefit to the poor people who are my main focus; it would be a highly unfortunate "banality" (no facile pun intended) to recall that in all centuries the law has as its object to consolidate the order of the moment, and that such an order is inevitably that of the strongest and most wealthy, armed or not—and I say "armed or not" because the Church of the time insisted that disorder was displeasing to God and that, good or bad, the law of men must always cede before that of the Creator. Shall we deduce from this, as an ignorant historiographic tradition incessantly repeats, that medieval justice was nothing but torture racks and gibbets? This is a complete misunderstanding of the state of mind of medieval judges. A focus on salvation—their own and that of accused criminals—led them to seek negotiation, accommodation, and compromise, with their inevitable financial effects: *Justicia est magnum emolumentum* (Justice is a great profit), as popular wisdom repeated. If arbitration by representatives of the two parties to a suit and a third person with the power to decide, when needed and after inquiry, had a startling success attested generally in many sources, it was not for lack of courts, but rather because the weight of families, witnesses, and guarantors formed the basis of judgment. It would be mistaken, however, to believe that at all times justice prevailed to the benefit of the party with the best backing. Here a glance at our own codified public justice should incite us to indulgence. Besides, the men of those times put themselves in the hands of God to redress their errors. To be sure, professional judges, experts in the law (particularly the written law) were, like their successors, bogged down in formalism and of an exasperating slowness, but in principle, they were equitable. Other judges, who were simply designated or *electi* by a local power might seem partial. At least they were rapid, and there are hardly any traces in our texts of complaints against the sentences of a lord or a college of city magistrates. Moreover, beginning in the twelfth century, recourse to a judgment pronounced by an assembly of "honest and just" men, such as the twelve "sworn" men on an English jury, offered an example of a nonprofessional justice, and in France a corresponding move was the opening of a right of appeal to a superior justice such as the king's.

When it came to pronouncing a sentence, the judge did not systematically send someone to the gallows or the "wall" (le *mur*; perpetual imprisonment). As we have seen, he far preferred to reach an agreement. In case of confusion, he could rely on divine decision, thus freeing himself from a difficult situation. The principle of the *ordalie*—that is, physical trial by red-hot iron or boiling water, imposed on the accused to give him the power to prove his innocence thanks to the aid of God—barely lasted to the twelfth century. It was replaced by the duel, which opposed two champions charged with settling a rival cause by combat. But such a confrontation between two paid professionals who had little interest in losing their lives was somewhat hazardous, and this irrational procedure was banned in the thirteenth century—in France, for example, by Saint Louis. Obviously, there were gradations in the sentences pronounced according to the gravity of the offense. The "blood crime" that had seen the letting of blood would be punished by more bloodletting. Such crimes included anything that harmed the general order: an armed attack or arson, for example. To burn down a barn was considered a crime as serious as killing one's father. Moreover, the sentence was accompanied by financial sanctions, and the early centuries of the Middle Ages have left us interminable lists of fines, the "price of blood," or *Wehrgeld*. These provide historians with a remarkable source of information on the relative value of men, animals, and household goods between the sixth and ninth centuries. Although these tariffs gradually disappeared from judiciary practice, a fine, accompanied by seizure of goods or by destruction (such as the *abattis* or destruction of the house), or even an obligatory pilgrimage, became the most common sanctions. Almost inevitably, their effect was either to ruin the life of the person judged guilty or to condemn him to definitive exile. The existence of corporal punishment—which was more likely to be mutilation than death by hanging—cannot be denied, any more than physical torture designed to force admissions, true or false. We have done much better since, and I shall leave the idea of deepest dungeons and *oubliettes* to the guides in ruined castles. There remained purification by being burned at the stake, and it was the Church that decided to use this punishment against the heretic or the witch, although it did not dare light the fire itself.

Whether or not a person had dealings with justice, whether or not he had sworn to follow religious or secular practices, and even whether he was a peasant, a bourgeois, or a knight, all felt that power—a *dominium*—was exercised over them. At times man felt that power simply because his place in the divine schema had imposed it on him. At times he himself was part of the power structure—in his family, when called to the village assembly, or at the *assise* held in the city on the square of the seigneury. The old Germanic word *bannum*, which historians have picked up, was not the term most used in the texts that speak of power. What the texts use instead are *potestas*, *auctoritas*, and *ministerium*, terms with slightly different meanings. We can leave aside the problems of words, because in reality all such terms embrace the principle of giving orders and seeing that they are carried out. Learned men have investigated the roots of that hierarchy of authority, and they have invoked their principal sources: Aristotle and Augustine among those who thought; the Bible or ancestral totems among those who believed. Such scholars have drawn from this two noncontradictory principles. On the one hand, power was warrior based, magical, and material, and it was the child of the conjuncture; it supported a relationship between forces; and obviously it was changeable, moment by moment, as is illustrated by the symbol of the Wheel of Fortune. On the other hand, power that in principle is exercised from on high downward was systematically limited or combated by a counterpower; the *frèrèche* stood opposed to the rights of the eldest, the testament to the *préciput* (the right to a distribution before division of an estate), the community to the "tyrant," the *consilium* to the *discretio*, and confraternity members to the *échevins* of the city. All invoked the "common good," which could only be obtained by an equilibrium, the moral argument for which was "take in order to give." For the first order this meant harsh management, but alms; for the second, a heavy *rente seigneuriale*, but protection and justice; for the merchant and the laborer it meant rapacity or stinginess, and sweat for both of them. Naturally, I am glossing over the many nuances found in a multiple society. In the fourteenth century, Chaucer spells out thirty forms of authority in the English world.

Investigation of the domains in which power was exercised, the forms that it took, and the actors that it mobilized would require me to embark on a study of society in its internal relations, for example, administration, public and other. A few remarks will have to suffice. Within the family or clan-based group, power was that of blood, and it implied the defense of material or moral goods accumulated by several generations. It was the task of the males (the father and the brothers) to maintain a stability that they had inherited from the ancestors, the instrument of which was faith—not the faith owed to God, but *fides*, the "good faith" that, when ruptured, prompted the exclusion of the group member (the rebellious son, the prodigal cousin, the unfaithful wife) guilty of having rejected the almost carnal obligations that cemented the group together. But we should not forget that there were strong counterpowers— that of women, about whom I have spoken at length above, and that of the Church, the natural defense for the forgotten.

The power of the Church offers the greatest diversity and the highest number of objects. In the first place, and by its very reason for being, the Church controlled the keys to salvation, and it never failed to threaten those who might work against its pastoral function or its more terrestrial positions with being deprived of it. The Church possessed a weapon even more efficacious than persuasive preaching or moralizing *exempla*. It controlled the written word, through which it imposed its temporal vision of the world. The enormous mass of Church manuscripts that have come down to us gives evidence of this. Until the expansion of the cities in the thirteenth and fourteenth centuries, the Church exerted control over all information. If we add that on the purely material level it held and exploited a good third of all land, we can appreciate that the *dominium* of the Church was primary in medieval society, which means that it was the foundation of "feudalism," as the devotees of Marx tell us. The Church controlled, visited, judged, exploited, but also supported, nourished, taught, and cautioned. That two-faced role was carried out by the solid hierarchy of the clergy, or at least until reasoning schoolmen, separatist monks, unworthy priests, and freethinkers slipped out of its hands. But those desertions (or counterpowers) did not arise before the fourteenth century. For four or five hundred years, the Church maintained a tight control over souls and bodies.

The case of the *bellatores* is simpler. They had the armed strength; they were, in varying degree, masters of the soil; they knew how to demand from other men enough to pay their expenses for war or prestige. According to the terminology of the scribes at their sides, they exercised the *potestas* that protected, the *districtum* that judged, and the *exactio* that levied monies. In order to make these powers felt, they had paid agents and armed forces, and they counted on a *fides*, a submission in return for their protection. When that *fides* weakened, as it did in the fourteenth century, the pact was broken. Within the second order the historian encounters another problem, however, that of the internal power relations of vassality and feudalism. I have already rejected the terms "feudal society" and "feudalism," and I have no intention to debate the matter again. First, I do not want to add to the crushing amount of literature devoted to the topic; next, I do not believe in their interest or even in their existence. Naturally, these statements appear provocative, but if anyone insists on pausing over the question, he will admit that these were only a social epiphenomenon, touching one or two men out of twenty, a simple institutional film on the surface of society. Given that nearly all of our written sources (and the same could be said of our archaeological sources) are deeply dependent on the two dominant orders, the historian finds it difficult to resist being led, unless he is careful, to taking a bishop essentially as a lord and a peasant as a "vassal." It is certain that the material domination of the warrior class is by no means a fiction, but what makes a castle "feudal" or not? Why should the man in the field and even the city dweller change his daily life under the pretext that his lord has or has not put his hands between those of another or exchanged a kiss on the mouth with that other? Is it really important that the common person know that his lord is "liege" or whether he has indeed furnished the services of counsel and warfare to which his oath bound him? For the common man, the lord was an armed master, and that is all. All of that "feudal" gesticulation concerned only a thin slice of society; ordinary folk understood nothing of it and cared little about it.

The case of the third order calls for fewer remarks, despite its social weight, or, rather, because of it. The power of a peasant, a burgher, or a merchant would be that of a father over his family or a proprietor over his tools, and although his obligations seem to be greater than his rights, it was here, more than elsewhere, that the counterpowers were the strongest in the face of the spiritual control of the clerics or the material control of the warriors; but these counterpowers were necessarily defensive in nature. The people of the cities, when they managed to form religious, economic, or political communities, were perhaps the only ones who disposed of a power of control. This occurred first within their own order. A master was not a *valet* and an *échevin* was not a craftsman, cloth seller, or weaver. But it also occurred in relation to all those (notably those of the two higher orders) who had to deal with competition from an urban justice, had to adjust to the growing spirit of liberty in the cities, and had to submit to the "law of the market" that reigned there, and whose money stood ready to combat an economy of simple subsistence.

In the climate of confusion between sacred and profane, did there exist a power above the social web that was, all things considered, balanced in its principles? In other words, was medieval man aware that he might have a higher recourse and source of protection? Did he even know what a duke was, or a prince, a king, an emperor? Even more, did he have any awareness of belonging to a "state" or a "nation" that was other than Christianity? Yes and no. And although this topic takes me away from my principal object, I have to pause over it. The chronicles report and iconography shows the people rejoicing along the routes when King Philip Augustus returned in triumph from Bouvines and at the festivities that accompanied the royal "entries" throughout the fourteenth century. They describe the sorrow of his subjects at the death of the "well-loved" but mad Charles VI and the fidelity of Joan of Arc's devotion to her *gentil Dauphin*. Our own age, which has carried the personalization of superior power to a level worthy of the absolute monarchies of the seventeenth century, shows great interest in the progressive "rise to power" of royal or princely authority in Europe of the late Middle Ages. In those centuries we encounter the same procedures to enhance the master of the state that we see today: propaganda diffused by paid chroniclers, agents to put his orders into effect, family clans or partisan groups, rites of sacralization. The emperor, who was German after the tenth century; the kings of France, England, Castile, and Sicily; the dukes or counts of Provence, Burgundy, Catalonia, or Milan; and even the mere lords of the city, as in Venice or Florence, were the object of and the actors in a "royal religion" equivalent to a civil religion in the Roman style. The leader is handsome, strong, just, courageous; he is the master of the soil and what lies beneath it, the protector of the common people, the guarantor of peace; on occasion he can be a patron, and on all occasions he is the military general. He had a charge of spiritual origin that he put into practice in his private life, as did the saintly King Louis, who, after his consecration, was a man of the Church to whom one could refuse neither faith nor taxes. He was, almost inherently, a "good king."

This being the ideal image reflected in the "Mirrors of Princes" that were popular from the thirteenth century on, what was the attitude of the "good people" before this distant master? In the Carolingian age the idea arose within the entourage of Charlemagne, especially after his crowning as emperor, to have all of the sovereign's subjects swear obedience to him. It was a magnificent idea, but close to inapplicable, like almost all ideas of the time. If we can believe the annals, the decision was taken and applied, but given the means of communication of the ninth century, we have every reason to doubt the latter. The experiment was not repeated, except in the atrophied form of personal loyalty oaths demanded of nobles whose lands and titles depended directly on the prince, as in Germany around 1050, for example. In the early fourteenth century there were indeed consultive meetings in France abusively called "Estates" or "Estates General," similar to consultations that had been held for some hundred years in England and in Castile. But such gatherings did nothing to satisfy the common people, whose representatives were overwhelmed by those of the Church and the "nobles." At most, a few cities attempted to make their voices heard when the topic of raising money arose. For the rest, it was thought that the princely ordinances, dictated by the clerical or aristocratic entourage of the sovereign, would suffice to respond to such problems of the "people" as duels, blasphemies, good conduct, work, and charity. That "democratic" fiction is all the more surprising because in the West the period from the Great Plague to the Reformation—say, from 1350 to 1550—was precisely when political disorders and economic ups and downs in the British Isles, in France, in the Holy Roman Empire, in Italy, and in Spain raised powerful winds of opposition, individualism, and general contestation. This is probably why the birth of the notion of the "state" or the "nation" that was to be the foundation of the "modern" age has become a highly popular field of research. Let us keep to these premises: it is doubtful that the idea of "France," or the concept of *Gallici* (to remain within one area) penetrated the commonality for some time. When in 1346 a Picard peasant reminded Edward of England of the existence of a ford that permitted him to cross the Somme before the Battle of Crécy, the man cannot be accused of "treason to the homeland," as was said in the nineteenth century. Quite to the contrary, he was above all remaining true to his local lord, the English king, who was in fact also the count of Ponthieu.

When Joan of Arc, almost a hundred years later, declared that she placed herself among the "good French," she meant the subjects of the king, who followed him in his destiny—a king who happened to be the king of France. Only the learned of the age would have used the term "*Francigeni*," the others—peasants, merchants, and even lords—called themselves Bretons, Catalans, Normans, or Savoyards. A time would come when the idea of being "national" would touch the village, but I do not see it within my horizon.

Gaps

Man is on this Earth by the will of the Creator; if he suffers, it is the doing of a destiny, the outcome of which escapes him; resignation is his lot. The absence or the rejection of all thought of eventual reincarnation imposes on him the task of making his way for all practical purposes alone. But the low murmurs that can be perceived in literature, the signs of pain on facial features or in gestures captured by artists show clearly that man lived in suffering and that the harmonious edifice of Peace, Faith, and Divine Love was only virtual.

First, violence was everywhere. It is a trait ceaselessly attached to the "medieval," and for once the use of the word is, unfortunately, justified. What is astonishing is rather that we are indignant about it. When we review over a thousand years of history, it is tempting to seek phases of increased or decreased violence. This search is purely theoretical, but also quite vain, given that our written sources remain largely aristocratic, hence mutilated, and that, when faced with a castle burned to the ground, the archaeologists cannot tell us why. If a century is mute, as was the case from the fifth century to the eighth century and also of the tenth century, it has a bad reputation and we call it "black"—the Dark Ages, as the English say. If a period overflows with written or painted works, as do the fourteenth and fifteenth centuries, it is simpler to separate the wheat from the chaff. Between these high and low points, Raoul le Glabre's "white robe of the churches," the aura of the schools, a gradual acculturation of the common people, the spread of a presumed moral consensus all make the twelfth and thirteenth centuries seem to shine, and a brief glimmer in the ninth century earns the Carolingians a flattering reputation. Here as elsewhere, is illusion perhaps lying in wait for us? Throughout the thousand years that I am swiftly flying over here, we can be sure that everyone exclaimed "What an epoch!" From beginning to end, exclamations provide a guiding thread—exclamations of joy, of warning, of pain, of hatred, or of love. These might be *Noël*, *Haro*, *Sus*, or *Notre-Dame*, without counting the "bad oaths" and swear words in which the name of the Lord, the Father, or the Son appeared, such as the inevitable *Mein Gott* or Goddamn, which, in the popular vocabulary of France, won the Germans the nickname of *maingots* and the English of *godins*.

Thus violence was first verbal. It took the form of insults regarding honor or sex, or curses that were believed to be efficacious and were accompanied by gestures of defiance, spitting, and blows or thrusts. Much more than the acts themselves, which harmed goods and even persons, it was the curse, the *démenti* that demanded immediate reparation or set off hatred—*odium*—among families or villagers. It could be the source of vengeance, usually armed, that rebounded from generation to generation unless a decisive fight settled the quarrel. The prominent place accorded honor and the rage to respond in the *faide* or vendetta overflows in all of the *lettres de rémission* of the late Middle Ages, where honor is invoked as an excuse for violence. Such tensions touched princes as well as villagers, and they could last for years, affecting the political attitudes of the great or the professional activities of lesser folk. History resounds with quarrels, beginning with the Merovingians, who substituted them for policy, until the age of Louis XI in France, when they still inspired fratricidal battles. Quarrels might involve jealousy, felony, rivalries for marriage or for interests, excuses for wars and pillage, and, little by little, political struggles, for example between the Armagnacs and the Burdundians, or the Montagues and the Capulets, among thousands of other examples that I will spare my reader. Judged by this standard, a rivalry opposing two forces animated by such theoretical motives as the superiority of pontifical power over that of the Germanic emperor, seems a struggle over an ideal to be defended, not a settling of accounts, despite two centuries of bloody conflicts and verbal jousts.

When the "Religieux de Saint-Denis" narrated the history of his time in the beginning of the fifteenth century, he stressed the importance of what was not said in these efforts of vindication; in doing so, he emphasized another form of equally aggressive but more crafty violence: the rumor, the murmur, the *ragot* that circulated about a prince, an officer, or a dignitary. The historian finds an obvious interest in a contagious calumny, private or public, because it reveals the popular subconscious. Allusions of the sort are, in fact, often signs of a latent anxiety regarding the current economic or political context; and the popular myth of "betrayal" or the *idée fixe* of a "plot" that has always been popular in France was much in evidence at the end of the Middle Ages.

Verbal violence, direct or stifled, was obviously contrary to love and peace, and it led to physical brutality. When the sergeant of a lord or a city magistrate seized some presumed delinquent by the collar, threw him to the ground, or hit him with his fist, it was behavior typical of the lower echelons of police forces everywhere and in all times. One can only suppose that the weakness, corporal or juridical, of the man suspected of fraud or rebellion helped to develop a climate of hostility between the threatened individual and the agent executing the master's wishes. The *lettres de rémission,* once again, are full of cases of sergeants who are accosted, even *navrés*—seriously hurt—or killed by individual delinquents or bands. In times of *effrois* the crowd, easily stirred up by an agitator, might attack an agent of the communal or royal power. But, contrary to our tendency today (and this remained true for some centuries), the supreme authority was not targeted. The king was not even aware of expressions of discontent, and instances of monarchs—who were the anointed of God, to be sure—or even of great princes who were assassinated can be counted on the fingers of one hand. This speaks volumes about the emotion of the common people when first a duke of Orleans, then a duke of Burgundy, were attacked in the early fifteenth century—events with disastrous political effects that the mass of men failed to measure.

Such cases were grave but rare; they should not lead us to forget small-scale daily violence, which was more subtle than brutal. Today we might call these "incivilities." A group of *villeins* agree to meet at night to move the stones that mark the master's lands; persons unknown engage in poaching with traps and nets; the Lord's oaks are felled chandestinely; or fraudulent measures appear. All these activities were based on an interest in financial gain. But the historian is happy to perceive in this hidden combat—to which we can add sabotaged *corvées*, ruined tools, short-weighted bread, and short lengths of cloth—disguised forms of "class struggle." We should not forget, however, that all of these men owned arms, even if we do not always see them with a weapon in hand; arms were even one of the signs of the freeman, and when Saint Louis moved to limit their use, he raised a scandal and his efforts failed. Men were quick to brandish a knife, an axe, or a dagger in the fields, in the tavern, at the mill, or at the market, either as a threat or as a gesture of defense. As for theft, the snatch-and-run variety was more frequent than breaking and entering, probably because when a band attempted the latter, it could be ambushed by the night watch and be charged with committing a blood crime. Murder, especially if premeditated, seems to have been less common than today, perhaps because the most frequent reasons for it—jealousy, inheritance interests, family rivalries—were often quickly settled by a financial agreement or by taking vengeance.

All of these men, and even women, who brandished a knife or insulted their future victim were ordinary people. In principle, they did not have the right to use violence any more than the clerics of the first order did. Recourse to arms was an offense to God. But for the *bellatores*, violence was, to the contrary, their trade, their function, their "ministry." I have no intention of listing wars or even investigating the mentality of the swordsman, but although they were clearly a minority in terms of numbers, the warriors had a considerable role in society, over which I must pause. Once again, traditional historiography is in error. The interminable conflicts, dynastic or not, the surprise attack of one castle on another, the noisy cavalcades of *damoiseaux* and *gentes dames* immersed the Middle Ages in an ocean of brutal, "anarchical," and incomprehensible disorder. This is a poor interpretation of such "wars." War was the most quotidian, the most natural form of the activity of the "nobles," people equipped with weapons whose ordinary lifestyle it was. The *werra*—or the *chevauchée*, if the affair lasted and had a political dimension—was a raid of several days, carried on by a band of young horsemen, more or less cousins, against a nearby castle for reasons of wounded honor, jealousy, scrimmage, or simple amusement, to win a girl or a sum of money. On the way, a few cottages or a city *hôtel* or two might be burned. Afterward came a noisy reconciliation with much drinking, kisses, and oaths of friendship. Beyond shades of difference from one century to another, this dangerous climate was not viewed kindly by the common man, who lost his belongings if not his life in it. It is these surprise attacks, practice exercises for battle, that have given the Middle Ages a bad reputation. That judgment is hasty, and all the more regrettable because there was also *bellum*—true, public war—which was well defined and lasting, but quite rare. This was an affair of great personages or, at least, if the king or the count was not its leader, an aspect of the "feudal" obligations of vassals or the *ost* of men obliged to serve. This time, war was a serious affair: several thousand men at the most, but with wagons, cavalry remounts, and dead bodies—or, better, captured opponents, a source of ransom money. The motivation for such wars was clear and often serious; they were political and even, at the end of the Middle Ages, economic. Military operations were scattered, however, and tended to be sieges, surprise attacks, and razzias; actual battles were the exception and were rarely decisive, unless there were enormous human losses. On the other hand, such engagements could last quite a long time, and might easily end through sheer lassitude. But it is an exaggeration, unfortunately endorsed by tradition, to believe that these were continuous military campaigns. Neither on the occasion of the German descents into the Italian peninsula and to Rome from 1050 to 1200, nor in the course of the two great conflicts between the kings of France and England—one between 1153 and 1259 and the other from 1337 to 1453—did the fighting go on without stopping. The best example, so often cited in France, is the Hundred Years' War. Not more than half of the 130-some years of that conflict saw *chevauchées*, and these were actually modest in scale.

Troops, arms, tactics, victims of combat, or political effects are far from being a part of my subject. I return to it when it comes to estimating the cost, which increased along with improvements in arms or the massive engagement of mercenary troops in the fourteenth and fifteenth centuries. These expenses could only be met through ransoms, booty, or requisitions: as early as the twelfth century, Pierre, the abbot of Cluny, spoke of "war perfumed by money." To win a war, one had to spend money, and in order to pay, one had to take. And if the affair went badly, one had to begin again—an unavoidable excuse for a constant renewal of conflicts. But who was going to pay, if not the commonality? By requisitions of arms and horses; defense taxes, the *exactio*, the *taille* or a tax by another name; by paying the ransom of the master captured in combat; and by payments in the form of ravaged livestock, grain fields, vineyards, and pillaged, destroyed, or burned houses. To be sure, in principle all free men had to serve in arms, but the leaders soon understood that this human material was inefficient in combat, which was why, toward the end of the eleventh century, the schema that reserved combat to the *bellatores* was put in place. That change had two important effects. Since free men were no longer risking their lives, they would have to pay, if not in the form of money then in labor—*corvées*—but when combatants were insufficient in number, mercenaries had to be hired. Mercenaries bridged the gap between two campaigns by pillaging cities and villages, which was perhaps worse than the demands of the master. This use of mercenaries began, often by royal initiative, in France, then in England, later in Castile, and by urban decision in Italy and in the Low Countries toward the mid-twelfth century, reaching its full extent in the fourteenth century. Men, grouped in "routes," "companies," and "militias," came from lands that were poor or had excess population, which led to calling the companies by names that were at times inaccurate, such as Brabançons, Genoese, or Navarrans. They had leaders who had drawn up a contract, or *condotta*, with a city or a prince, and they fought—quite well sometimes—for the highest payer. In the countryside and even in the city, it was clear who would ultimately pay the price. When the watch spied approaching *caïmans*, *écorcheurs*, *coquillards*, or other mercenary bands, the city gates were barricaded and the village population fled to the forest.

Two other manifestations of war were totally different. One did not affect the common people and comes under the category of the imaginary or aristocratic games. Errant knights in search of adventure and individual exploits is one aspect of this. They might seek a girl, a duel, or—a sure way to be more admired—the sacred chalice of the Holy Grail. All of the cast-off trappings of "courtesy" disguise these agitations, which delight historians of literature, but it is difficult to believe that the adventures of Percival and King Arthur's knights or Roland with his sword blows enlivened evenings in the cottage or served as a model for any simple man. Moreover, the jousts between teams of horsemen, and the tourneys that lasted several days with which the castle dwellers whiled away their time in the twelfth and thirteenth centuries, only held an interest for the spectator from the common ranks when they were reduced to the level of individual contests between champions raised to the level of sports heroes.

The second manifestation of war is more important. It is the crusade, the holy war against the pagan or the infidel. This was just war: the Church preached it, and kings and emperors fought it. It is a simple matter to ask what motivated the crusades, but many questions remain. Are we seeing a demographic surplus of landless younger sons? Were the crusaders searching for outlets in the commercial ports of the Levant? Were the crusades an externalization of the bellicose spirit that the peace failed to stifle? Or did they reflect a genuine fear of a Muslim offensive in the Mediterranean basin? It was probably all of these, but above all the crusades were a movement of aggressive piety, not an effort to convert Islam but one to put it down: a Christian *djihad*. To take Jerusalem from the Egyptians, Arabs, or Turks, to install one's own forces solidly on all the coasts of the Near East, to recover Spain, Sicily, and Puglia involved more than politics and monetary interest. Islam had understood this well, and it still conserves a humiliating memory of it today. It was not all (or not only) about the large princely expeditions that traditional historiography lists with dedication; rather, it was a powerful popular movement, a manifestation of faith, and an armed pilgrimage that everyone could aspire to make. There were not "crusades" but one "crusade"—every year, by water or by land, lords in arms, but also *valets*, peasants, and merchants left for the East. The voyage was ruinous, return uncertain, and the danger of death or capture very real. Still, although nothing durable resulted from them, the pilgrimage to the lands that Christ and his apostles had inhabited was a great moment of piety in the West from 1060 to 1300. Everyone was touched by it. Our texts show this, and in the cottages, they spoke of the Holy Sepulcher and of Saladin, not of Lancelot or Guinevere.

In its application of peace and law, war obviously occasioned "collateral damage," given the violence and ruin that accompanied it. This leaves me face-to-face with money, today the master of our daily lives if not of all our thoughts. I am not speaking here of public or private finance, of prices or salaries, of the minting and circulation of coins, of accounting or banking procedures, of monetary policy, or even of trade and exchanges, but only of the place of money in the mind-set of all men of those times, of their approach to life on this Earth no matter (for once) what order they belonged to. A preliminary remark will clarify the role of money as an instrument, a notion that was, in principle, inadmissible. Until the thirteenth century, and even later if we look only at country areas, money was a secondary element in daily life. Even more, it was a taboo to respect it. From the Golden Calf to Judas, Scripture subjected money to divine detestation; among the Gentiles, Aristotle even contested its power, although money was known in the economy of antiquity. The Christian Church admitted commerce and wealth, but it saw something *inhonesta* in them and emphasized poverty, since once cannot "serve both God and Mammon." Saint Luke denounced money as the symbol of corruption: that of the body when money dominated its efforts, and that of the soul when it was invaded by jealousy and envy. This categorical rejection was supported, at least until the twelfth century, by the basic nature of the economy, an economy of subsistence in which transactions could be carried through satisfactorily with barter, countergifts, or material goods, even for paying fines, rents or dues, and wages. It was with the growth of cities and the formation of a group of professional merchants between 1100 and 1250, depending on the region, that money crept into practical life. In spite of the evidence and in spite of its own involvement in money, the Church persisted in considering money and its manipulation a source of sin, hence for even greater reason, commerce, the placement of money, and the benefits expected from it. The Church's ire was directed above all at loans, even though they were the source of all investment and the Church itself did not eschew them. Receiving interest at the term of an advance that had been given, under the pretext of the risk run or lack of gain, was equivalent to selling time—the duration of the loan. But time belonged only to God, hence a loan was a punishable theft. Moreover, if the interest was judged to be excessive—for example, 20 percent of the capital—"usury" was claimed, which was a mortal sin and led to Satan. Did the common man show any resistance to the temptations of evil-doing in the face of a Church that winced but was itself guilty of transgression? In the cities, certainly not. In urban and even lordly circles, keeping accounts grew, as the documents show, and the literature of the fourteenth century clearly establishes social classifications in relation to wealth in goods and in money. Things are less sure in country areas, and the rebellions against the growing tax burden did not become the chief weapon of a growing peasant discontent until 1400 or 1450. The "Jacques" of the Paris Basin around 1350 were objecting to the failures of seigneurial power and its judiciary authority. In the final analysis, I do not think it reasonable to seek, even avidly, as many historians are tempted to do today, traces of a "capitalist system" in the cities of the Middle Ages before 1450 or 1500.

And People from Elsewhere

Imagine that a man has come from elsewhere, perhaps even just from a nearby land. He has heard that he would be easily accepted against the payment of an "entry fee," an *entrage*, and he will take care not to say whether he is a free man or not, in case a former master should claim him. He will tend to take refuge in the city, about which it is said, although with more audacity than certitude, that "city air makes men free" (*Luft macht frei*). In spite of all this, he will remain "from outside," *horsain*, someone from elsewhere, an *aubain* (from *alibi*, elsewhere, in Latin), a *forain* (from *foris*, outside), or a "stranger" (*estrange*). He has no right to swear the common oath that would protect him, or to appear in the *assises*, or to initiate legal action before the *plaids*, or judiciary assemblies. At the most, if he feels himself threatened, he might find a degree of security in a confraternity where he would pay a high fee or gain entry into a craft if he is permitted to ply a trade. A master who lacked manpower might seek out such people, *hôtes* to be sent to clear land or guide a plow. On the other hand, the migrant might simply be passing though—a student, a merchant, or an itinerant preacher (these were called *gyrovagues*); or he might be an artist moving from court to court, a buffoon, a *trouvère*, perhaps a pilgrim, and, of course, an officer being sent to another post. As they passed through, all of these people had superficial and fugitive contacts with other men. If the stranger should settle down, however, and form a specific group with his family or his companions, doors would open to relations with the local people.

Xenophobia is a universal animal sentiment founded on a reaction of almost biological rejection toward someone who is not of the same blood, the same tribe, or the same nature, and in this respect man differs from the other beasts only by the effort he makes to dominate that negative impulse. Antiquity did much to contribute to this hostile individualism. Even the philosophers most open to the world classified men according to their language, their appearance, and their mores, even when these "categories," as Aristotle called them, prompted no hatred or scorn, but simply mistrust or incomprehension. Thus it was only at the end of Roman times that "barbarian" lost its meaning of "bearded" or "stammerer" and took on a negative cast. Naturally, the Bible, the Three Magi, and the Christian message brought shifts of meaning. They did so on the basis of solid a priori principles, for if God states that he does not distinguish between his creatures, he nonetheless "elected" the Jewish people as the spokesmen for his law. Moreover, although the Christian faith claims to bring all men together, Saint Paul distinguishes Christians from "Gentiles" and "other peoples." This explains why the medieval centuries were profoundly hostile to the foreigner. Not so much for his biological otherness, his complexion, or his hairiness, nor perhaps even for his language or his religion, but because he was suspected of following the mores of his group of origin, the imaginary thus substituting for knowledge. The stranger, the foreigner, bore threats; he was outside of the collective networks. His sense of honor was suspect and he was quickly accused of heinous crimes, frauds, or poisonings. Even when outsiders were eventually admitted, as in the cities of Italy, they were placed under a particular status, paid specific levies, and were threatened with seizure of their goods by a special right, the *droit d'aubaine*, at their death. The situation worsened beginning in the fifteenth century, with the rise of the two complementary movements of a reinforced state and the birth of "national" sentiments. The stranger had to choose: become a "subject of the prince" by submitting to the common rule, or flee—or at best retire from society and become "estranged" in the current sense of the word.

This xenophobia was not "racism," to use a modern term. In order to become racism, scorn and ignorance had to be added to rejection. Nothing of the sort happened to the university student, the agent of a branch bank, or even the runaway serf, as they were all children of the true God, and at times the learned listened to them with interest, and the princes with curiousity. The climate changed, however, when the Christian aura was lacking. Then the "infidel"—the Saracen, the Moor, or the Turk (terms that were used interchangeably); in short, the Muslim—was a reprobate and a friend of Satan, and if he had a soul, it was surely sold to the Devil. Which was stronger, fear or scorn? Perhaps the two together. There were indeed a few curious minds who saw farther than the turban or the Crescent. They translated the Koran with honest intentions, like Peter the Venerable, the abbot of Cluny in the twelfth century; they read and discussed the medicine of Avicenna and the philosophy of Averroes; some of them spoke with emotion of the magnanimity of Saladin or fell into admiration like Emperor Frederick II (excommunicated, it is true), who "liked to hear the call of the muezzin rise in the night." All of this was for the rich and the learned, however, and the common people remained within the vision of the orthodox Church. To call a man a "Saracen" was a supreme insult as it signified "criminal" and "lawless." It is true that there were few Muslim groups within the body of Christianity, in fact only two, both numerically and economically secondary, both exclusively Mediterranean and whom no one had tried to convert. First, there were the slaves, sold after a raid or a commercial transaction to wealthy merchants and even the Church. In Liguria, the Levant, Catalonia, and Provence they worked as day laborers and domestic servants, were subjected to harsh conditions that went so far as putting them to death—as in antiquity—and the best they could hope for was to manage a stable or be invited into the master's bed. This time the idea of an inferior race may indeed have been introduced, as after 1400 slaves were above all blacks, and black was considered the color of Evil. The other group was quite special. These were the *mudejares* of Sicily, Portugal, and Andalusia who had not fled before the Christian *reconquista* of Spain and the islands between 1170 and 1300. Under Christian control they continued to speak Arabic, practice their own faith, and have their own law. They lived in isolated groups and were marked by a special mode of dress after the Council of 1214, and when they showed no serious opposition to their masters, they were left in peace. Moreover, they were useful in crafts and in commerce. Still, when a Christian encountered them, he viewed them with scorn.

Finally, a word needs to be said about the Jews. Their history is one of the indisputable veins in the cultures of Europe and the East. For two thousand years, amid striking advances and frightful misfortunes, under the stupefied, admiring, or wrathful eyes of both the Christian world and Islam, triumphant or persecuted, the people "elected" by God, the people of Abraham and of the Bible—that holy book of three religions—occupied an exceptional place in society. Although Jews were never many, their history is well known, for their life was highly organized and reliant on groups, and it has left us extremely rich sources of information that range from theological discussions to evidence of the price of kosher meat. There are several ways to approach the history of Jews in the Middle Ages. Let us follow them.

The first concerns the evolution of their relations with the Christian power (and I shall not go into their fate in areas controlled by Islam). From the destruction of the second Temple in 70 C.E. and the "diaspora" that followed until the fourth century, with the official triumph of the Christian faith, the existence of the Jewish people seems to have been concentrated in fixed groups throughout the Mediterranean region. Roughly until the tenth century, relations between Jews and the Christian kingdoms seem to have been quite peaceful. There were no serious attempts to convert them or even isolate them. In the southern parts of Europe, and particularly in the zones partially and slowly taken over by Islam, the place of the Jewish communities seems to have been good, even excellent in Spain and Italy. The period from the eleventh to the fourteenth century was the most dramatic, probably thanks to an awakening of Christian piety and to the power of the established and conquering Church. A hostility that until then had been muzzled and that probably was encouraged by royal authority and pious preaching shook the Christian population. Already isolated by their mode of life, both on this Earth and in their views of the Beyond, obstinately rebellious to all efforts of conversion, stubborn in their refusal of any accommodation in any domain whatever, the Jews were insulted, pursued, chased out, and eventually attacked and massacred. Concerted attacks on Jews broke out following the traces of the "crusading" masses of the eleventh and twelfth centuries, around 1100 in the Rhine Valley, then in the Rhone Valley after 1140 or 1160, followed by violent confiscations and expulsions, for example in the time of Philip Augustus and Philip the Fair in France. The Church went even farther. At the Lateran Council of 1215, Innocent III decreed that the Jews must wear a special headdress and display a *rouelle*, a round sign, on their clothing. As for Saint Louis, seized by aggressive devotion, he ordered that Jews who still rejected the "true faith" be forced to live in enclosed quarters of the cities. Such measures of segregation had the effect of reinforcing the cohesion of the Jewish communities in their piety, their customs, and their isolation. Persecution accelerated under the effect of the waves of terror in the fourteenth and fifteenth centuries caused by epidemics and wars, particularly in southern France, Spain, and Germany, where quite solid groups of Jews existed. This fury calmed down somewhat after 1450, aided by the papacy and the urban bourgeoisie, not acting out of charity or compassion for the Jews, but because the economy, in which the Jews played their role, required it. Moreover, at an earlier date, similar economic issues had already justified the recall, in France and elsewhere, of Jewish communities that had been exiled, with varying degrees of success. It is true that, beyond my time horizon, the Reformation and the Catholic intransigence that followed it rendered the situation of the Jews even more difficult.

The "history" of the Jews is full of ups and downs, punctuated by spoliations and massacres followed by reinstatements for reasons of financial interest, because the vitality of the "elected people" was many-faceted. During the centuries that preceded the eleventh, Jews occupied functions at court in Spain, and even military posts; they exercised particular trades that tended to pay well, such as raising horses or running dye works. Gradually ousted from those economic sectors by an untrusting Church, after the eleventh century they adopted activities as intermediaries that further encouraged their dispersion. As early as the ninth century, the Carolingians, in a cowardly move, charged Jews with the responsibility of conveying to Byzantium and Islam the human cattle rounded up among the Slavs by the valorous warriors of the "great emperor." Jews maintained a role in the slave trade in Islam, leading troops of blacks from Islam's outposts in the Maghreb to its Spanish, Sicilian, or Provençal communities. In the twelfth century, it was Jews who chartered ships loaded with Senegalese or Ethiopian gold and sent it to Europe, thus deeply disturbing the economy. In the smaller cites and even more in the villages, it was the Jews, always the Jews, who loaned money against gages at a high cost and for a short time span, often at usurious rates. Popular sentiment, obviously impermeable to the effects of the return of gold in the West, began to nourish a fierce hatred for the little peddler and his donkey who went from village to village, indifferent to the furious condemnations of the Church and indispensable to the common people. In contrast, Jews were not to be seen in the great commercial or banking enterprises, where the Italians reigned, as the Jews knew they would be too vulnerable to the brutal seizures that accompany the failure of adventurous companies. This meant that for princes, seizing the goods of the Jews was not a serious fiscal recourse.

The Church declared the Jews "God killers," yet it tolerated their cult, protected their synagogues, and consulted their rabbis. Naturally, in the thirteenth and fourteenth centuries in particular, it circulated horrible stories of child sacrifice and profaned hosts and did not refute rumors about the poisoning of wells or plots to exterminate clerics. The common people soon understood, however, that the Jew was outside the law, outside the sacred. People did not know and did not want to know what went on when the Jews celebrated their Sabbath. Even in itself the Jewish community, enclosed within ghettos after 1300, was split into rigorous pietists, the Ashkenazim, reputed to be more dangerous than their fellow Jews, and the Sephardim, Mediterranean Jews who remained closer to Christians. At this point fear and pious indignation between Jew and Christian became bitter mistrust, jealousy, and finally hatred, like the hatred aimed at sorcerers stained with diabolic sins. Society must be cleansed of such people, which meant that Jews must be killed. But how could one kill a people that had witnessed the Old Alliance, a people within which God had chosen to incarnate himself and who ought to be regarded as the negative but indestructible face of the divine message? Were the Jews not the reflection of the Old Testament? Would they not appear on Judgment Day as witness to what had come "before"? The common people of the Middle Ages felt neither scorn nor distaste for the Jews. "Racism" had no part in their sentiments, and "anti-Semitism" itself, which is so prominent in our own times, made no sense in the Middle Ages.

These, then, are our men, living in more or less dense groups, more or less aware of their common ties. Rights, duties, contacts with whatever the authority was, and with neighbors and strangers, customs within the peace or outside of it—these are the traits that I have found in the various "estates" of society. At this level, however, the differences between the strong and the weak, the rich and the poor, the villagers and the city dwellers begin to fade. Will we find the same similarities in their minds and in their hearts? What did these "people of the Middle Ages" know? What did they think about?

KNOWLEDGE

Readers who have followed me this far will not have failed to notice, perhaps with some irritation, how often I refer to the world of the animals, within which I place man among the most gifted. No one can deny that among the animals closest to us, which are the only ones we can seriously observe, there is no lack of attitudes identical to our own, obviously according to their species and biological characteristics. They live isolated or in groups, in the city or in the country; they manifest joy or sorrow; they plan, fight, grab food from one another, and mark their territories; they even have a memory, of which hearing and smell are certainly the surest vectors. We are too quick to shake off all curiosity in regard to such behaviors by calling them "instinctive." When we teach an elephant to count according to our customs, a monkey to play the clown in a costume, or a dog to do magic tricks, in French we call them "learned"—*animaux savants*—but what we mean by that is that they are "human."

Now, however, I have to stop invoking the beasts and concentrate on man, for I have to admit that no one has ever seen a dog hold a pen or discourse on Aristotle. In venturing into the brain and the heart of the human, my task becomes very delicate, however. Either my documentation is volatile, inconsistent, at times purely speculative, as it is concerning the notion of "mentality," or else it is solid, datable, and abundant but follows beaten paths and speaks only of a small portion of humanity. Dreams and their role is a topic that runs through my fingers, but speaking of students in the streets of Paris is old hat. Let us attempt it anyway.

THE INNATE

Man speaks, writes, and also expresses himself by actions or mimicry. All of these translate a sentiment or an idea that either arises at the very moment at which it is expressed or else is the end point of inner reflection, even long reflection. In both cases, they provide the base for the accumulated bits of knowledge that we treasure, some of them inherited or unconscious, others acquired over the course of years.

Memory

"Do this as a remembrance of me," the priest intones at the moment of the Eucharist. "And this was done from time immemorial," the scribe writes at the bottom of his minutes. *Memoria* is the bridge between God and his creature, the foundation on which society rises, the reservoir in which examples, models, and programs for life are kept. All that is to come is in the past, and a world as fearful and disarmed as that of the Middle Ages in western Europe needed the help of memory, individual or collective. It is memory that supported custom, alimented precedents, warded off the unexpected, justified pardon. It is not difficult to define what the common people expected from it. First came the souvenir of ancient times as related by professional tale-tellers or by the village elders; the lesson learned would then be repeated to give the generations to come a notion of the past that engendered the present and to provide that notion with a feeling of depth, a shared "sense of history." Next came a knowledge based on daily experience, which might be professional "know-how" for the workshop or the fields, where it might include the limits of parcels of land and the landmarks, plants, or natural features that define them, and the limits of a territory subject to a *dîme*, a right of usage, or of a particular "justice." When there was no map or the boundaries were disputed, all those who knew or who might know would have to be brought together in a public place, and we have many acts of accommodation in which, before redacting his text, the person conducting the inquiry gives the names and, if known, the ages of the witnesses whose opinions are solicited. Apparently the most difficult task was to find people's names. On the village level they seem not to have been used, at least before the thirteenth century. Although the range of baptismal names is, on the whole, fairly large, they come in compact groups within a circle of neighboring villages. Here there are massive numbers of Hugues and Guillaumes, but in the next village Guy and Robert might predominate. Identical names can even refer to an unexpected provenance: between two Jeans only "the lesser"—*le petit*—or "son of so-and-so" avoided confusion to some extent. As for a nickname that might become hereditary, it appears well after the "Jean, fils de Jacques" disappeared from use, usually not before the thirteenth century in country areas, as we have seen above. In the cities, a division of labor that becomes noticeable with urban expansion before 1200 introduced the "surname" much earlier, and usually one that stressed an activity or a trait of character. Given that the prime reason for forgetting names was the feeling that there was little point to remembering them, it is understandable that in the city, to the contrary, the system of crafts and trades implied not losing sight of the continuity of a lineage, both ascending and descending.

All of the above remarks regard the third order. The situation becomes more complicated when we turn to the two other orders. Aside from having to retain all that pertained to their current life— as was true of the third order—such men had a function that involved other demands. This was particularly true of the *bellatores*, who are easier to define. At first sight the question seems natural. These men of war managed properties, and everything that pertained to their possessions was important to them. They employed sergeants and relatives to recall what they owned and what they could hope for; as early as the thirteenth century, they would have immediate access to accountants or scribes to respond to their orders, as was also the case with the city merchants. They would learn from such men what it was profitable to remember; if need be they could have things read to them or repeated to them, or they could themselves recite recipes for success in the form of couplets or rustic poems, as did the lord of Guines whom I have already mentioned. Even before 1200, Normandy, England, and Italy produced a number of "treatises" on agriculture (books on husbandry, or *housebonderies*), the fruit of an experience, at times monastic, that the masters of domains and their managers could profit from. In their written form, to be sure, these were the works of clerics, but they were based on reports from men with practical experience.

The aristocracy had two other sources of memory, this time exclusive to them. The first lay in the shared imaginary of their social environment, which fed on narratives of lovers or warriors mixed in with the exploits of mythical heroes and their own ancestors. It was indispensable that these narratives be recited, sung, and mimed before a company of the old, who could enrich them with their own memories, and the young, who could find in them examples to imitate and reasons for pride. Naturally, the authors who took the trouble to redact and then recite these *gestes, canzoni*, or *romanceros* were professionals, half poet, half historian. So as to retain their own narratives or enable others to retain them later, they used very simple memorization procedures: rhythm, assonance, repetition, and stereotypes that attentive auditors could fix in their minds. The second field of memory within the aristocratic order was not only ideological but also political. It concerned remembering names. This was the base for prosopography of affiliations, genealogies, and power, a genre much cultivated by historians. Enumerating one's ancestors in chronological order, especially those of the most prestigious branches of the family tree, was an absolute necessity, politically and even economically. It justified authority over others, be they great or small; it brought the family closer to the royal or princely level, where the principle of hereditary legitimacy was the rule. The ties that were woven, then broken by a marriage or an inheritance translated into shifts in an onomastic baggage that historians of law and of the family find passionately interesting. We possess a number of genealogies established from the late eleventh century to the mid-twelfth century, a moment in which powerful lords felt the pressing need to reinforce aristocratic control over humbler folk. Later on, a similar desire to know the roots of their authority over others and the source of their wealth won over the men of the cities, the bourgeoisie, and especially the masters of the merchant companies. Here the power to be gained was uniquely economic and not ideological. Naturally, such *mémoriaux* were set down by professional writers, even though the master pretended to be their author, as was true of the count of Anjou, Foulques le Réchin, in the eleventh century. At times the number of additions and corrections (or remarks) is so great that we can discern the hand of a cleric engaged to produce the work. One example of this is the canon Lambert d'Ardres, working for the lords of Guines. He questioned the young and the old, read a few texts, and listened to legends, which means that his memory was operating at a second degree. It was a memory that spread out in concentric waves, going back to each branch of the central trunk of the family tree, one after the other. There are gaps, which he admits or fills with his inventions. In such lists there is no lack of women, in particular when they brought lands and glory. The ideal was to reach back to the *stirps*, the royal Carolingian root. Three centuries after his death, Charlemagne, and even his mediocre successors, always provide the major reference, both in epic literature and in the eleventh-century and twelfth-century genealogies. To descend from the "great emperor"—what glory! It is useless to say that in spite of accumulated legend and the determined zeal of many historians, particularly those who study German history, no one has managed to make that connection with certainty. In general, such lists go back a century or two before the time they were recorded. But can we go back farther? Without the aid of civil documentation, was it even possible? Moreover, we need landmarks. Count Foulques is supposed to have said modestly, "Before then, I know nothing because I do not know where my ancestors are buried." A necropolis, a construction, an "obituary" recited from one generation to another aided the memories of the survivors. Once again, it was the dead who supported the glory of the living.

The case of the men of prayer is clearer. They were the only ones who held a pen in these domains before the appearance of the "books of reason" or *ricordanze* of the bourgeois of the fifteenth century. If need be, they applied to themselves the techniques of memorization that a highly placed man would have asked of them for his own genealogy. In the mid-twelfth century Lambert of Waterloo, canon of Cambrai, wrote about his own family tree. Given that the Church was a past master in the art of managing its wealth and that of others, clerics also had to know how to count, verify, and remember. But another domain opened up to them. As holders and guardians of the written word, they were the channel through which it reached the faithful. They needed to read, recite, and comment on the Holy Book for the faithful, but also the Psalms that punctuated the liturgy, the *exempla* that nourished their sermons, the "martyrologies" that bore the names of saints to be revered, and the death registers in which the feast days to be celebrated were mentioned. All of this had to be retained and, if need be, enriched. It was among the clerics that the techniques of memory were developed earlier and more perfectly. These included using a chain of words reinforced by repetition of a central idea; beginning a statement with ideas that set off repetition and commentary; using formulas to support the paragraphs of a discourse (these were the *incipit* that so delight the specialists of Church diplomacy); and systematically learning by heart, which required rehearsal sessions with chanting or psalmody, a word that reveals its own derivation.

This recourse to memory depended on a common fund of knowledge that served as a reserve in which to dip. I have already mentioned the exempla several times—moralizing anecdotes related in the mid-thirteenth century by Dominicans such as Étienne de Bourbon (Stephanus de Borbone) or Caesarius of Heisterbach. These texts have aroused much interest among historians of popular thought (I hardly dare say "popular culture"). They consist of narrations that the preaching friars collected, for the most part in country areas, in order to condemn them or correct them; narrations that reflect ancient souvenirs, marginal beliefs, and tenacious phantasms, and that fed the collective memory of the *vulgum*, the *minores*, and the *illitterati*. They were the "folklore" or the culture of the people, as was said at the end of the nineteenth century. Folklore, which was regarded with contempt (or at least in a pejorative sense) as soon as it appeared in modern times (and is this not still the case?), is also seen today as one of the surest ways to gain access to the psychology of the common people or to evaluate the solidity of old traditions. We need to remember, however, that the notions the word conveys are not exclusively "popular." In a number of councils of the early Middle Ages the canons rivaled one another to condemn the beliefs, rites, and formulas that came down from ancient Celtic, Germanic, or Greco-Roman times. We no longer believe in fairies, but the "God bless you" (in French, *À vos souhaits*) that politely greets a friend's sneeze is a classic formula of exorcism against the spirit of Evil that was supposed to possess the unfortunate person with a cold—formulas that were condemned and forbidden by the Council of Leptines of 742!

The Imaginary

It is not "imaginary" when people today scare their audiences with fake dinosaurs, because those large beasts once actually existed. But when, from the tenth century up to today (in northern Europe at least), women think they see nocturnal and aerial cavalcades such as those of the "Mesnie Hellequin," in which female shamans and sorcerers are led by the goddess of the night, and transfer into their own subconscious an "invention" with no other origin than their fear of death and of the dark, this is "imaginary." The imaginary was thus fed by instinctive impulses and unreasoned interpretations. It forms a vast field of research, in which the historians of ideas and the masters of psychiatry play joyfully; it knows hardly any limits, either regarding the profundity of the myths expressed in such visions, or in its mixture of twisted memory and pure phantasm. The people of the Middle Ages were not indifferent to productions of the imaginary, but they condemned them when they were told of them. In the thirteenth century, Burchard of Worms saw in them pagan roots to be extirpated; in the thirteenth century, the Dominicans discerned heterodox deviations in them. The imaginary was common to all orders, estates, sexes, and ages, and if we are more in touch with clerics who explain their thoughts about such matters or peasants who admit belief in them, it is a pure question of sources.

Dreams, as is still true today, were the most solid support for such visions and the surest access to them. Saints and less saintly monks spoke of their dreams, as did kings and princes, along with a few others, who say little, however. What they do tell us about them is evidently closer to what they thought they had dreamed than to what they really did dream. Even when they involved holy matters, the Church was suspicious of dreams, fearing the snares of Satan. Was it not true that princes at times might make brusque and unreasonable decisions under the pretext of a dream? Or, what should we think of a member of the first order who dreams that a saintly man reveals to him the location of his bones? This was decreed a "good dream" and at this point the "invention" of these relics takes on a meaning that goes beyond what the term denotes today. What did all these men dream about? Probably just as is the case today, they dreamed of episodes of the previous day and problems of the morrow, the anguish or the hopes of their life in this world. To have a right to be narrated, dreams had to speak of God, of the Holy Book, of salvation, or of death. When that was the case, as in any hagiography, an ordered and didactic narrative could be made of it. The dream was a *visio*, not a simple *somnium*. But one had to be careful, as to go beyond this simple *apparitio* would be to permit oneself to be captivated by the poison of divination, which fed premonitions, predictions, and the rejection of the Word that spoke in dreams. In as early as the twelfth century the first Lateran councils formally forbade the interpretation of dreams. But these were the attitudes of clerics. In the times of Jean de Meung and the *Roman de la Rose* and in the time of Dante in Italy in the early fourteenth century, dreams left the realm of the sacred to become the secular echo of daily life. Still, this may be only because the dreams of the common people begin to appear in our sources at that time.

The subject matter of dreams was not restricted to visions of Saint Benedict, the damages brought on by storms, or one's ancestors. At times an astonishing episode or an extraordinary personage would slip into a dream. When the dreamer awakens, he describes the visitation; it may well be that when he has finished relating the dream he has deciphered, the dreamer has persuaded himself that he had actually seen those *merveilles* or *mirabilia*. Scholars have done their best to separate pure invention and more or less conscious distortion in the accounts of Marco Polo and Sir John Mandeville. Despite their claims, there are no men who protected themselves from the falling snow by using their gigantic feet; no unicorns, virgin or not; no hedgehogs hanging from the trees, but there could easily have been marching men carrying rackets, rhinoceroses, and the spiny-husked fruits of the plane tree. The inventions of the traveler or the dreamer contain spontaneous analogies that they sensed might be true, along with a dose of creative will. When this happens, the imaginary is nourished by a reality that has been at least partially absorbed. If, in the fourteenth and fifteenth centuries, people thought that everywhere they looked there were deformed beings, fantastic animals, or skeletons, the roving mercenaries, the wolves at the gates of Paris, and the plague have something to do with it. Naturally, we can add to dreams the entire range of sexual impulses. Today they play a determinant role in the psychiatrist's diagnosis, and imagined or realized, fleshly contacts have always occupied a place of choice in man's dreams. It is a domain, however, over which the Middle Ages drew a veil of decency and religious fear. Narrations that make any allusion to such forbidden images are extremely rare. At the most, they appear in the fugitive temptations that someone like Saint Anthony or another hermit will know how to conquer. There is one case that is apparently less frequent or flagrant: dreams that draw on androgyny. When and how, at the end of time, will the sexes be merged and their particularities be effaced so that all creatures, after the Judgment, will make only "one flesh" like the angels? A question of capital importance for the destiny of humanity was that of the sex of the angels. Bombarded in 1453 by the artillery of Mehmed II, the learned clerics of Constantinople attempted to respond to this question before abandoning themselves to the infidel. Our contemporaries who smile sardonically at their worrying about such things in a such moment have understood nothing of the ultimate anguish of the Christians of that region. In any event, the Turks cut short all discussion.

Among the "arts" (we would call them disciplines) that were taught in the schools—a topic to which I shall return—music had extremely fluid contours. But although it included what we usually understand as music, in those days it was translated as "harmony": that of the firmament, of Nature, and of extrahuman phenomena. And if I speak of it here, it is because I see in it an element of a natural gift, an inborn aptitude to grasp the demands of harmony. Without doubt in the centuries of the Middle Ages people were easily persuaded that harmony was the best expression of the desire for equilibrium desired by God, one that did not require the Word, and even less the Written Word. It was in Nature that one could find instruction about God, Saint Bernard stated in 1150, even though he himself was highly learned and an indefatigable preacher. But in order to profit from the harmony of the divine works one needed an innate feeling for and a taste for the Beautiful. Here historians remain perplexed. Over a period of a thou-

sand years, how can we discern what man found to be "beautiful,"
given that such a sentiment is personal and intimate and eludes definition and, even more, classification? We have available only two
ways to approach the problem, both of them quite narrow. Preachers, chroniclers, and—why not?—poets praised beauty as much as
they did any of the virtues. But their discourse is simplistic. For a
living being, a landscape or a human work, what is "beautiful" is
what is "good"—that is, it is pleasing to God or seeking to please
God, a homage to divinity, even a reflection of divinity. The "good
city" is calm, ordered, and active, hence it is "beautiful"; the "good"
chevalier practiced courage, devotion, and chastity, and therefore
he was "handsome." But the other approach is no more convincing. It is that of representations, in particular, painted depictions in
manuscripts, frescoes, on canvas, or sculpted on walls. Even if we
lack sure examples, we could probably add gardens. Disappointment lies in wait for us, however. In principle, a prince "in majesty," a lord portrayed as a *gisant* on his funerary slab, an angel of
Judgment, and even Christ in his mandorla in the apse of a church
must be "beautiful," but they all look the same. From one century
to another, gestures or expressions do change, but they all reflect
an abstract ideal. We have to wait for the fourteenth century to see
any real change in the "good" as it corresponds to the "beautiful"
and a return to actual traits. Can one judge the heads of Charles
V or Du Guesclin at Saint-Denis or at Amiens to be "beautiful"
because they were "good" men? In truth, we have passed, without
transition, from an imaginary beauty to a cruel realism. Unsur-
prisingly, a social dimension had injected its venom, for abruptly,
starting with Romanesque tympanums, common people were depicted as "ugly." The only domain in which a taste for the beautiful
can be seen is in that of the representation of females. The universally male character of the world of the artists (and the poets as
well) explains this. I have said a word above about the feminine
ideal, at least from a theoretical viewpoint. In the final centuries
of the Middle Ages a taste for the beautiful shifted more and more
from the face of the woman, which almost always remained ste-

reotypical, to her silhouette, for example, showing a pronounced taste for graceful arms and legs, an apparently supple waist, with a new importance given to the breasts and the neck in a representation that escapes the canons of harmony to tend toward the sensual. The fashion for closer-fitting clothing (for both men and women) emphasized the body, what was unveiled (at times indecently), and what was hidden (with hypocrisy). From the artist's viewpoint, what guided his brush or his pen was seeking the attention of the spectator or the listener.

There is a final domain in which France today shows its mastery: the role of color. It is an essential element in the internal decor and even the external aspect of buildings and it appears in coats of arms, the use of which became general in the twelfth century, but especially in clothing, including work clothes. Scholars have painstakingly investigated changing preferences in color—white, black, and red before the year 1000; blue in the twelfth and thirteenth centuries; green and yellow toward the end of the Middle Ages— but without giving any real explanation for these changes. What is more, popular wisdom states that this is not something to argue about, as it is a matter of taste and fashion. The symbolic meaning of colors is a domain in which a relation to the imaginary is hard to grasp. What the historian clearly sees is a Middle Ages that is neither black nor gold, but that shines everywhere in lively hues and brilliant colors, which become the natural aid to the beautiful.

Measurement

Popular wisdom declares that "You don't have to think; it's enough to count." But knowing that and being able to do it are two different things. Few domains are as different in our own day and in medieval times. For us a liter, an hour, or a kilometer are givens that are beyond discussion, and the whole world has rallied behind them, although not without some difficulties. As is known, only the British Isles and some territories that they once dominated have remained faithful to an obscure, archaic, and confusing system inherited from the Middle Ages, for reasons that are not important here. The feelings of disorder, caprice, and irrationality that such practices inspire in those who have given them up are like those of the historian who contemplates medieval systems of measurement. Although we are not born knowing how to count, the existence of a mental structure to do so serves as a base for society, and so counting can be considered innate. The notion of measure is, in fact, a personal impulse, perhaps a collective one, the details of which are common to a group, a family, a clan, or a village. This means that the scattering of data furnished by the sources leads each medievalist historian to accompany his study with a local "metrology" that is as confusing as it is useless. The enterprise is in fact all the more vain because, as Protagoras declared in Greek times, "Man is the measure of all things," which not only has the aspect of a moralizing maxim but also permits us to recall that to speak in "feet," "inches" (in French, *pouces*, or "thumbs"), "steps," and "elbow-lengths," or else in sacks, *journaux* (one *journal* is the area that one man can plow in a day, roughly an acre), or sheaves makes no sense arithmetically. Moreover, even if one manages to establish relations and averages, the fact remains that a measure of grain called "level" (*rase*) and another called "full" (*comble*) could go from single to double according to whether the calculation is stopped at the top edge of the measuring device or beyond; similarly, the value of a *journal* depends on whether the land is plowed by an ox or a horse. What good does it do, then, to point a finger at visibly erroneous evaluations in the obstinate belief that they are the result of dishonesty or ignorance? Even at the summit of societies, errors could be enormous. In 1371 the administration of England declared a tax on parishes of the kingdom, which it estimated numbering 45,000, when there were actually at most 6,500 of them. So? Does that mean that documentation is worthless? Or that we have to be happy with nearly mute estimates based on day-to-day experience—"my land," "my *dîme*," "my rights of usage"—or with expressions that say only "big," "numerous," or "important" whether they refer to houses, the dead, or profits? Yes, doubtless.

But, placing ourselves on the level of all these men, learned or unlearned, we see that the number does not matter. It is the work of God, and as it is given, it cannot be discussed, rectified, or, for even greater reason, avoided. Thus to alter a count is an insult to the Creator, almost a blood crime. Moreover, if it is sacred, the number is the sign of power, that of God, to be sure, but also that of the king, the prince, or, more modestly, the lord of the city. Whether a number is public or not, it is variable and personalized, hence it is also a symbol, which justifies not seeking its value in terms of accounting alone. This time, it is the ancient message, more or less Christianized, that obscures numerical value. The number one is an expression of the divine unity; three responds to the triad, that of the Egyptian or Vedic Pantheon before the Christian Trinity; four is the number of geometric perfection, that of the celestial Jerusalem and of the Temple and the house of God; seven is the number of Genesis and the Jewish calendar and also of the days in a week. As for six, it signifies "many" because it is more than can be counted on the fingers of one hand—six companions, sixty ships, six hundred dead, six thousand souls—or else what cannot even be counted: six times six, or thirty-six.

The questions that the history and the grouping of numbers pose to anyone who investigates them obviously derive from these basic notions. These questions are far from being clear, however. Here are some of them: The duodecimal system reigned in calculation until the triumph of the metric system in the nineteenth century. Inherited from Mediterranean antiquity, hence adopted by the Christian Church, its origin is disputed. Moon cycles, which are easily observed, determined the length of the year (as is still the case in Islam), but they do not coincide with the time it takes the Earth to make one revolution around the Sun. Inquiry thus focused on the constellations observed in the sky, which Ptolemy attempted to regroup into twelve, or else on the biblical twelve tribes of Israel. The number twenty, which was combined with the number twelve, for example in the monetary system of those times, is supposed to recall our ten fingers and ten toes, but this is hardly convincing. As for the zero—unknown to the ancient Greeks, who preferred to use the omega of the Greek alphabet to mark the end of all things (as the alpha opened the list)—it was introduced into Western accounting practices only in the tenth and eleventh centuries at the earliest, under Byzantine influence, which itself received it through contact with India, where it had been in use for over a thousand years. I might add that despite its advantages for accounting, the zero was not in current use before the development of commercial or fiscal practices in the thirteenth century. Perhaps the symbolism of the zero, a perfect circle that has no beginning and no end, placed it on the level of God and not on that of men. Another problem, and not a small one, was the substitution of "Arabic" numerals for "Roman" ones. This time, the causes and the stages of the shift are quite visible. It happened through contact with Islam and the East in general at a time of economic and cultural exchanges, after 1050, during the crusades, and perhaps earlier by way of Spain or Sicily. Arabic numerals and the obvious advantages of the zero for written accounts won out in spite of clerical resistance, writing "198" instead of "CXCVIII" was an undisputable progress. The earliest appearance of this new practice appears in Italian merchant documents or among the scribes of the Church who had contacts with the East at the end of the eleventh century and the beginning of the twelfth century.

The question of improvements in medieval counting and accounting techniques naturally leads us to the technical and mental equipment of those who had contacts with arithmetic and geometry, two of the "arts" that were taught in the schools. We know little of what the Celts and the Germanic peoples knew about measuring space, either linear or surface area, but their techniques must have been solid, given that Caesar himself speaks of the precise placement and the equal distance between Gallic trails and gathering places. As for the Scandinavians of the eighth to the tenth centuries, they had no need for outside help to mark on the ground in Ireland, Jutland, or Normandy the limits of the land parcels granted to warriors or their men. But it is evidently the Greco-

Roman heritage that served as a model for a thousand years. From Hesiod, eight centuries before the Common Era, to Boethius, five centuries after, and passing through Pliny, Varro, and Columella, lessons and examples flowed into Christianity. One might even say that before the fifteenth century, Christianity added nothing to them. Drawings such as those of Villard de Honnecourt in the thirteenth century, cadastral fragments from the fifteenth century, and all of iconography bear witness to this. There are depictions of graduated chains, surveyors' sighting devices, compasses and plumb lines, optical squares and water gauges, and, for the building trades, the windlass with a pulley and a compensating weight. The "cathedral builders" were probably simple Sunday volunteers pushing a wheelbarrow, just as the agents of the Florence *catasto* of 1427 were simple pen pushers; but above them there were the *maîtres d'oeuvre* on the worksite and the officials who designed the census. And, to end the list, we should recall that it was in those same times that the primitive calculator—the abacus with its complicated frames—was born, which a tenacious tradition attributes to the genius of Gerbert d'Aurillac, who, as Pope Sylvester II, reigned in the year 1000. Next came accounting in lines and columns, which for us seems the ABC of all account books, but was invented toward the end of the twelfth century by Italian merchants and bankers who wanted a clear and swift view of the situation.

I shall not pursue the question of the calculation errors that abound in medieval accounting, both commercial and fiscal. The people involved were not any more inexpert, inattentive, or dishonest than we are, but when it came to data estimated in numerical terms, they were ceaselessly led into error by the shifting values of the metallic coinage they had to convert into accounting units. Without entering into a history of coinage that has no place here and would take us too far afield, let it suffice to recall a few simple, basic notions that are quite different from our own. The value of sums to be paid or received was estimated according to a numerical scale that was an abstract sum and did not involve any "real" coins; one *livre* or pound (originally a weight of metal) was equivalent to twenty *sous* (a word that meant only "what one pays"), and one *sou* equaled twelve *deniers* (even worse, *denarius* meant "what is sold"). But that odd interrelation, which was supposed fixed, was so only in theory. Thus in France alone, there were some thirty different scales of valuation, which varied according to the place where the coins were struck and ancient customs of unclear origin. There were always twenty *sous* in one *livre*, but that *livre* was not the same in Paris, Tours, Vienne, or elsewhere, and at times, its value differed greatly; if estimated "in Paris style" (*en parisis*), a sum would be only 80 percent of the same sum expressed *en tournois*, and if the person doing the accounting had not taken the trouble to specify which (because it was perfectly clear to him), the historian can fall into error.

That first obstacle conquered, the next one is worse. A tax or a purchase could be paid by metal tokens of various weights, "titles," and appearances. These bore no numerical indication of worth and were distinguished only by a common name that identified them: an *écu*, an *agnel*, a *couronne*, a *franc* (this one bore an image of an armed man), and a hundred others, in France and elsewhere, such as the *florin*, the *ducat*, the *matapan*, the *marabotin*, and more. For this reason, the accounting value of these coinlike pieces was by no means fixed, but varied according to the market or the pleasure of the money changer, hence according to the zone in which these givens applied. And in what metal were they? In the Carolingian age the rarity (even the nonexistence) of veins of gold in western Europe, the Church's obstinate refusal to dip into or "liquidate" the treasures it had accumulated from ancient temples or from profits from the slave trade or that it had simply drawn from the rents paid by the *colons* who worked its lands, led the civil powers to renounce all coinage in gold. I shall not go into the consequences of this decision in terms of commercial paralysis in the face of an East, Greek or Muslim, that continued to trade in gold and silver. There was no lack of silver in the West, however, where it was used exclusively. At the moment in which the three Mediterranean cultures entered into durable contact with one another (in 1020 or

1050 for the southern portions of Europe), gold once again became necessary for trade transactions, which by then were considerable. That "hunger" for gold was invoked later to explain European expeditions of conquest in Africa or America, lands rich in gold, but one can also see gold as one of the determinant factors for the violent expeditions in Islam, whitewashed as pious "crusades." Gold in fact came from the Sudan, in upper Egypt, and from the Indies. Beginning in the early twelfth century, it could be shipped by caravan and then by boat to Sicily, to the Balearic Islands, or to Spain. After 1250 this incoming supply of gold through trade or violence prompted the renewal of striking gold coins in the West, and further confusion was injected into the system by the highly relative and fluctuating values of gold and silver. That imbroglio had two consequences: it opened the way to an unregulated commercial speculation; and it encouraged unpredictable changes in the cost of living. As a further result, historians of both yesterday and today have had the disagreeable feeling that a study of prices and wages (hence of "lifestyles") based purely on this quicksand is utterly unreal, which is why I shall not pursue the topic. What is there to say about musings regarding the value of coins in relation to the Poincaré franc? Still, the men of these time were well aware of the inconvenient aspects of monetary disorder: Justinian, Charlemagne, the popes themselves attempted projects of reform, and aristocratic literature credited a mythical Alexander the Great with attempted reform. The conditions for a serious monetary reform did not exist, and Europe had to wait for the Enlightenment and even the nineteenth century before any other attempts were made.

Besides, whether we are talking about space, volume, or numbers, the medieval approach is not our own. Their approach, inherited from Greek thought, had two dimensions. Neither landscapes nor quantities were valued "in depth," which led to a certain indifference to geography before the thirteenth century. Numbers had only as much "volume" as sight could register; thus Peter Damien crossed the Alps without noticing them, just as Saint Bernard did while traveling along Lake Leman. This was because the world, the work of God, was in a state of immobility that tolerated no critical examination or, evidently, any "reasonable" examination. After all, the Greek philosophers had distinguished the *macrocosmos*, which was the ensemble of the world created by the gods or by Nature, thus could not be changed (as Aristotle and even Plato state), from the *microcosmos*, the small daily world in which man, the citizen, and the traveler, as Pythagoras or Eratosthenes saw him, operated. We have to wait for the thirteenth century and contact with Islam to see the development of a geographical sense in Christianity shaking the placidity of the learned. At that time what learned Greeks or Indians had already theorized and Muslim travelers had verified, at least in part, became a question heavy with consequences: Was the Earth flat or round? Fixed or moving? This was what preoccupied those who knew the answer and knew how to confront a Church clinging to its biblical affirmations— and did not fear to do so. But what about the others, those others about whom I am most concerned? Well, they probably could not have cared less; they already had few means for scrutinizing, predicting, or undergoing the rhythm and the caprices of the weather, so how could they interest themselves in the space that lay beyond the nearby field, hill, or city? The curé might preach of Jerusalem, Rome, or Eden, but did his flock have any idea of those places and the distances leading to them? "Is that Jerusalem, to which we are going?" is how popular historiography reports that the poor people walking barefoot to the Holy Sepulcher greeted every city they encountered.

ACQUISITIONS

The term "culture" is extremely convenient, as is the term "society." Neither one has a content or even a precise meaning, which is what permits us to use them loosely. Does "culture" refer to accumulated knowledge, ideology and beliefs, "mentalities" and rules for living? And does "society" refer to varying internal compositions, to types of relations among humans, to the nature of work? This quibble over words, which is also filled with personal opinions and immediate contingencies, is not useless; notably, it frees the horizon that someone using the term claims to embrace. For me, this will be, here, the mass of knowledge that governed the actions of men during the course of the Middle Ages—I might say the strands, visible or invisible, that underlay their lives. These can come from the domain of the innate that I have just spoken of; they can also be quite largely acquired—we need to look at this second aspect.

Two preliminary warnings apply, however. It is much more difficult for us to understand and explain the importance that a problem like that of the "universals" or opposed concepts had in those times than to speak of the plague or how to work wool. The reason for this is clear. Today our thoughts no longer pass through the filter of the Christian Church, whether we are speaking of matters of "general culture" or scientific inebriation. Our minds are no longer corseted by the conviction that knowledge, hierarchy, and talent are connected, and that, in order to understand and learn, one must possess and cultivate the seven "theological virtues"—faith, hope, and charity, the minimum for a believer, but also prudence, justice, fortitude, and temperance, as Thomas Aquinas demanded. We are far from there.

The second correction is, in short, only a simple accounting observation that is too often forgotten. A thousand years is too long a time, too vast a duration to permit any comparison of its rhythms of evolution and those of our small nub of a century. If we think about it, the contraction of passing time obscures our judgment in a stupefying manner. It has rightly been recalled that as many years went by between the Merovingian Gregory of Tours and Saint Thomas Aquinas as between the latter and Jean-Paul Sartre, but in our schoolbooks, in particular those that survey literature and thought, ten pages suffice for "medieval thought," crushed under the weight of the five hundred pages devoted to the times that followed.

It is a banality to recall that anyone can learn anything in any fashion. It is another to pause over the case of all those whose profession it was—better, whose "ministry" it was—to transmit knowledge. Since they were not all members of the first order, I shall get back to them in a minute. It is a third banality to assert in scholarly fashion that in medieval times as in the Neolithic or today, the human being normally provided with the use of his senses learns by looking, imitating, listening, and reading. What he may do then with what he has learned in this manner is not in question here, but only the procedures by which he acquires knowledge, and the centuries of the Middle Ages offer a number of particularities in this regard.

Two of the four ways for absorbing new data are still ours, and perhaps more and more so. The first of these is sight: journalists speak of "the shock of photos," fixed or moving. Whether they put before our eyes a war atrocity, a sports exploit, a skin cream, the virtues of an automobile, or anything else that interests us, from our toddler years to old age, pictures are today the first source and the prime instrument for intellectual acquisitions. In medieval times, the miniature, the fresco, and sculpture were the most obvious channels for such learning; they provided illustrations of religious, warlike, or legendary scenes in which the spectator could glean a technical awareness of the habits, tools, and gestures of daily life. The symbolic content of such representations touched the intellectuals more. It deserves a closer look, and I shall return to the topic. To remain within traditional historiography, it seems to me that it is going too far to see in that figurative art a "Bible in stone" or a "popular encyclopedia." The manuscripts adorned with painted initials and small figures, even those that aimed at being "practical," like the illustrated bestiaries, were accessible only to the rich and to the clergy. Can anyone seriously believe that the sumptuously decorated *Très Riches Heures* created in the early fifteenth century for Jean de Berry provided anything other than an egoistic pleasure for a collector? As for the "Bible in stone," aside from difficulties of interpretation that still perplex the historians of art, how can anyone imagine that the faithful could have gained instruction from a piece of sculpture placed at the base of a tower lantern or on a four-sided capital ten meters from the floor, unless by looking at it the faithful worshiper ceases to pay any attention to the divine office that brought him there? The historian of thought takes pleasure in examining such works, but personally I think that ordinary folk found in them only pleasure for the eyes and little instruction.

The second channel for learning was via gesture or act. When such information came from on high, it revealed and taught what power, practice, and experience were. Imitating that action or that attitude was a source of information that might be immediate or demand time for assimilation. As is still true today, apprenticeship was the preliminary step, the first stage in comprehension and knowledge; it involved learning to guide a plow, use a sickle or a distaff at a young age, then learning to run a household, keep up the fire, spin wool, forge iron, eventually sail a ship, travel, or sell under the watchful gaze of a mother, a father, a companion, or a "master." We may use different techniques today, but the principles remain the same. To imitate an act is, gradually, to learn how to replace the author of that act and take over his function and his role. I have said a few words above about the symbolic meaning of such gestures and the connections they create between those who do them and those who imitate them. The medieval centuries are rich in cases that today are stripped of their former power. There are some examples that we can still understand, however: to be seated in a large hall when the others are on their feet, or in a professorial chair when the others at the university have only bails of hay, to be seated on a throne when the others are on their knees, or at the end of the table when one is the oldest or the most important. In such cases, would anyone not look at how the "master," the lord, or the professor is acting? Another example is wielding a stick, the sign of the authority of the one who gives orders: the cane of the angry father chastising his young, the crook of the chief shepherd or the staff of the bailiff in the fields, the baton of the officer in function, and finally, the scepter in the hand of the king. A last case is typically medieval: authenticating a decision that requires a visible act of power. Our signature must be autograph, which means that no one else will counterfeit it. Because he could not write his name, the medieval man traced a cross if he was poor (although we have crosses traced by royal hands), or else he sketched a *signum*, an *S* with a line through it preceding or accompanying his name, written by a professional scribe. If the signer held power, his signature would be his entire name in ornamented letters—his "monogram"—some parts of which he would himself trace if he was king. But what is essential is the apposition of some sign on the document, either affixed to it or hanging from it on a pair of leather laces or a handful of fibers, or a wax seal that bears a mark, an emblem, or a figurine proper to the author of the decision, who publicly poses his hand on the act and signs it in witness to its authenticity. In 1194, because he was fleeing before his enemy Richard the Lionhearted, Philip Augustus, in his haste, threw his great seal and its matrix into the river, and the king was obliged to substitute a new seal for the lost one. Naturally, there were false seals in those times, just as today there are counterfeited signatures, but what counts here is the force of the power that is implied in the act, graphic or not. Imitating that act is in fact the sign that someone intends to substitute his force for another's.

Thus speaking, reading, and writing are now the most ordinary paths to knowledge that are open to us. Our contemporaries speak with no rhyme or reason, they read less and less, and they are content with "abstracts" and "e-mails." They write not at all; they click and they fax, when possible abbreviating phrases and even words. My job here is not to sigh at this state of affairs, but to emphasize that in medieval times the situation was quite different. Then the Word of God and the Holy Scriptures supported knowledge. Reading and writing are evidence to us of a means of communication, but even today not everyone has access to them, which means that from the start, the question of literacy arises. Next comes the question of the language used. I have to pause here for a moment because it immediately opens up a highly important social gap. A truly minuscule portion of society was made up of individuals who possessed skills that they acquired thanks to their profession, because their "order" was that of those who know, and they learned how to read and write in the schools so as to communicate the Word of God. Almost all of these were clerics. As the centuries passed, their numbers remained roughly constant: some twenty thousand in England out of a population of 3 million in 1450 and a proportion of probably around 10 percent in France. As for the people of the other orders, if one half of them knew how to read, those who could write were an infinitely small number. The chronicler Matteo Villani tells us that before 1370, 70 percent of Florentines counted themselves among those who could write, but this was probably pure boasting on the part of arrogant city dwellers. We can accept the idea for merchants and a few princes with some culture, but it is certain that before 1250 Gregory of Tours states that because he did not know his letters, the Merovingian King Chilperic I claimed to have invented others, and Einhard explains that Charlemagne, in spite of his tenacious efforts, was never able to hold a pen. Was this the fault of the distant eighth century? In the middle of the eleventh century, the Capetian Henry I was still signing acts with an X. What can we say about his contemporaries in the countryside? In the fifteenth century, wooden stamps were made that, when inked, enabled the *condottieri* to sign their contracts as mercenaries—and these were Italians, the most nimble-witted people of the time.

Whether speaking, reading, or writing, the men and women of those times were confronted with the problem of linguistic expression. That vast question must detain me for a moment. The language of power, law, and faith was Latin, even in places where no Roman soldier or magistrate had ever set foot, which meant over half of "Christian" Europe. We can agree that toward the south of the continent, roughly south of a line from the Loire to the Danube, a degraded, mutilated Latin contaminated by the expressions and accentuations of a vernacular language might have formed the base for opening the door—or people's ears—to the language of religion, but this did not occur later in the "barbarian" lands of the Franks, the Saxons, the Scandinavians, and the Slavs. Besides, even where traces of low Latin did remain, the version of it in the Iberian Peninsula was not the Gallo-Roman version, which in turn was not the trans-Alpine version. The clerics who surrounded Charlemagne, and who came from different lands, took on the task of purifying the holy language, an admirable accomplishment, but they rendered that "pure" Latin absolutely incomprehensible to the common folk, both in the cities, where a certain "elite" might be able to grasp something of it, and in the village, where the curé would have to translate it rapidly into the vernacular from the pulpit if he wanted his message to be understood. A fairly easy task in "Latin" lands, it became infinitely more difficult when the Carolingian Latin had to be reduced to Pict, Breton, or Saxon. Between 800 and 950, from the north to the south of Europe, the vernacular was pushed into the domain of everyday communication, and the triumphant new Latin was restricted to being the language of the learned. One might well wonder, under such conditions, whether from the fourth century to the thirteenth, the code, the chronicle, the poem, or the romance written in Latin had the slightest chance of being perceived or followed by the common people. The same question might be asked of our own time, given that in France, for example, children are taught (or were taught!) that the "literature" of the Middle Ages had nothing to offer before Joinville or Villon except for three phrases dating from an oath sworn in Strasbourg in 842, a *cantilène* in praise of a holy woman from the early eleventh century, and the *Chanson de Roland* only a bit later. Because all the rest—and this remained true for a long time—was in Latin, it did not exist. No one read it, *non legitur*. But when it came to redacting a commercial contract, measuring a field, designing a tool, or even pronouncing a sentence, it was important to be understood, hence the spoken language demanded its place among written documents as a way to avoid contestation, error, and fraud. From the late eleventh century, names, words, formulas in common language began to appear in Latin texts. In Catalonia, in Provence, in Auvergne, and (naturally) in Italy this presented no problems; more to the north in the twelfth century, there was still some hesitation. A text might say *gallice, quo vulgo dicitur*, followed by the vernacular term. Eventually, as a way to simplify things, the entire text was redacted in the vernacular—in Anglo-Norman, in Oïl, in Picard, in Lorrain; in the *pays d'oc* Poitevin was used, along with Gascon, Toulousain, and Provençal. Such texts were at first destined for city dwellers, who needed them in their daily lives, or for the aristocracy, who wanted to hear sung to them exploits that they might imitate. After 1240 or 1250, the vernacular was used everywhere, and if we cannot hear the voices, at least we can read the writings.

Writing

In a civilization of the act and the word, orality was quite surely the prime support of communication and knowledge, but the written word retained the magical power that Holy Scripture had conferred on it. To kiss the Bible and to deposit in the tomb the phylactery bearing the invocation and the identity of the deceased were not mere "signs" of piety, but marks of submission to the power of written things when they pertained to the eternal. This may be a Mediterranean concept, but Scandinavian runes quite probably had a similar function. So, if the historian does not have voices, he or she has texts of all sorts. They are innumerable, and it is pure erudite coquetry to affect great sorrow at the disappearance of so many of them. In reality, and speaking honestly, no more than a quarter of what is conserved in the archives has been consulted or utilized. To speak only of France, and not counting either juridical texts, literary works, or the earliest notarial or accountants' documents—that is, keeping to acts "of practice" alone—we possess in our public collections, for the period from the ninth to the fourteenth centuries, more than five thousand cartularies, or collections of copies, of some two hundred items each, and nearly as many original documents or isolated copies, for a total of nearly a million and a half texts. What is more, that volume tripled in the two final centuries of the Middle Ages. To be sure, the distribution of this material through time and in space is quite irregular, and there are gaps that owe as much to the will of our own contemporaries as to natural or human accidents; documents judged to be useless or of no durable value have been eliminated, which has increased the relative mass of the "juridical" texts that have been saved. It was precisely the interest in sorting out and classifying that marked the progressive triumph of the written word at the end of the eleventh century. But the witness that these texts bear is partial in both senses of the term, as it shows us the world only as the clerics saw it. This is a constraint and a mutilation that we should never lose sight of.

The art of writing was learned at school; it is not an innate skill. It was difficult, as it was not only a question of holding a pen or a chisel; the writer also must possess some knowledge of Latin, of the ancient authors, of the "philosophers," of the Fathers, and of all that is involved in "grammar" and "rhetoric" in the schools and in the monasteries. The writer must also be a master of words, of their various meanings, of their opposed content, thus opening the way to discussion and persuasion. An entire technique, in large part Greek in origin—the *disputatio* — was intended to encourage reflection among the learned, and belief among the faithful. "Dialectics" permitted the study of general ideas, concepts, or "universals," referred to in the Middle Ages as God, the Good, Evil, the Virtues, dogma, and so forth. The contribution of the Middle Ages to this soaring rise of thought was prodigious. But are we sure that the wine-maker or the weaver shared in it in any way?

I would like to set aside for the moment the weight of knowledge acquired through writing, in order to examine several problems of a technical nature and respond to some practical questions. Here are some of them. First, who wrote? Almost all of those who wrote were men. We do indeed have a few female signatures, but the rare works credited to female authors of romances or poetesses, from Dhuoda in the ninth century to Christine de Pizan in the fourteenth, have not come down to us in their own hand. Moreover, the *lais* of Marie de France were probably not written by her, and it is probably Abelard who wrote the letters of Héloïse. In those days and for many centuries to come, women might speak, but not hold a pen. The men who wrote were sometimes laymen, like the Italian scriveners of the eighth century, or merchant accountants and scribes in the cities of the thirteenth century, when the economy demanded many more written documents. In the overwhelming majority, however, they were clerics, workers in the episcopal writing bureaus known as *officialités*, chaplains of princes or lords, monks above all, ten or twenty of them working under dictation in the *scriptoria* of monasteries to produce copies of works of piety, running the evident risk of inattention or incomprehension that leads to errors, to the great joy of finical and erudite scholars today.

The ultra-rapid "progress" in abbreviating language today—swallowing syllables and contracting words, along with the drunken profusion of initials incomprehensible to the non-initiate either when spoken or written—forbids us criticizing the procedures of systematic abbreviation used by medieval scribes. This has been a constant practice in certain types of philosophic or scientific texts or in certain periods, the eleventh to the thirteenth centuries in particular. It has never been explained satisfactorily. Does abbreviation reflect a desire to write faster, to save space? Does it have something to do with the nature of the writing implement? Opinions differ, as they do for our modern customs. But the habit adds other difficulties to reading a medieval document and it presents our own contemporaries with sizable obstacles. As for the graphic act itself, deciphering a text requires techniques of paleographic reading that can be arduous. To be sure, the history of writing is well known today; it explores the material support on which people wrote, the nature of the writing instrument, and the constraints introduced by both of these, but it is also interested in the number of texts written and the significance of those texts to their public. The "brief notes" of the notary or the minute-books of the clerk of the court can easily seem "illegible" to an untutored eye, but a royal diploma, a contract that is *parti* (redacted in two copies), or a lease for a plot of farmland will be carefully drawn up and at times provided with colored ribbons and decorated letters. Naturally, such remarks pertain to literary, juridical, or philosophical works, the ornamentation of which can go as far as including miniatures, which require the collaboration of an artist and contribute to a larger range of information, spiritual and, even more, material. It should also be remembered that in certain centuries a desire for clarity, often of royal or at least public origin, gave writing a regularity that we find enchanting. A survey of ligatures and abusive distortions, the almost direct heritage of the writing styles of late antiquity and its epigraphy, writing on stone, gave rise first to the "uncial" book hand of the sixth to the seventh centuries, then to the "Carolingian minuscule" of the "Palace school" of the age of Louis the Pious in the late ninth century. That was followed, between 1150 and 1250, by a more fluid cursive called "primitive Gothic," and eventually by the "Roman" script of Italy to which printing, beginning with the presses of Aldus Manutius (Aldo Manuzio), around 1500, conferred the dignity of a clear design abusively called "humanistic" that has become ours without serious resistance from computer keyboards.

If the Middle Ages did not, before it ended, durably mark our manner of writing, it left a highly important base for our written culture. I will say only a word about ink, which was already known in China and ancient Egypt. It was a watery mixture of lampblack, glue, and iron sulphate, with nuances that interest only the chemists. And I will say little more about writing implements: a chisel on stone, a stylus on soft brick or wax, the calamus of hard wood for a support made of plant material, and a bird's feather—preferably a goose feather—on animal skin. What this all led to—ligatures, thicknesses of letters, full or thin strokes—concerned the learned; the common people remained indifferent. In contrast, and this is essential, there are two problems that merit a pause; they are all the more important to us because our modern procedures have strongly upset their long use.

The first touches on the material support for writing. Aside from lapidary inscriptions or sepulchral epigraphy, the centuries of the Middle Ages used plant-based or animal materials for writing. We have no examples (or they have not yet been discovered) of writing on tree bark, for example the birch bark of Slavic lands, but we do have wooden plaques of various origin—poplar or conifers in particular—covered with wax that were used to bear inscriptions or dispositions to be carried out immediately and erased equally immediately. This technique, which was widely used in ancient times, was long thought to have been secondary in medieval times, but, with the aid of a few archaeological artifacts, we might well wonder if it was not comparable to our "first drafts," "running notes," and memos. The plant material preferred in ancient times was, as is known, papyrus, a semiaquatic reed whose stalks, like those of the elderberry, furnish a solid screen almost like cloth when split, interwoven, and glued together. The use of papyrus is confirmed in the Far East and in Egypt long before the Common Era, and Mediterranean antiquity made large use of it. Unfortunately, although it is very supple and fire resistant, papyrus is of subtropical origin, hence it is sensitive to cold and humidity, and rodents find it appealing. Moreover, once Islam became the master of the southern shores of the Mediterranean, papyrus became so difficult to obtain that the trade was given up in the seventh century, although Italy and the Roman curia held out until the mid-eleventh century before abandoning its use. The lamentable state of "Merovingian" fragments attests to this failure. Paper, which draws its name from papyrus, was fabricated in similar ways. Known in China before the Common Era, paper was made from a paste of cotton or sawdust; it was supple and more resistant to the caprices of the weather than papyrus, but it was very vulnerable to fire, and rats and worms found it very tasty. Paper arrived in western Islam, Sicily, and Andalusia in the eleventh century, but it was not found in Christian lands until the mid-twelfth century, in Roussillon and in Provence (and then only wood-based paper). Paper was not used in daily practice until the fifteenth century, and even then it absorbed ink so greedily that its use was restricted to first drafts and minute-books, where the ink leaked through to the back side of the page. This drawback of paper, like the exorbitant cost of papyrus in its time, assured the triumph of animal-based parchment, the name for which probably comes from the region of Pergamum in Asia Minor, which was known and utilized before the fall of Rome. Parchment was made from young skins without cuts or holes, either of stillborn calves (this was the precious "vellum") or, more commonly, of sheep, carefully shorn. Resistant to rot and fire, to water and gnawing rodents, capable of being reused after being scraped, parchment's only defect was its strict dependence on herdsmen and tanners. It did not cost much, and it was the object of an active commerce, especially when writing developed to include psalm books for the bourgeoisie or, in the schools, the practice of *peciae* in which to note the words of the master. Fairs like the one in Lendit, across from Saint-Denis, did an active business in such notebooks, especially among students at the university in Paris.

A second element suffices to give medieval times a place of the first rank in the history of culture in the West, although we may be witnessing its end. Those centuries invented the book, or the *codex*, as the learned say. Older custom had privileged texts in the form of rolls, *rotuli*, fixed top and bottom to a stick that the reader unrolled or rolled up again according to the portion he wanted to read. It was in the second century C.E. that the idea arose of sewing separate leaves along one side and placing them in a binding. Although papyrus lent itself poorly to this treatment because of its natural flexibility, parchment enabled the reader to keep his place in several passages of a text by the simple use of his fingers, and without having to manipulate a roll. If *rotuli* were certainly easier to conserve, the conservation of the *codices* was much facilitated when their bindings were strengthened, at times with wood, which permitted vertical storage. The possibility of multiple consultations eliminated the use of the roll. That manipulation, which once was simple good sense, is disappearing today before the remarkable "progress" of screens that unroll their text without having to use complex maneuvers and that mark a surprising return to customs long ago abandoned as inconvenient.

What to Learn?

In a society still closely connected with nature and with the survival needs that nature satisfies, people had no need to be familiar with Aristotle on logic or even to know how to read; only the mastery of actions mattered. As soon as the group becomes a society of men, however, it needs a language of exchange understood by all; at that point, the oral and the good use that was made of it in earlier ages made it unnecessary to read or write that language; the spoken word took care of diffusing it and repeating it. This provided a level of "culture" that might be enough for a simple man. But when man moved up to the level of a group living in society, he needed numbers for a life of exchanges, and a holy text to express belief. At this point he had to rely on a "specialist" or recite a text that he had learned by heart. In either case, the intervention of that "specialist," someone who had sufficient knowledge and could serve as a "bridge" between man and science, and between the believer and God, became indispensable. This particularly banal remark is intended to note two constraints. On the one hand, in principle, the common people had no need to learn and could turn to those who did; on the other hand, those who were learned were the ministers of the Divinity. In a society of that sort, it is thus the clerics, and they alone, who are masters of knowledge, at least at first. Since I am particularly interested in the "little people," I could stop here. But those clerics also had, as part of their mission, to guide such men on the road to salvation, so they felt impelled to diffuse downward what they had acquired from on high. A village curé, a chaplain in the castle, and a canon in the city took on that task; they commented on the epistle or the scriptural passage of the day, and they had their flocks recite psalms with obscure, even incomprehensible texts that were, though, the path of the faith, just as the suras of the Koran were for Muslims. Such men might explain decisions on the part of the local powers (when they understood them), or they might recall local customs. In the cities, an audience interested in such topics might be increased through the circulation of small collections, at times illustrated, known as manuals, but even these passed only through the hands of a minority of city dwellers or lords who could read (in the vernacular, of course). Beginning in the fifteenth century, when the cultural level rose, bestiaries and treatises on agriculture, like the Anglo-Norman *Fleta* or the *Viandier de Taillevent* in the fourteenth century, reached beyond the elite. The numbers of didactic secular texts rose noticeably in the two final centuries of the Middle Ages, when "book culture" penetrated into the mass of people, until then *illitterati*.

The learned acquired "book culture" in the schools, which I shall get to soon. It was almost entirely inherited from antiquity. It constituted the base of the knowledge expected of a "citizen," a free man in the eyes of the law, and one sufficiently well-off not to be obliged to work with his hands and capable, if need be, of playing a civil and political role (both adjectives that evoke the city). In short, he was expected to possess the same qualities as the *honnête homme* of the French "classical" age. The tendency to subject everything to rules that underlies Roman thought had introduced, in the beginning of the Christian era (for example, under the influence of "rhetoricians," professional lawyers like Quintilian in the first century), the idea of a program of studies organized by disciplines or "arts," which meant by the types of professions likely to have need of them. This framework lasted beyond the Roman centuries to be recuperated at the dawn of medieval times in the fifth and sixth centuries, in Italy by princes' counselors such as Boethius and Cassiodorus, after which it was adopted by the Church and by its men of letters as the technical foundation for all reflection on Scripture or dogma. There were three paths that gave access to this learning—the *trivium*—and that were difficult to separate, as they were interconnected. These were grammar, to master the language of the sacred; rhetoric, to accumulate and define juridical and moral notions; and dialectic, to help organize a reasoned argument and formulate responses. Both in the age of the Greek masters of antiquity and when university courses were developed in the Middle Ages, there was a fixed and logical system of thought. What was known about a topic was brought together in the *quaestio*; the *sententia* drew a teaching from it, and the *disputatio* subjected it to a critique. Whether the topic was rules for current life, a problem of law or of morality, or even an abstract notion having to do with faith or dogma, this was the procedure that was followed in the "schools" and by "Scholasticism." The Church had adopted this system, even though it feared and even on occasion condemned the stage of the *disputatio*, at which subtle minds tended to escape its control. This was because a question touching on faith, divinity, or, more simply, good and evil bore the risk of deviating from the mouth of a master and leading to error and heresy, both for the learned man and for the students who listened to him. This was the principal contribution of medieval reflection in the history of Western thought, and, without entering too far into a domain that exceeds my competence and my convictions, I feel I cannot ignore two important questions that were much debated in the schools and from the pulpit in the eleventh and twelfth centuries.

First of all, and as Anselm of Canterbury phrased it in 1100: "Must one believe in order to understand? Or understand in order to believe?" God would have to opt for the first response. Hence ontological reflection is at the base of faith and supports the entire teaching of the dominant Church. To hesitate to respond is to subject the "proofs" of the existence of God to reflection, to stray from the true path, as Abelard did not long after: *Sic et non*, "Yes or no." It was only in the fourteenth century that the Anglo-Saxon contribution of the virtue of experimentation to enlighten debate gradually led to a preference for the "No." The second problem, and one closely connected to the first, stressed the weight of words and the taste for words in medieval society. Do concepts or "universals," which serve to designate an ensemble of notions or ideas, exist as such? Are they things, "realities," *realia*? Accepting that stance, one was a "realist"—a term that today would imply a hint of skepticism. Or are words merely *nomina*, intellectual notions imagined by man, and nothing more? To accept this idea was to be a "nominalist." As long as the topic in question was inherently human, such as the notion of "woman" or that of "nature," this could be simply mind play, but discussion of more moral notions—good, evil, the beautiful, or the true—implied a risk, but only a modest one since they did not affect faith. But what if the question touched on God? Is God "real," and thus, with no need of demonstration? Or is he a creation of the human mind? The realists invoked Plato on the soul; the nominalists held for the "first" Aristotle and nature. In one camp there were Augustine and the Fathers; in the other, the Muslim Averroes and the "categories" of the "second" Aristotle. When, in the thirteenth century, the whole body of Aristotle's works, with all their contradictions, was introduced into the West through the "Arabic" thinkers, it was this thought that scholars fought over bitterly. Thomas Aquinas attempted a compromise that left some place for reason and brought Aristotle closer to Christian thought. In 1277 he was condemned for his pains, then canonized in 1333, and today's philosophers have raised him to the summit of their reverence. This is the way thought works.

If I have lingered at some length over these quasi-metaphysical problems, it is to stress the blindness of many "moderns" before the progress of human thought in the centuries that they categorize as "Gothic." But I am not fooled. Neither the wine-maker in Burgundy nor the shepherd of the Causses nor the weaver in Flanders had ever heard of Aristotle, and perhaps the same was true of the parish priest in his village. By a curious reversal that our own times render even clearer, an entire range of knowledge has a better chance of interesting the common man today than his counterpart in ancient times. This is what we conveniently call "the sciences," all of those disciplines that do not concern the soul but in which the everyday man finds something useful. The *trivium* only offered an ideological glimpse of such topics, and the Church was not very conversant with them. Better, it was suspicious of them as a possible lair of doubt and heresy. Their study entered into the Scholastic scheme, however, as they were the "four ways" or *quadrivium*. At the time not one of these four ways led very far; rather, they produced only glosses—that is, commentaries—or translations or descriptions without any overall viewpoint. Even "inventions" tended to be the development, at best the reduction to a system, of ancient discoveries—which is not nothing, to be sure, but does not add much to the "sum" of achievements of the Middle Ages. What was the brace and bit, or lap-jointed boards in comparison to the *Summa* of Thomas Aquinas? The *quadrivium* opened the way to other domains, one of which I have already spoken about: "music," the study of the harmony of sounds and forms. The monks, Cluniac monks in particular, made ample use of the discoveries of Guido of Arezzo by fixing on his musical staff the six basic notes that, since the eleventh century, were designated by the initials beginning each line of a hymn to Saint John. Some have asserted that we should also see in "music" the art of governing men, but this is difficult to prove! Arithmetic and geometry, which came next, have certainly permitted construction and land measurement. Notebooks of drawings, like those of Villard de Honnecourt in the thirteenth century in northern France, attest to a mastery of the rules of geometry, but errors in estimating distances or in bird's-eye views, as well as the architects' uncertainties in the calculation of the thrusts and the weight of vaults erected over many buildings, all show well that worksite experience often prevailed over calculation in the study where construction and measurement were concerned. As for astronomy, which was constantly feared and accused of slipping toward astrology, it was long limited to computing the ecclesiastical calendar and observing motion in the skies (which Aristotle denied). Not until the fifteenth century and the arrival of multiple Greek and Arabic manuscripts was the science of astronomy torn away from simple parroting.

"Greek manuscripts"? Certainly, and a "humanist" like Coluccio Salutati could read them in the original Greek even before 1400. Knowledge of the Greek language in which so many works had come down from antiquity had never disappeared, but it was confined to a few monasteries that had kept contacts with the East, or else to a few curious scholars, among them John Scotus Erigena in the Carolingian age. However, merchants were likely to have some acquaintance with Greek out of professional necessity. Translations were available through intermediaries in the Iberian Peninsula, Sicily, and Byzantium. Many others abandoned all attempts to read Greek: *graecum est: non legitur*. Italy, as usual more open to the world, created courses in Greek in Florence in the mid-fourteenth century, but with little success. Even the most nimble minds—Petrarch in that same epoch, or Boccaccio—knew only a few words of Greek, while professing a lively admiration for the "language of the gods." Petrarch had acquired a Homer that he placed on a reading stand at the center of his home and that he kissed every day, inviting his guests to do the same. It was the decomposition of the last fragments of the Empire of the East before 1453 that urged erudite scholars and book collectors to save their treasures from the Turks and move them to Italy. Some of these collections, like that of Cardinal Bessarion, were genuine libraries; popes—Nicholas V for one—founded translation workshops; and printing furnished the first edition of a Greek grammar in 1476. When Greek texts had become accessible and even, after 1500, the object of an erudite fashion, Greek, now rehabilitated, presented a danger to the Church in that earlier and inaccurate translations needed to be rectified. Although I usually hesitate to use the word "Renaissance" because it casts an unjust opprobrium on earlier periods, I have to admit that the return of Greek caused a profound shock, even beyond the small circle of professional "humanists." The Holy Scriptures had not been redacted in Latin, but in Aramaic, in Hebrew, and in Greek, with a series of translations. What, then, was the place of the fourth-century Latin Vulgate of Saint Jerome, or of the commentaries of Saint Augustine of the fifth century, Isidore of Seville in the sixth century, and Gregory the Great in the seventh century, given that these learned men and theologians thought and wrote on the basis of translations, perhaps even dubious ones? Doubt was added to the more general discomfort of the faithful of the fifteenth century, and one might suggest that access to Greek was one of the roots of the Protestant Reformation of the Church.

And Where?

All humans have an innate desire to transmit the fruit of their efforts in this world. To instruct those who follow after us is thus a natural preoccupation. One way to satisfy it is to teach one's sons and daughters behaviors that serve for daily life. This is evidently the case with "primitive" societies: in them it is parents and kin who teach, which does not exclude innovation and progress. But if the idea of a divinity to be served or a desire to accumulate things is introduced into the group, learning has to reach beyond simple parental instruction, for example, to using numbers and letters, and this implies that the teacher knows them himself. For girls, rudimentary instruction might be enough: to procreate and keep up a fire did not require more knowledge. But if the man claimed to occupy himself with the affairs of the group, if he had to argue, buy, and sell, he would have to learn outside the home. These banal considerations are intended to show that man could in fact remain, like a simple beast, in the "holy ignorance" within which Saint Bernard invited him to stay, so that he could consecrate himself entirely to praising God. But if he did not want to or could not be content with that "idleness," he would have to pass under the control of those who knew, and who, in medieval times, were all men of the Church. Which brings us to the school.

Antiquity knew nothing resembling a school. Greek masters, who were rhetoricians, *grammatici*, or sophists, paid obedience to no overall organization; they taught with no fixed place of study and no controls, following the demands of wealthy men who paid them to have access to what they knew, which obviously limited their audience to an elite. At the end of Roman times certain teachers were even of servile status; many of these shared their knowledge when they joined the earliest Christian groups. This sort of free professorate, largely secular and almost exclusively reserved to the wealthiest families, was more like a lay preceptorship. We have proof, in spite of the disastrous intellectual reputation of the "barbarian" epoch, that this type of teaching continued, with a certain brilliance, up to the seventh century in Gaul, Spain, and Italy. At that moment, however, those practices were much influenced by a program of studies that introduced more properly Christian information. The monasteries attracted a "clientele" of children and even adults, usually of aristocratic status, who were taught not only the "arts" that we have just seen but the rudiments of dogma. In this manner, the Irish, the Anglo-Saxons, but also the Italians, working with the support of the Roman Church, gradually supplanted the ancient grammarians.

The Carolingian epoch brought the clearest break with the past. For once in conformity with his almost hagiographic reputation, Charlemagne imprinted his mark on the history of teaching in Europe, or in any event, his entourage of English, Italian, and Spanish clerics did so. One capitulary, an *admonitio generalis* of 789, prescribed the installation of a school in each parish for the poorest of his subjects from ages seven to twelve. This disposition, like most imagined in those times, was probably not followed by actual practical effects. It nonetheless remains at the root of the legend of the bearded emperor praising the poor and docile schoolchildren and lambasting the rich and lazy ones. The famous "Palace school," however, was never anything more than a modest circle of idle counselors in which the emperor was not the only one who did not know how to write. But even if these concerns remained theoretical, their obvious effect was to definitively pass responsibility for teaching into the hands of the Church.

The history of the school, in a country like France that clings strongly to its "culture," is quite well known, and I shall content myself with a sketch so as to avoid falling immediately into a traditional and smug admiration of the universities, that "fine child" of the Middle Ages. First, if I followed the logic of the objective that I have repeatedly stated, I would stop here. To be sure, opportunities for study destined for the "little people" runs modestly through the centuries like a red thread. The *petites écoles*, as they were called in nineteenth-century France, were there. Boys from seven to twelve or fourteen years of age were invited to listen to (or actually did listen to) the parish curé; in a city, the teacher would be a *magister* designated by the bishop's *official*, a judge. Six or ten pupils were brought together in a special locality where they were taught ... we are not sure just what. Reading, certainly arithmetic, singing, in particular, psalm singing. The teacher would be a cleric, on occasion a canon; how much he knew was often disputed by the children's parents, which means that we have the impression that school was more of a day-care center than a place of study. The youngsters fought one another, played ball or dice, and broke their writing tablets, but they were also quite likely to be beaten by the master. In the fourteenth and fifteenth centuries, however, these preparatory schools for the university were reinforced by the addition of some notion of what it was necessary to know, in the city at any rate, to enlarge knowledge useful on a daily basis. The "rectors" of such schools seem to us somewhat more learned and more effective. Was this only a small achievement? Perhaps, especially if we add to it an inevitable division between city and countryside, between rich and poor, and between boys and girls (girls are neglected in our sources and probably were confined to learning the rudiments of "domesticity"). At least children amused themselves at school, if we can believe Guibert of Nogent, whose abusive mother subjected him to a brutal and uneducated preceptor, and who sighed as he watched from his windows the schoolchildren of his village playing in the yard outside. What is essential, however, is that a thin current of secular knowledge continued to flow during the reign of the dominant Church.

Beyond such rudiments lay the serious courses of study dispensed by the established Church and from which nearly all of medieval "culture" emerged. We can distinguish two overall chronological phases, each one containing a break. The first phase covers the tenth, eleventh, and early twelfth centuries. The teachers were almost exclusively monks, and what they taught remained self-referential. The curriculum was devised by the Benedictines of Cluny, who were more fond of research than the monks of Cîteaux, who were more modest when it came to studies. These monks learned by reading and discussing the manuscripts their order brought together, and they opened their *studium* to other religious, to a few curious aristocrats, and to *donats* and *oblats*, young children given or oblated to the monastery and destined to become monks. This was an instruction of the rich for the rich, but it was also responsible for a formidable search for texts and commentaries, which it saved from oblivion. The rise of cities in the twelfth century made it clear that the laity also required instruction, and that even their business affairs demanded some secular culture. This led bishops and their canons to open their cloisters to a less arcane and purely religious instruction. Out of the clash of these two strands was born the "Twelfth-Century Renaissance," a movement that was not merely bookish, but also emphasized the *disputatio* against the mechanical repetition of "realism" in the style of Saint Anselm. These urban schools flourished instead of closing their doors. They justified access to a hierarchy of knowledge and made it possible for the student to teach in his turn, thanks to the *licencia docendi*, the right to teach, conferred by the bishop. Hugh of Saint Victor and Peter Lombard made the schools of Paris as famous as that of Bologna, where Gratian, at the same time, was renewing the study of law—that is, of Justinian and the *Corpus juris civilis*. At times, certain masters thought that the schools should go farther. Around 1120 or 1130 Abelard even broke off all ties with a program that he judged to be overly cautious.

At this point a second phase began, that of the history of universities, that holy of holies about which professional medievalists and an enlightened public commune with emotion. So much ink and saliva has already been spent on this majestic medieval "heritage" that I shall add only a few minor notes. The creation of what is called a *studium generale* was an exclusively urban phenomenon, and four out of five men who lived in the countryside probably had never heard tell of such a thing. Moreover, in the final analysis, it was simply a form of trade association, like many others in the cities: an opportunity for masters and students, the *universitas magistrorum et scholarium*, to gather in a strong organization provided, as was natural everywhere, with solid statutes and a firm framework. However, it was original in that it depended uniquely on the pope or, at most, as in France, on the king, which allowed it to escape the theoretical control of the established Church and enabled it to open its doors to everyone. The masters were paid by their students, unless they too were monks. At least a half of the masters and students who frequented such places were laymen who had pronounced no vows. Lessons were given in the streets, with no fixed locale; the "colleges" that flourished thanks to the donors—often princely ones—who created them were lodgings for poor students, although it did happen, as in the college founded by Robert de Sorbon in Paris, that instruction took place there as well. The students who had not managed to obtain money from their families or a "benefice" from the Church (for example, an assignment as chaplain to a wealthy bourgeois) frequented the streets, where they made a good deal of noise. Gradually, the auditors came to be arranged by their "nation" of origin or even by their "faculty" or the nature of their studies. Those categories led to courses of study punctuated by controls that are far from having completely disappeared. From sixteen years of age to twenty, they studied the "arts," which we have seen above and which were sanctioned by the degree of "bachelor" (probably originally a word in Iberian slang that meant "biscuit-chewer"!). Two years later they might earn the *licencia*, which had no value as a practical diploma until some six years later, according to the discipline studied, and was awarded to barely 20 percent of the students after detailed examinations. Several more years of study were required for medicine or law. As for theology, a student had to be over thirty to teach it.

Historians admire this fine edifice: in reality, it was a shapeless magma ceaselessly in formation. To be sure, it had some brilliant results. An opening toward the outside world and a limitless stirring up of juvenile appetites were new and praiseworthy achievements. But for power in all of its forms, the results were purely negative. The king and his police, the bishop and his canons, the abbot and his monks, the pope and his dogmas were all faced with disorders, blockages, deviations, rivalries, and incessant quarrels. It is we who venerate the medieval university; there is no echo of that admiration among contemporaries. Moreover, a glance at one portion of the period included in this rudimentary overview shows this clearly. University institutions appeared, fairly massively, at the end of the twelfth century and during the thirteenth. By a sort of belated nationalism, the Lombards, the English, the Catalonians and Parisians dispute priority for these creations—Bologna? Paris? Oxford? Montpellier?—between 1195 and 1220, which were followed by more than twenty other universities in a hundred years. At Paris there were from five to eight thousand students and some fifteen colleges, with a hundred or so lay masters. The structure soon cracked, however. In 1230 in Paris, the minor religious orders, the "mendicants," sensed the danger that threatened control of the faith, knowledge, and dogma. They entered the university from the top down, taking command of their specialty and their claim to superiority, theology. Gradually they inundated the entire university organism, thus quickly contributing to changing its reason for being and, by the fourteenth century, turning it into a simple sounding board for their own doctrines. At this point universities multiplied throughout Europe, but by mutilating one another. They became instruments of the local powers, solidifying into a ratiocination that eventually gave the term "Scholasticism" its pejorative weight. The teaching personnel, who remained laymen, shifted to becoming a largely impoverished and hereditary caste. Let there be no mistake; the great minds of the age—a Thomas Aquinas, an Albertus Magnus, a Buridan, a Bonaventure, and many others—were "university" men, but first of all they were "mendicant friars." And the great doctors of the fifteenth century—Gerson, Pierre Cauchon (so severely criticized for quite different reasons related to the trial of Joan of Arc)—were by no means second-rank minds, because they, too, were university teachers. But the time of the university's greatest brilliance was no more. In practical terms, it had lasted for a century. Henceforth curious minds sought knowledge elsewhere. In Florence, Rome, and Paris "academies" sponsored by princely patronage opened their doors to wealthy thinkers and "intellectuals" rather than "professors." The age of Abelard had passed; that of Petrarch and Marsilio Ficino had arrived; and that of Erasmus would soon follow.

EXPRESSION

Littré states that "to express" means to make something that is within gush forth to the outside, if need be by applying force. The word "exteriorization," if only it were not so ugly, would be much more appropriate than "expression" to qualify what I want to talk about next. What I have talked about thus far is what the human being feels intimately within his body, what he has imagined, what he has learned, and what he wants to communicate to others and help them to understand. Man can attain those goals in a number of ways. He can act, and I have spoken of action in relation to trades or rites; he can talk, even shout, using all the resources of the voice, in the family, at the market, or from the pulpit. Orality is even a prime historical source to which I have often appealed, and specialists of the spoken word have given it a place of choice. Some scholars have collected the "cries of Paris," others have studied those whose mission it was to propagate the voice of God, still others have taken on the task of supporting good mores and morality, as did the preaching orders of friars, the Dominicans and the Franciscans. Song and dance encourage exchanges with their rhythms, profane or sacred. Still, all of these "natural" manifestations remain difficult for us to grasp because the Church, which controlled knowledge, feared the indiscretions of language or of attitude that might come from them. Thus the Church managed to discredit (or, at any rate, conceal) "popular" attitudes such as the echos of joy and wild exuberance of young students expressed in the streets by bands of "Goliards" (a word whose origin is disputed). These *juvenes*, these young *scolares,* stood opposed to Order, either that of the Church or that of the bourgeoisie, by their shouts, their parades, their songs and other excesses that were quickly and with relief described as "anarchy."

If these forms of expression largely escape us (unfortunately), our schoolbooks sag under the weight of others that seem to us the most evident and that we grasp easily—what was written and what was built and decorated: literature and art. And even if the "little people" whom I pursue never read Froissart's chronicle or could not have understood much of the tympanum of Vézelay, I need to pause over them.

Who Wrote and What Did They Write?

The answers to these two initial questions are not of equal interest. The first leads to a list containing hundreds of names and dates, organized by century, by region, by social categories, even by the subjects treated—in short, a "history of literature." An immense attic! The best I can do is sweep out a corner or two. What seems to me to be the closest to my observation post is not a nomenclature of inspired writers, who, until the twelfth century, were almost all men of the Church who wrote in Latin and were thus inaccessible to the overwhelming majority of the "illiterate." I have already spoken of the decrease in the use of the language of religion and of the shift to profane and lay writers. What is important to me is not the name of the "author" but a search of his personal contribution in the work attributed to him. If he is a man of God who bathed, at times from childhood, in the ocean of the sacred sources, this personal or direct characteristic can only be measured by looking beyond what he has borrowed (at times plagiarized, if he allows himself to do so), which is a matter of sources of inspiration and outside influences. Whether he had a professional scribe do the actual writing or redacted the work himself is secondary; in any case, this would require an investigation of handwriting, a nearly impossible and always disappointing task. When the writer is a layman, the difficulty is great, and research is essential, especially if this "author" has furnished us with a text redacted in Latin and he did not know the language; but the task is difficult even if the work is in a vernacular language. To pick an example that is relatively easy to grasp: The Sire de Joinville was the "author" of a *Livre des saintes paroles et des bons faits de notre saint roi Louis*, a work that is in reality a collection of the personal memories of Joinville, the seneschal of Champagne, as a confidant (according to him) of Saint Louis and a former combatant in the Egyptian crusade. The work, redacted in the aim of adding to the dossier for the canonization of King Louis, was presented in 1309, when its author was over eighty years of age; hence it speaks of events that occurred a half century earlier. The problem is not to scrutinize the accuracy of an octogenarian's memories or that of a work written for hagiographic purposes, but to know how these narrations were brought together. Joinville knew how to write. We have two lines written by his hand (but extremely poorly) in an act relating to the administration of one of his lands. This means that he was not holding the pen in 1309, yet the vivacity of the narration, the original style, and the liveliness of the anecdotes attest to a quite personal thought. Did he dictate the work? And if so, on the basis of what? On memory alone, from an investigation, from notes taken over the intervening years? If we add the relative scarcity of the manuscripts of his *History of Saint Louis*—only a few before the sixteenth century—we can conclude that one of the most famous works of French medieval literature was not received or widespread even among the people of the court, and that therefore it remained unknown by the "public."

The example of Joinville is famous, which is why I cite it, but it can be extended to almost all lay "authors" of the period. The range of these is instructive: William IX, duke of Aquitaine, a truculent *langue d'oc* poet; Foulques, count of Anjou, who adored genealogies, in the eleventh and twelfth centuries; the countess of Die or Marie de France and her *lais* (if these even existed); Guilliaume le Maréchal and his autobiography; and Chrétien de Troyes and his romances in the thirteenth century. Did they hold the pen themselves? Certainly not. But then, who served as an intermediary between their "work" and the parchment on which it was transcribed? Curiously, it is perhaps among the most humble authors that we will have a better chance of capturing authentic author-writers, for they often present themselves and tell us of the road they have traveled. This is often the case with the "troubadours" who were the authors of *chansons d'oc*, writing in a *razo* preceding a poem. Similary, the *jeux* and the *dits* of the Artois in the twelfth century often have known authors who give their names and boast about their work. This is also true of Adam de la Halle and Jean Bodin, who may not have had the funds in their purses to pay a scribe. Evidently, we can be more sure in the fourteenth and fifteenth centuries, for it is clear that Froissart, the "Bourgeois of Paris," and Villon redacted their texts and wrote them down on parchment. Moreover, works not destined for public consumption such as the "journals," "memoirs," and *livres de raison* of the bourgeoise or the merchants of the later Middle Ages received no assistance in organizing their personal memories.

It is not only easier but tells us a good deal more to pose the second of the two questions that head this section: what did these people write? The question leads to a survey of what are called literary "genres" and the answer is clear. The ten centuries of the Middle Ages have left us evidence of all the forms of expression known to Western thought, thanks to the Greco-Roman and the Celtic and Germanic heritages, with a nuance here and there, it is true, and, above all, with two exceptions, to which I shall return. First, there were treatises and works of piety, half of which were derived from Greek or "Arabic" philosophy and the Christian faith. Their echo and their raw material penetrates our culture to this day. Next came all the various forms of recall of the past—chronicles, annals, biographies—for which Mediterranean antiquity had opened a royal road, at times ranging from the origin of man to the "end of time." The Church had these well in hand. Next, in poetic prolongation, the war epics, the relations of *gestes* (a word that means "prowess"), the Scandinavian sagas, the Germanic songs of the *Niebelungen*, the Carolingian "cycles"—all of which depended on the dominant class of clan or war leaders. But did not antiquity have its *Iliad* and its *Aeneid* and poetry in all its varieties (lyric, burlesque, moralizing, didactic, satirical), travel narrations, descriptions of cities or lands, technical manuals, and, finally and rather late, theater? All of this, which remains more or less intact, still attracts our attention, and all the more so because certain "genres" are particularly tempting today to those whom we call and even believe to be "literate." Enough, then, of an inventory that can become tedious.

There were also innovations, works that are all the more interesting because they have no ancient paternity and are much cultivated today. First, we live surrounded by dictionaries and encyclopedias, and I am not about to analyze the reasons for this enthusiasm. The attempt to bring together all that we know or hope to know is a medieval invention. Perhaps the motivation underlying the *Etymologies* of Isidore of Seville in the sixth century was an attitude of defense in the face of a world that seemed about to collapse, and an attempt to gather up its heritage. Or, on the contrary, it may have been motivated by a desire for a more enlightened future, which was true of the *Speculum* of Vincent of Beauvais or the many *Mirrors* of the thirteenth century. The point of such compilations was not (or only in small part) to approach the data by sorting words or notions alphabetically; this was true only of small illustrated collections like the bestiaries. Instead, the Middle Ages triumphed in the domain of general tableaus, in verse or in prose, and for the most part in the vernacular. The twenty thousand lines of the *Roman de la Rose* (especially the second part by Jean de Meung in the late thirteenth century) and the ten thousand lines of Dante's *Divine Comedy* in the early fourteenth century offer an overall picture of the world. The considerable number of manuscripts of these works that have come down to us—several hundred—seems to attest to a distribution that reached well beyond an elite. We would have to leap over the "modern" centuries steeped in "humanism," where man was all, to find a similar level of reading in the much later "Enlightenment."

The other literary genre born in medieval times is the novel. For us, it is the very essence of the written work. In France today more than seven hundred novels are published every year. Antiquity, in the age of Horace or Ovid, of course had stories with characters in them, but they seem not to have been overly popular. The first "songs" in Latin or in the vernacular that inaugurated this approach date from the eleventh century and are often in verse. *Fabliaux* and *nouvelles* multiplied between 1170 and 1230, as if in proof of an acculturation of the popular classes. Between the mid-thirteenth and fifteenth centuries fiction flourished, from Chaucer in England to Boccaccio in Italy and including Rutebeuf and the authors of the *Roman de Renart* and *Aucassin et Nicolette*. The *roman*—which was originally any work written in a Romance language—began to be defined as a written work with certain set characteristics: an anecdote, typical characters, secular subject matter, and some indication of personal sentiments. The Christian dimension and heroic virtues retreated before a realism that mixed a captivating little story with daily life. The tellers of such tales were professionals, probably clerics, but of modest culture, like their intended public. Most of these tales are anonymous. Initially, many of these romances incorporated a taste for (but by no means a real knowledge of) antiquity, thus opening a vein of extraordinary adventures featuring a dazzling Alexander the Great. Another series of works known as "matter of Brittany" drew from Celtic, Scandinavian, Saxon, and perhaps Spanish elements to center on Arthur and his knights, Tristan or Siegfried, in "cycles" composed during the period from 1150 to 1350. Beyond that date, it was in Italy and Germany that a taste for the story penetrated, but different conditions of reception gave a different resonance to their inspiration.

For Whom and Why Did Authors Write?

The preceding overview leads directly to these two questions, which can be separated only artificially. The response to the first is necessarily simplistic if the results of the second—essential for my purposes—are not combined with them. People wrote either to instruct or to amuse their public. Contrary to many later authors, without counting our own times, where it is a common occurrence, the people of the Middle Ages rarely picked up a pen to talk about themselves, though there were exceptions: Guibert of Nogent, talking about his unhappy childhood; Joinville boasting of his position and his exploits; Abelard, who overflows with intimate lamentations; Villon, writing in flattering terms about his life as a *mauvais garçon*. Other authors were busy narrating war-related, diplomatic, or merely sexual exploits or accumulating examples, lessons, and formulas that they hoped others would find useful. If they were of the Church, they hoped to persuade the faithful of the divine power; if they were laymen, they hoped to nourish *memoria* or simply to amuse without drawing any personal benefit from it. To do this they made use of heroic narrations as well as scatological writings, for the point was to capture the attention of the listener, which varied over time. The best the historian can do today is to catch a glimmer or two of life in society from such things as an increase in the urban public's taste for theater and for the more or less lubricious tale; the gradual withdrawal of the aristocracy into its class values, which served as a basis for the growth of "courtly" or epic works; the development of scientific curiosity, which fed on translation from the Arabic and on travelers' narratives and nourished a literature of contestation; and poetry, with its many faces, an evident reflection of the moral climate, or, more simply, the material climate of the times. We do not know enough about the attitude of readers toward the works to which they had access. All we have to judge this is the evidence of the number of copies of any particular work that have come down to us. This is an imperfect measure, not so much because of losses that may or may not have been accidental, but because of the very nature of the public concerned: here, wealthy warriors who enjoy illustrated *gestes*; there, "lesser" men who passed on from hand to hand a *dit* written on poor-quality parchment. One trait is typical of all of these centuries, so different from our own: there is no sign of a counter-literature attacking a work or an author in the name of principles presumed not to have been respected, or else we catch only a murmur of it in letters or sermons. The Church may have erased all traces of this, however. The result is that we have the impression that the public contested nothing in the message proposed to it. The famous doctrine of the "betrayal of the clerics" did not exist in the Middle Ages. In the late Middle Ages, the learned continued to tear one another apart in Latin in their dry quarrels, but these held no interest for the man in a cottage.

It is that cottager who is primarily important to me, he or his companion in the city, or the merchant on the dock. Under these conditions, the inference is simple. The common man wanted to hear, and even to read, if possible in his everyday language, "moralities"—things that the curé might confirm from the pulpit and that might contribute to a discussion at home or to a tale told by a *conteur*. In the city, he would enjoy himself at the *jeux*, the *sotties*, or the *mystères* that were put on for him and in which he might even participate. He would know and approve of the *fabliaux* and popular poetry, which appealed to his taste for satire, for the scabrous, and for "fine stories." But despite their resemblance to these amusements, it is not sure that the various "offshoots" of the *Roman de Renart* had the success they are usually credited with.

Moral or warlike virtues; love, sublime or delicate; Christian sensitivity or clan spirit—an entire portion of medieval literature seems to have been received and conceived by one social class, which alone enjoyed it or even understood it. As is true of so many other aspects of life in those times, we can observe many of our own contemporaries opening their eyes wide when it comes to the literature of "courtesy," a somewhat obscure and generally misunderstood word. This literary genre displays only heroes, combatants of the Faith, men and women of high—very high—rank who give themselves over to subtle sexual combat, which they discuss endlessly: is this reality or fiction, seduction or machismo, heroism or hypocrisy? This was a literature that came from professionals who adored symbols and were deeply imbued with stereotypes; at base it remained quite learned and tended to draw on the antique and on folklore (Celtic in particular), saintly history, or ethnic phantasms. In general, this produced the kings of a pack of cards: David the psalmist, Alexander the adventurer, Caesar the master of the world, and Charles the king of kings. Curiously, the only one missing is Arthur (in spite of the fact that the bear [in Greek, *arctos*] is king of the animals) and his squadron of seekers of the Holy Grail, the cup that caught the blood of Christ on the Cross. The domain occupied by the imaginary of the powerful is an interesting one, but can we really believe that those personages and their extraordinary contentions in any way touched the emotions of more than one man out of ten? Moreover, the Church soon discerned Satan concealed in Lancelot's armor.

The Artist's Part

Satan was highly visible, outside of courtly songs. He was sculpted on the tympanums of the cathedral of Saint-Lazare in Autun, in depictions of the Temptation and of the Judgment, and on hundreds of other buildings; he was painted in the intertwined initials of the *Moralia in Job*, in the frescoes of Asnières-sur-Vègre, and in frightening images everywhere. He did not need any special discourse to show himself. He was a serpent, a wolf, a monstrous animal, at times a flame. The man who represented him in such guises was also expressing a sentiment. Art was thus one of the paths to knowledge. Even more than with written works, I am not about to draw up interminable lists of monuments, or painted and sculpted works. To do so would only show that we still possess, from the medieval age and often intact, a mass of built works; painted and sculpted décors; objects, simple or sumptuous, in wood, metal, glass, ivory, cloth, or stone—all of which form a total a hundred times greater than all the written works mentioned above. This prodigious mine has been the object of inventories that remain incomplete today, even in lands as curious about their ancient culture as France and Italy. To further complicate our approach to this treasure, a number of these works—buildings especially—have been altered and reconstructed, at times several times, in later centuries, as dictated by the needs of the moment or simple changes in taste. Whereas a written object does not easily accommodate refashioning, unless under the form of a "gloss" added by a painstaking reader, there is hardly a church or a castle that has not been subjected to additions, transformation, remodeling, and decorative changes over a period of a thousand years. We admire the Gothic cathedrals of the thirteenth century and the fortresses of the fourteenth century, but we have completely forgotten that these masterworks replaced others that were systematically destroyed. The Gothic was born on the ruins of Romanesque art, which had itself wiped out Carolingian art. When it happens, by a surprising stroke of luck, that successive construction phases coexist, as they do in the cathedral of Beauvais, the effect is striking.

I have no intention of studying the evolution of all these works. They are the offspring of the possibilities of the place and the needs of the moment; stone often replaced wood, not for its ability to withstand fire, but because it permitted, for example, the building of round structures, and in the castles round towers replaced square towers because they did away with vulnerable angles in case of attack. Similarly, when the Roman techniques for using cement became known and the long saw was introduced into the quarries, building stone or ashlar replaced dry stone, beds of brick, and *opus spicatum*. Painted wall frescoes disappeared when oil painting on canvas, more appropriate to the new tastes, came into common use. Agricultural equipment, harnesses for horses, machines for weaving or crushing were improved by acquaintance with techniques that came from the Mediterranean or from central Europe. As for miniatures, which became outrageously expensive when multiple copies were wanted, they gave way to printing, thanks to the ink woodcut, then to the copper engraving. I could give many other examples of technical modifications in all domains, but it may suffice to add that all of these "improvements" had a social basis, a moral one, and at times an economic one. Demographic growth in the cities eliminated churches that had become too small; the choice of a site for a new castle was connected to the appearance of siege artillery. Moreover, in the final centuries of the Middle Ages, the plague and war set off a "macabre" artistic current in which death played a highly prominent role, much as, in earlier times, the cult of the Virgin inspired many nativity scenes, crucifixions, and assumptions.

In all of its expressions, medieval art covered a thousand years. This means that seeking "constant" traits becomes a limitless quest, because, as we have seen, art was the offspring of its times. If I nonetheless take up the question, it will be keeping in mind that our own time and its sensitivities cannot hand us the keys to medieval art without risk of error. I should add, moreover, that both building and decoration were the work of specialists for whom—as is true today—inspiration does not necessarily echo the sentiments or the tastes of the popular classes. Besides, it is hard to see how or why anyone would have consulted the peasants of a village or the workers in a workshop before building or decorating a church or a castle. I have already said that the "cathedral builders" were likely to be volunteers with wheelbarrows, and that in the cities especially, when the burghers thought they had paid out enough money for a project that never seemed to end, they refused to pay more and the project remained unfinished, as was the case in Beauvais and in Cologne. It was fortunate when there was enough time to construct all or part of one of the towers on the facade, as in Sens, Strasbourg, Troyes, Amiens, and many other places.

This said, and it is essential to my viewpoint, it seems certain that the *maîtres d'oeuvre* who supervised the worksites, those who commanded the artisans' workshops, and the monks who painted miniatures in the monasteries worked under constraints that were more spiritual than material. To be sure, such masters reflect what both the poor folk and the wealthy thought and understood, but at times it is easy to discern the personal contribution of the artist even when he was working under orders to reproduce a certain theme or plan. The masks and the grotesques on church stalls and on the capitals of columns, the satirical figures sketched in with light pen strokes that slip in and out of the initials of a beautiful book, or the sense of humor that animates even depictions of the Last Judgment, such as the one in Autun, show proof of a freedom of execution and perhaps even of a liberating intention to circumvent the "program." So at this point, it becomes difficult to interpret a form or a theme in absolute terms, as everything seems to be symbol—that is, a simplified framework for thought. What matters for our purposes is to ask whether these appeals to the subconscious had any chance of being grasped by humble folk. To enumerate some of these, they include an appeal to light, the emblem of the house of God that enters into daily life; the principle of verticality, emblem of the regeneration of man in face of the horizontal of rampant evil; the need for a centrality in the sacred portions of the building or in decoration; and emphasis on a point of convergence of the lines in a drawing, a crucifixion, the ribbed transept crossing, the figure of Christ. Seen in this light, the simplest geometrical forms take on a symbolic significance. The square—that of celestial Jerusalem, of the royal *aula*, of the Roman camp—is the established image of a closed world. The circle is the road followed by the stars in the sky and in divine Creation, which, with no beginning and no end, is the image of perfection. The spiral, however, which is made up of successive and continuous circles around one center, is an image of the infinite. The cross, finally, even more than the emblem of Christ crucified, is the image of the four directions that tear man apart, which are astronomical and physical directions even more than they are spiritual ones. The cross rotated on its axis is the symbol of the mobile world, and Greek art made great use of it well before, *gammée* like a swastika, it became the emblem of political regimes claiming to be new. For the historian, all of these traits and many others have a purely theoretical dimension rich with intertwined interests. But in a more worldly dimension, where the humble scurried about, can we hope to grasp an echo of these speculations?

During the course of my narration, few surveys have left me as unsatisfied as this one. Often (and I have apologized for it) I have had to simplify or thrust aside topics that merit serious study but would take me too far away from my observation point, particularly as regards the economy or social hierarchy. This time, the sacrifice has been other, or at least of another kind. It is not so much that I have had to reject things that seemed to me "out of my subject"; rather, I have had to carve into a limitless mass. Out of an ocean of names, works, and affiliations I have fished out a few relics. This time what I lack is space to cover even the main points. I have of course had my regrets, but some reassurance as well, as at this point I have emerged from the domain of the forest and stand face-to-face with that of the spirit. Whether they were learned or ignorant, attentive or distracted, made of fine or rough stuff, all of these people had a soul or believed that they had one.

7

AND THE SOUL

In his description of the castle of Ardres, which was built before his eyes at the dawn of the twelfth century, Canon Lambert moves from one level to another. At the base, almost planted in the ground and supporting the entire building, is the stone motte and space for various animals, water, hay, and supplies; above this came the kitchen, a storage area, and a nook where a fire could be lit for sick persons or infants; above that, the hall, where men grouped around the lord; on the next level there were the bed chambers of the lady mother, the nucleus of the master's family, with a dormitory for the boys and rooms for girls; on the next floor there were sleeping quarters for the garrison that surveyed the surroundings; finally, at the top and as close as possible to God, the chapel, the "temple of Solomon." Archaeologists are deeply moved by this sketch, but it does not much matter whether it is or is not a work of pure imagination. Now that I have climbed all the stories, I have come to the door of the holy oratory.

The pediment over the door does not bear Dante's threat, "Abandon all hope, you who enter here," but rather embodies the phrase of a historian today: "The Middle Ages were never Christian." This specialist studying the Catholic Church of the sixteenth century is saying, of course, that being "Christian" includes the Counter-Reformation canons of the Council of Trent. As it happens, for the God whom we have encountered on almost every page of this book, being "Christian" according to the Tridentine definition is secondary, as is whether God was viewed as one divinity in three persons, but with a predilection for the Son rather than for the Father. What is strikingly clear is that "God" is the supreme form of superiority of spirit over matter. We can call this God Christian according to usage and in a literal sense, but that is all.

It would be unfair to leave the matter here, as the Middle Ages may indeed have practiced a simplistic, even a rough-hewn "deism." Without lingering too long over the discourses of those who make a profession of dissecting dogma and pursuing rebels, any historian of these times has to attempt to narrow the focus of his inquiry. If the medieval Christian calls the Muslim a "miscreant" and accuses the Jew of "deicide," the first responds that the Christian is polytheist and the second that he is idolatrous. All three of them venerate Abraham and the Book, however, which means that they do not differ over dogma, but in their mentalities. The word "mentality" is a trap, however. Can anyone hope to define a "mentality"? And more basic, call it "medieval" and "Christian"? The first question can be answered in a fairly broad way. The mentality of a man or a group implies a particular manner of feeling and of thinking within a specific social setting; it includes the unconscious (notably the collective unconscious), a baggage of facts or habits and a certain way of translating them, and little "reason." As for the second question, the response seems clear; there is no one medieval mentality, because over a thousand years it is obvious that social, cultural, and spiritual frameworks changed; there were multiple successive mentalities, reflecting the tensions of each moment. This is why we can say that the forms of representation or expression of those mentalities have coherence only when we take care to cast a light on their twin faces, which are cultural and social.

A third question presents more difficulties. It has been said of man that he is an "ideological animal," which means subjected to pressure from the ideas, acts, and words that assail him. The extreme weakness of man's means of defense against nature, not to mention against his fellow man, plunge him into a constant fear, about which I have said a few words above, and push him into the trammels of religiosity. This means that it was in the idea of God that he sought refuge, comfort, and submission. He might unite himself with God by means of the spirit if he aspired to follow the written acknowledgment of revealed faith, or else by the heart if he was capable of losing himself in mystical meditation. Abelard followed the first path, and Saint Bernard the second. As for the ministers of the cult, their task was to reinforce these supports. But could the God they evoked be specifically "Christian"? And how did the people of the Middle Ages who were not learned conceive of such a God?

GOOD AND EVIL

I have little enthusiasm, and even less competence, for diving audaciously into the middle of dogmatic quarrels. I shall thus limit my remarks to the most modest level, which was, precisely, that of the little people of the Middle Ages whose bodies and minds I am trying to sound. I differ from those people in one important way, however, as I hold man, in all times, to be an animal, a very "evolved" one, to be sure, and even a "superior" one if you insist, but a creature among other creatures. This "materialistic" view made no sense in the Middle Ages, as man was then considered the end point of Creation, and, as Pascal said, he was "neither angel nor beast"; he had within him a reflection, an *imago*, of the Supreme Being, hence he escaped all rational study. However, he was himself well aware that perfection was not his lot on this Earth and was at best a promise. The Creator had immersed him in an ocean full of reefs, temptations, and illusions in order to try his strength, perhaps to constrain him to a personal effort toward what was better, or to lead him to ask questions about himself. "Know thyself" as Socrates advised. Therefore, before appearing at the end of time, he had to choose between Good and Evil.

The End of Dualism

In the eyes of all men motivated by material interests, nature was animated—if the word is not too strong—by movements, some but not all of which were good for living species; these included temperature, humidity, and changes in the soil. There is little reason to linger over these evident notions, except to recall that all societies that have been called primitive use such notions to define an idea of what is good or bad for the survival of the species, hence, moving to the level of the spirit, an idea of what is good and what is evil. Such forces are beyond the control of man, however, so they must have come from a superior world, that of the "gods," be they benevolent or wrathful. From ancient Egypt and moving through the gesticulations of the Greco-Roman pantheon to the Scandinavian worlds, good and bad gods fight over man and the world, and even over life and death. But when these outer trappings are torn off, if a group rises to the idea of a one superior power, it becomes clear that such a power is itself torn between two equally powerful forces in constant combat, and disputing control over creatures. This was the conviction of a number of believers in central or eastern Asia, for example, in ancient Persia or in Asia Minor of the fifth and sixth centuries B.C.E The one god Ahura Mazda combined the two antagonistic forces, which fire would separate at the end of time. A prophet such as Zarathustra (or Zoroaster, as the Greeks called him) took this same idea and made it a dualistic dogma in the age of the Achaemenid kings in the fourth and third centuries B.C.E. Variants of this eschatological vision retained a solid presence in these regions until the third century C.E., when the "prophet" Manes gave it a second wind and lent it the name Manichaeism.

This division of God into two and this consequent triumph of Lucifer over Yahweh—which the Jews rejected—was obviously unacceptable to Christians. The duality of God the Father and God incarnated as Jesus did not constitute a duality, and even less a dualism, because God is the very spirit of the Good. There is no allusion to this problem in the Gospels. It was, as in so many things, Saint Paul who was the first to denounce what was not a "heresy" but a negation of the divine oneness. This line of thought was, moreover, encouraged in the same epoch by the dangerous vigor of the cult of Mithra, which offered some resemblance to the message of Christ, tempted many adepts, and was even favorably received in Rome. At the same time, what is more, dogmatic quarrels over the nature of the Son in comparison with the Father developed within learned Christian communities, quarrels that also found an echo among the "barbarian" elites newly called to the Christian faith. The Church had to come to a decision about such matters or face the very real risk of internal schisms, and a series of general councils held between 325 and 471—that is, when the fiction of a unified Roman Empire still existed—condemned these doctrines, dualism in particular. What remained of the interpretations regarding Christ's filiation faded in the West in the seventh century, when the populations that had rallied to the Arian hypothesis submitted to Roman dogma at the same time that, in the East, Islam swallowed up any remaining traces of such beliefs.

It is useless to say that the greater part of the Christian populations of the West paid little attention to the contortions of the Fathers in the councils. Still, several lords asserted, on returning from a crusade at the end of the eleventh century or during the first decades of the twelfth century, that they had encountered among the *bougres* (that is, Bulgars), whose territory they crossed, strange "Christians" who believed that God had a dual nature. They called them Bogomils although they were unclear about the origin of the word. Somewhat later, around 1140 or 1160, the indefatigable defender of Roman dogma, Saint Bernard, denounced the presence of similar beliefs in the Rhine Valley. Which brings me to one of the most solid stereotypes of medieval history and one that continues to earn money for popular publishing ven-

tures: the Cathars. I have two preliminary observations, of unequal interest. The first is linguistic. The word "cathar" (Greek for
"pure") has no specific content. It was hardly ever used before the
thirteenth century, at which point it was often used interchangeably with the word *vaudois* (from which we get Waldensian), a
simple confusion of disciplines about which I shall soon have a
word to say. Cathars were also called *bougres*, a term derived from
Bogomils, or the word *albigeois* (Albigensians), in an excessive ex-
trapolation from the role the region of Albi played in armed conflict. The Patarini, a movement of social revolt in Milan, had no
connection with Catharism. Even among the Cathars, the titles
of "good man" or *parfait* ("perfect") given to their leaders did not
have any specific religious meaning. The second problem emerges
from a rectification that makes it indispensable to read roughly
all of the literature on the question: a "heresy" is a choice—which
is the root sense of the word—in the face of a dogmatic or disci-
plinary decision that one contests; it represents a tear in the very
body of the Church. The Byzantine East teemed with heresies,
perhaps because religious thought was more agitated and diverse
than it was in the West. There were heresies in the West—and I
shall say a word or two about them—but they remained quite personal, without any real audience, and of short duration. However,
Catharism was not a "heresy." It was another belief, and a strongly
anti-Christian one, hence inadmissible. The Church was not mistaken in its relentless attempts to annihilate it. The Cathar dualism set the soul, dominated by God, against matter, dominated
by Evil. Everything that had anything to do with matter—sex, the
flesh, blood—was a symbol of the Devil, which meant no meat,
no sex acts, no fighting. But then God, who is soul, could not have
been made flesh in Jesus. Hence the Incarnation was one of Satan's
snares and Christ was an impostor or the spirit of Evil. This was
no longer a heresy, it was a negation.

The episode of the Cathars raises two questions. The first has
been widely studied, and our sources, some of which are Cathar,
leave little doubt about it. Grouped along the Rhine, in Lom-

bardy, in Catalonia, then more densely in the middle course of the Garonne in Provence, Cathars became solidly organized around 1150–1170 in a process that is difficult to trace but included efficacious preaching, the holding of "councils," discussion tournaments with Catholic dignitaries, and the organization of something resembling a church. Around 1200 the danger that they presented seemed clear enough for Rome to express concern. The king of France—Philip Augustus—said nothing, seeming to wait for a chance to introduce his own presence in the Midi. It was Pope Innocent III who took the affair in hand after the assassination of a papal legate. What happened next is well known. Barons from the north of France rushed south for a war blessed by the pope as a "crusade" (which in fact it was) that produced abominable massacres, battles, and cities and towns sacked and destroyed. Then the king joined the fray, went south to the *pays d'oc*, and settled in. The whole affair lasted twenty years, from 1209 to 1229, although some strongholds resisted until around 1250 or 1260, and for long after, some who declared themselves Cathars were found here and there. The two essential and immediate results of this struggle are quite obvious. In order to avoid a return of a similar threat, the Church created a corps of investigators, or "inquisitors" of the Faith and charged the learned brothers of Saint Dominic with responsibility for it, and the king of France reached the Mediterranean.

There is another aspect to the problem of the Cathars, however. Why and how did a doctrine like theirs, one of exceptional rigor (to the point of permitting oneself to die of hunger rather than touch a forbidden foodstuff), succeed in gaining a foothold, backed by enormous determination, in the land of sunshine and the troubadours? No explanation is truly satisfactory. Was there an unsupportable degradation in the mores of the local clergy? The same was true elsewhere. Was it due to the preaching of Bulgarian apostles? There is no serious evidence of this. Was Catharism based on an ancient dualistic foundation, Basque or Catalan? But it is hard to see why it should emerge at just that moment; besides, this explanation is pure hypothesis. Nor was there any prophetic leader or provocateur from the north, though this is an avenue that might bear investigation. The brutality of the men of war from the north shows clearly that a spirit of cupidity launched them on an attack of lands richer and less populated than their own, and their king allowed them to do what they wanted—or might he have incited them? On their side, the people of the south did not hide their scorn of the northerners and their independent spirit. So was this a settling of accounts that had been resonating in the Occitan subconscious? Another hypothesis: by mixing the count, the lord, the artisan, and the peasant in one and the same movement, the Cathars adopted an almost revolutionary attitude toward the "orders" that had to be punished, at least in the eyes of the Church. But was this a cause or an effect?

These are obscure questions that prevent us from firmly situating the twelfth- and thirteenth-century Cathar episode. I have attempted to rid it of the worn monastic habits (regionalist ones in particular) in which it has been dressed, for lack of anything better, and that are still venerated by a few nostalgic historians. As for the idea of the double face of the Supreme Being, it was pursued fiercely by the Dominican preachers who were masters of the powers of pursuit and judgment after 1235. But the inquisitors of the thirteenth century should not be confused with their ferocious sixteenth-century successors. Although any court brought together to judge a cause condemned ahead of time led more often to the stake or to perpetual imprisonment than to a fine or a pardon, the judges of those times, for example, Bernard Gui, their master, although not tender lambs, showed a finely tuned appreciation that kept them within the bounds of moderation. As for the popular classes, they were shaken by the echoes of the conflict. Without any examination of the truth of the matter, the qualification of "Satanism" with which the Cathars had been accused and, in a variety of times and a range of topics, later deviants or sects were attacked was founded on the memory of the "Albigensian Crusade." This was one of the accusations brought against the Templars in their trial in the early fourteenth century.

Like others, I use the word "Church" in multiple contexts in my picture of these times, but it is unfortunately a highly contradictory term, since it includes both the hierarchical structure that refers to Christian dogma and guides or supervises the faithful in their passage in this world, and those faithful as a group, the *ecclesia* in its Greek sense of "assembly," which reaches far beyond the ministers of God. Taken in this second sense, which is, moreover, that of those times, the medieval Church was the whole social organization, the dominant expression of those who had been baptized, and the foundation for all representation. What dominated it was thus not the pope, a bishop, or monks, but the idea of a spiritual coherence among all men, beyond all contradictions or "religious" nuances. That coherence was founded on the notion of Virtue, that is, on the courage, the merit, and the physical or moral energy that, according to the ancients, distinguishes man from beast. Effort in favor of the common interest must be spontaneous and has no need of a code. Nonetheless the learned, in those centuries, made an attempt to provide this vision with a framework, according to a spirit of system that is one of the marks of Western "culture." I have spoken above of the seven "virtues," so often symbolized in effigies and as the ways to perfection for all men, Christian or not. As Thomas Aquinas spoke of them in the mid-thirteenth century, three of these virtues, Faith, Hope, and Charity, had a moral dimension, while four others, Prudence, Justice, Strength, and Temperance, had a more "human" aspect. As part of its responsibility to keep the control of the flock of the baptized within its own hands, the Church—and this time, under the form of an organized body—multiplied its incitements to further that march toward the ideal, even at some cost. This is why for such a long time it set aside the question of the grace accorded by God to the faithful to help the individual do good and avoid introducing a discrimination between those who may or may not have received that gift and other gifts on the level of "works." The importance of these questions during the Protestant Reformation in the sixteenth century is well known.

In contrast, putting those virtues into operation soon appeared to the Church to require modulation according to the "estates" of society. Beyond the division of society into three "orders" decreed by God and that I have spoken of on many occasions, the preachers showed themselves to be very open to quasi-"social" judgments. This flexibility was perhaps most clearly manifested in the virtue of charity. A certain comprehension, even indulgence, shown to one's neighbor, which would seem to us the most evolved form of charity, was not the aspect of that virtue most respected in those centuries—or, rather, charity took on the more measured aspect of aid to the needy. Hospitals under the guidance of monks or bishops certainly existed beginning with the earliest Christian centuries, and they expanded in moments of epidemics or economic crises in the fourteenth and fifteenth centuries, but these institutions were more likely to be places of asylum and refuge, often provisory, and offered no therapeutic assistance. The gesture of Saint Louis, who created a house to care for three hundred needy blind people (the *quinze vingts*) was an exception. That fairly rudimentary, almost superficial form of charity was not due to what we might call "hardness of heart," but rather to the clash of two antinomic concepts. In the first place, it was God who chose to burden the blind man, the invalid, or the pauper. These disgraces (in the root sense of the word) were not chosen voluntarily, except by the clergy, who drew from them the purity demanded by their "estate." Others were simply afflicted by them and were not to expect spontaneous help. In the fourteenth century, when the weaknesses of the seigneurial economic system produced large numbers of the "new poor," some were suspected of being a "bad pauper," a voluntary deviance that raised suspicion of heresy. A more rigorous selection kept foreigners and strangers to the city out of the hospitals, along with men healthy enough to be sent to work in a building site. The second concept also contains a disputable correction: possessing material ease in this world was considered legitimate, and the question of the "poverty" of Christ tore apart the Church in the early fourteenth century. Faithful to the lesson of their master, Francis of Assisi, the Friars Minor, faced with the obvious and scandalous wealth of a Church staggering under the weight of legacies and gifts, preached the abandonment of all material goods and giving them to the poor. Such an act of "pure" charity was considered shocking, however, and there were plenty of Christians for whom Jesus had owned property and who rejoiced at the crusaders' pillages of the infidel. Because excessive wealth was a powerful source of several of the capital sins, however, everyone was expected to give, usually in the form of voluntary alms. This was a classic theme for preaching in a Church that soon understood that the faithful could be persuaded that a gift to the Church was a gift to God or to the poor, thus assuring the giver of an "indulgence" on Judgment Day. The gift that the wealthy man could be persuaded to make on the occasion of a festival, a good harvest, or, quite simply, when death lurked, thus became, among those who could afford it, a duty related to their "estate" and a social obligation; the giver's heart may have been in it, but as a complement. This means that charity, in both of its senses, risked becoming little more that the modest alms of an equally humble member of the faithful. Unfortunately for the historian, these real acts of charity have not been honored by being put in written form.

This long development about one of the cardinal virtues most necessary to men's spiritual life could be coupled with discussions of the others, but the conclusion would be the same: as the guardian of the paths to salvation, the Church did not function as a Christian Cerberus. It distinguished perfectly well among the forms and the limits of Virtue according to the "orders" that translate the will of God and the "estates" that resulted from the will of men. Thus clerics, both regular and secular, who were called tenants of prayer were expected to give an example to laymen, known to be inevitable sinners. An entire hierarchical and closed structure contributed to playing the role of a fortress of Virtue, a refuge, and a citadel. This is perhaps why the Church, with some difficulty, was endowed with an exceptional status, in some instances from the first centuries of its existence, regarding in the notion of the ecclesiastical *for* that put its members and their goods "outside of" (*foris*) lay control. This privilege was not purely a gesture of self-defense. It was instead the mark of a moral specificity, and it was a veritable heresy to denounce it as an abuse, as was attempted by a number of clerics, in the fourteenth and fifteenth centuries in particular, who were indignant to see that exception cover up exaggerated instances of wealth or laxity.

The other orders eluded the rigorous discipline of Virtue. The warriors might be accused of an excessive interest in outward appearance, their appetite for honors, or the indomitable force of clan interests, but they were quite easily pardoned for straying if they remained faithful to the duty of their estate to defend and to fight. The third order made up for its failings by the "virtues" of labor once opprobrium was no longer attached to manual labor. It was the merchants whose salvation was the most difficult to prepare. Masters of time and of numbers, which should be attributes of God alone, leading an equivocal and suspect life, animated by a desire to win their salvation by themselves, they were often suspected of acting in the name of the Devil, and the Church hesitated to offer them its confidence and its charity. In 1198 the canonization of a Cremona merchant known only as a "fine man" (*homo bonus*), was a sensational bit of news, but the experiment was not often renewed.

Difficult as it was for the faithful who led a "common" existence to stay away from the traditional temptations and traps that Satan laid for them, an enumeration of the missteps on the road to salvation would soon take on the aspect of a simple list of men's weaknesses—weaknesses that had pursued them at least since the end of the "golden age" imagined by ancient wisdom. One of these temptations merits a closer look in the medieval period because it seemed to the thinkers of those centuries to be the most difficult to control. This was the temptation to think outside of the law dictated by God, or at least expressed in his name by his ministers.

Some historians speak of a "birth of the secular spirit" at the end of the thirteenth century, an expression that others have judged excessive. What is sure is that the notion of a freedom to think outside of the imposed framework—and even more, the notion of free will—does not seem to have been widespread before the age of the pre-Renaissance and pre-Reformation. Thomas Aquinas, William of Ockham, and Jean Buridan, to cite only three powerful thinkers between 1250 and 1350, praised and valued individual thought and acuity in regard to Creation, while Jean de Meung and even Dante denounced the hypocrisy of a society stifled by the Church, but none of these men were free of the idea of a strict dependence on the Creator. The menace of "humanism" as a rival to an indisputable revealed thought was not felt until the very end of the medieval era, and in fact marks its end. At the start, however, it took the form of a global rejection and almost a negative mysticism: the "Brothers of the Free Spirit" in northwestern Europe in the early sixteenth century pass for being pious—very pious—mystics. In fact, their distance from the core of the Church was not considered a heresy or a rupture only because their action was rarely militant and did not frighten the hierarchy.

The opposite was true of the anti-ecclesial movements of revolt, which were systematically denounced, pursued, and exterminated because they attacked the excesses of clerical domination or the weaknesses of the established hierarchy. To our eyes, however, these movements seem much less redoubtable for the Church than the dogmatic rejection of the Cathars or internal challenges to faith. In these movements of contestation, which at times could be quite radical, what worried the hierarchy was "popular" reaction to many of them and the indisputable accuracy of the reproaches made concerning the false virtue of the clergy, their wealth as opposed to the poverty of Christ, and their claim to involve themselves in problems to which they were manifestly incapable of offering a response, such as the conditions of marriage, inheritance, and even "mechanical" labor. The list of uprisings is long. Because the repression that followed came in the form of an agreement, more or less openly avowed, between the first and second orders to recall the third to obedience, the historian finds it an easy task to discover the "social" dimension of these uprisings. But this rudimentary aspect of "class struggle" has little to retain me here; on the other hand, the often "peasant" nature of these "furors" merits a pause. Uprisings occurred in all regions of western Europe, and under masks that varied according to the century: Normandy in the tenth century; Lombardy, Champagne, Picardy, Flanders, the banks of the Rhine in the eleventh century; Catalonia, Germany, the Loire Valley, around Lyon in the twelfth century; Italy and Languedoc in the thirteenth century. At times the Church managed to recuperate a portion of the forces that were let loose in this manner, as in the cities of Italy in the eleventh century; at other times it closed its eyes to attempts that it found difficult to condemn, such as the reforms urged by Robert d'Arbrissel in the eleventh century or Francis of Assisi in the thirteenth century; while still others gave it food for thought. Some such attempts were well aimed and could be tolerated if kept under a superior control. This was true of Peter of Bruys in the mid-twelfth century, who demanded a literal reading of Scripture, and of Pierre Valdès (Peter Waldo), who preached in favor of a reconstitution of the primitive Christian communities. After 1300 or 1320, however, and the intractable pontificate of John XXII in Avignon, repression became so much more dramatic that the rebels, who were systematically called *vaudois* (or Waldenses), urged on by the economic crisis, turned their criticism to the entire hierarchical structure of the Church. By collapsing into the anarchy of a pontifical schism that lasted three-quarters of a century, the Church opened the way to a posthumous triumph of the "heretics."

Rebellion against the Church structure could also arise out of a temptation in which pride played a primary role. But, after all, the Church was armed—and had proven it—to keep control of its flock and to reestablish the meaning of virtue. But what could it do against the force of a good half of baptized humanity: women? On several occasions above I have attempted to circumscribe the place, role, and power of the women of these centuries, and if I have not really managed to do so, it is precisely because it was always men (clerics above all) who talked about them, and this fact has obscured and even eliminated the female figure. For man, woman was the incarnation of temptation and, from Eve to the Last Judgment, she inevitably formed one half of daily life on this Earth. This temptation was not sexual attraction; it is possible that even the clerics may have been sensitive to it, as were the other males of the species, and that the exclusion of women from the priesthood, as Saint Paul prescribed, despite the teachings of Jesus himself, aggravated the situation. Woman was suspect well above and beyond her sexual place: admirable and attractive but repellent and hostile, it was in her that God placed the "negative" aspect of his work. By attributing to woman both the power to give life and the power to frequent the dead, he placed her opposite man as a sign of contradiction and as a reflection. Both the Christian Church and Islam were blind to woman, and they both took refuge in an absurd condemnation.

Sin and Pardon

Man was created in the image of God, but he was but a reflection of the divinity; he was "superior" to the beasts because he had been endowed with reason, but he was inferior to the angels because he had been corrupted at his birth. It was thus inevitable that he should sin, but it was indispensable that he wash himself clean of his sins. Original sin, confession, and pardon in this world are among the major traits that make up the Christian faith; they do not exist with such unity or such force in other belief systems. A latent notion of guilt weighs on the human species, and it was appropriate that men should be persuaded of this. A fondness for regulation dear to Mediterranean peoples led to the establishment of an entire table of errors and faults against the law of God, or simply against human law. Aristotle commented on "vices"; Saint Augustine converted them into sins; in the seventh century Gregory the Great established a list of them; in the twelfth century, Peter Lombard introduced the notion of "capital" sins of volition, but the expression "capital sins" did not appear before 1260, under the pen of Thomas Aquinas. Each of these sins was the echo of an impulse of the heart or of the mind, willingly accepted or prompted. Sins would accompany man to the Last Judgment, which meant that they were clearly related to the characteristics of human society, in the West at least. Pride, *superbia*, was at the base of the spirit of domination, but also of the spirit of rebellion against Order or the "orders." Vanity supported the pretensions of wealthy men. Envy was the motive factor of the "seigneurial" system, just as avarice was its product. Wrath was the symbol of human relations, as gluttony was the symbol of an insult to poverty. Lust was the obsession with the flesh in preference to the soul, and it went much farther than sexual appetite. Accompanying these seven sins, but on a lesser scale, was acedia, which the fifteenth century called sloth, but which was the abandonment of all human initiative in the face of the natural forces and an insult to God's plans. Any hierarchy among these errors could only be the fruit of personal reflection. The exception was pride, which led to a negation of the Creator, as with the fallen archangel. As one might suspect, however, contingencies of the moment could privilege one sin or another, for example lust as matrimonial customs changed, or envy and avarice in face of the advance of the use of money.

If the original sin could be redeemed by baptism, that sacrament, which opens the door to salvation, was only a rite of initiation; it did not eliminate sins to come. Besides, the gradual decline of adult baptism, beginning early in Carolingian times, in favor of the baptism of infants, who were without genuine awareness, or children at their confirmation, who were still too young to possess the understanding necessary for any conscious engagement, brought baptism back to the simple role of a doorway to Christian life and in no way exonerated the new believer from error. Sin was thus a voluntary act of offense against God, an obstacle on the way to the salvation that was the goal of all existence. The need to be aware of this, spontaneously or on the invitation of a minister of God, led to remorse first, contrition next, and finally confession. The sentiment that admitting one's fault was an eminent form of submission to the Divinity and an example of the struggle to be conducted against Evil, led the first Christians to preach public confession before others who had been baptized and in church, the setting dedicated to prayer. In order to humiliate himself even more, as human justice demanded for material crimes, it was proper that the sinner express himself out loud and by marking with his admission the sentiment that he recognized that he had sinned and promised not to fall back into error. Naturally, it was not long before the dangers of such declarations, sincere or not, became evident, when other believers, at times animated by an appetite for calumny, commented on them. It may have been fear that the good behavior and sincerity of the person at fault would change if scandal was threatened that led to the introduction of the obligation, first to confess at least once a year, and second that such a confession be "auricular," that is, spoken into the ear of a priest endowed with the power of absolution. These practices gradually spread after the tenth century, but did not become obligatory until 1215, for the first, and 1255, for the second.

Now that pardon for sins had been established as a penitential sacrament, admission of sin was closely associated with confession, provided this was accompanied by serious contrition, of course. Absolution, ardently desired by the dying in the form of extreme unction and pardon, was the strongest weapon of Church power over the faithful; there was no salvation if the soul remained impure. Moreover, pardon demanded penitence, hence expiation. This domain is one of those best known in Christian practice. In fact, it is not enough to lose oneself in interminable prayers or order a series of masses to efface the faults of the deceased. A personal effort is required; the "penitentials" that have come down to us, from the eighth century in Ireland up to the eleventh and twelfth centuries elsewhere, list the fasts and the flagellations that various faults demand. Expiation could be more burdensome, however.

The gift—whether in the form of movable or immovable goods, short-term income or payments in perpetuity—was decided at the moment of receiving absolution or, especially, *in articulo mortis*. This was the simplest and the most current form of that expiation, and, according to the sinner's social level, it might be the most onerous. Such gifts went to the Church, the natural intermediary with the Beyond, and it is easy to imagine with what zeal and what hidden thoughts monks or canons, acting as testamentary executors for sins, encouraged such acts of penitence. But there was a much less dubious yet more arduous path toward salvation: expiatory pilgrimage to holy places, which could easily ruin the penitent to the end of his days.

Thus the Christian people made its way between the stains of sin and hopes. In these "simple" centuries, the way to follow in order to correctly accomplish the "passage" through this world was carefully supervised by the depositories of the law. But did the faithful even know how to recognize that law?

FAITH AND SALVATION

We have now arrived at the end of the road that began with the body, tools, practices, and conditions of life. My command of language shrinks before the task of mastering the metaphysical dimension of my personages. Still, this is a key to the Middle Ages, and perhaps the principal one, and I have ceaselessly invoked faith, salvation, and the Supreme Being as playing major roles at the time. It does not really matter whether or not these centuries can be called Christian; this is just a quarrel over words. All of the medieval world was bathed in an ocean of piety and indisputably meaningful beliefs; anyone who was not immersed in it was not of that world. I fear drowning in it.

Let us begin by studying words. Faith, *fides*, that of one man toward another or of a "faithful" believer toward God, is by no means a form of pious or religious thought, but only the avowal of a contract accepted by two parties, a contract that excludes any transcendental notion. Some writers detached from the sacred have even suggested that faith supposed a thought structure close to that of secular "feudalism." Serving faith required rites, formulas, and obligations that implied an attentive surveillance blazing the trail to be followed; the ecclesial structure was thus the mold into which faith was placed. Belief, or *credentia*, is just a more or less provisory confidence in others; *credere* means "to lend," to give credit (*faire crédit*), or to have belief (*avoir créance*), and the word is much more secular than sacred. If it is applied to the sacred, it is mutilated, as the sacred is what escapes reason, what contains only the spiritual and the unknowable. In proper logic, credence—*la croyance*—does not belong there. Nor can we be any happier with the term "*religio*," which means "re-reading," scruples, even respect, and in no way contains the notion of an order of the world. To say that someone has the "religion" of work is simply a moral engagement, not a dogma or a rite. As for *pietas*, it expresses tenderness and devotion; the ancients venerated *Pietas* as a familiar, even a domestic, divinity.

This review of words thus leaves us with no one response. In the attitude of medieval man, and probably of man in all ages, the relation with a Supreme Being contains at once a confidence, an agreement, and an engagement of the spirit and the vital breath, the first meaning of the soul or *anima*. Like all human manifestations, that relationship demands consideration of its content, its container, and its object. And, in spite of the reservations that the word inspires in me, and to simplify my argument, I shall call its essence "faith."

Dogma and the Rites of Medieval Christian Faith

This heading is a bit long, but I wanted to stress the specificity of the manifestations of belief in these times. Indeed, some of the essential foundations of the Christian faith come from convictions that are much older and came not only from cultural areas with no obvious connection to the Mediterranean Christian world—

such as India or Iran, perhaps also the Far East—but also from the original Jewish matrix, and at times even from the secular world of ancient philosophy. Thus, the soul is superior to the body and touches on the immortal; God is *one* no matter what appearance he chooses; all creatures are his work and owe everything to him, notably love and obedience. Christians added to this thousand-year-old base an element that was fundamental to their belief; for one short moment, God made himself man on this Earth in order to redeem a sinful humanity. This "Incarnation" is unique to Christian belief; not to accept it is to place oneself outside of the *ecclesia*, the assembly of believers. Obviously, I have no intention of commenting on this dogma, but it is indispensable to point out its effects. I see three of them.

First, although the word of God was revealed by the prophets of ancient times, the Word—that is, the supernatural "word"—draws its authority and its doctrine from the holy book that brings together these messages. The messages that came before Christ—the "old witness" (which is the meaning of Old Testament)—operate as a contract of alliance between man and an incorporeal God. But if Jesus is indeed "the son of God," his message and all that it contains of "good news" (which is the meaning of the word "evangels," and also apply to the later ones and even the apocryphal ones) form a "New Testament" and a new Alliance. This message becomes the prime base of belief because it is the Logos, the true word proffered among men, whereas what preceded it in the Book was simply a prefiguration, a *mythos* or myth. In emphasizing the New Testament, which the Jews did not accept, the Christians magnified the entire "human" portion of the divine message.

This was the origin of the hypertrophy of the Christic figure in convictions, rites, and representations. Because Christians were convinced (or at least said they were) that Jesus was God made man, he had to be honored, depicted, and drawn as if he were a man. The common people did not worry their heads about the learned discussions prompted by such a duality in one person. God was treated as a man; he was called Lord and addressed by joining one's hands together as the humble did before the master; a family life was found (or invented) for him; he was almost always depicted with the unchanging traits of a bearded young man, as people imagined that he had been amid the Jews of those times; or else he was painted or described with tools in hand. Popular festivities celebrated the stages of his passage through this world along with the old agrarian fertility rites; moments of the liturgical year were coordinated with payment dates for the *cens* and other dues. For the Jews and for the Muslims, this humanization of God was an abominable scandal. Today, little or nothing has changed of that Christic heritage; during the Middle Ages some went so far as to exonerate Jesus himself for any role and any prescription in these domains, shifting responsibility to the discourses of Paul of Tarsus, who had never known him. The fact that Paul was called an apostle shows that he was recognized as the "inventor" (in the medieval sense of the word) of Christian doctrine.

Another effect is more philosophical in nature. The populations of western Europe, both northern and Mediterranean, were in need of "reality," and an appetite for the concrete led them to give a dimension to the "true" and to truth as a line of spiritual conduct. This truth was expressed in attitudes the object of which was to make the spiritual more accessible; a manuscript copy of the Bible was, corporally, *the* Bible; the host that symbolized the sacrifice of Christ must be displayed and eaten like the real body of Jesus. And then there were the remains, or "relics," of saintly personages that were to be touched, not just looked at. Because one could not be sure that the objects related to the person of Christ—spines from the crown of thorns, pieces of the true cross, his winding sheet— were "authentic," one could revere images of Jesus, the Virgin, or the angels. Although this custom was much stronger in the Eastern Roman Empire, where it set off furious political quarrels and wars, iconoduly, or the veneration of images, also shook the Carolingian world. In the West, it is thanks to the pressure of popular piety and monastic tolerance that the figure of Christ has lasted to our days, at least in scenes of the Crucifixion, the basic element of Christian theology. And such practices still provoke indignation among Jews and Muslims.

In order to penetrate the uneducated masses, who do not always understand correctly (if at all) the spiritual aspects of their own piety, and to keep them from falling into idolatry or "savage thought," they must be trained to submit to rites. What is more, this was just as true of pagan beliefs. It was evidently up to the Church to take on the task, which was all the more difficult because the *vulgum* tenaciously held to a number of extremely solid customs connected with pre-Christian cults. In the first place, the faithful must remain in contact with the divine, hence they must frequent the house in which the image and the signs of God were accessible. For reasons that the learned easily found, the faithful cannot be left to their own devices and simply invited to pray alone several times a day like the Muslim or the Jew. To be sure, they were invited to praise God on a regular basis, but the Church seems to have doubted their zeal. The appetite for the spiritual and spontaneous devotion among all those simple men, former adorers of Nature or of human "virtues," seemed to the Church to require constant encouragement. The mission of the priest who had been given the care (*cura*) of souls in a village or a city parish was to keep up that flame. He of course was responsible for delivering the sacraments—notably, celebrating the Eucharist regularly and even on a daily basis in his church—but the "office" of the mass must also be an occasion for predication. The various stages of Christ's Passion had to be recalled, the marks of divine clemency or wrath stressed, signs of virtue praised, and the timid and the skeptical threatened with eternal punishment. If need be, the learned specialists of the Word of God, the "preachers"—Dominicans in the schools and Franciscans in the marketplaces—would fill in for a curé who lacked followers or imagination.

In the final analysis, the parishioners in question were not very zealous. The Lateran council of 1215 decreed that all must attend services in the parish church to which they were attached and must take communion by the consecrated host at least once a year, for example, at Easter. Thirty years later, however, the bishop Jacques de Vitry furiously stigmatized the tepidity of the faithful, whom he showed were more apt to frequent the tavern than Sunday mass. This led to a multiplication of mechanical forms used to internalize devotion: genuflexion (a pagan rite of submission), the sign of the Cross (a gesture of union with the Trinity), the wearing or the removal of headgear in the holy place (an inversion, conscious or not, of Jewish practice), hands joined in prayer like a slave (instead of raising outstretched arms to the heavens like the ancient "orant"). Such gestures cannot be anything other than a totally external materialization of piety. Direct invocation of God remained confined to the *Credo*, the minimal foundation of belief, the knowledge or recitation of which does not seem to have been obligatory before the thirteenth century. The other "prayers"—the *Pater noster* beginning in the twelfth century, and even more the *Ave Maria,* bear witness to the humanization of faith of which I have already spoken.

The need to render visible spiritual realities that the commonality seemed to grasp poorly led the Church to make sacred practices that punctuate the pious life of the faithful, which meant making them morally inviolable. In the mid-thirteenth century Peter Lombard set the list of the seven "sacraments," the importance of which varied with the evolution of religious sentiment within the Church itself. Baptism and its confirmation signified entry into the *ecclesia*. The Eucharist was the truly Christian "passport" because it magnified the principle of the Incarnation. Penitence was a weapon against a laxity of mores that the Church felt to be a betrayal of its message. And extreme unction opened the way toward salvation. It was not until somewhat later that "reception" into the order of the clerics was assimilated to a sacrament, as was marriage among the laity, probably in order to combat the weakening of pious vocations in the first case and to work against the scandalous matrimonial liberty that reigned among the warrior aristocracy in the second. We have the feeling that, in its simple desire to prepare for salvation, the common people chose to adopt as undisputed sacraments only the saintly precautions of baptism and extreme unction and often saluted the others from a distance.

In order to break the resistance of the last unbelievers—or rather, of the tepid (for not to believe and to say so had no place in the minds of these people)—the Church had one more highly effective weapon: the miracle. This was an unexpected, undisputable, admirable, and spectacular event by which the power and, in general, the benevolence of God was manifested even to the eyes of the incredulous. Be it a lesson or a warning, a comfort or an act of charity, the miracle went against the laws of nature, the old pagan traditions, and magic. It appeared following a prayer, a touch, the intervention of a "virtuous" man, and concerned only pure souls or souls that would hopefully be purified by this means; 80 percent of miracles occurred to women, children, and poor people. Most of them involved healing, as was also true of the miracles of Jesus; out of the five thousanad and more miracles that have been analyzed, 40 percent concerned mobility and 30 percent sense deficiencies. As the centuries went on, and especially after the thirteenth century, their efficacy became suspect, and miracles were converted or shrunken into "marvels" (*mirabilia*)—that is, prodigious and fantastic but more and more secularized events, even though the popular classes persisted in seeing the mark of the supernatural in them. Up to the Counter-Reformation the Church struggled against this slide toward paganism, but its remedy—retiring into oneself to lose oneself in the true faith—had little chance of persuading the common people.

The Church

The *ecclesia* was the totality of believers, and all that has been said above was a part of it. But the flock had to be guided, and the Church, in the sense in which I have usually used the word, was the hierarchical framework in which the ministers of the Divinity were grouped. Without them the *ordo laicorum* would remain without a shepherd, which means tempted by savage thought, the thought that fed the pagan beliefs of which I have often spoken: nocturnal processions, votive meals with sacrifices, idolatrous cults involving stones, trees, and waters. The men of the Church had to make a prodigious effort of acculturation, either by guiding such beliefs toward more orthodox ways, for example, by encouraging the cult of the dead, or else by justifying brutal practices such as the *faide* or vengeance (both familial and other), using social arguments to absorb it within a "judgment of God" played out in a closed field. Another way was to sacralize the processions of Rogations, Lent, and Carnival and transform spontaneous shamanism into a spiritual belief in the omnipotence of the Creator. Moreover, from the earliest centuries of Christianity, monastic communities offered the future baptized a model of life in perfect conformity with the hoped-for ideal of disparagement of the fleshly, rejection of the vanities of this world, and a personal effort to renounce Evil. But in spite of its successive attempts to render that ideal accessible, the Church was confronted by a people that disliked theocentrism because it was beyond the reach of its modest spiritual baggage. One can always join a group of penitents or exonerate oneself from all remorse by generous donations, but this was as far as it went; not everyone who wants to be (or even who could be) a hermit, a Cistercian, or even a Friar Minor actually was one.

Thus intermediaries were needed—those whose duty it was to lead others to salvation—and this time, we have the "established" Church, from the modest vicar of a rustic chapel to the sovereign pontiff in Rome. I am supposing that my reader is not hoping here for a history of the Church, any more than he or she hoped for an overall picture of the lay nobility or the portrait of a wealthy merchant. So many excellent works—including dictionaries, surveys, essays, and manuals—have been written on the religious history of the Middle Ages, the history of the papacy, the monks, and the bishops, or else on the schools and dogmatic quarrels that I would feel ridiculous if I added to them. Still, I have not lost sight of my ordinary public, the lesser people. It seems certain that they would have heard of the reigning pope as a sort of distant leader, or of their local bishop, for example when he came, once a year at least, to confirm baptismal vows. But all the *officiaux* (ecclesiastical judges), archdeacons, and deans of Christianity were for them nothing but entities, even in the cities. As for the monks, it is quite possible that the people admired them, but I am sure that the high walls of their cloister seemed to outsiders much more a sign of a formidable economic power—and a domination that was more material than spiritual—than a protection of Virtue against Evil. The only representative of the Church who was visible, real, and near at hand was the curé of the village or the neighborhood church, flanked by his "vicars," his eventual replacements, who lived in their midst in the "parish" that was their common religious space.

Today the historian of religious culture willingly abandons the vantage point of Rome or the abbey to make a larger place for the "parish," about which I have already spoken. The various examples of this model of faith in fact punctuate the history of Christianity much more than is true of the dogmatic quarrels about the Trinity or the history of the "reforms" of the Church *in capite*. If indeed the *ecclesia* is the complete group of believers, its meaning was too vague and its mark on the ground too extensive for families, neighbors, or clans to recognize one another in it. What was needed was to gather inhabitants, houses, or individual cells, but joined together: a *paroikia* in Greek fashion, a Latin *parrochia*, a *paroisse*, or even a *plebs*, which is the crowd assembled, or a Celtic *plou*. That a place of worship, a cemetery, and baptismal fonts were set up in such gathering places was not a general evolution, nor was it natural or immediate. Such groupings form in fluid and fluctuating zones. Historians today are nearly sure that the *fundus* (farm or estate) of late antiquity did not necessarily give birth to the parish; that the latter was not the reflection of some ancient political or fiscal district, even in the zones strongly held by Rome; and that the *terroir*, in the geographical sense of the area necessary to produce enough to nourish a group of men, did not automatically coincide with a religious framework any more than did a land area under "seigneurial" rights. This means that the formation of a network of contiguous parishes, each grouped around a church with a curé, was certainly a late phenomenon in the solidification of rites and customs; only shortly before 1215 did the Church decree, in the Lateran council, that each believer have his parish rather than frequent several churches or pick one at random.

We can trace the successive stages of that formation, however. From the fifth to the ninth centuries, while Christianity itself was slowly spreading, the centers of the cult were designated either under the influence of whomever commanded in the area (in which case it was known as a "private church" or *Eigenkirche* and the priest was designated by a layman) or else by episcopal and, even more, monastic, decision. Next, a patron saint was chosen by the faithful themselves—and of course this process is easier to see in an urban context. The idea of extending the parish organization throughout a territory arose in the Carolingian epoch, thanks to a prevalent urge to reorganize society, at least on the high end of the lay or clerical hierarchy. Hincmar, the archbishop of Reims, introduced the idea that the local pastor be remunerated by a payment of one-tenth of the revenues of his parish, the *dîme* (*decima*), which obviously implies that an area within which this tax would be collected had already been determined. At the moment of the capital phase of village encellment between 950 and 1150, a genuine clarification of the parish system accompanied reform of the Church. The parish building, the *atrium* for burials that surrounded it, the ground and the land donation on which the altar (*dos et altare*) were established were classified as *res sacrae*, thus including them, as Gratian stated in his *Decretum* of the twelfth century, in the exceptional jurisdiction, the *for* enjoyed by the Church. Reinforcing the sacrality of churches and spacing them out more rationally thus led to the gradual disappearance, usually by successive purchases, of private churches and secondary churches (*Niederkirchen* and isolated chapels), demoted to the level of simple oratories. Collection of the *dîme* accompanied this movement, and "synods" under the control of the bishop assured control of it. Results were mediocre on the two last points, however. In various localities the lay aristocracy seized the *dîme* and refused to turn it over to the Church, and on occasion the Church personnel lacked zeal. Still, the network put into place in the thirteenth century held firm until the end of the ancien régime. The parish network tended to be replaced by a secular and communal network, but not without adjustments that extend beyond my topic here.

One last element, however: for the faithful on the bottom of the social structure, the notion of parish was equivalent to a recognition of the place in which the sacraments were dispensed, baptism and the Eucharist in particular; but as the parish was also, as we have seen, a gathering place, a place of asylum, and a place for festivities, the curé's role within the social group was fundamental. As a man of God, he was the spokesman for the community, seconded by the blacksmith, the first among the artisans of the village. If he knew a few words of Latin to throw at the master of the place and had an ounce of dogmatic culture and a certain personal charisma, the curé was taken to be the depository of knowledge, the supporter of dogma, and the director of conscience of the faithful and the lord alike. Medieval curés do not have a good reputation. Until the twelfth century, they were either elected by their future parishioners, with the backing of the master of the environs, from among the local clerics and the priests who served a nearby monastery or convent, or they were designated by the bishop of the diocese, who tended to push his own candidate. This rudimentary designation procedure does not imply that the curé was ignorant, dishonest, or corrupt. He was often reproached for such faults, but it seems clear that, during the final centuries of the Middle Ages, the personage of the curé won a place in people's minds. The recommendation of celibacy, which dates from the tenth century, became an obligation after 1225 or 1250; the minimum level of culture demanded of a parish priest resulted in a gradual improvement in the cultural level of the faithful; nepotism and absenteeism were seriously combated, even by the bishops and archdeacons who did not always escape a similar accusation themselves. In short, the medieval curé was worth more than it would seem from the way he was portrayed in the traditional satire of the *fabliaux*. He remained a man, like his parishioners subject to temptation, but served by faith. What distinguished him from others was his absolute obligation to try to lead them to salvation in the Other World.

The Other World

All living beings are something more than a collection of cells animated by chemical or electrical impulses. No culture has failed to discern in them a material envelope and a spiritual breath, a body and a soul. It is hard to see why the human being should be alone in this. (I think that my reader will have noted in passing my opinion on the subject, but I will leave it at that.) Paleontologists attempt to find out when and in what ways prehistoric man became aware of this body/soul duality and how he expressed it. But all of the "civilizations" of which we have any trace had no doubts. They wondered about the moment and the conditions under which that "alliance" was established: by the unmediated will of God, the Bible and Eastern belief systems declare, with the philosophy of Plato even invoking a demiurge. This idea of the preexistence of the duality of body and soul in the mind of the Creator is a point of dogma that interested the learned, but the faithful in the Middle Ages saw only one obvious thing: the body is perishable, the soul survives, and death is the moment of separation of the two. But the body and soul would be reunited at the end of time, when the believer would find himself face-to-face with God.

The road would be long, and the approaching moment of "after," when the body would be abandoned and the soul displayed, was anguishing. Life, the "passage" through the world here below, was a constant combat, a psychomachy between vices and virtues, as Prudentius described it in the fifth century and as sculptors and miniaturists illustrated it. The life of man was a combat in a closed field between good and evil, a combat that would come to a definitive end in a Judgment, after which the body would be thrust aside and the soul weighed, placing some among the just and some among the rejected. Thus the body should not disappear while awaiting resuscitaton at the end of time; in the meantime, it must be buried, even if it rotted in the ground. Christianity had to be formal on this point; cremation and incineration, which many cultures had adopted in the East and the Far East, were prohibited. Such practices gradually disappeared in Europe in the ninth century, despite the purifying reputation of fire (they are more in favor today). As for the souls, they wandered in anguished expectation of the Last Day, waiting for Resurrection and Judgment, perhaps in Limbo, where the Gentiles and the stillborn took refuge, the Hades of the Greeks, the Sheol of the Jews, or else they remained in their former dwellings, sighing and invisible, amid the living, or in the field of the dead where their mortal remains reposed.

The expectation of the day on which the trumpets of Judgment would resound quite naturally encouraged confused meditations about the signs of the coming of the end of the world among many thinkers, some of them highly learned and others simply anguished. The biblical prophets, Isaiah and Ezekiel in particular, then the apostle John, had described this Apocalypse. The Antichrist would arise, for the moment delivering the world over to all possible torments. In the eleventh century, Judgment was thought to take place forty days after the disappearance of the Antichrist; in the twelfth century, an imperial "reign" of 120 days was introduced, at the end of which those who had refused the true faith, the Jews in particular, would be converted; in the thirteenth century, Thomas Aquinas rejected the notion of a thousand paradisiac years preceding Judgment; in the fourteenth century, the woes of the age turned people's minds to John's four horsemen announcing the Apocalypse and bringing death, war, pestilence, and famine. All of those phantasms of a fearful piety alimented the verve of the poets and the inspiration of the painters, especially toward the end of the Middle Ages. A number of spiritual movements founded their quasi-revolutionary programs on them: the end of time would mark the end of the world of men, hence one had to prepare for it. This is the way Tanchelm spoke in the eleventh century, Joachim of Fiore in the twelfth century, the flagellants and the Taborites in the fourteenth and fifteenth centuries, and, as late as the sixteenth century, Thomas Münzer, the leader of the German peasants in revolt. We abusively group under the term "millenarianism" the conviction of the imminence of a calamitous end to humanity because those thousand years were supposed to be a time of peace. The term should not be applied to the one-thousandth anniversary of the Passion: the "terrors" of the year 1000 had nothing to do with millenarianism. This is a simple verbal coincidence.

And finally we get to Judgment. The resuscitated will crowd into the Valley of Jehoshaphat at the foot of the Temple in Jerusalem, biblical tradition declares. They will come out of the tomb, their more or less clean souls reincarnated. Through the centuries, iconography has provided many versions of that august moment. The scene varies little, except to leave some space for the imagination (or the humor!) of the artist. In a "glory," God, depicted as Jesus, at times accompanied by Mary or by John, separates the good from the wicked; Saint Michael weighs good and bad actions; at his side, the Devil attempts to tip the balance his way. The elect hurry toward Paradise, the physical version of the "bosom of Abraham"; the condemned are pushed with pitchforks into the wide-open mouth of the monster, Leviathan, or directly into the flames. The popular imagination did not much focus on describing Paradise. It was a vague place in which the souls of the blessed floated; images usually show a sort of permanent ecstasy, possibly repeated choirs singing hymns, but no particular enjoyment. And no white robes and no kneeling in beatitude, as a "modern" artist would imagine the scene. The depiction of Hell is totally different. In sculptures, frescoes, and miniatures, it is nothing but enormous kettles belching steam, pitchforks and hooks, dreadful beasts, rot and shadows, refined tortures, and everything that inspires fear in this world: fire, cold, night, and animals with stingers, teeth, and venom. One might well wonder whether, at the end of medieval times, these dreadful tortures might not have aroused some doubt among persons with a somewhat more advanced mind. So many ills—and for all eternity—was an excessive price to pay, even for repeated sins. But God is just. Thus he must have thought of gradations of punishment. Dante, at least, praises him for this in the beginning of the fourteenth century. Besides, as early as the fifth century, Augustine had expressed astonishment that a soul could be burned, which, when you think about it, does not make much sense. What is more, God is merciful. He has the powers of grace and pardon. The idea of a middle term thus slowly gained ground over the course of time, among other ways, in a refinement of the penal arsenal in this world that tried to make the nature and the length of the punishment proportional to the nature or the gravity of the crime. Around 1120 or 1150 several authors expressed the idea of a "purgatory," a sort of provisory detention facility in which one could expiate his sins through remorse. The sinning soul who had committed only venial sins (*venia* meant "pardon") would remain isolated, tormented, overwhelmed with contrition, before being washed clean and received into divine grace, a grace that might also be obtained by the fervent prayers of the relatives of the deceased.

Angels accompanied the soul on this journey toward life eternal face-to-face with God. This is one of the most animated facets of medieval piety. Beginning in the sixth century, the learned and, for once, the simple people even more, said or showed that they knew of or felt perfect beings at their side, invisible and incorruptible beings that God had charged with acting as their guardians and their guides. These beings appeared in an internal hierarchy headed by the three archangels who had remained faithful to God: Gabriel, the protector and guardian of Mary, then of her cult; Raphael, who watched over Paradise; and especially Michael, from the fifth century the sword of God. Angels were sexless, and they are usually depicted with uniform, almost insipid traits. The need for security, which had increased in the fourteenth and fifteenth centuries, emphasized even more the protective role that had been attributed to them. They were responsible for guarding threatened cities, and their statues kept watch over the city gates.

They had plenty to keep them busy, for the "enemy of human kind," the "prince of this world" was there, waiting for a chance to tempt the just, support the impious, and combat the work of God. Satan, after inspiring the original Fall, had a grip on man and suggested to him—as did the archangel Lucifer, his emblematic figure—the pride to oppose himself to God. Judaism did not personalize Satan. The Devil was a medieval invention; it was around the year 1000 that the Church denounced his deadly role. At that point he was Temptation, which infiltrated dreams and appeared in uncontrolled impulses. He was seen as the negative side of Creation, which led the learned to hold woman to be his most faithful ally. To be sure, Jesus rejected all temptation, and his Passion redeemed the power of the Demon over the human soul, but one always had to fear his renewed persuasion and the temptation to sell one's soul to the Devil, like the monk Theophile, the ancestor of Faust, a frequent theme in moralizing literature. How could one fight against that cunning, disguised, and determined force? By exorcism of one "possessed" by the evil spirit? By prayer, fasting, amulets, reading the lives of the saints who were able to thrust the Devil aside? By struggling against fear, ridiculing the Devil, as in the *fabliaux*? These were largely a waste of time. The medieval Devil was a creature of God himself; he was not an entity, as the dualists or the Cathars were to claim; he was present and by his nature was at the side of every man. He had, or could claim to have, a thousand grotesque or menacing forms, or else charming and tempting ones. Saint Michael and many others could undoubtedly slay him, but only if they could find him! For he often hid himself, and extremely cleverly, in a cranny in the brain or in the heart of the sinner nibbled by the fear of failing to attain salvation because he has not unmasked the Devil in the smile of a woman, the wound of a horse, or the false weight of a bundle of wool. Constant doubt was life's companion.

So here are our "people" at the end of their passage. Man is always represented—by the pen or the chisel, in the chaldrons of the Devil as in the *danses macabres*—with all of the "estates" of this world mixed together, given that all men have a soul. If the artist seems to have taken a bitter pleasure in showing more bishops and high-born ladies than peasants or tanners boiling in the kettle or leading in the dance of Death, he was simply a humble man taking satisfaction against the proud. At life's end, as the curé repeated from the pulpit to console the suffering or calm the embittered, everyone, put into the cold ground or honored with a stone tomb capped by a *gisant*, will be no more than bones and dust. But the survivors did not really know where their souls had gone.

CONCLUSION

Here I am, at the end of my road. Academic custom demands a "conclusion" at the end of the journey, but, to tell the truth, I do not know what to "conclude." I have tried to follow very ordinary people in their lives and daily cares, their material concerns in particular. Although I have attempted to penetrate into the domains of the mind and the soul, I have felt myself less at ease there, perhaps for a lack of metaphysical sensitivity. I have taken my ordinary people for a millennium, and then I have left them, but they were there before, and they remain there after. What can be said, then, about this small nub of time in this small stretch of land, in the ocean of the human adventure? Nothing that is not known, nothing that is not banal.

There are perhaps two things left to say. The first is an explanation, or even a justification, of my own behavior in this inquiry. The second is a question, perhaps an insoluble one.

When an inquiring writer takes on a subject, he sketches out, in an "introduction," what he proposes to demonstrate, and ends by stating that he has succeeded in doing so. I have a slightly different position because in reality I have nothing to "demonstrate." The reader will have noticed that above all I have pillaged the works of others, perhaps without having always understood them well, and my mosaic, which mixes the oak and the rat with cabbage soup and the Trinity, offers nothing original or new. It does require explanation, however. My narration arises out of two preoccupations to which I hold strongly and that have cropped up here and there, perhaps expressed too personally. First, I do not believe in the superiority of our species, wherever it comes from, and in spite of its egoistic and dominating comportment. I cannot but grieve at its total inability to master nature, which it treats with an imprudent scorn, and I cannot get used to its perfect ignorance of the animal world. It is thus a simple living being, called "man," that I have sought and pursued, I fear, without spiritual depth, from when he was a baby shaking a rattle to his moment of death. In the interest of keeping to what is essential, I have attempted to shake up the mass of stereotypes and a priori statements of those who take pleasure in praising medieval times and those others who read them or listen to them: No! The "Middle Ages" is not the university, the Cistercians, the Teutonic Hanseatic League, or the statutes of the Arte della lana, any more than it is the *Summa* of Thomas Aquinas or the cathedral of Amiens. I am tired of hearing only about knights, feudalism, Gregorian reform, or seigneurial bans under the pretext that nothing is known about other people. These "others" are nine-tenths of the humanity of those times. Can we not try to perceive them? I have tried to do this. It is useless to accuse me of mixing up centuries, of being content with simplistic generalizations, of eliminating nuances of time or place, of using deceptive words and impure sources. I know all this and assume responsibility for it. At least this explains why everything that is indisputably in motion—the political, the economic, and the social scale—has been systematically thrust aside as mere vicissitudes in the history of men.

And this leads me to my second statement. The human being whom I have followed during this thousand-year period, is he the same as us? Does my analysis lead to the conclusion that only nuances separate us from medieval men and women? In spite of the convictions brandished by almost all medieval historians, I am persuaded that medieval man is us. Many objections could of course be raised. The economy is not the same, thanks to capitalism and competition in particular; in those far-off times social hierarchy was based on secondary criteria (learning, common service public or private); the spiritual climate is not the same since the disappearance of the "Christian" vision of the world; daily life itself has been turned upside down by new conceptions of time, space, and speed. All of this is indisputable but superficial. It is a view taken from on high, as medieval historians are so often wont to do. An attentive reading of any daily newspaper will make it abundantly clear what is essential. As in the long-gone times of which I speak, life does not lie in the performance of the Stock Exchange, or in political gesticulations, or in coiffure fashions; what the newspapers are really talking about is professional concerns and money, problems of board and lodging, of violence, love, and sports and leisure activities, or else they offer consoling discourses. The ignorant chatterboxes who reign over our sources of information may indeed call a particular decision or event "medieval," but they fail to see that they are still living "in the Middle Ages."

I have swept through many domains in this essay, some of which are not very familiar to me. What does this mean for my eventual reader? In truth, I am not quite sure whom I am addressing. These pages are not intended for an erudite person who specializes in matrimonial law or in the study of alimentation, and even less if he or she is a specialist in Christian piety and dogma. I can hear their protests already. But I make a number of allusions to works, people, and events that are not in the domain of collective memory, even of the "enlightened reader." Simplistic for the erudite, confusing for the student, obscure for the non-initiate? I don't know; I felt like saying all this, and that is enough.